THE PENTAGON'S BRAIN

ALSO BY ANNIE JACOBSEN

Operation Paperclip

Area 51

THE PENTAGON'S BRAIN

AN UNCENSORED HISTORY OF DARPA, AMERICA'S TOP SECRET MILITARY RESEARCH AGENCY

ANNIE JACOBSEN

LITTLE, BROWN AND COMPANY
New York • Boston • London

Little, Brown and Company
Hachette Book Group
1290 Avenue of the Americas, New York, NY 10104
littlebrown.com

First Edition: September 2015

Little, Brown and Company is a division of Hachette Book Group, Inc. The Little, Brown name and logo are trademarks of Hachette Book Group, Inc.

ISBN 978-0-316-37176-6 (hc) / 978-0-316-38769-9 (large print) /
978-0-316-34947-5 (int'l ed.)
Library of Congress Control Number: 2015941909

10 9 8 7 6 5 4 3 2 1

RRD-C

Printed in the United States of America

For Kevin

CONTENTS

PART III
OPERATIONS OTHER THAN WAR

PART IV
THE WAR ON TERROR

PART V
FUTURE WAR

THE PENTAGON'S BRAIN

The best way to predict the future is to create it.

—Erich Fromm

PROLOGUE

The Defense Advanced Research Projects Agency, or DARPA as it is known, is the most powerful and most productive military science agency in the world. It is also one of the most secretive and, until this book, the least investigated. Its mission is to create revolutions in military science and to maintain technological dominance over the rest of the world.

DARPA was created by Congress in 1958 and has functioned ever since as the central research and development organization of the Department of Defense. With an annual budget of roughly $3 billion, DARPA is unlike any other military research agency in the United States. DARPA as an agency does not conduct scientific research. Its program managers and directors hire defense contractors, academics, and other government organizations to do the work. DARPA then facilitates the transition of its successful results to the military for use. It acts swiftly and with agility, free from standard bureaucracy or red tape. DARPA maintains an extraordinarily small staff. For six decades now the agency has employed, on average, 120 program managers annually, each for roughly five years' tenure. These entrepreneurial leaders, the majority of whom are accomplished scientists themselves, initiate and oversee hundreds of research projects—involving tens of thousands of scientists and engineers working inside national laboratories, military and defense contractor facilities, and university laboratories—all across America and overseas.

DARPA program managers maintain an unusual degree of authority in an otherwise rigid military chain of command. They can start, continue, or stop research projects with little outside intervention. Once ready for fielding, the resulting weapons and weapons-related systems are turned over to the Army, Navy, Air Force, and Marines, and to intelligence agencies including the CIA, NSA (National Security Agency), DIA (Defense Intelligence Agency), NGA (National Geospatial-Intelligence Agency), NRO (National Reconnaissance Office), and others.

DARPA carefully controls its public persona. Stories about DARPA as America's cutting-edge science agency appear regularly in the press, while the bulk of DARPA's more consequential and sometimes Orwellian programs go largely unreported. "Tiny DARPA implants could give humans self-healing powers," headlined CBS News in the fall of 2014. That same week, *Business Insider* ran the headline "DARPA's Incredible Jumping Robot Shows How the US Military Is Pivoting to Disaster Relief." These and other DARPA stories angle toward health and wellness, when in fact DARPA's stated mission is to create weapons systems. This book reveals why. Many news stories remind readers that DARPA created the Internet, Global Positioning Systems (GPS), and stealth technology. But to describe DARPA this way is to describe Apple as the computer company that built the Macintosh 512K. These DARPA milestones are forty-year-old inventions. Why has so much else about America's most powerful and most productive military science agency been shrouded in mystery? This book shines a light on DARPA's secret history.

Until 1972, DARPA was located inside the Pentagon. Today the agency maintains headquarters in an unmarked glass and steel building four miles from the Pentagon, in Arlington, Virginia. DARPA's director reports to the Office of the Secretary of Defense. In its fifty-seven years, DARPA has never allowed the United States to be taken by scientific surprise. Admirers call DARPA the Pentagon's brain. Critics call it the heart of the military-industrial complex. Is DARPA to be admired or feared? Does DARPA safeguard democracy, or does it stimulate America's seemingly endless call to war?

DARPA makes the future happen. Industry, public health, society, and culture all transform because of technology that DARPA pioneers. DARPA creates, DARPA dominates, and when sent to the battlefield, DARPA destroys. "We are faced with huge uncertainties and shifting threats," DARPA director Arati Prabhakar stated in a press release in 2014, "but we also have unparalleled opportunities to advance technologies in a way that can provide the nation with dramatic new capabilities." But what if some of these "dramatic new capabilities" are not such great ideas?

To research this book, I interviewed seventy-one individuals uniquely affiliated with DARPA, going back to the earliest days of the agency. The list includes presidential science advisors, DARPA program managers and scientists, members of the esoteric and highly secretive Jason scientists, captains, colonels, a Nobel laureate, and a four-star general. In interviewing these individuals, I heard stories about pushing known scientific boundaries in the name of national security, about weather warfare, social science experiments, and war games. I heard about brilliance and hubris, about revolutionary triumphs and shortsighted defeat. One concept stands out. DARPA, by its mandate, pioneers advanced military science in secret. A revolution is not a revolution unless it comes with an element of surprise. Once DARPA technology is revealed on the battlefield, other nations inevitably acquire the science that DARPA pioneered. For example, in the early 1960s, during the Vietnam War, DARPA began developing unmanned aerial vehicles, or drones. It took three decades to arm the first drone, which then appeared on the battlefield in Afghanistan in October 2001. By the time the public knew about drone warfare, U.S. drone technology had advanced by multiple generations. Shortly thereafter, numerous enemy nations began engineering their own drones. By 2014, eighty-seven nations had military-grade drones.

In interviewing former DARPA scientists for this book, I learned that at any given time in history, what DARPA scientists are working on—most notably in the agency's classified programs—is ten to twenty years ahead of the technology in the public domain. The world becomes the future because of DARPA. Is it wise to let DARPA determine what lies ahead?

PART I

THE COLD WAR

CHAPTER ONE

The Evil Thing

One day in the winter of 1954, a group of American scientists found themselves entering into a time when a machine they had created could trigger the end of the world. It was March 1, 1954, 4:29 a.m. local time on Bikini Atoll in the Marshall Islands, a small island chain in the vast Pacific Ocean, 2,650 miles west of Hawaii. Some of the scientists in the group had warned of this moment. Enrico Fermi and Isidor Rabi, both Manhattan Project scientists, called this machine an "evil thing," and they told President Truman it should never be created. But it was built anyway, and now it was about to explode.

The machine was a thermonuclear, or hydrogen, bomb, small enough to be loaded onto a U.S. Air Force bomber and dropped on an enemy city like Moscow. Because the bomb's existence had been kept secret from the American public, the test that the scientists were about to witness had been given a code name. It was called Castle Bravo.

On one end of Bikini Atoll, ten men, each with a top secret Q clearance for access to nuclear secrets, waited inside a concrete bunker, facing an unknown fate. In a little more than two hours, the most powerful bomb in the history of the world to date was going to be detonated just nineteen miles away. No human being had ever before been this close to the kind of power this bomb was expected to deliver. With a predicted yield of 6 megatons, Castle Bravo would deliver twice as much power as all the bombs dropped on Germany and Japan during World War II together, including both atomic bombs.

Thanks to recent advancements in defense science, by 1954 machines were being miniaturized at an astonishing rate. Nuclear weapons in particular were getting smaller and more efficient in ways that scientists could not have imagined a decade before. The Castle Bravo bomb would likely explode with one thousand times the force of the atomic bomb dropped on Hiroshima in August 1945, and yet it weighed just a little more than twice as much.

The light had not yet come up on Bikini. An intense tropical rainfall the night before had left the fronds on the coconut palms and pandanus trees soaking wet. Salt-loving sea lavender plants covered the lowlands, and little penny-sized geckos scampered across wet white sands. The bunker, code-named Station 70, was an odd sight to behold, squat, rectangular, with blast-proof doors and three-foot concrete walls. Everything but the bunker's entrance had now been buried under ten feet of sand. A freestanding concrete-block seawall stood between the bunker and the lagoon, engineered to help protect the men against a potentially massive tidal wave. A three-hundred-foot-tall radio tower built nearby made it possible for the men in the bunker to communicate directly with U.S. defense officials and scientists running this secret operation from aboard the Task Force Command ship USS *Estes,* sixty miles out at sea.

The men inside the bunker were members of the bomb's firing party, a team of six engineers, three Army technicians, and one nuclear scientist. Miles of waterproof submarine cable connected the racks of electronic equipment inside the bunker to the Castle

Bravo bomb, which was located on a separate island, nineteen miles across Bikini's lagoon.

"In the bunker we felt secure," recalled Bernard O'Keefe, one of the nuclear weapons engineers who had advocated for this test. Like Fermi and Rabi, Barney O'Keefe had worked on the Manhattan Project. But unlike those two nuclear physicists, O'Keefe believed this hydrogen bomb was a good thing. That it would keep Americans safe. Defense science is, and likely always will be, a debate.

"At 4:30 a.m. we heard from the scientific director," O'Keefe later remembered. Dr. William Ogle, Los Alamos scientific director, used a ship-to-shore radio link to relay messages from the USS *Estes*. Zero Hour grew near.

"Start the countdown," Ogle said.

"The Time is H minus two hours," O'Keefe announced. Beside him, another member of the firing party pushed the red button marked "TWO HOURS." The machinery took hold.

Inside the bunker, time marched on, and as it did, the general tenor shifted from bearable to "agonizing," O'Keefe recalled. The interior of Station 70 was rough and ugly, with the damp baldness of new concrete. Pool hall–style reflector lights gave off a harsh fluorescent glare. There was a laboratory table covered with tools of the engineering trade: radio tubes, bits and pieces of wire, a soldering iron. On one wall hung a blackboard. On it someone had written a mathematical equation then erased part of it so it no longer made sense. A clock ticked toward Zero Hour. For a long stretch no one said a word, and a heavy and foreboding silence filled the room. Just sixteen minutes before detonation, someone finally spoke. One of the Army's radio technicians wondered aloud how tonight's steak dinner, stored in a meat locker at the back of the bunker, was going to taste after the bomb finally went off.

"H minus fifteen minutes," said O'Keefe, his voice sounding out across dozens of loudspeakers now broadcasting the information to more than ten thousand scientists, soldiers, sailors, airmen, and government officials spread out across fourteen seagoing vessels, forty-six aircraft, and two weather stations. There was no turning back now. Zero Hour was just fifteen minutes away.

Out at sea, aboard another vessel, the men on the USNS *Ainsworth* heard Barney O'Keefe's voice "loud and clear," recalls Ralph "Jim" Freedman, a twenty-four-year-old nuclear weapons engineer. Standing beside Freedman on deck was a group of scientists from Los Alamos. These were the physicists who had designed and built this bomb. They were here now to witness the results of their engineered creation—the machine that Enrico Fermi and Isidor Rabi had warned President Truman was an "evil thing." The sun had not yet risen. Outside, all around, it was dark.

"All observers having high-density goggles put them on," O'Keefe's voice boomed. Freedman was feeling anxious and uneasy. He had not slept well the night before. "I was in the same bunkroom as the Los Alamos scientists, some who were up all night, drinking Chivas Regal and discussing the bomb test," Freedman recalls. "They were discussing things they were not supposed to be discussing but did anyway, because who could sleep the night before the test?" Castle Bravo had been built according to the "Teller-Ulam" scheme—named for its co-designers, Edward Teller and Stanislaw Ulam—which meant, unlike with the far less powerful atomic bomb, this hydrogen bomb had been designed to hold itself together for an extra hundred-millionth of a second, thereby allowing its hydrogen isotopes to fuse and create a chain reaction of nuclear energy, called fusion, producing a potentially infinite amount of power, or yield. "What this meant," Freedman explains, was that there was "a one-in-one-million chance that, given how much hydrogen [is] in the earth's atmosphere, when Castle Bravo exploded, it could catch the earth's atmosphere on fire. Some scientists were extremely nervous. Some made bets about the end of the world."

This was not Freedman's first atmospheric nuclear bomb test. By 1954 he had worked on more than a dozen nuclear tests at the continental atomic test site located in Nevada, seventy miles north of Las Vegas. Freedman had witnessed atomic explosions before, through dark welder's glasses. He had seen mushroom clouds form. But Castle Bravo was different. It was going to be colossal. Titanic. A history-making bomb test. With his goggles in place over his eyes, Freedman turned to face the bomb. There was less than two minutes to go when a Los Alamos scientist standing beside him let out a frustrated cry.

"He'd left his goggles down below deck," Freedman explains. "And there wasn't enough time for him to go get them and make it back up."

Freedman took off his goggles and handed them to the man. "I was young," he says, "not so important to the test." Without eye protection, Jim Freedman had to turn his back to the bomb. So instead of watching Castle Bravo explode, Freedman watched the scientists watch the bomb.

The prerecorded voice of Barney O'Keefe came over the loudspeaker, counting down the last seconds. Everyone fell silent. "Five. Four. Three. Two. One." Zero Hour. A flash of thermonuclear light, called the Teller light, sprang to life as a flood of gamma radiation filled the air. The presence of x-rays made the unseen visible. In the flash of Teller light, Freedman—who was watching the scientists for their reactions—could see their facial bones.

"In front of me...they were skeletons," Freedman recalls. Their faces no longer appeared to be human faces. Just "jawbones and eye sockets. Rows of teeth. Skulls."

Out at sea and in the distance, the world's largest-ever nuclear fireball—nearly four-and-a-half miles in diameter and nine miles tall—lit up the sky. So intense was that fireball that Navy personnel manning a weather station 155 miles to the east watched, awestruck, as the dark sky remained alight for sixty agonizing seconds. Next, the mushroom cloud started to form. Freedman's eyes remained on the Los Alamos scientists, his own perspective now returned to normal in the absence of the Teller light. "I was watching their faces," he recalls, "to see their reaction. Most had their mouths open, with the eyeballs darting back and forth. I remember the eyes. The eyeballs kept moving. There was fear and terror, I think. The mushroom cloud just kept getting bigger." The scientists knew something was wrong.

One scientist held two fingers up in front of his eye, trade craft among nuclear weapons engineers to roughly measure the rate of expansion of a mushroom cloud. What was predicted to be a 6-megaton explosion had gone out of control. Castle Bravo was a 15-megaton explosion. No one had any idea the explosion could be this big.

"The mushroom cloud should have been fifteen [or] twenty miles wide at this point. Instead it was forty," Freedman explains. "As the cloud kept growing behind me, I could see in the faces that [some] of the scientists thought the atmosphere was catching on fire. The look said, 'This is the end of the world.' "

Time passed. Freedman stared at the horrified scientists. Then, finally, the rapid expansion of the mushroom cloud began to slow. To Freedman's eye, the scientists' expression of intense terror and despair suddenly lifted and was gone. "The look on their faces went from fear to satisfaction," Freedman recalls. "The world didn't end and they were triumphant. Self-satisfied with what they had accomplished. With what they had done."

Within sixty seconds, the top of the mushroom cloud reached fifty thousand feet, roughly twice as high as commercial airplanes flew back then. Its cap would eventually grow to an astounding seventy miles across. The cloud's colossal stem was sucking millions of tons of pulverized coral up from the ocean and into the atmosphere, where it would be dispersed into the jet stream as radioactive dust. The remains would leave a footprint of fallout on every corner of the earth.

An unexpected ninety-degree shift in wind direction meant

that weather forecasters had been wrong about which way the wind would blow. Intense fallout was now heading in an easterly direction, where it would pass over several of the Task Force vessels and the inhabited atolls of Rongelap and Rongerik. And it was headed directly for Station 70, on Enyu Island.

Back inside the bunker, the firing party was silent. They could not feel or see the fireball. They'd missed the Teller light. All the ten men had to go by, to gauge what might be going on outside, was the violent electronic chatter on the equipment racks.

"The explosion had to have been a big one to cause that much electrical commotion," O'Keefe later recalled. O'Keefe had also calculated that it would take another forty-five seconds for the shock wave to travel the nineteen miles from ground zero across the lagoon and hit the bunker head-on. And so when, after only ten seconds, the bunker began to shudder and sway, O'Keefe knew instantly something unexpected had happened.

"The whole building was moving," O'Keefe recalled, "not shaking or shuddering as it would from the shock wave that had not arrived yet, but with a slow, perceptible, rolling motion, like a ship's roll."

O'Keefe felt nauseated. He wanted to throw up. "I was completely unable to get it through my head that the building was moving," he said, trying to push away the sickening feeling that the bunker might be sinking into the sea. "The walls are three feet thick," he told himself. "It's anchored like a rock on this island." But things were most definitely moving outside. Objects on the surfaces and walls began to rattle, slide, and crash to the floor. O'Keefe looked at the clock. He knew how long it was supposed to take for the shock wave to travel from ground zero to the bunker. "It was impossible for the shock wave to have reached Enyu Island yet," he recalled thinking. "But the bunker was moving. The motion was unmistakable as it built up."

Lights flickered. The walls appeared to bulge. Then there was a loud and frightening crash, like a thunderclap, as the giant steel door beat like a drumhead. A "slow, sickening whoosh" sounded through the bunker "as the air found its way out after the shock wave had passed." One of the men was thrown to the ground, and O'Keefe watched him stagger as he struggled to his knees. Sparks were flying. There was the sputter of electronic batteries. A vapor cloud began to fill the room. Then the worst possible element in this catastrophic mix appeared.

"Water!" someone yelled. "There's water coming in!"

O'Keefe's legs went rubbery. It was too early for a tidal wave, he told himself, and began to think that perhaps the whole ocean had erupted around them. That soon he and his colleagues would be jettisoned to the bottom of the lagoon, their concrete bunker a watery tomb. The scientist in charge, Dr. John Clark, dispatched one of the Army technicians to investigate. The technician walked to the single round porthole built into the blast-proof steel doors and looked outside. Station 70 was not underwater. It was still anchored to the land. The water in the bunker was coming from burst water pipes. O'Keefe volunteered to take a Geiger counter and venture outside. Several others followed along, Geiger counters in hand.

The situation outside looked far worse than anyone had anticipated. Palm trees were on fire. Dead birds littered the land. There was no visible life, and they sensed that there might not be life anywhere. The sun was blotted out behind the nuclear mushroom cloud. "The air was filled with a whitish chaff," O'Keefe recalled. "I stuck out my hand, which was soon covered with a substance like talcum powder." When O'Keefe turned on his Geiger counter to check for radiation, the needle spiked. Someone else shouted out a dangerous radiation level. If a human were exposed to this level of radiation for twenty-five minutes, he would be dead.

The men ran back into the bunker. But inside, behind three-foot concrete walls, there were also life-threatening radiation levels. The group retreated to a region far back in the bunker, behind a second concrete-block wall where the urinals were. Jack Clark called for an emergency evacuation but was told it was too dangerous to send a helicopter pilot to Enyu Island just yet. Station 70 had been designed with a ten thousand factor of radiation shielding. Whatever was going on inside the bunker, outside it was ten thousand times worse. The firing party would have to wait it out. Eventually the deadly radiation levels would subside, they were told.

Eighty miles to the east another calamity was unfolding. A Japanese fishing trawler, called the *Lucky Dragon Number Five,* had been caught unawares roughly fifteen miles outside the designated U.S. military restricted zone. After the Castle Bravo bomb exploded, many of the Japanese fishermen on the trawler ran out on deck to behold what appeared to be some kind of mystical apparition, the sun rising in the west. Awestruck, they stood staring at the nuclear fireball as it grew, until a chalky material started falling from the sky. This was pulverized coral, made highly radioactive by the thermonuclear blast. By the time the fishermen returned to Japan, all of them were suffering from radiation poisoning. Six months later, the *Lucky Dragon*'s chief radio operator, Aikichi Kuboyama, died.

Castle Bravo was a weapon of unprecedented destruction. It was 250 percent more powerful than the force calculated by the scientists who had engineered it. In time Castle Bravo would become known as the worst radiological disaster in history. Radioactive contamination became so consequential and widespread that two days after the explosion, the Navy evacuated Rongelap, Rongerik, Ailinginae, and Utirik atolls, which lay between seventy-five and three hundred miles to the east of ground zero. Many of the islanders living there were powdered in radioactive dust.

In the days that followed, the world's 2.7 billion inhabitants remained ignorant of what had happened in the Marshall Islands. The Atomic Energy Commission ordered a news blackout on the aftereffects of the bomb, including that no mention be made of the extensive fallout or the evacuation of the four atolls. Castle Bravo was only the first explosion in a series of U.S. hydrogen bomb tests, a series that had been obliquely announced to the public as "weapons tests." All other information was classified. This was 1954, before the invention of communications satellites. It was still possible to move ten thousand men and a fleet of warships and airplanes unobserved to an obscure corner of the earth to conduct a secret hydrogen bomb test.

Americans back home remained in the dark. On March 10, a full nine days after the United States had exploded what would turn out to be a 15-megaton hydrogen bomb, causing deadly fallout to circle the earth, President Dwight Eisenhower took to a podium in the White House press room. In his weekly presidential news conference to the nation, he had this to say: "I have only one announcement. It is very inconsequential. Sometime during the coming week I shall probably go on the air to discuss the general contents of the tax program."

But in Japan the *Lucky Dragon* fishing trawler had returned to port, and news of the radiation-poisoned fishermen was making international headlines. The Atomic Energy Commission issued a terse statement saying that some individuals had been "unexpectedly" subjected to "some radiation [during a] routine atomic test in the Marshall Islands." On March 17, at the weekly news conference from the White House, reporter Merriman Smith asked the president to shed light on this mysterious, all-powerful weapon.

"Mr. President," said Smith. "The Joint Congressional Atomic Energy Commissioner said last night that we now have a hydrogen bomb and can deliver it anywhere in the world. I wonder if you could discuss that?"

"No, I wouldn't want to discuss that," the president said. And he did not.

It was the Cold War, and secrecy reigned.

Behind the scenes, what President Eisenhower was just now learning about the Castle Bravo bomb was horrifying beyond most people's comprehension. The president's scientific advisors showed him a top secret map of the fallout pattern made by the Castle Bravo bomb across the Marshall Islands. The scientists then superimposed that same fallout pattern onto a map of the east coast of the United States. If ground zero had been Washington, D.C., instead of Bikini Atoll, every resident of the greater Washington-Baltimore area would now be dead. Without a Station 70–style bunker for protection, the entire population living there would have been killed by 5,000 roentgens of radiation exposure in mere minutes. Even in Philadelphia, 150 miles away, the majority of inhabitants would have been exposed to radiation levels that would have killed them within the hour. In New York City, 225 miles north, half of the population would have died by nightfall. All the way to the Canadian border, inhabitants would have been exposed to 100 roentgens or more, their suffering similar to what the fisherman on the *Lucky Dragon* had endured.

But President Eisenhower had no intention of relaying this information to the public. Instead, he said there was nothing to discuss. The physical fallout map would remain classified for decades, but even the president could not control the escalating international outrage over the Castle Bravo bomb. Soon he would be forced to address the issue.

The secret decision to engineer the thermonuclear, or hydrogen, bomb began five years earlier when, on August 29, 1949, the Soviets exploded their first atomic bomb. Suddenly, the United States lost the nuclear monopoly it had maintained since World War II. The question of how to respond took on great urgency. Should America reply with powerful counterforce? Or was restraint the more suitable reply?

One month after the Soviet atomic bomb test, the General Advisory Committee (GAC) of the U.S. Atomic Energy Commission—an elite group of nuclear scientists—convened, in secret, to identify whether or not the United States should pursue a crash program to build the hydrogen bomb. The chairman of this committee was J. Robert Oppenheimer, the former scientific director of the Manhattan Project and a man known as the father of the atomic bomb. In "unanimous opposition," the scientists agreed that the United States should not move forward with the hydrogen bomb, and they stated so in no uncertain terms. The reasons were uncomplicated, they said. "It is clear that the use of this weapon would bring about the destruction of innumerable human lives," they wrote. "Its use would involve a decision to slaughter a vast number of civilians." Tens of thousands of people had been killed in the atomic bombings of Hiroshima and Nagasaki; a hydrogen bomb would kill millions in a single strike. The hydrogen bomb was a weapon with a built-in "policy of exterminating civilian populations," the GAC members warned.

Two committee members, the physicists Enrico Fermi and Isidor Rabi, felt compelled to add a letter, or "annex," for then President Truman to read. "It is clear that such a weapon cannot be justified on any ethical ground," they wrote. "The fact that no limits exist to the destructiveness of this weapon makes its very existence and the knowledge of its construction a danger to humanity as a whole. It is necessarily an evil thing considered in any light." While there was unanimity among the scientists on the General Advisory Committee—the official advisory committee on all matters related to nuclear weapons—the GAC members were not the only nuclear scientists with power and persuasion in Washington, D.C.

As in any serious scientific race, there was fierce competition going on behind the scenes. There existed another group of nuclear scientists who were deeply committed to engineering a hydrogen bomb. Leading this team were the Hungarian-born Edward Teller and his mentor, the American-born Ernest O. Lawrence, both former members of the Manhattan Project. Neither Teller nor Lawrence had been elected to the General Advisory Committee, nor did they take part in the unanimous decision to advise President Truman against building the hydrogen bomb.

Teller and Lawrence had extraordinary power and influence in Washington, at the Pentagon and the Atomic Energy Commission. Mindful that the GAC had plans to stymie their efforts for a hydrogen bomb, Edward Teller met personally with the chairman of the congressional committee on nuclear energy. "We must know more about principles of thermonuclear devices to make a decision about [the] military implications," said Teller, who felt that Oppenheimer was foolishly being guided by moral arguments in a fight against an atheistic communist enemy. Senator Brien McMahon, the powerful chairman of the Joint Committee on Atomic Energy, agreed. The view of the Oppenheimer group "just makes me sick," McMahon told Teller.

Ernest Lawrence met with David E. Lilienthal, the chairman of the Atomic Energy Commission. "If we don't get this super [i.e., the hydrogen bomb] first," Lawrence warned, "we are sunk, the U.S. would surrender without a struggle." Lawrence considered the atomic bomb "one of mankind's greatest blessings," and felt that the hydrogen bomb was "a technical means of taking profit out of war." He met with Lewis Strauss, chairman of the Atomic Energy Committee. Lawrence took umbrage at the idea of anyone's bringing moral principles into the mix. Their conversation inspired Strauss to appeal directly to the president. "A government of atheists is not likely to be dissuaded from producing the weapon on 'moral' grounds," Strauss wrote. The "super" must be built. "If we let the Russians get the super first, catastrophe becomes all but certain," Brien McMahon told the president and his national security advisors. "It's either we make it or we wait until the Russians drop one on us without warning," said National Security Committee member Admiral Sidney Souers.

In January 1950 President Truman authorized a crash program to build the hydrogen bomb. The Joint Committee on Atomic Energy decided that a second national nuclear weapons laboratory was needed now, in order to foster competition with Los Alamos. This idea—that rivalry fosters excellence and is imperative for supremacy—would become a hallmark of U.S. defense science in the decades ahead. Lawrence was put in charge of the new lab, with Teller acting as his special scientific advisor. The lab, a branch of the University of California Radiation Laboratory, was located in Livermore, California, about forty miles southeast of the university's Berkeley campus.

Livermore, which opened in the spring of 1952, began with 123 employees. Three of them, all graduate students at the Berkeley Radiation Laboratory, were Edward Teller protégés. Their names were Herb York, Harold Brown, and John Foster. Herb York, age thirty, was Livermore's first scientific director. Harold Brown, age twenty-four, was put in charge of its A Division, for hydrogen bomb work. John Foster, age twenty-nine, headed up the B Division, which worked on smaller and more efficient atomic weapons. In retrospect, it seems that York, Brown, and Foster were all remarkably inexperienced young men to be put in charge of developing the most powerful nuclear weapons in the world. Each scientist would play a major role in the history of DARPA and leave footprints on U.S. national security that are ineradicable and absolute.

Nuclear weapons work at Livermore went slowly at first. For all the ambition and big ideas, Livermore's first nuclear weapons tests, detonated at the Nevada Test Site in 1953, were duds. One exploded with such a low yield—equivalent to just two hundred tons of TNT—that the steel tower on which it detonated was left standing in the desert, merely bent and crumpled. A photograph of the misshapen tower was published in newspapers around the country, accompanied by jokes about Livermore's impotence.

"Los Alamos scientists filled the air with horse laughs," scientific director Herb York later recalled. And so, despite the Livermore team's desire to shepherd the world's first deliverable hydrogen bomb into existence, scientists at Los Alamos were instead given scientific authority over the Castle Bravo bomb. Edward Teller had designed the bomb before Livermore existed, which is why he is considered the father of the hydrogen bomb. But Los Alamos was in charge of the test.

In that fateful winter of 1954, there were additional hydrogen bomb tests planned for Bikini Atoll. The Bravo bomb was only the first of what would be a six-bomb thermonuclear test program in the Castle series, from March 1 to May 14. Five of the six bombs had been designed and built by Los Alamos. One, called Koon, was designed at Livermore. Like the new laboratory's previous two efforts, Koon was a failure. Instead of exploding in the megaton range, as was planned, Koon was a 110-kiloton dud. The new Livermore laboratory project was now at serious risk of being canceled. What good is a competition if one side cannot seem to compete?

Teller and his protégé Herb York would not accept failure. Fueled by humiliation, they planned to outperform the competition at Los Alamos. Four months after Castle Bravo, the General Advisory Committee met in Los Alamos for classified discussions about how to move forward with the hydrogen bomb. The majority of these men were the same ones who had opposed the creation of the super bomb just four and a half years before. One person missing was Robert Oppenheimer. He had been stripped of his security clearance, on the grounds that he was a communist, and banished from government service for life. Oppenheimer's forced exile sent a strong message to defense scientists. There was little room for dissent, and certainly not for objection on moral grounds. Gone was any further discussion of ethics, or of the fact that the super bomb was a dangerous machine. The hydrogen bomb was part of the U.S. military arsenal now. As commissioners, these scientists had much work to do.

Isidor Rabi replaced Oppenheimer as committee chairman. Rabi now embraced the super bomb as having created a "complete revolution... in atomic weapons." Science had fathered a new generation of technologically advanced weapons and had paved the way for a whole new "family" of thermonuclear weapons, Rabi said, "from tactical to multi-megaton strategic weapons, which would render some stockpile weapons obsolete or of little utility."

In an atmosphere of such rapid scientific advancement, the Livermore laboratory remained in a precarious position. Its first three weapons tests—code-named Ruth and Ray, at the Nevada Test Site, and Koon, in the Marshall Islands—had been failures. During the July 1954 meeting in New Mexico, the General Advisory Committee discussed whether or not creating the second laboratory had been a mistake. Isidor Rabi called the Livermore tests "amateurish," a failure highlighted by the fact that all Livermore had to do was work on the hydrogen bomb. The lab didn't even have to share any of the national security burdens that Los Alamos shouldered, Rabi said, including responsibility for building the nation's stockpile. In the summer of 1954, it looked as if the Livermore laboratory might be closed down.

But Livermore's chief scientist Herb York, and Edward Teller, acting as special advisor to Ernest Lawrence, had already crafted a bold response, and they had come to New Mexico to present their idea to the General Advisory Committee. On day three of the meeting, York and Teller presented an idea for a new weapon on Livermore's behalf. Castle Bravo had been a 15-megaton bomb. Livermore had drawn plans for two mega-super bombs, which they had code-named Gnomon and Sundial. This was a play on words; gnomons and sundials are two of the oldest scientific devices known to man, used in the ancient world to measure shadows cast by the sun. Livermore's mega-super bombs were each designed to have a 10,000-megaton yield, York and Teller said. This weapon was capable of destroying an entire continent in a single strike.

The idea was met with laughter. Scientists on the General Advisory Committee were appalled. In the only surviving record of the meeting, one committee member, Dr. James Whitman, expresses shock and says that a 10,000-megaton bomb would "contaminate the earth." Teller defended his idea, boasting that Lawrence had already approached the Air Force, and the Air Force was interested. Rabi called the idea "a publicity stunt," and plans for a 10,000-megaton bomb were shelved. But Livermore was allowed to keep its doors open after all.

Decades later, Herb York explained why he and Edward Teller had felt it necessary to design a 10,000-megaton bomb when the United States had, only months earlier, achieved supremacy over the Soviets with the 15-megaton Castle Bravo bomb. The reason, York said, was that in order to maintain supremacy, American scientists must always take new and greater risks. "The United States cannot maintain its qualitative edge without having an aggressive R&D [research and development] establishment that pushes against the technological frontiers without waiting to be asked," York said, "and that in turn creates a faster-paced arms race. That is the inevitable result of our continuing quest for a qualitative edge to offset the other side's quantitative advantage."

For Herb York, the way for America to maintain its position as the most militarily powerful country in the world was through the forward march of science. To get the most out of an American scientist was to get him to compete against equally brilliant men. That was what made America great, York said. This was the American way of war. And this was exactly the kind of vision the Department of Defense required of its scientists as it struggled for survival against the Soviet communists. The age of thermonuclear weapons had arrived. Both sides were building vast arsenals at a feverish pace. There was no turning back. The only place to go was ahead.

It was time to push against technological frontiers.

CHAPTER TWO

War Games and Computing Machines

On the west coast of California, in the sunny Santa Monica sunshine, the defense scientists at RAND Corporation played war games during lunchtime. RAND, an acronym for "research and development," was the Pentagon's first postwar think tank, the brains behind U.S. Air Force brawn. By day, during the 1950s, analysts inside RAND's offices and conference rooms churned out reports, mostly about nuclear weapons. Come lunchtime they moved outdoors, spreading maps of the world across tabletops, taking game pieces from boxes and playing *Kriegspiel,* a chess variant once favored by the powerful German military.

Competition was valued and encouraged at RAND, with scientists and analysts always working to outdo one another. Lunchtime war games included at least one person in the role of umpire, which usually prevented competitions from getting out of hand. Still, tempers flared, and sometimes game pieces scattered. Other times there was calculated calm. Lunch could last for hours, especially if John von Neumann was in town.

In the 1950s, von Neumann was *the* superstar defense scientist. No one could compete with his brain. At the Pentagon, the highest-ranking members of the U.S. armed services, the secretary of defense and the Joint Chiefs of Staff, all saw von Neumann as an infallible authority. "If anyone during that crucial period in the early and middle-fifties can be said to have enjoyed more 'credibility' in national defense circles than all the others, that person was surely Johnny," said Herb York, von Neumann's close friend.

Born in 1903 to a well-to-do Hungarian Jewish family, John von Neumann had been a remarkable child prodigy. In the first grade he was solving complex mathematical problems. By age eight he had mastered calculus, though his talents were not limited to math. By the time von Neumann graduated from high school, he spoke seven languages. He could memorize hundreds of pages of text, including long numbers, after a single read-through. "Keeping up with him was impossible," remarked the mathematician Israel Halperin. "The feeling was you were on a tricycle chasing a racing car."

"Johnny was the only student I was ever afraid of," said his childhood teacher, George Pólya, also a famous mathematician. "If in the course of a lecture I stated an unsolved problem, the chances were he'd come to me at the end of the lecture with the complete solution scribbled on a slip of paper."

By all accounts, von Neumann was gentle and kind, beloved for his warm personality, his courtesy, and his charm. "He was pleasant and plump, smiled easily and often, enjoyed parties and other social events," recalled Herb York. He loved to drink, play loud music, attend parties, and collect toys. He always wore a three-piece banker's suit with a watch chain stretched across his plump belly. There exists a photograph of von Neumann traveling down into the Grand Canyon on a donkey's back, outfitted in the legendary three-piece suit. It is said that the only things von Neumann carried in his pants pockets were unsolvable Chinese puzzles and top secret security clearances, of which he had many.

To his core, von Neumann believed that man was violent, belligerent, and deceptive, and that he was inexorably prone to fighting wars. "I think the USA-USSR conflict will very probably lead to an armed 'total' collision and that a maximum rate of armament is therefore imperative," von Neumann wrote to Lewis Strauss, head of the Atomic Energy Commission, three years before the Castle Bravo bomb exploded—a weapon that von Neumann helped engineer.

Only in rare private moments would "the deeply cynical and pessimistic core of his being" emerge, remarks his daughter Marina von Neumann Whitman, a former economic advisor to President Nixon. "I was frequently confused when he shifted, without warning.... [O]ne minute he would have me laughing at his latest courageous pun and the next he would be telling me, quite seriously, why all-out atomic war was almost certainly unavoidable." Did war stain him? During World War II, when his only daughter was a little girl, John von Neumann helped decide which Japanese civilian populations would be targeted for atomic bombing. But far more revealing is that it was von Neumann who performed the precise calculations that determined at what altitude over Hiroshima and Nagasaki the atomic bombs had to explode in order to achieve the maximum kill rate of civilians on the ground. He determined the height to be 1,800 feet.

At the RAND Corporation, von Neumann served as a part-time consultant. He was hired by John Davis Williams, the eccentric director of RAND's Mathematics Division, on unusual terms: Von Neumann was to write down his thoughts each morning while shaving, and for those ideas he would be paid $200 a month—the average salary of a full-time RAND analyst at the time. Von Neumann lived and spent most of his time working in

New Jersey, where he had served as a faculty member at the Princeton Institute for Advanced Study since the early 1930s, alongside Albert Einstein.

To the RAND scientists playing lunchtime war games, less important than beating von Neumann at *Kriegspiel* was watching how his mind analyzed game play. "If a mentally superhuman race ever develops, its members will resemble Johnny von Neumann," Edward Teller once said. "If you enjoy thinking, your brain develops. And that is what von Neumann did. He enjoyed the functioning of his brain."

John von Neumann was obsessed with what he called parlor games, and his first fascination was with poker. There was strategy involved, yes, but far more important was that the game of poker was predicated on deception: to play and to win, a man had to be willing to deceive his opponent. To make one's opponent think something false was something true. Second-guessing was equally imperative to a winning strategy. A poker player needs to predict what his opponent *thinks* he might do.

In 1926, when von Neumann was twenty-three years old, he wrote a paper called "Theory of Parlor Games." The paper, which examined game playing from a mathematical point of view, contained a soon-to-be famous proof, called the minimax theorem. Von Neumann wrote that when two players are involved in a zero-sum game—a game in which one player's losses equal the other player's gains—each player will work to minimize his own maximum losses while at the same time working to maximize his minimum gains. During the war, von Neumann collaborated with fellow Princeton mathematician Oskar Morgenstern to explore this idea further. In 1944 the two men co-authored a 673-page book on the subject, *Theory of Games and Economic Behavior.* The book was considered so groundbreaking that the *New York Times* carried a page one story about its contents the day it was published. But von Neumann and Morgenstern's book did more than just revolutionize economic theory. It placed game theory on the world stage, and after the war it caught the attention of the Pentagon.

By the 1950s, von Neumann's minimax theorem was legendary at RAND, and to engage von Neumann in a discussion about game theory was like drinking from the Holy Grail. It became a popular pastime at RAND to try to present to von Neumann a conundrum he could not solve. In the 1950s, two RAND analysts, Merrill Flood and Melvin Dresher, came up with an enigma they believed was unsolvable, and they presented it to the great John von Neumann. Flood and Dresher called their quandary the Prisoner's Dilemma. It was based on a centuries-old dilemma tale. A contemporary rendition of the Prisoner's Dilemma involves two criminal suspects faced with either prison time or a plea deal.

The men, both members of a criminal gang, are believed to have participated in the same crime. They are arrested and put in different cells. Separated, the two men have no way of communicating with each other, so they can't learn what the other man is being offered by way of a plea deal. The police tell each man they don't have enough evidence to convict either of them individually on the criminal charges they were brought in for. But the police do have enough evidence to convict each man on a lesser charge, parole violation, which carries a prison sentence of one year. The police offer each man, separately, a Faustian bargain. If he testifies against the other man, he will go free and the partner will do ten years' prison time. There is a catch. Both men are being offered the same deal. If both men take the plea deal and testify against the other, the prison sentence will be reduced to five years. If both men refuse the deal, they will each be given only one year in jail for parole violation—clearly the best way to minimize maximum losses and maximize minimum gains. But the deal is on the table for only a finite amount of time, the police say.

Von Neumann could not "solve" the Prisoner's Dilemma. It is an unsolvable paradox. It does not fit the minimax theorem. There is no answer; the outcome of the dilemma game differs from player to player. Dresher and Flood posed the Prisoner's Dilemma to dozens of RAND colleagues and also to other test subjects outside RAND. While no one could "solve" the Prisoner's Dilemma, the RAND analysts learned something unexpected from the results. The outcome of the Prisoner's Dilemma seemed to depend on the human nature of the individual game players involved—whether the player was guided by trust or distrust. Dresher and Flood discovered the participants' responses also revealed their philosophical construct, which generally correlated to a political disposition. In interviewing RAND analysts, almost all of whom were political conservatives, Dresher and Flood discovered that the majority chose to testify against their criminal partner. They did not trust that partner to follow the concept of self-preservation, gamble against his own best interests, and refuse to talk. Five years in prison was better than ten, the RAND analysts almost universally responded. By contrast, Dresher and Flood found that the minority of game players who refused to testify against their criminal partner were almost always of the liberal persuasion. These individuals were willing to put themselves at risk in order to get the best possible outcome for both themselves and a colleague—just a single year's jail time.

Dresher and Flood saw that the paradox of the Prisoner's Dilemma could be applied to national security decisions. Take the case of Robert Oppenheimer, for example, a liberal. As chairman of the General Advisory Committee, Oppenheimer had appealed to Secretary of State Dean Acheson to try to persuade President Truman not to go forward with the hydrogen bomb. To show restraint, Oppenheimer said, would send a clear message to Stalin that America was offering "limitations on the totality of war and thus eliminating the fear and raising the hope of mankind." Acheson, a conservative, saw the situation very differently. "How can you persuade a paranoid adversary to 'disarm by example?'" he asked.

Von Neumann became interested in the Prisoner's Dilemma as a means for examining strategic possibilities in the nuclear arms race. The Prisoner's Dilemma was a non–zero sum game, meaning one person's wins were not equal to another person's gains. From von Neumann's perspective, even though two rational people were involved—or, in the case of national security, two superpower nations—they were far less likely to cooperate to gain the best deal, and far more likely to take their chances on a better deal for themselves. The long-term implications for applying the Prisoner's Dilemma to the nuclear arms race were profound, suggesting that it would forever be a game of one-upmanship.

In addition to game theory and nuclear strategy, the RAND Corporation was interested in computer research, a rare and expensive field of study in the 1950s. The world's leading expert in computers was John von Neumann. While no one person can accurately claim credit for the invention of the computer, von Neumann is often seen as one of the fathers of modern computers, given the critical role he played in their early development. His work on computing machines goes back to World War II, a time when "computer" was the name for a person who performed numerical calculations as part of a job.

During the war, at the Army's Aberdeen Proving Ground in Maryland, scores of human computers worked around the clock on trajectory tables, trying to determine more accurate timing and firing methods for various battlefield weapons. Bombs and artillery shells were being fired at targets with ever-increasing speed, and the human computers at Aberdeen simply could not keep up with the trajectory tables. The work was overwhelming. Von Neumann, one of the nation's leading experts on ballistics at the time and a regular presence at Aberdeen, got to talking with one of the proving ground's best "computers," Colonel Herman Goldstine, about this very problem. Goldstine was an Army engineer and former mathematics professor, and still he found computing to be grueling work. Goldstine explained to von Neumann that on average, each trajectory table he worked on contained approximately three thousand entries, all of which had to be multiplied. Performed with paper and pencil, each set of three thousand calculations took a man like Goldstine roughly twelve hours to complete and another twelve hours to verify. The inevitability of human error was what slowed things down.

Von Neumann told Colonel Goldstine that he believed a machine would one day prove to be a better computer than a human. If so, von Neumann said, this could profoundly impact the speed with which the Army could perform its ballistics calculations. As it so happened, Colonel Goldstine was cleared for a top secret Army program that involved exactly the kind of machine von Neumann was theorizing about. Goldstine arranged to have von Neumann granted clearance, and the two men set off for the University of Pennsylvania. There, inside a locked room at the Moore School, engineers were working on a classified Army-funded computing machine—the first of its kind. It was called the Electronic Numerical Integrator and Computer, or ENIAC.

ENIAC was huge and cumbersome: one hundred feet long, ten feet high, and three feet deep. It had 17,468 vacuum tubes and weighed sixty thousand pounds. Von Neumann was fascinated. ENIAC was "the first complete automatic, all-purpose digital electronic computer" in the world, von Neumann declared. He was certain ENIAC would spawn a revolution, and that, indeed, computers would no longer be men but machines.

Von Neumann began developing ideas for creating an electronic computer of his own. Borrowing ideas from the ENIAC construct, and with help from Colonel Goldstine, he drew up plans for a second classified electronic computer, called the Electronic Discrete Variable Automatic Computer, or EDVAC. Von Neumann saw great promise in a redesign of the ENIAC computer's memory. He believed there was a way to turn the computer into an "electronic brain" capable of storing not just data and instructions, as was the case with ENIAC, but additional information that would allow the computer to perform a myriad of computational functions on its own. This was called a stored-program computer, and it "broke the distinction between numbers that mean things and numbers that do things," writes von Neumann's biographer George Dyson, adding, "Our universe would never be the same." These "instructions" that von Neumann imagined were the prototype of what the world now knows as software.

Von Neumann believed that this computer could theoretically speed up atomic bomb calculations being performed by his fellow Manhattan Project scientists at Los Alamos, in New Mexico. He and the team at the Moore School proposed that the Army build a second machine, the one he called EDVAC. But the atomic bomb was completed and successfully tested before EDVAC was finished, and after the war, EDVAC was orphaned.

Von Neumann still wanted to build his own computer from scratch. He secured funding from the Atomic Energy Commission to do so, and in November 1945, John von Neumann began building an entirely new computer in the basement of Fuld Hall at the Institute for Advanced Study in Princeton. Colonel Goldstine arrived to assist him in the winter of 1946, and with help from a small staff of engineers, von Neumann first constructed a machine shop and a laboratory for testing computer components. Officially the project was called the Electronic Computing Instrument Computer; von Neumann preferred to call the machine the Mathematical and Numerical Integrator and Computer, or MANIAC.

MANIAC was smaller and much more advanced than ENIAC, which weighed thirty tons. ENIAC was rife with limitations; gargantuan and cumbersome, it sucked power, overheated, and constantly needed to be rewired whenever a problem came along. ENIAC technicians spent days unplugging tangled cables in order to find a solution for a numerical problem that took only minutes to compute. MANIAC was compact and efficient, a single six-foot-high, eight-foot-long machine that weighed only a thousand pounds. But the most significant difference between ENIAC and MANIAC was that von Neumann designed his computer to be controlled by its own instructions. These were housed inside the machine, like a brain inside a human being.

Indeed, von Neumann had consciously modeled MANIAC after the human brain. "I propose to store everything that has to be remembered by the machine, in these memory organs," von Neumann wrote, including "the coded, logical instructions which define the problem and control the functioning of the machine." In this way, MANIAC became the world's first modern stored-program computer. Von Neumann's friend and colleague Edward Teller saw great promise in the computer and used MANIAC to perform calculations for the hydrogen bomb.

After two and a half years of work, the team at Princeton tested MANIAC against von Neumann's own brain. Initially, von Neumann was able to compute numbers in his head faster than the machine. But as his assistants entered more and more complicated computational requests, von Neumann finally did what human beings do: he erred. The computer did not. It was a revelatory moment in the history of defense science. A machine had just outperformed a brain the Pentagon relied on, one of the greatest minds in the world.

The Pentagon's strategy for nuclear deterrence in the 1950s was based on a notion called mutual assured destruction, or MAD. This was the proposition that neither the Soviets nor the Americans would be willing to launch a nuclear attack against the other because that action would ensure a reciprocal action and ultimately guarantee both sides' demise. At RAND, analysts began applying the Prisoner's Dilemma strategy to a nuclear launch, keeping in mind that the driving principle of the dilemma was distrust. This led a RAND analyst named Albert Wohlstetter to start poking holes in the notion that MAD offered security. The way Wohlstetter saw it, MAD most definitely did not. He argued that if one side figured out a way to decapitate the other in a so-called "first strike," it might be tempted to launch an unprovoked attack to ensure its superiority. The only solution, said Wohlstetter, was to develop a new nuclear strategy whereby the United States had more nuclear weapons in more hardened missile silos secreted around the American countryside than the Soviets could decapitate in a preemptive strike. Wohlstetter's famous theory became known as "second strike." U.S. policy regarding second strike deterrence took on the acronym NUTS, for nuclear utilization target selection.

President Eisenhower began to see the madness of it all. The year after Castle Bravo, the Soviets successfully tested their own deliverable hydrogen bomb. If something wasn't done to stop it, the arms race would only continue to escalate. Speaking to his cabinet, Eisenhower wondered if it was possible to put an end to nuclear weapons tests. He launched his administration's first investigation into the possibility of stopping nuclear science in its tracks. His vision was short-lived. After a month of study and discussion, the State Department, the Atomic Energy Commission, the CIA, and the Department of Defense were all unanimous in their opposition to ending nuclear tests. Atmospheric nuclear weapons tests must continue, they all said. The safety and security of the country depended on more nuclear weapons and more nuclear weapons tests. The president's advisors instead encouraged him to focus his attention on strengthening a national effort to protect civilians in the event of a Soviet nuclear attack, an unpopular program called civil defense. This job fell to the Federal Civil Defense Administration, a three-year-old agency with headquarters in Washington, D.C.

The plan for civil defense in the mid-1950s was to have people prepare to live underground for a period of time after a nuclear attack. An effort to build a national network of underground bunkers had been moving forward in fits and starts. The president's advisors told him that his endorsement would boost morale. But the very idea of promoting civil defense put Eisenhower in an intractable bind. Ever since he had been shown the fallout map from the Castle Bravo bomb, Eisenhower knew how implausible a civil defense program was—how many tens of millions of Americans were destined to die in the first few hours of a nuclear attack. The idea that there was safety to be found in a civilian underground bunker program was apocryphal. One needed to look no further than what had happened to the men in the Station 70 bunker. Station 70 was a windowless bunker carefully constructed of three-foot-thick concrete walls with steel doors, buried under ten feet of dirt and sand. It was surrounded by a moat and had a secondary blast buttress wall. And even with a 10,000 factor of shielding, the radiation nearly killed the men inside; they barely made it off Enyu alive. After taking cover in the bunker's urinal for eleven hours, the men were ultimately evacuated from the death zone by two Army helicopters in a carefully orchestrated military operation. The helicopter pilots were part of a ten-thousand–man task force, with unlimited access to state-of-the-art rescue and communication equipment. The rescue teams had fewer than one dozen rescue operations to perform, the majority of which had been rehearsed. Castle Bravo was a highly organized scientific test. In a real nuclear attack, there would be carnage and mayhem. Each person would be on his or her own.

To be caught outside, en route to a civil defense shelter, even forty miles away from ground zero, would be life threatening. The bomb blast and shock waves would rupture lungs, shred eardrums, and cause organs to rupture and bleed. Debris—uprooted trees, sheets of metal, broken glass, electrical wires, wood, rocks, pipes, poles—everything would be ripped apart and hurled through the air at speeds of up to 150 miles per hour. How, in good conscience, could the president urge the public to support a program he knew was more than likely going to kill so many of them?

Paradoxically, in the event of a Soviet nuclear attack, there was a fully formed plan in place to keep the president and his cabinet alive. An executive branch version of the Station 70 bunker had recently been completed six miles north of Camp David, just over the Pennsylvania state line. This underground command center, called the Raven Rock Mountain Complex, was buried inside a mountain of granite, giving the president protection equivalent to that of walls a thousand feet thick. The Raven Rock complex, also called Site R, had been designed to withstand a direct hit from a 15-megaton bomb. The idea of an underground presidential bunker was first conceived by U.S. Army military intelligence (G-2) during postwar examination of the underground bunker complexes of the Third Reich. The survival of so many of the Nazi high command in Berlin was predicated on the underground engineering skills of a few top Nazi scientists, including Franz Xaver Dorsch, Walter Schieber, and Georg Rickhey, all three of whom were hired by the U.S. Army to work on secret U.S. underground engineering projects after the war, as part of Operation Paperclip.

Plans for Raven Rock were first drawn up in 1948, including some by Rickhey. Work began shortly after the Russians detonated their own atomic bomb, known in the West as Joe-1, in August 1949, and by 1950, construction crews with top secret clearances were working around the clock to build the first underground presidential bunker and command post. Site R was a three-story complex with living quarters for the president and his advisors, a hospital, chapel, barbershop, library, and water reservoir. By the time the bunker was finished, in 1954, the costs had reached $1 billion (roughly $9 billion in 2015).

In the event of a nuclear strike, the president would be helicoptered from the White House lawn to the landing pad at Raven Rock, a trip that would take roughly thirty-five minutes. But the prospect of retreating underground in the event of a nuclear strike made President Eisenhower despondent. To his cabinet he expressed his view of what governance would be like after a nuclear attack: "Government which goes on with some kind of continuity will be like a one-eyed man in the land of the blind."

While the president lived with his conundrum, the civil defense program grew. The details of the Castle Bravo test remained classified, as did the existence of the Raven Rock command center, leaving the public in the dark as to the implausibility of civil defense. Nuclear tests continued unabated, in Nevada and in the Marshall Islands. But the press attention created by the Castle Bravo fallout debate began to generate strong negative responses to the viability of civil defense.

In February 1955 the Senate Armed Services Committee opened a federal investigation into what civil defense really meant for the American people. The investigating committee was headed by a Tennessee Democrat, Senator Estes Kefauver, known for his crusades against organized crime and antitrust violations. The Senate sessions would become known as the Kefauver hearings, and in the course of them, shocking new information came to light.

Civil defense had a two-pronged focus: on those who would stay in the city and seek shelter, and on those who would try to leave. In the event of a nuclear attack, which would likely target a big city, some people living in urban centers were advised to hurry to air-raid-type shelters that had been built underground. As for those who could leave, the Federal Civil Defense Administration said that they should evacuate the cities, promising that this was a better alternative. During the hearings, the senators had questions. In the mid-1950s, most land outside big cities was little more than open countryside. Where were citizens supposed to evacuate to? And what were they supposed to eat?

The director of the Federal Civil Defense Administration, Frederick "Val" Peterson, took the stand. The former Nebraska governor was under oath. He revealed that the plan of the administration was to dig roadside trenches along public highways leading out of all the big cities across the nation. The trenches were to be three feet deep and two feet wide. When the bombs hit the cities, Peterson said, people who had already made it out were to stop driving, abandon their automobiles, lie down in the trenches, and cover themselves with dirt. Senator Kefauver, learning this along with the public for the first time, was dumbfounded. The government could use science and technology to create power as great as that generated by the sun, but when it came to civil defense, this was the best they could come up with? What about "food, water [and] sanitation in [these] trenches?" the incredulous Kefauver asked. Peterson fumbled for an answer. "Obviously, in these trenches, if they are built on an emergency basis, there would be no provisions for sanitation," he admitted. But there was an alternative plan. Instead of the dirt trenches, another idea being discussed involved using concrete pipes, four feet in diameter, to be laid down alongside the highways. When the bombs hit the cities, Peterson said, people who had already made it out would stop driving, abandon their automobiles, and crawl into the pipes. Sometime thereafter, Peterson explained, federal emergency crews would come along and bury the pipes with earth.

Senator Leverett Saltonstall, a Republican from Massachusetts, expressed astonishment. He told Peterson that he found it impossible to imagine millions of "shell-shocked evacuees waiting out a nuclear war inside concrete pipes," without fresh air, water, sanitation, food, or medical care. And for who knew how long. Senator Saltonstall said he would rather lie down in a dirt ditch "than get into a concrete pipe a mile long, with no exit." Saltonstall shared his vision of being crushed in the mayhem by fellow American citizens fighting to stay alive.

Next came the issue of food. Committee members wanted to know how the government was going to help feed evacuees after a nuclear exchange. Peterson replied that the United States would open food kitchens, but there would be little food to be served. "We can't eat canned foods," he explained, because radiation could penetrate tin cans. "We won't eat refrigerated foods," he conceded, because most electricity would be out. The truth was not pretty, he acknowledged, but was "stark, elemental, brutal, filthy and miserable," he said under oath. "We will eat gruel made of wheat cooked as it comes out of the fields and corn parched and animals slaughtered as we catch them before radioactivity destroys them." The committee told Peterson his agency's plans for evacuation were inadequate. In a matter of hours, the notion of civil defense became the subject of national ridicule. And yet the nuclear tests continued unabated.

Over the next two years, the United States exploded eighteen nuclear weapons; the Soviet Union exploded twenty-five. Nuclear spending was at an all-time high, and design originality was key. The Pentagon ordered hundreds of high-yield hydrogen bomb warheads, like the one detonated during Castle Bravo, but also smaller, lighter-weight tactical atomic bombs. Herb York flew to Washington, D.C., with a full-scale mockup of Livermore's newest design, the forty-eight-pound Davy Crockett nuclear weapon, in his carry-on bag. The Davy Crockett had the same yield as the atomic bomb dropped on Hiroshima, but advances in science meant that the powerful weapon was small enough to be handheld. Thanks to ambition and ingenuity, the Livermore laboratory had begun to pull ahead from behind. The computer designed by John von Neumann played an important role in allowing Livermore scientists to model new nuclear weapons designs before building them.

In the summer of 1955, John von Neumann was diagnosed with cancer. He had slipped and fallen, and when doctors examined him, they discovered that he had an advanced, metastasizing cancerous tumor in his collarbone. By November his spine was affected, and in January 1956 von Neumann was confined to a wheelchair. In March he entered a guarded room at Walter Reed Hospital, the U.S. Army's flagship medical center, outside Washington, D.C. John von Neumann, at the age of fifty-four, racked with pain and riddled with terror, was dying of a cancer he most likely developed because of a speck of plutonium he inhaled at Los Alamos during the war. Two armed military guards never left his side.

For a while, von Neumann's mind remained sharp, but as the end grew near, his mental faculties began to degrade. Beside him at his bed, von Neumann's brother Michael read aloud from Goethe's tragic play *Faust*. Michael would read a page and then pause. Lying on the hospital bed, eyes closed, faculties failing, for some time von Neumann could still pick up in the text precisely where his brother left off. But soon, even John von Neumann's indomitable memory would fail. Friends said the mental decline was excruciating for him to endure. An atheist all his life, von Neumann used to joke about people who believed in God. In a limerick for his wife, Klara, he'd once written, "There was a young man who said, Run! / The end of the world had begun! / The one I fear most / Is that damn Holy Ghost. / I can handle the Father and Son." Now von Neumann sought God and he called upon the services of a Roman Catholic priest.

But death grew near. In von Neumann's final, frightened last days, even the priest could not offer a reprieve. Weeks before von Neumann died, Herb York went to Walter Reed hospital to pay his final respects. "Johnny was in a bed with high, criblike sides, intended to keep him from falling out or otherwise getting out on his own," York recalled. "I tried to start a conversation about some technical topic I thought would interest and divert him, but he would say no more than a simple hello." Von Neumann's brain was failing him. Cancer was robbing him of the thing he valued most, his own mind. Soon he would not remember. In weeks there would be nothing left of him. John von Neumann died on February 8, 1957.

He left behind a single unfinished manuscript that he had been working on in his final months of life. It was called "The Computer and the Brain." A copy was made for the Los Alamos Scientific Laboratory library, where it remains today. In this paper, von Neumann draws a comparison between the computer and the human nervous system. He theorizes that one day the computer will be able to outperform the human nervous system by infinite orders of magnitude. He calls this advanced computer an "artificial automaton that has been constructed for human use." John von Neumann believed computers would one day be able to *think*.

CHAPTER THREE

Vast Weapons Systems of the Future

It was October 4, 1957, 6:00 p.m. Cocktail hour at the Officers Club at the Army Ballistic Missile Agency in Huntsville, Alabama, or "Rocket City, USA." Neil H. McElroy, a corporate executive soon to be confirmed as secretary of defense, had just arrived in a military jet with an entourage of defense officials from the Pentagon. Inside the Officers Club, drinks flowed freely. Appetizers were passed among the men. McElroy stood chatting with Wernher von Braun, the famous German rocket scientist who now served as director of development operations at Huntsville, when a press officer named Gordon Harris rushed into the room and interrupted the party with an extraordinary announcement.

"The Russians have put up a successful satellite!" Harris shouted.

The room fell silent. For several moments only the background music and the tinkling of ice cubes could be heard.

"It's broadcasting signals on a common frequency," Harris said.

"At least one of our local 'hams' has been listening to it." A barrage of questions followed.

It did not take long for news of *Sputnik* to become official. The Soviet news agency, TASS, released a statement providing technical information and specifics about *Iskusstvennyy Sputnik Zemli,* or "artificial satellite of the earth." The Soviets had beaten the Americans into space. Not since Pearl Harbor had the Pentagon been caught by a surprise of such consequence.

The nation slipped into a panic over what was seen as superior Soviet scientific prowess. Eisenhower's attempts to minimize the significance of *Sputnik* had a reverse effect, with many Americans accusing the president of trying to conceal U.S. military weakness. *Sputnik* weighed only 184 pounds, but it had been launched into space by a Soviet ICBM. Soon the Soviet ICBM would be able to carry a much heavier payload—such as a nuclear bomb—halfway across the world to any target in the United States.

The situation was made worse when, on December 20, 1957, someone leaked a top secret analysis of the Soviet threat, called the Gaither Report, to the *Washington Post.* The report "portrays a United States in the gravest danger in its history," wrote the *Post.* "It shows an America exposed to an almost immediate threat from the missile-bristling Soviet Union." If *Sputnik* had caused mild panic, the Gaither Report produced national hysteria.

But the Gaither Report had its own controversial backstory, one that would remain classified for decades. In the spring of 1957, seven months before *Sputnik* was launched, President Eisenhower asked his National Security advisors to put together a team that could answer one question: how to protect the American people in an all-out nuclear war. A RAND Corporation co-founder, the venture capitalist H. Rowan Gaither, was chosen to chair the new presidential research committee. Making up the body of the panel were officials from NORAD (North American Air Defense

Command), the Strategic Air Command, the office of the secretary of defense, the Federal Civil Defense Administration, the Weapons Systems Engineering Group, and the CIA. There were representatives from the defense contracting industry, including Livermore, Sandia, Raytheon, Boeing, Lockheed, Hughes, and RAND. The corporate advisors on the panel were from Shell Oil, IBM, Bell Telephone, New York Life Insurance, and Chase Manhattan Bank.

In the resulting top secret Gaither Report, officially titled "Deterrence and Survival in the Nuclear Age," the defense contractors, industrialists, and defense scientists concluded that there was no way to protect U.S. citizens in the event of a nuclear war. Instead, the panel advised the president to focus on building up the U.S. arsenal of nuclear weapons. The most menacing threat came from the Soviet ICBMs, they said. The individuals who calculated the exactitude of the Soviet missile threat were Herb York, scientific director at the Livermore laboratory, and Jerome Wiesner, a presidential science advisor and MIT engineering professor.

No figure mattered more. The Soviets had just successfully launched their first long-range missile from the Baikonur Cosmodrome, in what is now Kazakhstan, all the way across Siberia—a distance of three thousand miles. To determine how many ICBMs the USSR could produce in the immediate future, York and Wiesner set up shop inside the Executive Office Building, next door to the White House, in the summer of 1957 and got to work doing calculations.

"The issue was both real and hot," York later recalled. "We took the best data there were on the Soviet rocket development program, combined them with what we could learn about the availability of factory floor space [in Russia] needed for such an enterprise, and concluded that they [the Soviets] would produce thousands [of ICBMs] in the next few years."

One Castle Bravo–size bomb dropped on Washington, D.C.,

would take out the Eastern Seaboard in a single strike. York and Wiesner's ICBM analysis indicated that the Soviets wanted to be able to strike America a thousandfold. The information was shocking and alarming. If the Soviets were trying to produce a thousand ICBMs in only a few years, clearly there was only one rational conclusion to draw. The Soviet Union was preparing for total nuclear war.

It would take years to learn that the number York and Wiesner submitted to the Gaither Report was nothing more than a wild guess. In the summer of 1957 the Soviets had a total of four ICBMs built, and in the "next few years" they would build roughly one hundred more. This was a far cry from the thousands of missiles York and Wiesner said the Soviets would be producing in the next few years.

"The estimate was quite wrong," York conceded thirty years later. In defense of his error, York said, "The problem was simple enough. I knew only a little about the Soviet missile development program and nothing about the Soviet industry. In making this estimate, I was thus combing two dubious analytical procedures: worst-case analysis and mirror imaging." How could such an egregious error have happened, York was asked? "My alibi is that I was new to the subject and that, like the rest of the panel, I was an easy victim of the extreme degree of secrecy that the Russians have always used to conceal what they are doing." York also pointed out that no one on the Gaither Report panel questioned his and Wiesner's math. "I don't remember [the others] arguing with our views," York said.

When President Eisenhower received his copy of the Gaither Report on November 7, 1957, the timing could not have been worse. The *Sputnik* launch had taken place a mere month before. Eisenhower disagreed with the findings of the report. He had much better intelligence, from the CIA, but it was highly classified and no one but a small group of individuals knew about it. CIA pilot Hervey Stockman had flown a classified mission over the Soviet Union in a U-2 spy plane the year before. Stockman returned from his dangerous mission with thousands of photographs of Soviet Russia, the first ever (this was before the Corona satellite program), showing that the Russians were not preparing for total war. There was only one person on the Gaither panel who had knowledge of this information, and that was CIA deputy director Richard Bissell. It was Bissell who was in charge of the U-2 program, which he ran out of a secret base called Area 51, in Nevada. No one else on the Gaither panel had a need to know about the top secret U-2 program and the multiple missions it had been flying over the Soviet Union. All the Gaither panel had to go by was what York and Wiesner told them, in error, about Soviet ICBMs.

After President Eisenhower rejected most of the findings of the panel, someone leaked the top secret report to the press. It was York and Wiesner's findings about the missile threat that the public focused on, which was what caused the *Sputnik* panic to escalate into hysteria. Eisenhower responded by creating the President's Science Advisory Committee to advise him on what to do next. Among those chosen was Herb York, the youngest member of the group. It remains a mystery whether or not the president knew that York was responsible for the most consequential error in the Gaither Report. York soon left Livermore for Washington, D.C. He would remain there for the rest of the Eisenhower presidency.

With the narrative of Soviet aggression spinning out of control, the president authorized Secretary of Defense McElroy to proceed with a bold new plan. McElroy was a master of public relations. A thirty-two-year veteran of Procter & Gamble, McElroy is considered the father of brand management. He began as a door-to-door soap salesman and worked his way up through management. In the mid-1950s, P&G had four major soap brands—Ivory, Joy, Tide, and Oxydol. Sales were lagging until McElroy came up with the concept of promoting competition among in-house brands and targeting specific audiences to advertise to. It was McElroy's idea to run soap ads on daytime television, when many American housewives watched TV. By 1957, P&G soap sales had risen to $1 billion a year, and McElroy would be credited with inventing the concept of the soap opera. "Soap operas sell lots of soap," he famously said. Now McElroy was the U.S. secretary of defense. He took office with a clear vision. "I conceive the role of the Secretary of Defense to be that of captain of President Eisenhower's defense team," he said. His first job as captain was to counter the threat of any future Soviet scientific surprise.

On November 20, 1957, just five weeks after assuming office, Secretary McElroy went to Capitol Hill with a bold idea. He proposed the creation of a new agency inside the Pentagon, called the Advanced Research Projects Agency, or ARPA. This agency would be in charge of the nation's most technologically advanced military projects being researched and developed for national defense, including everything that would be flown in outer space.

"What we have in mind for that agency," McElroy told lawmakers, was an entity that would handle "all satellite and space research and development projects" but also have "a function that extends beyond the immediate foreseeable weapons systems of the current or near future." McElroy was looking far ahead. America needed an agency that could visualize the nation's needs before those needs yet existed, he said. An agency that could research and develop "the vast weapons systems of the future."

Congress liked the idea, and McElroy was encouraged to proceed. The military services, however, were adamantly opposed. The Army, Air Force, and Navy were unwilling to give up control of the research and development that was going on inside their individual services, most notably in the vast new frontier that was space. McElroy called the most senior military leaders into his office in the E-Ring of the Pentagon to discuss how best to handle "the new dimension of outer space."

In separate meetings, Army, Air Force, and Navy commanders each insisted that outer space was their service's domain. To the

Army, the moon was simply "the high ground," and therefore part of its domain. Air Force generals, claiming that space was "just a little higher up" than the area they already controlled, tried to get Secretary McElroy interested in their plans for "creating a new Aerospace Force." The admirals and vice admirals of the U.S. Navy argued that "outer space over the oceans" was a natural extension of the "underwater, surface and air regime in which [the Navy] operated" and should therefore be considered the Navy's domain. General Bernard Schriever of the U.S. Air Force told the Senate Preparedness Subcommittee that he wanted to state on record his "strong negative against ARPA."

The Atomic Energy Commission had its own idea about this new agency McElroy was proposing. Ever seeking more power and control, the Atomic Energy Commission lobbied to remove authority over outer space from the Defense Department entirely and have it placed under AEC jurisdiction. The AEC chairman had a bill introduced in Congress to establish an "Outer Space Division." Defense contractors also lobbied hard against McElroy's idea for a new agency. Many feared that their established relations with individual military services would be in jeopardy. Ernest Lawrence of Livermore rushed to the Pentagon to meet personally with Defense Secretary McElroy and present his alternative idea to ARPA. Accompanying Lawrence was Charles Thomas, the president of Monsanto Chemical Company, a nuclear defense contractor that would be vilified during the Vietnam War for producing the herbicide Agent Orange, and made notorious in the 1990s for being the first agrochemical company to genetically modify food crops. Lawrence and Thomas met with McElroy in his private office and shared their idea "to adopt some radical new measures... to meet the Sputnik challenge and cope better with problems of science and technology in the Defense Establishment." They proposed that McElroy allow the two of them to create and administer a new government agency, classified top secret and modeled after the

Manhattan Project. The meeting lasted several hours before McElroy rejected the two defense contractors' idea as "infeasible in peacetime." Lawrence had a second suggestion. If this new agency was to work, it would need a brilliant scientist at the helm. Someone who understood how the military and industry could put America's best scientists to work solving problems of national defense. The perfect person, said Lawrence, was Herb York. McElroy promised to give the suggestion some thought.

McElroy had one last hurdle to overcome, involving colleagues just one floor away at the Pentagon. The Joint Chiefs of Staff hated the idea of an Advanced Research Projects Agency and registered a formal nonconcurrence on December 7, 1957. But the attack against ARPA by the military services was bound to fail. "The fact that they didn't want an ARPA is one reason [Eisenhower] did," said Admiral John E. Clark, an early ARPA employee.

President Eisenhower was fed up with the interservice rivalries. Having commanded the Supreme Headquarters Allied Expeditionary Forces in Europe during World War II, he held deep convictions regarding the value of unity among the military services. As president, he had been a crusader against the excessive waste of resources that came from service duplication. "The Army and Air Force 'race' to build almost duplicate CRBMs [Continental Range Ballistic Missiles] incensed him," wrote presidential historian Sherman Adams.

On January 7, 1958, President Eisenhower sent a memorandum to Congress authorizing $10 million in the 1958 fiscal year "for expenses necessary for the Advanced Research Projects Agency, including acquisition and construction of such research, development and test facilities, and equipment, as may be authorized by the Secretary of Defense, to remain available until expended."

In his State of the Union message two nights later, Eisenhower announced to the nation the creation of this new agency. "Some of the important new weapons which technology has produced do not fit into any existing service pattern," Eisenhower explained. These new weapons should "cut across all services, involve all services, and transcend all services, at every stage from development to operation." The rapid technological advances and the revolutionary new weapons this technology was producing created a threat as revolutionary to warfare as the invention of the airplane, Eisenhower said. But instead of working together, the services had succumbed to petty "jurisdictional disputes" that "bewilder and confuse the public and create the impression that service differences are damaging the national interest." This was why ARPA had been created, Eisenhower said, in "recognition of the need for single control in some of our most advanced development projects."

That the president would publicly admonish the services outraged top officials, including the Joint Chiefs of Staff. "So the Agency was controversial even before it was formed," wrote Lawrence P. Gise, ARPA's first administrator, in an unpublished history of the agency's origins. "Beset by enemies internally, subjected to critical pressures externally, and starting from scratch in a novel area of endeavor, ARPA was a tumultuous and exciting place to be."

It was the second week of February 1958, and Washington, D.C., was blanketed in snow. A severe blizzard had wreaked havoc on the nation's capital. Subzero wind chills and five-foot snow drifts paralyzed traffic. On Monday morning, the Eisenhower administration advised all nonessential government workers to stay home. Herb York received a telephone call at his house. It was the personal secretary to Neil McElroy, asking York to come to the Pentagon right away for a meeting with the secretary of defense, alone. Never mind the storm, York recalled. He was determined to get to the Pentagon.

Herb York was in a remarkable position. If he did not have

time to reflect on this now, he would pay homage to his humble background later in life. Here he was, living in Washington, D.C., and advising the president of the United States on scientific matters, when he had been the first person in his family to attend college. York's father was a New York Central Railroad baggage man. His grandfather made caskets for a living; his specialty was lining a customer's permanent resting place with satin bows and carved velvet trim. Herb York had been born of humble means but had a brilliant mind and plenty of ambition. To think he was only thirty-six years old.

"From the earliest times," York recalled, "I remember [my father] saying he did not want his son to be a railroad man. He made it clear that that meant I should go to college, even though he knew little about what that actually entailed." York followed his father's advice, spending most of his free time at the Watertown, New York, public library reading newspapers, books, and science magazines. He attended the University of Rochester on a scholarship and excelled in the field he chose for himself, physics. Like many other top university physics graduates of his generation, York was recruited into the Manhattan Project during the war. In the spring of 1943 he traveled by bus to faraway Berkeley, California, where, as circumstance would have it, he was assigned to work under Ernest O. Lawrence. During the war, York helped produce uranium in Lawrence's cyclotron, material that would eventually make its way into the core of the Hiroshima atomic bomb. After the war York returned to Berkeley to get his Ph.D. During his doctoral research, he co-discovered the neutron pi meson, which elevated him to elite status among nuclear scientists. In 1952 York became chief scientist at Livermore. Now, during the February 1958 nor'easter, Herb York wondered what lay ahead.

"I made my way with difficulty across the river to the Pentagon and did a lot of walking in deep snow," York recalled. He had tried to hail a taxi, but there were none around. The parking lot at the Pentagon was almost empty. But the man he had come to see, Secretary of Defense McElroy, was in his office, busy at work. York had a feeling he was being considered for the position of chief scientist at ARPA. Because of the snowstorm, he would benefit, he said, from having an "unhurried, hour-long, one-on-one conversation that I could not have had with the secretary on an ordinary, busy day."

After the meeting York went home and McElroy weighed his options. There was one other contender for the position of ARPA chief scientist, and that was Wernher von Braun. Von Braun and his team had just launched America's first successful satellite, *Explorer I,* and as far as the public was concerned, von Braun's star was on the rise. But Army intelligence had information on von Braun that the rest of the world most definitely did not, namely, that he had been an officer with the Nazi paramilitary organization the SS during the war and that he was implicated in the deaths of thousands of slave laborers forced to build the V-2 rocket, in an underground labor-concentration camp called Nordhausen, in Nazi Germany.

While McElroy weighed his options for scientific director, new information came to light. Von Braun was nothing if not entitled, and in his discussions regarding the new position, he insisted that were he to transfer his services over to the Pentagon, a sizable group of his German rocket scientist colleagues would have to accompany him there. Army intelligence had classified dossiers on each of von Braun's 113 German colleagues. They were all part of Operation Paperclip, the secret intelligence program that had brought Nazi scientists to America after the war. Many of von Braun's rocket team members had been ardent Nazis, members of ultra-nationalistic paramilitary organizations, including the SS and the SA.

"For a while Wernher von Braun appeared to have the job but to get him it was necessary to take his 10–15 man package of [German] associates and that was not acceptable," wrote ARPA administrator J. Robert Loftis in a declassified report. Secretary McElroy offered Herb York the job. York accepted. It was the opportunity of a lifetime, he said.

York moved into his office in the Pentagon the following month, in March 1958. He would remain on the president's scientific advisory board. On the wall of York's new office he hung a large framed photograph of the moon. Next to it he hung an empty frame. When people visited they would ask, why the empty frame? York told them he would leave the frame empty until it could be filled with a photograph of the backside of the moon, taken from a spacecraft to be developed by ARPA. This new agency Herb York was in charge of at the Pentagon would be capable of phenomenal things.

With his new Advanced Research Projects Agency in place, President Eisenhower was more determined than ever to put an end to nuclear weapons tests. The week after York hung the moon photograph on his office wall, Eisenhower took all of his scientific advisors, including Herb York, to Ramey Air Force Base, in Puerto Rico, to discuss banning nuclear weapons tests. The president wanted to know, was this good for national security, and if so, could it be done? Everyone voted yes on both counts, except Herb York, who abstained.

Decades later, York explained his bias. "I might well have responded 'no' but abstain was the most I could do under the circumstances." Just weeks on the ARPA job, York felt conflicted. He now served the president of the United States and the secretary of defense. But he also remained loyal to Ernest Lawrence, whom he had worked for his entire adult life, and who was something of a father figure to him. Edward Teller was York's mentor, the teacher who had taught him most of what he knew about nuclear physics. "Lawrence and Teller were all participants in the nuclear weapons program," York later explained. "It was their ox that was about to be gored." If the president was able to ban nuclear weapons tests, the Livermore laboratory would most likely cease to exist.

The following day, after hearing arguments from the other scientists, York changed his position and voted in favor of a nuclear weapons test ban. It did not take long for word to reach Livermore, where Edward Teller became enraged. "Traitorous!" Teller said of York to his Livermore colleagues.

Just two weeks after the Puerto Rico trip, President Eisenhower took action. In his memoirs the president wrote, "I formally proposed to Chairman Khrushchev a measure we had been considering—a meeting of experts whose technical studies would precede any political conference." Come summer, scientific experts from the United States and the Soviet Union would meet in Geneva to discuss how to put an end to nuclear weapons tests once and for all. The centerpiece was test detection. ARPA would be in charge of overseeing this new technology, which included seismic and atmospheric sensing, designed to make sure no one cheated on the test ban. The program was called Vela. Its technology was highly classified and included three subprograms: Vela Hotel, Vela Uniform, and Vela Sierra.

The leaders of the world's two superpowers each had a vested interest in making this test ban happen. Each man was tired of having to live and govern under the nuclear sword of Damocles. Both Eisenhower and Khrushchev would send their most qualified scientists to Geneva, with a mission to sort out any differences and to make the moratorium happen. President Eisenhower made a bold and brilliant move with his choice. Instead of sending one of his science advisors who wanted nuclear weapons tests to stop, he chose a scientist who did not: Ernest Lawrence. So committed to nuclear weapons tests was Ernest Lawrence that he had recently told Congress, "If we stop testing.... Well, God forbid...we will have to use weapons that [will] kill 50 million people that need not have been killed."

President Eisenhower was determined to bring about a test

ban, but he was also determined to ensure that the Soviets could not and would not cheat. In sending Lawrence on his behalf, Eisenhower knew that the Soviet scientists' intentions would be under intense scrutiny. For the first time since Castle Bravo, there was a sense of hope in the air.

Meanwhile, at ARPA, Herb York was about to get to work on the Vela programs. Vela would soon become ARPA's second-biggest program after Defender, which was ARPA's colossal effort to advance antiballistic missile technology. Vela was a joint effort with the Atomic Energy Commission, the Air Force, and later NASA to advance sensor technology so the United States could certify that no nuclear weapons were being detonated in secret. Vela Hotel developed a high-altitude satellite system to detect nuclear explosions from space. Vela Uniform developed ground sensors able to detect nuclear explosions underground, and produced a program to monitor and read "seismic noise" across the globe. Vela Sierra monitored potential nuclear explosions in space.

So much rested on the success of the Geneva Convention of Experts. Putting an end to nuclear weapons tests would slow the arms race and dramatically reduce the chances for all-out nuclear war. But could it be done?

CHAPTER FOUR

Emergency Plans

For Herb York, the sense of hopefulness that followed him back home from Puerto Rico did not last long. Shortly after the president announced his plans for a nuclear test ban, a twenty-two-page secret document called "The Emergency Plans Book" arrived on York's desk at the Pentagon. Its classified contents were nothing short of apocalyptic. They would remain classified for the next forty years. When, in 1998, the Defense Department learned that an author named L. Douglas Keeney had discovered a copy of "The Emergency Plans Book" inside a declassified U.S. Air Force file at the National Archives, the Pentagon immediately reclassified the report. Keeney made public the contents of the copy he had come across, but the original document remains classified.

For defense officials, "The Emergency Plans Book" served as the "only approved guidance to departments and agencies" regarding what to expect before, during, and after a Soviet nuclear attack on U.S. soil. Issued by the Office of Emergency Planning, a federal agency whose function was to coordinate and control wartime mobilization activities, the book was not a hypothetical war game.

It was official protocol. To those familiar with its contents, it would become known as the Doomsday scenario.

The scenario begins on a hypothetical "D-Day" in the not-so-distant future. Because of the inadequacy of U.S. capabilities at the time, the first strike comes as a surprise. Soviet sleeper cells have managed to "emplace by clandestine means" several hydrogen bombs inside the continental United States, and these weapons are the first to explode. Thermonuclear war has begun.

In quick succession, Soviet submarines swarm the Eastern and Western Seaboards, firing nuclear missiles at dozens of inland targets. At roughly the same time, the Soviets launch a catastrophic air attack against the United States using bombers and fighter jets. The U.S. Air Defense Command destroys a substantial portion of the attacking swarms, but at least half of the Soviet aircraft are able to fire off their tactical nuclear weapons before being shot down. The opening salvo comes to a climax as hundreds of incoming ICBMs, launched from the Soviet Union, reach the U.S. mainland. The majority of these nuclear-armed missiles are able to outfox the Army's Nike-Ajax missile batteries and strike military and civilian targets across the nation. In less than one hour, 25 million Americans are dead.

The Soviets have all but decapitated U.S. military installations, write the authors of "The Emergency Plans Book," including most atomic weapons facilities, naval bases, airfields, and Army bases. All major communication centers, financial districts, and transportation hubs have been targeted for attack, and the majority of them have suffered catastrophic losses. America's infrastructure has been obliterated. Virtually nothing remains of Washington, D.C. Even those living in rural America experience death and destruction on a cataclysmic scale. Because of automated-targeting errors, many of the nuclear weapons miss their intended targets and instead strike at random across the heartland.

Though crippled, the U.S. military has not been destroyed and the counterattack begins. "Notwithstanding severe losses of military and civilian personnel and materiel," the authors predict, "air operations against the enemy are continuing and our land and naval forces are heavily engaged. Both sides are making use of atomic weapons for tactical air support and in the land battle." Lightweight portable nuclear weapons, like Livermore's Davy Crocket bomb, are deployed across the nation by the thousands as Soviet ground forces invade. Next comes a final full-scale nuclear exchange. ICBMs rain down from the skies by the hundreds. Coastal naval bases are pummeled with hydrogen bombs. Ports are clogged with sinking ships. Merchant shipping comes to a halt. Surface transportation and airlift capacity are nonexistent.

There are now hundreds of ground zeros across America, and everything within a five- to ten-mile radius of each one has been obliterated. The confluence of fireballs has created a series of major firestorms. Forests and cities are in flames. Those who escape being burned to death are subjected to varying degrees of deadly radiation. "The surface bursts have resulted in widespread radioactive fallout of such intensity that over substantial parts of the United States the taking of shelter for considerable periods of time is the only means of survival."

In the document's "Post-Attack Analysis," things get much worse. One hundred million American survivors now live in a nation entirely without the rule of law. The government is paralyzed. Roughly 50 million people are in need of immediate emergency medical attention, half of whom will require hospitalization for up to twelve weeks. Twelve and a half million others have received lethal doses of radiation and will die in the next few days, regardless of treatment. Health resources are in a critical state. The doctors and nurses who survived the first strike cannot begin to handle what is now being asked of them. Of a pre-attack total of 1.6 million U.S. hospital beds, 100,000 remain. Radiation is but one malady. "Communicable diseases, including typhoid fever, smallpox, tetanus and streptococcal diseases, begin to run rampant." Day-to-day production of food comes to a halt. Most salvageable food stocks have been contaminated. Widespread looting has begun, with survivors hoarding what little remains.

The housing system has gone critical. Millions of homes were destroyed in the nuclear exchange; millions of people now have nowhere to live. Fallout has made vast portions of the Eastern Seaboard uninhabitable. There is no electricity, no refrigeration, no transportation, and no community water systems. Another deadly health menace emerges with the inability of the survivors to dispose of human waste or the dead bodies of millions killed in a single day. Then comes the knockout punch. "Along the coasts, bubonic plague, cholera and typhus are expected to emerge," write the authors, "part of a Soviet biological warfare secondary attack." The authors of the secret document clearly believe the Soviets to be the kind of enemy who will stop at nothing. Americans who managed to survive nuclear Armageddon must now prepare for the emergence of incurable diseases like bubonic plague.

By the twenty-first century, catastrophic narratives like the Doomsday scenario would become a staple of post-apocalyptic fiction, films, and video games. But in 1958 this was the first and only known official document of its kind. Out in Santa Monica, RAND analysts regularly gamed out first- and second-strike scenarios as war games, which Air Force officials would then use to persuade Congress to allocate more funds for the Strategic Air Command. But "The Emergency Plans Book" was not a "what if"; it was a "here's when." It was doctrine. An official reference manual.

It was also not a report that could be ignored. "The Emergency Plans Book" was sent to the highest-ranking defense officials in each of the military services, the Joint Chiefs of Staff, the director of ARPA, the secretary of defense, each of the assistant secretaries of defense, and the director of the National Security Agency. In a cover letter, the director of the Office of Emergency Planning instructed recipients to submit changes or indicate they had none. As for Herb York, when faced with this portrait of extreme cataclysm, the ARPA director did not lose sight of the agency's mission to prevent strategic surprise. Submitting or not submitting notes to the Office of Emergency Planning was, for York, a moot point.

Herb York had another plan in play, a seemingly preposterous idea that was already several years in the making. What if ARPA could create a defensive shield over the entire United States and stop incoming Soviet ICBMs in their tracks? York believed it could be done on account of a theory that had been proposed to him by an eccentric, brilliant, and obscure scientist named Nicholas Christofilos. As York later explained, Christofilos believed it was possible to create "an Astro-dome like defensive shield made up of high-energy electrons trapped in the earth's magnetic field just above the atmosphere." It sounded ludicrous. Something straight out of a Marvel comic book. But York thought it just might work.

Which is why, in the summer of 1958, Herb York gathered together a group of the nation's top scientists and had them briefed on this radical, classified idea. York wanted to know what the top men of science thought of what he called the "Christofilos effect." The top secret program had already been given the go-ahead by the president of the United States. In March 1958 York met with Eisenhower and personally briefed him on plans for an ARPA operation to test the Christofilos effect. By summer, the idea was no longer just an idea but ARPA's first full-scale operation. The top secret, restricted data, limited distribution Operation Order 7-58 went by the cover name Project Floral. Its real name, which was classified, was Operation Argus—for the mythological giant with one hundred eyes.

On July 14, 1958, with top secret clearances in place, twenty-two defense scientists gathered at the National War College at Fort McNair in Washington, D.C., with the goal of producing "ARPA

Study No. 1." The gathering went by its own code name, Project 137. Its purpose, explained York, was "to identify problems not now receiving adequate attention" in the national security domain.

"Fort McNair was a delightful place to work," remembered Marvin "Murph" Goldberger, one of the Project 137 scientists. The facility was one of the oldest Army posts in the nation and one of the most genteel. Each morning the scientists gathered in Roosevelt Hall, a grand neoclassical building of red brick with granite trim overlooking the Potomac. There they listened to Defense Department officials deliver briefings on America's "defense problems selected for their urgency." Then the scientists gathered in groups to discuss what had been said and brainstorm science-based solutions. Afternoons were spent writing. In the early evening, everyone would dine together, in the War College mess hall, and discuss Soviet threats. They were dealing with a total of sixty-eight national security problems and programs, from submarine warfare and balloon warfare to biological weapons, chemical sensing, and the possibility of inventing a laser beam weapon. But the most interesting program by far, as Goldberger recalled, was the Christofilos effect.

"Hearing about it required its own special clearance," Goldberger said.

The Project 137 group was led by John Wheeler, a Princeton University physicist famous for coining the term "black hole." Working alongside Wheeler were five others from Princeton, four from Berkeley, three from the University of Illinois, one from Stanford, one from the University of Chicago, and one from Cal Tech. Four scientists came from the federally funded nuclear laboratories, Los Alamos, Livermore, Oak Ridge, and Sandia. Two scientists came from the defense industry, one from General Dynamics and the other from the DuPont chemical company.

These were advanced scientific thinkers of the most serious kind. The Supermen of hard science. Among them were particle physicists, theoretical physicists, astrophysicists, chemists, mathematicians, an economist, and a nuclear weapons engineer. They were men who coined terms like hexaquark, wormholes, and quantum foam. Two of them, Eugene Wigner and Val Fitch, would win the Nobel Prize in physics. All of the scientists were experienced in Defense Department work, and many had been part of the Manhattan Project during World War II. Stated requirements for membership in Project 137 were "ingenuity, practicality and motivation."

"We listened to Nick [Christofilos] discuss the [Christofilos] effect," recalled Goldberger. "He was a strange kind of genius."

Christofilos's theoretical Astrodome-like shield was the hoped-for result of exploding a large number of nuclear weapons in space as a means of defending against incoming Soviet ICBMs. By Christofilos's count, this likely meant "thousands per year, in the lower reaches of the atmosphere." These explosions, he said, would produce "huge quantities of radioactive atoms, and these in turn would emit high-energy electrons (beta particles) and inject them into a region of space where the earth's magnetic fields would trap and hold on them for a long time." Christofilos figured that this electromagnetic field could last months, or perhaps longer, and that "the trapped electrons would cause severe radiation—and even heat damage—to anything, man or nuclear weapon, that tried to fly through the region." In short, the idea was that the arming and firing mechanisms on the incoming Soviet ICBMs would be fried.

Christofilos had presented the idea a few years earlier, back when York was the chief scientist at Livermore. "His purpose was of epic proportions," York recalled. "His idea was the most amazing and original of all not only at Livermore but, to my knowledge, in the entire country," a plan to create "an impenetrable shield of high-energy electrons over our heads, a shield that would destroy any nuclear warhead that might be sent against us." But exploding thousands of nuclear weapons in space each year was an impractical proposition. "At the time Nick presented these proposals, I could not conceive of a procedure for actually carrying them out," said York. "In sum, there was simply no place to take an invention like Nick's." Then York became chief scientist at ARPA.

Nicholas Christofilos had an unusual backstory. He was born in Boston to Greek immigrant parents but at the age of seven returned with his family to Athens, where he went to school, dreamed about science, and became an amateur radio operator. He graduated from the National Technical University in Athens in 1938 and went to work in an elevator factory. His first job was as an elevator installer. When the Nazis took over Athens, Christofilos's elevator factory was converted to a truck repair facility. Left with "very little to do," Christofilos kept himself busy learning German. Eventually he was able to read the German-language physics textbooks and scientific journals that his new Nazi bosses left lying around the factory. According to Herb York, Nick Christofilos began "focusing his attention on the design of high-energy accelerators—cyclotrons and the like."

With no formal training, and in a matter of a few years, Christofilos transformed himself from an elevator technician into one of the most ingenious scientists in the modern world. There are almost no details about his work during this dark time of occupation and war, but three years after the end of the war, in 1948, he wrote a letter to the University of California Radiation Laboratory in Berkeley, "purporting to describe a new invention," according to York. "The letter was, apparently, not easy to decipher." But when a scientist at Livermore finally did "puzzle it out," says York, "he discovered that it was only another way of describing the synchrocyclotron," a device that had been invented independently several years before by Edwin McMillan, a chemist at Berkeley, and Vladimir Veksler, a physicist in the USSR. "Papers describing that invention had already been published more than a year before Nick's letter arrived, so it was set aside and forgotten," said York.

The supposition was that the letter writer could have gotten the information from the academic paper. Then, two years later, scientists at Livermore received a second letter from Nicholas Christofilos, this one describing another type of particle accelerator. "It was considerably more complex than the first," said York, "and whoever was assigned to read it could not make out what it was trying to say." Same as the first letter, it was cast aside.

Two years later, two nuclear physicists at the Brookhaven National Laboratory on Long Island published a paper describing an accelerator, this one so technologically advanced that for the first time in the history of science, a machine could "produce particles with more than one billion electron volts of energy," noted York. As it so happened, Christofilos had recently moved to the United States. When he read the article in a science journal, he contacted the authors to tell them he had already invented that machine in his mind, and had described it in a letter that was on file with the Livermore lab. When Christofilos demanded due credit for the invention, a search of the records was made. Sure enough, according to York, Christofilos had a clear priority of invention. "Naturally," recalled York, the discovery that a Greek elevator installer had priority in this very sophisticated invention produced a flurry of interest and reaction." In 1954 Christofilos was offered a job at Brookhaven, where a huge accelerator based on his invention was being built. But soon Christofilos became bored with the invention he had imagined years before. He was already well on to other ideas. When Herb York learned the strange story of Nicholas Christofilos, he saw great potential and hired him.

Resistance came from the federal security clearance people. "They found it hard to believe that an 'elevator mechanic' had accomplished all that Christofilos had claimed," said York. "He must be, they thought, some sort of mole that the Russians had pumped full of ideas not his own." Clearance officers finally authorized Christofilos to work at Livermore, giving him access to top secret information. But he was denied the coveted Q clearance, which allows a scientist access to nuclear secrets. At Livermore, Christofilos produced one seminal idea after another. Eventually he was granted higher clearances than just about everyone else around him. When *Sputnik* flew, Christofilos became convinced that the Russians had gained a too significant scientific advantage over the United States. That they were likely planning a surprise attack. He threw all his energy and ingenuity into finding a way to keep this from happening. Now the Project 137 scientists were at a crossroads. It was risky and expensive. But if the Christofilos effect worked, it would be a magic bullet answer to ballistic missile defense.

At Fort McNair, the scientists agreed that the Christofilos effect was worth investigating. In practical terms, it was the best idea anyone had come up with. The scope of national security threats facing the nation left many of the Project 137 scientists with a deep sense of foreboding. It caused "responsible people sleepless nights," John Wheeler said. Although all of the scientists had worked on Defense Department programs before, learning of sixty-eight threats concurrently "weighed heavily on the conscience," Goldberger recalled.

"Many of the members of Project 137 were deeply disturbed and others even shocked by the gravity of the problems with which they found themselves confronted," Wheeler wrote in his after-action report for ARPA. "The group has developed a strong feeling for and deep appreciation of the great crisis with which the nation is faced. The group senses the rapidly increasing danger into which we are inexorably heading."

Much rested on the success of Operation Argus, now set to unfold at the bottom of the world.

Halfway across the earth, in the middle of the South Atlantic Ocean, the men of Task Force 88 were assembled as far away from civilization as man can get without being in Antarctica. The spot had been chosen because it was outside shipping lanes, in a remote expanse between the tip of South America and the tip of Africa, east of a dip in the magnetic field known as the Brazilian Anomaly. The weather was unpredictable, and there was the issue of high seas. It was in this rough ocean that the U.S. military planned to launch three nuclear weapons into space, off the back of a moving seaplane tender called the USS *Norton Sound.* The hope was that the Christofilos effect would create a great enough disturbance in the earth's geomagnetic fields, in the layers of the ionosphere, and in radio waves that it would ruin the delicate electronics housed inside any incoming missile.

An extraordinary number of men and machines were involved in Operation Argus, the only fully classified test in the history of U.S. nuclear testing; no part of the operation was made public, nor would the public know about it until the *New York Times* broke the story six months after its completion. There were 4,500 military personnel, hundreds of scientists and engineers, twenty-one fixed-wing aircraft, eight Sikorsky helicopters, three destroyers, a fleet oiler, an aircraft carrier, a seaplane tender, more than a dozen Lockheed X-17A missiles, and three nuclear warheads involved. ARPA was the agency in charge, with divisions from the Air Force, the Army, and the Navy shouldering major elements of the operation. Satellites, each carrying a payload of a hundred pounds of recording instruments, would be placed in equatorial and polar orbits by the Army Ballistic Missile Agency shortly before the tests. The sensors would record effects and relay data. With so many moving parts, on so many different continents, any number of things could go wrong.

Weather was a major unknown to contend with. Operation Argus involved firing three nuclear-tipped Lockheed X-17A missiles off the back of a moving ship. The USS *Norton Sound* was capable of launching a missile in winds up to forty-six miles per hour, but no one had expected waves nearing twenty feet. The ship could make speed corrections to compensate for the wind, but the waves threatened to dangerously alter the missile trajectory in its boost stage. The commander of Task Force 88 was concerned with the safety of his crew, and with good reason.

During a practice run of a missile launch, one of the X-17As failed in flight, after only twenty-five seconds. Had there been a nuclear weapon in the nosecone, it would have produced a catastrophic disaster. The missile would have been just a few thousand feet up, and exploding at that height would likely have killed or injured many of the crew. Making matters seem even more precarious, in the following test run, the missile failed again, this time just three seconds after launch.

Secrecy was paramount to success. If the Christofilos effect was achieved, it would produce massive disturbances across the earth's upper atmosphere. These disruptions would be detected by every nation monitoring these kinds of phenomena, most notably the Soviets. Total secrecy meant the disturbances would infuriate the Soviets; they would have no idea what caused them and would most likely conclude the United States was working on a top secret high-altitude weapon. This was one of the desired effects.

Four days before the first nuclear launch, all ships and aircraft were in place. U.S. reconnaissance aircraft patrolled the skies over the South Atlantic. Ships carrying antiaircraft rockets were at the ready, in the unforeseen event of Soviet sabotage. The commander of Task Force 88 sent his final coded message to the ARPA office at the Pentagon, a prearranged indication that the operation was a go at his end.

"Doctor Livingstone, I presume?" the commander stated clearly into a ship-to-shore radio microphone. The first test would take place on August 27, 1958. Although no one had a name for it at the time, Operation Argus was the world's first test of an electromagnetic pulse bomb, or EMP.

Halfway across the world, in Switzerland, a remarkable series of events was taking place. It was the height of the summer season, and Ernest O. Lawrence and his wife, Molly, were attending a party at the historic Parc des Eaux-Vives, an eighteenth-century mansion on Lake Geneva. Mist rose off the lake, the weather was magnificent, and from the villa's terrace where the couple sat behind protective glass, there were stunning panoramic views. Ernest and Molly Lawrence dined and watched fireworks. Wine flowed. And Ernest Lawrence was having a miserable time.

For the first time in the history of nuclear weapons, top scientists from the United States and the Soviet Union had been meeting here in Geneva, under the strictest of security provisions, to hash out technical terms so that a nuclear test suspension could go forward. The Geneva Conference of Experts marked the ultimate low point in the prolific nuclear weapons career of Ernest Lawrence. For more than twenty years, Lawrence had been one of the nation's most vocal advocates for nuclear weapons development and testing, along with his deputy Edward Teller. That Eisenhower wanted Lawrence to represent him distressed Lawrence when he was first asked, and it upset him even more now that he was attending the conference.

"The President has asked, so I must go!" he told Molly before they left California. The very thought rendered Lawrence "depressed over the idea," according to his biographer Herbert Childs, but still he "felt it was his duty to accept" and to go to Geneva. The conference lasted all summer, and for Lawrence the meetings were becoming increasingly stressful. There were so many important technical aspects to iron out, including ways in which each side could be certain that the other side would not cheat. For that, Lawrence brought his Livermore deputy Harold Brown, the young physicist who had taken over York's job as chief scientist at Livermore.

Here in Geneva, Brown acted as Lawrence's technical advisor. In order to stop testing, both superpowers had to agree to the creation of a network of 170 seismic detection facilities across Europe, Asia, and North America. This technology effort was being spearheaded by ARPA through its Vela Uniform program. Technology had advanced to the point where these detection facilities would soon be able to monitor and sense, with close to 100 percent certainty, any aboveground nuclear test over 1 kiloton and, with 90 percent certainty, any underground test over 5 kilotons. Both sides knew that in some situations it was difficult for detection facilities to tell the difference between an earthquake and an underground test. These were the kinds of verification details that the experts were working to hash out.

Ernest Lawrence had been attending meetings by day and social events by night. The situation was stressful, and now he was exhausted. Lawrence worried that there was something wrong with his health. He deeply distrusted the Soviets. Perhaps working with their scientists was making him ill? He had just returned from a first-class trip across India and Europe, traveling in private planes and being driven by chauffeurs. He and his family had visited with statesmen and maharajahs. There, he'd felt fine. Travel always made him feel better, and Molly suggested a day trip to the ski resort at Chamonix-Mont-Blanc, in the nearby Alps. Lawrence agreed and off they went, but upon his return, Lawrence came down with a fever. The next day he was unable to get out of bed.

"He just didn't seem to get well, though he didn't seem terribly sick," recalled his colleague Robert Bacher, one of three nuclear scientists officially representing the United States. Fearing her husband had pneumonia, Molly Lawrence called for a physician. Dr. Bernard Wissmer examined Lawrence and noted that he "was cheerful and did not seem acutely ill, despite fever."

Lawrence confided in the Swiss doctor. He suffered from colitis, or inflammation of the bowels, he said, and he relapsed when he became tense. Dr. Wissmer gave him a proctoscopic exam and said he was in good health. The following day Lawrence made some effort to attend the conference, but mostly he had Harold Brown participate on his behalf. Venturing out of his hotel room, he collapsed in the hallway. Molly suggested they return home.

"I could never live with myself if I left before this conference was over," Lawrence told his wife. Dr. Wissmer prescribed penicillin. Then later that week, after a lakeside lunch with his translator, the Berkeley professor and Russian émigré Leonid Tichvinsky, Lawrence decided that he had had enough. "This is it, we're going home tonight," he told his wife.

Arriving back in California, Lawrence checked into a hospital. He never left. He was given a blood transfusion and was told he needed to have his colon removed. The thought of never being able to defecate like a healthy human horrified him, his biographer later revealed. Shortly after the surgery, Lawrence slipped into a coma. On August 27, he died. He had just turned fifty-seven years old. The Livermore laboratory would be renamed the Lawrence Livermore National Laboratory.

Halfway across the world in a far corner of the South Atlantic, outside shipping lanes and near a dip in the magnetic field, on the same day that Ernest Lawrence died, the first of the three Argus high-altitude nuclear weapons was detonated. Argus 1 suffered an errant missile trajectory and missed its target—which was 340 nautical miles above the earth—by more 230 miles. Three days later Argus 2 also failed to reach its desired altitude and exploded roughly 84 nautical miles above the task force launching area. The last and final test, Argus 3, was the most precarious, first with a misfire in high winds followed by a nuclear explosion on September 6, 1958, at an altitude of 115 nautical miles. Operation Argus proved to be a grand disappointment. The results were nothing close to what Nicholas Christofilos had predicted and Herb York had hoped for. While the Christofilos effect did occur, it was limited in intensity and very short-lived. More nuclear tests were needed. But the moratorium was coming.

In Switzerland, at the Geneva Conference of Experts, the scientists submitted their final report. Given advances in the technology of detection, American and Soviet scientists now agreed that it was possible to cease nuclear testing. If one side cheated, they would be caught. President Eisenhower was delighted. The very next day he held a press conference to announce that the United States would halt nuclear testing, starting on October 31, if the Soviets formally agreed to halt testing as well.

At Livermore laboratory in California, Edward Teller was furious. He had no intention of giving up nuclear testing without protest. Two days after the death of his colleague and boss Ernest Lawrence, even before Lawrence was buried, Teller sent a classified telegram to Brigadier General Alfred Starbird, the defense official at the Pentagon in charge of nuclear weapons tests. The telegram, marked "Priority," had the subject heading "Thoughts in Connection to the Test Moratorium."

Teller told Starbird that the test ban was a threat to national security. That it showed weakness and vulnerability and opened America up to a sneak nuclear attack. "The purpose [of this telegram] is in part to clarify laboratory plans and in part to point out dangers in connections with future discussions concerning the test moratorium," Teller wrote. "The laboratory must continue research and development of nuclear weapons," he wrote, "in order to comply with the [president's] directive." More tests needed to be done in order to make sure that it was safe to comply. Furthermore, he argued, many of Livermore's nuclear tests were not tests per se but rather scientific experiments, as Operation Argus was.

There was a loophole to be explored, Teller suggested. "Explosions below a kiloton cannot be detected and identified by any of the methods considered realistic by any of the delegations at the Geneva Conference," he wrote. The United States could secretly conduct low-yield tests. Yes, it would be cheating, but the Russians could not be trusted, and surely they would cheat too.

CHAPTER FIVE

Sixteen Hundred Seconds Until Doomsday

Eugene McManus, an electronics technician, worked at the top of the world. He had joined the Air Force, at age seventeen, for adventure and to learn radar technology, and now here he was four years later working at a classified ARPA-activated outpost just nine hundred miles from the North Pole. This was the Ballistic Missile Early Warning System (BMEWS) facility, the world's first operational missile-detection radar site, and it was connected directly with the North American Air Defense Command, or NORAD. McManus and everyone else who worked here knew the remote, isolated facility as "J-Site."

"Our job at J-Site amounted to ninety percent boredom and ten percent panic," Gene McManus recalls. "The panic was if the power went off or if there was a missile scare."

J-Site was part of ARPA's secretive 474L System Program Office, which was responsible for developing techniques and equipment to track all objects in space and any ICBMs that might be coming in over the North Pole. The Air Force ran the place, and McManus technically worked for RCA, Radio Corporation of America, under its defense contractor division, RCA Service Company.

The Arctic environment played a role in everything, McManus explains. J-Site was located thirteen miles from the main Defense Department base in Thule, Greenland, an area that was landlocked by ice nine months of the year. For roughly four of those months, the sun never came up over the horizon and the temperature stayed around -40 degrees Fahrenheit. There was darkness all day and all night, the black sky interrupted only by the low-rising moon. For the two hundred people who worked at J-Site each day, the commute was called "the coldest thirteen miles on wheels."

The J-site workers—mostly radar technicians and maintenance crews—rode to the BMEWS site in a twelve-bus convoy that always traveled in tight formation. If any bus were to fall behind, get stuck, or have engine failure, it would not take long for the passengers to freeze to death. In a phase-one blizzard, which was common, bus drivers battled 70-mile-per-hour winds and maintained visibility of about fifty feet. But if a phase-three blizzard hit, the worst kind of storm, with winds up to 120 miles per hour, visibility was reduced to inches, and the road turned into a giant snowdrift. Bus drivers had to slow down to a treacherous 10-mile-per-hour crawl. Driving slower meant the bus engine could stall. Driving faster meant the bus driver might drive off the road into deep snow. One Christmas, Gene McManus and his fellow crewmembers got caught in a phase-three blizzard, and the commute that normally took thirty to forty minutes took thirteen hours. "The anemometer [wind meter] at the BMEWS site pegged at a hundred and sixty-five miles per hour," McManus recalls. He and his crew got stranded at J-Site, which was particularly unfortunate because the Bob Hope USO tour was visiting Thule Air Base that holiday, and instead of seeing the show live, the stranded J-Site workers had to listen to the gala over the public address system.

J-Site was a futuristic-looking environment with some of the most modern, most powerful technical equipment in the world, perched high on a frozen, treeless bluff overlooking the Wolstenholme Fjord. Four massive radar antennas, each 165 feet high and 400 hundred feet long, were programmed to track objects three thousand miles out. When McManus arrived in the spring of 1961, workers were building the radome, a bright white 150-foot-tall microwave radar dome that looked like a giant golf ball made of honeycomb pieces in the shape of pentagons and hexagons bolted together.

In the summer it was beautiful. "We would watch the icebergs calve from the glaciers, and when the fjord thawed, the water was clear blue," McManus remembers. He and other technicians would take summer walks around J-Site. The landscape was barren above the Arctic Circle, but when the snow melted, from June to early September the tundra bloomed with moss, cotton, and poppies. Sometimes you could see arctic foxes and hares if you had sharp eyes.

At J-Site there were nine buildings attached by enclosed roadways, like tunnels. Because the ground was permanently frozen, nothing was built underground. J-Site was a self-supporting facility with its own mess hall, receiving docks, and machine shop—all in support of the computer rooms, which were the heart of the BMEWS facility. The outpost required 85 megawatts of electricity "to provide full power to the radar and auxiliary equipment, lights, and computers," McManus explains, enough wattage to power about fifteen thousand U.S. homes. For this, J-Site had its own power source in the oil-fired turbines on a Navy ship at anchor in the bay. "The heat generated by the power ship kept the water in the ship's permanent mooring thawed, even at minus forty degrees," says McManus.

It was Gene McManus's job as an electronics technician to take care of the cables at J-Site, and these were far from any old cables. "Hundreds of miles of inch-thick multi-conductor cable carrying control, communication, and radar receiver information [were] laid perfectly straight in the cable tray, never crossing over or under another," McManus recalls. "Each was tied down at precise intervals, with the knots in the cable ties all facing the same direction. When the cables had to bend around corners, the radius of the bends of all the cables in the tray were exactly the same." Precision was everything. The information flowing through these cables could start or prevent World War III.

"The ten percent panic part of the job came when something unusual was happening with the electricity," says McManus. "Once we had a water leak in one of the antennae, in one of the waveguides. The power was down for about fifteen minutes." It was nerve-racking, but it was nothing compared to what happened the third day J-Site went into twenty-four-hour operational mode, on October 5, 1960.

Three thousand miles from J-Site, deep inside Cheyenne Mountain in Colorado Springs, a clock on the wall read 3:15 p.m. Air Force colonel Robert L. Gould was sitting in the NORAD War Room when an alarm light flashed red. NORAD, or North American Air Defense Command, was an organization created in 1958 by the United States and Canada to defend against a Soviet attack. The War Room was where military personnel monitored airspace for ICBMs and incoming Soviet military aircraft. Colonel Gould was facing a freestanding, twelve-by-twelve-foot transparent plastic display board with a map of North America and Eurasia drawn on it. Above the map was an alarm-level indicator made up of five red lights. Nearby, Air Force technicians monitored information coming in from the BMEWS J-Site at Thule.

Suddenly, the Level Three light flashed. Had the Level One light flashed, NORAD protocol would have required Colonel Gould to "assemble the battle staff [and] watch closely." If the light had flashed on Level Two, Gould would know "the contact is significant. Be ready to move in seconds." Instead, the alarm system sounded at Level Three, which required Gould immediately to contact the Joint Chiefs of Staff in Washington, the Chiefs of Staff Committee in Ottawa, and Strategic Air Command (SAC) headquarters in Omaha, Nebraska. A flashing Level Four was something every individual in the War Room knew about from training but dreaded ever having to deal with because it meant "You are apparently under attack." A Level Four flashing light required an officer to "bring defense weaponry up, warn SAC to prepare its ICBMs for launching, get its bombers off the ground and turn loose the airborne alert force." Level Five was the endgame. It indicated "it is 99.9 percent certain that you are under ICBM attack."

With Level Three flashing, Colonel Gould picked up the telephone in the War Room. As he waited to connect with NORAD's commander in chief, Air Force general Laurence Kuter, the alarm level suddenly went to Level Four, then Level Five. Gould quickly learned that General Kuter was flying over South Dakota and could not be reached, so he was instead put in touch with NORAD's deputy commander, Air Marshal Charles Roy Slemon, of Canada. By now, also on the line was NORAD's chief of intelligence, Air Force brigadier general Harris B. Hull.

"Where is Khrushchev?" Air Marshal Slemon asked Brigadier General Hull.

"In New York City," Hull quickly replied.

This changed everything. There was a moment's pause.

"Do you have any intelligence indications that would tend to confirm the radar reports" of an ICBM attack? Slemon asked.

"None, sir," Hull said.

What was said next remains classified.

To Air Marshal Slemon, it seemed extremely unlikely that the Soviets would strike North America when Premier Khrushchev was in New York City, at the United Nations. But Slemon also believed that an attack could not be ruled out entirely and that it was time to get the BMEWS J-Site on the phone.

The technicians at J-Site, who were manning the IBM 7094

computers that received data from the radar, analyzed it, and made calculations were seeing very strange radar returns. A radar echo from an incoming ICBM took one-eighth of a second to receive. These radar returns were seventy-five seconds long. How could anything be that far away? But whatever it was that was coming over the horizon, according to the computers there were literally thousands of them. Here at J-Site, where environment was everything, someone thought of looking outside. There, coming up over the horizon, over Norway, was a huge rising moon.

The BMEWS had not malfunctioned. It was "simply more powerful than anyone had dreamed," said a NORAD spokesman after the story broke on December 7, 1960. The "BMEWS—thought to have a range up to three thousand miles—had spotted the moon nearly a quarter of a million miles distant," explained reporter John Hubbell. The J-Site computers had not been programmed to read or express that kind of distance and instead "divided three thousand miles into the precise distance to the moon and reported the distance left over—twenty-two hundred miles—as range."

It was a defining moment in the history of weapons development and the future of man and machine. A computer had reported that a thousand-strong Soviet ICBM attack was under way. And a human, in this case Air Marshal Charles Roy Slemon, used his judgment to intervene and to overrule. At J-Site, the ARPA 474L System Program Office worked with technicians to teach the BMEWS computers to reject echoes from the moon.

On October 5, 1960, nuclear Armageddon was averted, but the underlying reality of national defense was that the scientists who had created the hydrogen bomb had created a weapon against which there was no defense. In ARPA's first years as an agency, its single biggest program was Defender, with a mission to advance antiballistic missile technology and further develop "early warning systems" like the one at J-Site in Thule. Defender began with a publicly announced first-year budget of $100 million, roughly half of ARPA's entire budget. This figure was misleading, as Herb York explained in now declassified memos, because it included only research and development costs, not operational costs. In its first two years alone, the Pentagon spent closer to $900 million on Defender, York said, roughly $7.3 billion in 2015.

The Defender program, also called Ballistic Missile Defense (BMD), was ARPA's most important national security program and the one that received the most press. People wanted to believe that the brilliant scientists who had created weapons of mass destruction in the first place could create a means to defend against them, especially now that the Soviets had an arsenal of their own. To Herb York, the situation was dire, mostly because of the time frame involved. York ordered ARPA scientists to determine the *exact* amount of time it would take for a Soviet ICBM carrying a megaton warhead to travel from a launch pad in Russia to a target in Washington, D.C.

In a secret dossier, "Assessment of Ballistic Missile Defense Program" (PPD 61-33), obtained through the Freedom of Information Act (FOIA) and not known to have been reported before, ARPA mathematicians whittled that number down to an exact figure—a mere 1,600 seconds. It seemed impossibly fast. Just twenty-six minutes and forty seconds from launch to annihilation.

The ARPA report chronicled the journey of the nuclear-armed ICBM in its three stages: boost, midcourse, and terminal phase. The initial boost stage took three hundred seconds—five minutes. This included the time it took for the rocket to fire up off the launch pad, head skyward, and reach cruising altitude. The second stage, called midcourse, lasted 1,200 seconds—twenty minutes. This stage included the time it took for the missile to travel in an arc-like trajectory over the planet at an altitude of approximately eight hundred miles above sea level. The final stage was called the terminal stage. It accounted for the last one hundred seconds of flight—1.6 minutes. This terminal phase began when the warhead reentered the earth's atmosphere and ended when it struck its target—an American city. Sixteen hundred seconds. That was it.

The secret "Assessment of Ballistic Missile Defense" came with a stern forewarning: "The nuclear-armed ICBM threatens us with annihilation; the stakes are so high that we must explore every alternative of strengthening our military posture." One of the great tragedies, or ironies, here was that defending against a single ICBM was actually not too difficult a task. According to the authors of the ARPA report, the Army's antiballistic missile system, called Nike-Zeus, gave "high confidence that... targets [i.e., incoming Soviet ICBMs] could be destroyed." The problem was numerical, the scientists said. It was the sheer volume of megaton weapons in existence—with more still being engineered—that made the situation so hopeless. "The most important limitation of [Nike-Zeus] is that its firepower will probably not be able to handle the number of simultaneous targets which can reasonably be expected in an all-out war with the USSR," the scientists wrote.

For Herb York, it was time to go back to the Supermen of hard science. Several of the men from Project 137 had formed a defense consulting group of their own. They called themselves the Jason scientists.

"I suppose you could say I started Jason," said Murph Goldberger in a 2013 interview, at the age of ninety-one. The former Manhattan Project member, former science advisor to President Johnson, former president of the Federation of American Scientists, and the first American scientist to travel to communist China on an official government-sponsored science mission, among other impressive feats, was living with his full faculties intact at a retirement home in La Jolla, California, called Casa de Mañana, or House of Tomorrow. Eating Hungarian goulash in a dining room filled with people of a similar age, and with a commanding view of the vast Pacific, Goldberger explained, "I was Jason's first director or president. It was an impressive group. We were scientists committed to solving defense problems."

Murph Goldberger had been involved in nuclear physics since he was twenty-two years old. During World War II, as a college student and member of the enlisted reserves, he was called up to the Army's Special Engineering Department—the Manhattan Project—after being singled out for his scientific talent. After the war he earned a Ph.D. in physics under Enrico Fermi, the scientist who told President Truman that the hydrogen bomb was "an evil thing." Murph Goldberger had been a key player in Project 137 at Fort McNair. At the time he was working as a professor of physics at Princeton University, alongside John Wheeler, Oskar Morgenstern, and Eugene Wigner. A *Life* magazine article about America's most important scientists carried a photograph of the four Princeton physicists and described them with a kind of reverence. Scientists in the 1950s were seen as modern-day wizards, alchemists who could unlock the secrets of the universe. American scientists could win wars, defeat polio, even travel to the moon.

After Project 137 ended, Goldberger returned to Princeton, where he soon got an idea. He wanted to craft a defense consulting group of like-minded colleagues. Goldberger contacted four friends outside the university enclave, scientists whose areas of expertise had been entwined since the end of World War II. Kenneth Watson, a nuclear physicist at the University of California, Berkeley, and protégé of Edward Teller, had done a postdoctoral fellowship at the Institute for Advanced Study in Princeton. Keith Brueckner, a physicist, meteorologist, and former Los Alamos weapons developer, had studied at the Berkeley Radiation Laboratory with Watson and Goldberger and at the Institute for Advanced Study alongside John von Neumann. Murray Gell-Mann, the youngest member, had been a doctoral student of Manhattan Project giant Victor Weisskopf, and was someone Goldberger considered a prodigy. The four physicists agreed to start a for-profit defense consulting company together. Their first idea was to call it Theoretical Physics, Inc. "The idea was that we would not work simply as consultants; we'd work as a formal group, a little business," Keith Brueckner recalled, in a 1986 oral history.

Goldberger decided to run the idea by a fourth colleague and friend, the physicist Charles H. Townes. Two years earlier Townes had published the first academic paper on what he called the microwave laser, or maser. In time the maser would become known as the laser, and it is now considered one of the most significant inventions of the twentieth century, used widely in both defense and civilian work. Townes had recently taken a leave of absence from his position as a professor at Columbia University to serve as vice president of the Institute for Defense Analyses (IDA), a federally funded research center in Alexandria, Virginia, that served one customer: the Department of Defense. Specifically, IDA served the Office of the Secretary of Defense (OSD) and the Joint Chiefs of Staff (JCS). If another service wanted IDA's assistance researching a problem, they had to secure permission from OSD or JCS first. In the early ARPA years, the salaries of all ARPA directors and program managers were paid through IDA. Townes thought Goldberger's idea of a defense consulting group was excellent, and he suggested that Goldberger speak with Herb York. Perhaps the Advanced Research Projects Agency would fund the group itself, Townes said. He offered to find out.

"Townes called back to say [ARPA] loved the idea," Goldberger remembered. The scientists, mostly university professors, were free to consult during the summer, as they had at the war college at Fort McNair. The group could remain flexible and independent, detached from any Pentagon mindset. To avoid red tape or bureaucracy, they could be paid through IDA; besides, most of their work would be classified. IDA would provide the group with an administrative assistant.

Goldberger and his colleagues got to work creating a list of scientists they felt would add to their group of defense consultants. They wanted to limit membership to theoretical physicists, said Goldberger, generalists who had knowledge in a wide variety of areas and used mathematical models and abstractions to understand, explain, and predict phenomena in the natural world. "It was a very elite operation," recalled Brueckner. "It was an honor to be asked." Goldberger remembered that "everyone was excited, full of ideas, and very patriotic." Murph Goldberger, Keith Brueckner, Kenneth Watson, and Murray Gell-Mann drew up a list of their most respected colleagues and asked them to participate.

The group's first meeting took place at IDA headquarters in Virginia on December 17, 1959. George Kistiakowsky, one of President Eisenhower's science advisors, led the meeting. Kistiakowsky kept a daily desk diary in which he recorded his thoughts. "Met at IDA headquarters with the 'bright young physicists,' a group assembled by Charles Townes to do imaginative thinking about military problems," Kistiakowsky noted that day. "It is a tremendously bright squad of some 30 people." After the first meeting Goldberger went home to Princeton University very excited, he recalled. "We knew the group could contribute significantly to the problems" of national defense.

Three weeks later, on January 1, 1960, and by ARPA Project Assignment number 11, the group became an official entity. What to call it, Murph Goldberger wondered? "The Pentagon had a machine that generated code names for projects," he said. Whether the Defense Department naming process was random or systematic remains a mystery, but the machine decided that this scientific advisory group was to be called Project Sunrise. Goldberger felt disappointed. "The name did not fit," he recalled. That night he shared his feelings with his wife and fellow scientist, Mildred Goldberger; the couple had met when they were both working on the Manhattan Project during the war. "Mildred thought Project Sunrise was a dreadful name," Goldberger recalled. This group was going to be doing dynamic problem solving and groundbreaking consulting work. Project Sunrise sounded sentimental and bland. Goldberger recalled Mildred picking up a piece of paper on the table in front of her, a document from IDA. The header included the image of an ancient Greek Parthenon-style building. Ancient Greece made Mildred Goldberger think about Jason and the Argonauts, characters from Greek mythology. Jason, the leader of the Argonauts, is one of history's great mythological heroes, the archetype of a man on a quest. The Argonauts were Jason's band of warriors who accompanied him on his journey to find the Golden Fleece.

"You should call yourself Jason," Mildred Goldberger said. Which is how one of the most secret and esoteric, most powerful and consequential scientific advisory groups in the history of the U.S. Department of Defense got its name. Over the course of the next fifty-five years, the Jason group would impact ARPA, and later DARPA, with greater significance than any other scientific advisory group. Jason's first senior advisors were Hans Bethe, George Kistiakowsky, and Edward Teller.

In April 1960, each member of Jason was granted a clearance of top secret or above. The Jason scientists' first official meeting took place in Washington, D.C., where they were briefed on a set of challenges to consider. Ballistic missile defense was at the top of the list. The Jasons were briefed on the classified elements of the Defender program and asked to think outside the boundaries of possibility that were currently being explored by other scientists.

Two months after their first official briefing, the Jason group held a summer study at the Lawrence Berkeley National Laboratory in California, formerly called the Rad Lab. It took place between June 1 and August 15, 1960, and there were about twenty

Jason scientists present. Goldberger recalled that during that meeting they learned that ARPA wanted them to think about measures and countermeasures, about offense and defense. The Jason scientists were briefed on the classified results of Operation Argus and the Christofilos effect. They were asked to think about new programs to be researched and developed, and also to imagine the programs that Russian scientists might be working on. The 1960 summer study produced multiple classified reports.

Goldberger described one concept in general terms. It was a variation of the Christofilos effect. "The idea was proposed to the [Jason] study group that the enemy could detonate a nuclear weapon high up [in the atmosphere] to confuse satellite detection." The Jasons were to think about the creation of an effect similar to the electromagnetic pulse seen during Argus. One of the Jason scientists who was present at that meeting, Sidney Drell, tried to explain the concept in an oral history in 1986. "If you have a high altitude explosion of a nuclear weapon, and it makes a [cloud] of NO [nitric oxide molecules], would that cause a big enough cloud to last long enough that we wouldn't see the missile attack launch and we wouldn't get the early warning?" In their first summer study, the Jason scientists were asked to calculate the size of the cloud, the amount of nitric oxide in the cloud, and the rate of dispensation in the atmosphere required to negatively impact the electronics on a nearby U.S. satellite system. From their calculations, said Goldberger, the Jasons concluded that the enemy would have to explode "many megaton warheads" to have a significant effect on the signals, and that this was "impractical." For ARPA, this was good news.

These were the kinds of hard science problems the Jasons were excellent at solving, and ARPA wanted the group to apply this type of "imaginative thinking" to the Defender conundrum. They came up with a new idea, one that involved the age-old warfare concept of using decoys—devices meant to distract or mislead—

like the mythological Trojan horse. The Jasons suggested the development of a new technology whereby American ICBM warheads could be equipped with decoys designed to evade, or trick, the Soviet's antiballistic missile defense system. If every U.S. warhead was equipped with five or six decoys, then the entire U.S. arsenal of ICBMs would have a five or six times greater chance of getting through to a target in the Soviet Union. The Jasons called this concept "penetration aids."

On the basis of the Jason scientists' work, ARPA created a new program called PENAIDS, short for penetration aids. PENAIDS suggested the development of a far more aggressive offensive posture in the MAD dilemma, the inventing of new ways for U.S. missiles to outfox the Soviets' ballistic missile defense. Starting in 1962, PENAIDS proof tests at the missile bases at White Sands, New Mexico, and at Kwajalein in the Marshall Islands delivered promising results, which the Jason scientists reviewed. PENAIDS led to another ARPA study called "Pen X," which endorsed the engineering of a new kind of advanced hydrogen bomb warhead called MIRVs, multiple independently targetable reentry vehicles. Their birth initiated a fierce new competition in the nuclear arms race as both sides rushed to build more accurate, more powerful, more deceptive MIRVs. The programs were initially classified, but when they were made public, MIRVs were vilified as dangerous and destabilizing because they put a premium on a nuclear first strike.

For their second summer study, in 1961, the Jason scientists met in Maine, on the Bowdoin College campus. Jack Ruina, the new director of ARPA, called Charles Townes at IDA to coordinate his attending the summer study. Ruina also wanted to bring several ARPA program managers along.

"Well, we don't want anybody from ARPA to attend except you," Townes told him.

Ruina was stunned. The Jasons worked for ARPA—and ARPA

only. "What do you mean, we can't attend?" Ruina said. "We are paying for the whole thing. You can't say you're [going to] have a private meeting when it's the government that is paying for it."

"Sorry, you can't come to our meetings," Townes repeated.

"Charlie, you can't do that," Ruina told him.

Townes explained to Ruina that this was how the Jason scientific advisory group worked. The Jasons sought objectivity, and they wanted to remain free from government bureaucracy and red tape. They did not want Pentagon interference during any of their summer studies. The Jasons gathered together to solve problems related to national defense. That was it.

After some back-and-forth, Ruina and Townes reached an agreement of sorts. As suggested, Jack Ruina, as director of ARPA, could attend a Jason summer study, alone.

For the Maine summer study, the focus again was on the Defender program. The Princeton physicist John Wheeler had a summerhouse not far from the college campus, on a wooded island off the coast called High Island. Wheeler had the group out to his house for many of the meetings that summer, where the scientists held clambakes, ate lobsters, and considered another highly classified program. This one involved the concept of directed energy. "This was very exotic science," Ruina recalled. Directed energy beams come in two forms: light, which involves lasers, and charged particles, which involve electrons or protons. "Particle beam weapons [are] esoteric weapons systems," Ruina explained. They come with a "Buck Rogers death ray image," noted an early ARPA summary, because they "work at the speed of light and involve instantaneous kill."

The Jason scientists wondered if an incoming ICBM could be shot down by a directed energy beam. The conundrum, according to Ruina, "was whether you can use a particle beam, earth-based, to form a beam through the atmosphere and destroy an incoming warhead." The concept's originator was Nick Christofilos; he had first presented the idea during Project 137, Goldberger recalled. Scientists at Livermore laboratory had already conducted earlier proof test experiments under the code name Seesaw. The classified results were shared with the Jason scientists, who were impressed. Directed energy weapons were well worth researching and developing, they decided, and ARPA moved forward with Project Seesaw—its first directed energy weapons program. Goldberger recalled the program being so highly classified that not even all of the Jasons were cleared for future work on it.

"Seesaw was a sensitive, limited-access project which deserves mention in the ARPA history as the most enduring specific project ever supported by the agency," an agency review stated. ARPA's mission was and remains getting programs up and running, then transferring them over to the military services or other government agencies for field use. Project Seesaw remained in development at ARPA for fifteen long years. Then in 1974 it was transferred to the Atomic Energy Commission. Some unclassified summaries have been released. Over the next fifty-five years, ARPA's directed energy weapons programs would develop and grow. The majority of them remain highly classified.

"Directed energy is the weapon of the future," said retired four-star general Paul F. Gorman in a 2014 interview for this book. "But that is a sensitive area and we can't get into that."

CHAPTER SIX

Psychological Operations

A handsome dark-haired war hero named William H. Godel was commanding the attention of a crowd of reporters outside Vandenberg Air Force Base in California. It was June 3, 1959. Godel wore the wire-rimmed glasses of an intellectual and walked with the slight limp of a Marine wounded in battle, in his case the hellhole of Guadalcanal. As director of policy and planning for the Advanced Research Projects Agency, Godel had a few facts to share with the press corps about America's tiniest space pioneers, four black mice. Not far away from where Godel was standing at the podium, a seventy-eight-foot Thor Agena A rocket, carrying the *Discoverer III* life-sustaining satellite, pointed upwards at the sky. The four black mice were inside the rocket's nosecone. They were about to be shot into space.

The mice, Godel announced, were "happy and healthy." They were all males and were about two months old. These were not "ordinary mice" but members of the C-57 strain, making them "the best specimens of a special strain of hardy laboratory animals, selected and trained specifically for their road trip into space and planned return to earth." They had been selected, at random, from a pool of sixty similarly trained mice. Their mouse capsule, roughly two feet long and two feet wide, was air-conditioned and soundproof. They had a food supply of unsalted ground peanuts, orange juice, and oatmeal. Each rodent had a tiny instrument pack on its back containing mini-transmitters that would record its heartbeat, pulse, and body temperature and then send that information back to Air Force veterinarians on the ground.

Godel cautioned people to be realistic about the fate of the mice. Most likely they would not return to earth alive, he said. The chances that the mice astronauts would live through the journey were roughly one in seven hundred.

"We don't want to humanize them in any way," said a colleague of Godel's, an Air Force officer. The mice were purposely unnamed because "it would just make it worse for those people who have tender feelings about these things."

So much rested on the success of the mission. The space race was about creating ICBMs capable of annihilating the other side, but it was also a psychological race, about humans and science and who was best. Both the United States and the Soviet Union had succeeded in getting animals into space, but neither side had been able to launch living beings into space with enough acceleration to escape the earth's gravity and achieve orbital motion, that mysterious balancing point somewhere between gravity's pull on the satellite and a satellite's inherent inertia. The satellite had to reach an altitude of 150 miles above the earth's surface while traveling at a speed of about 17,000 miles per hour. Too slow and the satellite would fall back to earth; too fast and it would disappear into deep space. The plan was for the *Discoverer III* life-sustaining satellite to achieve orbit, circle the earth seventeen times, then return back to earth with the mice, ideally, alive. The Navy had been rehearsing "a dramatic rescue effort" to retrieve the capsule once it landed in the ocean.

In the Cold War space race, each side sought to be the first nation to achieve specific scientific milestones. Getting mice into orbit was a big one. The Discoverer program was, as a "satellite technology effort," a scientific experiment that would eventually allow humans to travel into space. That was all true, but there was another side. *Discoverer III* was a highly classified spying mission, a cover for America's first space-based satellite reconnaissance program, called Corona. The CIA had done the heavy lifting in Corona's early years, with the support of the U.S. Air Force. ARPA had inherited the program from the Air Force in 1958. The mission of Corona was to photograph the Soviet Union from space so that the United States could better understand Soviet military hardware on the ground. Corona would remain one of America's most closely guarded secrets, and would stay classified for thirty-six years, until February 1995. Like the U-2 spy plane, also a highly classified CIA program, this was where technology, espionage, and the quest for military superiority fused.

It was ARPA's job to put satellites in space for intelligence-gathering purposes, and William Godel oversaw these early programs. Satellite technology gave birth to a whole new world of intelligence-collection disciplines, including IMINT, or imagery intelligence (like Corona); SIGINT, signals intelligence; GEOINT, geospatial intelligence; and MASINT, measurement and signature intelligence. Some of ARPA's most successful early satellite programs included SAMOS (signals intelligence), GEODESY (mapping), NOTUS (communications), TRANSIT (navigation), and MIDAS (early warning). Most of these programs were highly classified, while others, like TIROS, the Television-Infrared Observation Satellite Program, amazed and informed the general public in remarkable ways.

TIROS was the world's first true weather satellite. ARPA had inherited much of the technology from an Army program called JANUS. The TIROS satellite, a first-generation remote-sensing instrument, was developed by RCA. It weighed 270 pounds and contained a television system that transmitted images of the earth's weather—most notably its cloud cover—from a 450-mile altitude orbit back to a ground station at Fort Monmouth, New Jersey. The first launch took place on April 1, 1960; by then the program had been transferred to the newly created National Aeronautics and Space Administration, or NASA. In its seventy-six-day life, TIROS transmitted 22,952 images back to earth. Every image was revolutionary. The spiral banded structure of oceanic storms, the vastness of mountain-wave cloud structures, the unexpected rapid changes in cloud patterns—none of this had been seen before. Technology offered a view of the planet previously beyond human comprehension, a new and spectacular perspective on Mother Earth. Before TIROS it was unknown.

The first set of photographs were pictures of cloud formations along the St. Lawrence River, over the Baja Peninsula, and across Egypt near the Red Sea. They were so magnificent that the director of NASA personally delivered them to President Eisenhower for him to see. The president called a press conference and shared details of the breathtaking photographs with the American public. The *New York Times* ran a four-column page-one article about TIROS. The very notion that it was now possible to see photographs of a storm front out at sea, before it hit land, inspired awe, if not disbelief, in millions of people. The photographs were marvels of modern science. *National Geographic* dedicated a large portion of its August 1960 issue to the seminal images.

To William Godel, satellites provided access to legions of foreign intelligence. Hired just weeks after ARPA's creation, Godel held the second-most-important job after Herb York. His nebulous title, originally director of foreign developments, then director of policy and planning, purposely concealed the classified nature of Godel's work. Godel was in charge of ARPA's psychological warfare programs as well as its overseas research programs, both of which would intensify during the Vietnam War. When Godel departed the agency under FBI investigation for financial misconduct in 1964, he left behind the most controversial and most toxic legacy in the agency's fifty-seven-year history. Notably, his presence at ARPA has been largely erased from the official record. "The Pentagon library has no information about him in our collection," confirmed Pentagon librarian Myron "Mike" Hanson in 2013. Declassified files located at the National Archives and other documents obtained through the Freedom of Information Act reveal a story of intrigue.

William Godel began his career in espionage. By the time of the *Discoverer III* launch of the four black mice, Godel had more than a decade of experience working with and among spies. He moved back and forth between military intelligence and civilian intelligence, between the CIA and the Pentagon, with great self-confidence and aplomb. From his earliest beginnings as a Marine Corps intelligence officer until he began working for ARPA in February 1958, Godel had already forged a brilliant record in the uppermost echelons of the U.S. intelligence community. He was intensely patriotic, physically brave, and intellectually bold. He joined the Marine Corps in 1940, at the age of nineteen, and one month after turning twenty-one he fought at Guadalcanal, the remote jungle-covered island in the Pacific where Allied forces won their first major offensive against the Empire of Japan. At Guadalcanal, Godel was shot in the leg and suffered a near-fatal injury that left him with a leg brace and a limp.

After the war, Godel worked at the Pentagon, in military intelligence. His boss was Major General Graves B. Erskine, a hard-charging war hero who had already fought in both world wars. In World War II, the forty-seven-year-old General Erskine led the Third Marine Division in the battle for Iwo Jima. In the spring of 1950, Godel was chosen by General Erskine to accompany him on an elite mission to Southeast Asia, a mission that would profoundly affect how William Godel saw the world and how he would do his job at the Pentagon over the next fourteen years.

On its face, the mission to Southeast Asia in July 1950, led by Erskine and the diplomat John F. Melby, was a joint State Department–Defense Department diplomatic effort to determine the long-range nature of American objectives in the region. Its real purpose, classified secret, was to examine how communist-backed fighters, also called insurgents or guerrillas, were resisting and undermining French colonial rule in Vietnam. When the Melby-Erskine team arrived in Vietnam, French military officers handed General Erskine and his associates five thousand pages of reports to read. Erskine found the request ridiculous.

The French "haven't won a war since Napoleon," he told Godel and the team. "Why listen to a bunch of second raters when they are losing this war?" Instead, General Erskine told his team to go out into the field with South Vietnamese army units of the French Expeditionary Corps and make military intelligence assessments of their own. For several weeks the Erskine team accompanied the soldiers on tours of military installations, including forays into Vietnam's neighbors Laos and Cambodia. One night the Erskine group accompanied a South Vietnamese army unit on a nighttime ambush of a camp of communist insurgents. The French ordered the South Vietnamese unit to capture the communist soldiers, called Viet Minh, and bring them back to French Expeditionary Corps headquarters for interrogation. The French believed that the Viet Minh soldiers had information that could help them gain a strategic edge.

The ambush was a success but the mission was a failure. In an after-action report, Godel's colleague Captain Nick Thorpe explained why. "The Vietnamese refused to bring back heads with bodies still attached to them," Thorpe wrote. To Godel, the ramifications were profound. The French wanted the soldiers' minds; the South Vietnamese brought them heads. French commanders wanted intelligence; South Vietnamese soldiers wanted revenge.

The way Godel saw it, the French colonialists were trying to fight the Viet Minh guerrillas according to colonial rules of war. But the South Vietnamese, who were receiving weapons and training from the French forces, were actually fighting a different kind of war, based on different rules. Guerrilla warfare was irrational. It was asymmetrical. It was about cutting off the enemy's head to send a message back home. When, in the spring of 1950, William Godel witnessed guerrilla warfare firsthand in Vietnam, it shifted his perspective on how the United States would need to fight future wars. Guerrilla warfare involved psychological warfare. To Godel, it was a necessary component for a win.

Halfway across the world in Korea, during some of the heaviest fighting of the Korean War, a most unusual element of ARPA's psychological warfare programs found its origins near a hilltop called Outpost Bunker Hill. It was the fall of 1952 on the western front, and soldiers with the First Marine Division were freezing and tired in their rat-infested trenches. For months the Marines had been battling the enemy here for control of area hills. Once a hilltop was conquered, the Marines would dig in and build bunkers and trenches with their shovels. Sometimes they could rest.

The Korean War, like so many wars, began as a civil war between the North and the South. In June 1950 the conflict became international when the United Nations joined the war to support the South, and the People's Republic of China joined the war to support the North. The international war began as a mobile campaign, with UN forces led by an American, General Douglas MacArthur. The initial ground assault was supported by U.S. airpower. But after more than two years of battle, by the fall of 1952 the conflict had devolved into trench warfare, the old-fashioned, grueling style of warfare that defined World War I and had come to symbolize stalemate.

"We hated to dig," recalled A. Robert Abboud, First Marine Division Company commander at Outpost Bunker Hill. "The Chinese were wonderful diggers. They had tunnels they could drive trucks through," said Abboud. "We couldn't get to them with our air power because they were underground all the time."

Yet these tunnels were a lifeline for the Marines at Outpost Bunker Hill. And so with their shovels they dug and dug, creating a labyrinth of trenches and tunnels that provided them with some degree of safety from enemy attack. "We had lumber, really six-by-sixes...in the trenches," explained Abboud, "that we'd set up and then we'd put a roof of lumber on top and sand bags on top of that." In this manner, the Marines created firing positions along a number of the topographical crests. Individual men maintained guard over their own sliver of the hill. "You had to make sure that there was integrity, that nobody came in and infiltrated your area," said Abboud. The Marines relied on one another.

It was tough and brutal work, keeping enemy infiltrators at bay. The weather was hellish and cold. It snowed much of the time, and there were rats running around the trenches. Late at night the youngest soldiers, whom Abboud called "just kids with bayonets," got sent out into the darkness, down the hill and into the rice paddies on patrol. Their job was to poke their bayonets around on the ground in an effort to locate Chinese land mines. Other times, more senior officers led dangerous patrols to check the integrity of the perimeter wire. Abboud himself went so many times he lost track of the number. Sometimes his deputy went, a young machine gun officer whose safety Abboud felt particularly responsible for, and whose name was Allen Macy Dulles. The young soldier's father, Allen Welsh Dulles, was the deputy director of the CIA.

It was also personal. Abboud and the younger Dulles had known each other since they were boys. "I'd known Allen because he'd gone to Exeter and he was on the debating team," Abboud recalled. "I was on the debating [team] at Roxbury Latin," the venerable Boston day school. The two boys became friends, sharing a similar passion for antiquity and a desire to study ancient Greece. Both did; Allen Macy Dulles studied classics at Princeton, Abboud at Harvard. Now here they were in Korea, together serving as Marines. Despite his being the son of the deputy director of the CIA, Allen Dulles sought no special treatment in Korea. He insisted on taking his equal share of the dangerous night patrols, said Robert Abboud.

While both men came from privilege, Dulles came from extraordinary privilege. In addition to his father's powerful position at the CIA, his uncle John Foster Dulles was about to become U.S. secretary of state. From his knowledge of classics, Abboud knew that the history of warfare—from Carthage to the present time—was riddled with stories of princes being captured by enemy forces only to be used as bargaining chips. These stories almost always had a tragic end. The thought of the young Allen Macy Dulles being captured and taken prisoner of war by the Chinese communists worried Abboud. Sometimes it kept him up at night.

Still, "we took turns going out there to the front lines," Abboud recalled. On occasion, Abboud suggested maybe it wasn't a good idea. "If I said, 'Allen, I can't send you out there. Your father is [deputy] head of the CIA. What happens if you get captured?' He'd say, 'I'm a Marine Corps officer and it's my turn to go out there. I'm going to go.' "

Which is exactly what Allen Macy Dulles did one fateful night in November 1952.

"For God's sake don't get hurt!" Abboud called after his friend.

Dulles made his way out of the bunker. Abboud watched him climb over the sandbags and head down the steep slope of the hill, then listened on the communications system.

"I'm on the radio and I'm listening and my heart's in my

throat," Abboud remembered. "God, don't let anything happen here," he prayed.

Dulles walked down the slope a good distance until he came to where the Marines had constructed a simple barbed-wire fence. The enemy had cut the concertina wire there. He pulled a tool from his pocket and began making repairs. Suddenly the area was consumed by a loud and deafening noise. The enemy was launching a mortar attack.

"Lieutenant Dulles has been hit!" cried a voice over the radio.

Robert Abboud summoned four Marines and a stretcher. The team ran out of the bunker, down the hill, and into the open terrain in search of Dulles. They discovered him not far from the fence, lying on the ground.

"We found him," Abboud recalled. The situation was grim. Dulles's helmet had been knocked off his head. Blood and shrapnel covered the ground. He was unconscious. A low pulse. Abboud picked his friend's helmet up off the ground.

"There was a lot of his head in the helmet," Abboud said.

The team lay Dulles on the stretcher and ran back to the bunker with what was left of him. When a rescue chopper finally arrived, they loaded Dulles inside. Abboud remembered watching the Sikorsky fly away. News reached Washington, D.C., fast.

"Marine Lieutenant Allen Macy Dulles, son of the deputy director of the Central Intelligence Agency, has been critically wounded in Korea," the Associated Press reported the following day. The helicopter took Dulles to the hospital ship USS *Consolation,* anchored off the coast of Korea. There he remained, unconscious but with signs of life. He was twenty-two years old.

"He was unconscious for three weeks, maybe a month," recalled his sister Joan Dulles Talley at age ninety, in 2014. "Initially there was no cognition. No response to people or to environmental stimulus. Then, slowly, he came back. He reemerged. Doctors told us there would be no hearing in one ear but he could speak, just like someone who was normal. At first there was hope. Allen *seemed* normal when we took him home. But as month after month passed, he was not able to make a life for himself. Then we realized what had been injured was his mind."

Dulles had suffered a catastrophic traumatic brain injury. The promising young scholar, brave Marine, and son of the deputy director of the CIA was, in the words of his sister, "caught between worlds. It was as if he were trapped in a faraway place," Talley continued. "Allen was there, but not really there. It was so terribly tragic. He was so young. He was someone who had been so gifted in the mind. Like so many young soldiers he had everything ahead of him, and then . . . no more."

In November 1952 the human brain was uncharted territory. Cognitive science, the study of the mind and its processes, was still in its dark ages. Neuroscience, as an interdisciplinary field that now includes biology, chemistry, genetics, and computer science, did not yet exist. Not for another three months would James D. Watson and Francis H. C. Crick announce that they had determined the structure of DNA, the molecule that carries genes. Advanced computers that can image the human brain and produce high-resolution scans had not yet been developed. Lobotomies—a neurosurgical procedure that removes part of the brain's frontal lobes—were still being performed in U.S. hospitals as a means to treat psychiatric illness. Brain science was as mysterious in 1952 as was the center of the earth or the surface of the moon. Like a man lost in space, Allen Macy Dulles had very little hope of ever returning fully to this world.

A few weeks after Allen Macy Dulles was transported back to the United States, in January 1953, his father, Allen W. Dulles, was chosen by President Eisenhower to be the director of the CIA. Already Dulles had decided he would do everything in his power to help his brain-injured son. Most notably, he hired a top brain specialist named Dr. Harold G. Wolff, a world-renowned neurologist and director of the New York Hospital–Cornell Medical Center. In addition to being the world's authority on migraine research, Dr. Wolff was a pioneer in the study of general brain behavior, with a specialty in psychosomatic illness, or mental illness, which in 1953 did not mean all that much. Dr. Wolff, on the surface, was a man of distinction. Privately he was a dark, shadowy figure, though this would take decades to be known. After graduating from Harvard Medical School in 1923, Wolff traveled to Europe to study neuropathology, or diseases of the nervous system, in Austria. Next he traveled farther east, to Leningrad, where he worked under Ivan Pavlov, the famous Russian physiologist known for his discovery of classical conditioning, the idea that human behavior could be strengthened or weakened though punishment and reward. (Pavlov won the Nobel Prize in medicine in 1904 and will forever be remembered for his famous dog.)

When Lieutenant Allen Macy Dulles came back from Korea with his brain injury, CIA director Allen Welsh Dulles contacted Wolff in New York City, hoping Wolff could help his son get well. Dr. Wolff said he would be happy to see what he could do. But the following month a national security crisis gripped the nation, and Allen Dulles was pulled away. On February 23, 1953, a U.S. Marine colonel named Frank S. Schwable appeared on TV as a prisoner of war of the North Koreans. Schwable, a member of the U.S. First Marine Air Wing, had been shot down on a combat mission over North Korea seven months earlier, in July 1952. Now, in a six-thousand-word statement broadcast on Chinese radio, Colonel Schwable shocked the world with a startling confession.

Colonel Schwable said that he had been given detailed orders by his superior officers to participate in "various elements of bacteriological warfare." Schwable cited specific "field tests" which he claimed had already taken place and said that military commanders had discussed with him their plans for using biological weapons against North Korean civilians in "regular combat operations."

Schwable named names, described meetings, and discussed strategy. Everything Schwable said, if true, violated the Geneva Conventions. General Mark W. Clark, UN Supreme Commander in Korea, immediately denounced the germ warfare charges, declaring them fabrications, but at the Pentagon, officials were aware how quickly such a narrative could spin out of control.

At the Pentagon, the man tasked with handling the situation was William Godel, now deputy director of the Psychological Strategy Board (PSB). The PSB coordinated psychological warfare operations between the Department of Defense and the CIA. In response to the Colonel Schwable affair, Godel convened an emergency meeting of the PSB. This was psychological warfare of the worst order, Godel declared; declassified minutes of the emergency PSB meeting indicate that its members agreed. The position of the U.S. government was then, and is now, that it never engaged in biological warfare in Korea. So how should the United States respond?

Secretary of Defense Charles Wilson suggested an "all out campaign to smear the Koreans." He wanted the Pentagon to accuse the communists of "a new form of war crime, and a new form of refinement in atrocity techniques; namely mind murder, or menticide." The CIA thought this was a bad idea. "Menticide" was too powerful a word, Director Dulles cautioned, and it conceded too much power to the communists. But time was critical, and the Pentagon had to respond. The members of the PSB agreed to a watered-down version of Secretary Wilson's suggestion. Hours later, the Department of Defense issued a statement calling Colonel Schwable's action the result of the "mind-annihilating methods of these Communists in extorting whatever words they want." Defense Department officials had a very specific name for what the communists were doing to our soldiers, a word recommended by the CIA. The communists were "brainwashing" American soldiers, the Pentagon said.

It was a CIA move that was three years in the making. In fact, the word "brainwashing" had entered the English lexicon in September 1950, courtesy of the CIA, when an article written by a reporter named Edward Hunter appeared in a Miami newspaper, the *News*. "Brain-Washing Tactics Force Chinese into Ranks of Communist Party," the headline read. Although Hunter had been a journalist for decades, he also worked for the CIA. He'd been hired by the agency on a contract basis to disseminate brainwashing stories through the mainstream press. "Brain-washing," wrote Hunter, was a devious new tool being used by the communists to strip a man of his humanity and "turn him into a robot or a slave." The very concept grabbed Americans by the throat. The notion of government mind-control programs had been a mainstay of dystopian science-fiction novels for decades, from Yevgeny Zamyatin's 1921 classic *We* to Aldous Huxley's 1932 best-seller *Brave New World*. But that was science fiction. This was real, Hunter wrote. To be incinerated in a nuclear bomb attack was an ever-present Cold War threat, but it was also an abstraction, difficult to conceptualize on an individual scale. In 1950, the idea of being brainwashed, as if controlled by an evil wizard's spell—that was somehow much easier to relate to. Brainwashing terrified people, and they wanted to know more.

Edward Hunter wrote article after article on the subject, expanding his stories into a book. The communists, he declared, had developed tactics "to put a man's mind into a fog so that he will mistake what is true for what is untrue, what is right for what is wrong." Brainwashing could turn a man into an amnesiac who could "not remember wrong from right." Memories could be implanted in a brainwashed man whereby he would "come to believe what did not happen actually had happened, until he ultimately becomes a robot for the Communist manipulator," Hunter warned.

In the September 1950 *Miami News* article, Hunter claimed to have information proving that the Chinese had created "brainwashing panels" of experts who used drugs, hypnosis, and other sinister means that could render a man "a demon [or] a puppet." The goal of the communists, said Hunter, was to conquer America by conquering its citizens—one at a time. In a follow-up book on the subject, Hunter explained the science behind the "mind atrocities called brainwashing." Through conditioning, the communists intended to change human nature. To turn men into ants. "What the totalitarian state strives for is the insectivization of human beings," Hunter declared. "Brain changing is the culmination of this whole evil process," he said. "The brain created science and now will be subordinate to it." Even Congress invited Hunter to testify before the Committee on Un-American Activities, in a session discussing "Communist Psychological Warfare (Brainwashing)." He was presented as an author and a foreign correspondent, with no mention of his role as a CIA operative.

Psychologists across America echoed Hunter's thinking, adding to the growing fear of mind control. In an article for the *New York Times Magazine,* the renowned psychologist and former prisoner of the Nazis Joost A. M. Meerloo agreed that brainwashing was real and possible. "The totalitarians have misused the knowledge of how the mind works for their own purposes," Meerloo wrote.

With all this focus on brainwashing and its evil power, starting with Hunter's first mention of the concept in the fall of 1950, it is surprising how quickly the story of the brainwashed Marine colonel Frank S. Schwable in the winter of 1953 went away. At first the situation garnered considerable press, but then diffused. This was largely due to the behind-the-scenes efforts of William Godel. Godel had been assigned to act as liaison between the Pentagon and the government of North Korea in an effort to get Schwable and thousands of other Korean War POWs released. The documents at the National Archives are limited in number, and many remain classified, but what surfaces is the notion that William

Godel was extremely effective at his job. By the late summer of 1953, the majority of the captured pilots had been returned. Many of them appeared on television and explained what had been done to them, that they had been tortured into making false confessions. A solid narrative emerged. The evil communists had tried to "brainwash" the Americans, with emphasis on the word "tried," and failed. Schwable recanted everything he had said and was awarded the Legion of Merit. The American public welcomed this idea with open arms; in his constitution and character, the American serviceman was stronger than and superior to the communist brainwashers.

As for Allen Macy Dulles, he was not getting any better. The brain injury had damaged his prefrontal cortex, leaving him with permanent short-term amnesia, also called anterograde amnesia. He had lost the ability to transfer new information from his short-term memory to his long-term memory. He knew who he was, but he could not remember things like where he was. Or what day it was. Or what he had done twenty minutes before.

"He was present, one hundred percent present, in the moment," his sister Joan Talley said. "But he could not hang on to anything that was happening anymore. He could remember everything about his life up to the war, up to the injury. Then nothing." His days at Exeter, when he was a teenager, were his fondest memories, all sharp. He retained much knowledge of the classics, and of ancient Greek warfare, which he had studied at Princeton. He could recall training with the Marines, but from the moment of the injury, it was all darkness. Just a blank page. "You would talk to him, and ten minutes later he would not remember anything that you had just said," Joan Talley recalled. "Poor Allen began to act paranoid." Conspiratorial thinking gripped his mind. It was the fault of the Nazis, he claimed. The fault of the Jews. His father was not his father. His father was a Nazi spy. "The psychiatrists tried to say it was mental illness. That Allen was suffering from schizophrenia. That was the new diagnosis back then. Blame everything on schizophrenia."

The ambitious Dr. Harold Wolff could not help Allen Macy Dulles, nor could any of the other doctors hired by his father. He was moved into a mental institution, called the Chestnut Lodge, in Rockville, Maryland. This was the infamous locale where the CIA sent officers who experienced mental breakdowns. How much doctoring went on at the Chestnut Lodge remains the subject of debate, but the facility offered safety, security, and privacy. Joan Talley visited her brother regularly, though it pained her to see him locked up there.

"Allen was suffering from a terrible brain injury," she said. "Of course he wasn't crazy.... Allen had been absolutely brilliant before the brain injury, before the war. It was as if somewhere down inside he knew that he was [once] very intelligent but that he wasn't anymore. It drove him mad. That his brilliance in life was over. That there would be brilliance no more." Allen Macy Dulles was shuffled around from one mental hospital to another. Eventually he was sent overseas, to a lakeside sanatorium in Switzerland, where he returned to a prewar life of anonymity. Joan moved to Zurich, to study psychology. She visited her brother every week.

Dr. Harold Wolff did not disappear. He had become friendly with CIA director Dulles while treating his amnesiac son. Now Dr. Wolff had a bold proposal for the CIA. A research project in a similar field. What, really, was brainwashing other than an attempt to make a man forget things he once held dear? Wolff believed this was rich territory to mine. The brainwashing crisis with the Korean War POWs had passed, but there was much to learn from brainwashing techniques. What if a man really could be transformed into an ant, a robot, or a slave? What if he could be made to forget things? This could be a major tool in psychological warfare operations. The CIA was interested, and so was William Godel.

In late 1953 Dr. Wolff secured a CIA contract to explore brainwashing techniques, together with Dr. Lawrence Hinkle, his partner at the Cornell University Medical College in New York City. Their classified report, which took more than two years to complete, would become the definitive study on communist brainwashing techniques. From there, the work expanded. Soon the two doctors had their own CIA-funded program to carry out experiments in behavior modification and mind control. It was called the Society for the Investigation of Human Ecology. One of their jobs was to conduct a study on the soldiers who had become POWs during the Korean War. This work would later be revisited by the CIA and DARPA starting in 2005.

At the Pentagon, having so adroitly dealt with the POW brainwashing scandal, William Godel was elevated to an even more powerful position. Starting in 1953, he served as deputy director of the Office of Special Operations, an office inside the Office of the Secretary of Defense. Godel's boss was General Graves B. Erskine. Godel acted as liaison between the Pentagon and the CIA and NSA. So trusted was William Godel that during important meetings he would sometimes serve as an alternate for the deputy secretary of defense. In declassified State Department memos, Godel was praised as an "expert from DoD on techniques and practices of psychological warfare." He worked on many different classified programs in the years from 1955 to 1957 and left a footprint around the world. As part of the Joint Intelligence Group, he was in charge of "collecting, evaluating and disseminating intelligence in support of activities involving the recovery of U.S. nationals held prisoner in Communist countries around the globe." He served as deputy director of the Office of Special Operations, Department of the Navy, and was in charge of the classified elements of the Navy's mission to map Antarctica. In March 1956, a five-mile-wide ice shelf off the coast of Queen Maud Land, Antarctica, was named after him, the Godel Iceport. But his true passion was counterinsurgency.

In 1957 Godel traveled around the country, giving lectures at war colleges to promote the idea that the United States would sooner or later have to fight wars in remote places like Vietnam. In many ways, Godel would say to his military-member audiences, America was already fighting these wars, just not out in the open. In his lectures he would remark that by the time of the French defeat at Dien Bien Phu, the U.S. had "been paying eighty percent of the bill." Godel believed that America had "to learn to fight a war that doesn't have nuclear weapons, doesn't have the North German Plain, and doesn't necessarily involve Americans."

Godel believed he knew what the future of warfare would look like. How its fighters would act. They would use irregular warfare tactics, like the ambushes and beheadings he had witnessed in Vietnam. America's future wars would not be fought by men wearing U.S. Army uniforms, Godel said. They would be fought by local fighters who had been trained by U.S. forces, with U.S. tactics and know-how, and carrying U.S. weapons. The way Godel saw it, the Pentagon needed to develop advanced weaponry, based on technology that was not just nuclear technology, but that could deal with this coming threat. Godel formulated a theory, something he proudly called his "bold summation." Insurgents might have superior discipline, organization, and motivation, he said. But science and technology could give "our" side the leading edge.

In February 1958, William Godel was hired on in a key position at the newly formed Advanced Research Projects Agency. It was Godel's role as director of the Office of Foreign Developments to handle what would be ARPA's covert military operations overseas. For Godel, his experience in Vietnam back in 1950 left him convinced that if America was going to defeat the global spread of communism, it needed to wage a new kind of warfare called counterinsurgency warfare, or COIN. Godel was now in a position to create and implement the very programs he had been telling war college audiences across the country needed to be created. Through inserting a U.S. military presence into foreign lands threatened by communism—through advanced science and technology—democracy would prevail and communism would fail. This quest would quickly become Godel's obsession.

In 1959 ARPA's Office of Foreign Developments was renamed the Policy and Planning Division. Godel retained the position of director. Herb York moved from chief scientist at ARPA to the director of the Defense Department of Research and Engineering, or DDR&E, with all ARPA program managers still reporting to him. Herb York and William Godel shared a similar view: the United States must aggressively seek out potential research and development capabilities to assist anticommunist struggles in foreign countries by using cutting-edge technology, most of which did not yet exist. In early 1960, York authorized a lengthy trip for Godel and for York's new deputy director, John Macauley. The two men were to travel through Asia and Australia to set up foreign technology–based operations there. Godel still acted as ARPA liaison to the NSA and CIA.

Godel traveled to a remote area in South Australia called Woomera. Here the Defense Department was building the largest overland missile range outside the Soviet Union. The site was critical to ARPA's Defender program. Next he went to Southeast Asia, where he made a general assessment of the communist insurgency that was continuing to escalate there, most notably in Vietnam. Upon his return to the United States, Godel outlined his observations in a memo. In 1960 the South Vietnamese army had 150,000 men, making them far superior, numerically, to what was estimated to be an insurgent fighting force of between only three thousand to five thousand communists, the Viet Minh or Vietcong. And yet the South was unable to control this insurgency, which was growing at an accelerating rate. South Vietnamese president

Ngo Dinh Diem's "congenitally trained, conventionally organized and congenitally equipped military organizations are incapable of employment in anti-guerrilla operations," Godel wrote.

For the secretary of defense William Godel prepared lengthy memos on the unique nature of the insurgency, singling out the growing communist-backed guerrilla forces in Vietnam and neighboring Laos and the "potential value of applying scientific talent to the problem." Godel suggested that ARPA create "self-sustaining paramilitary organizations at the group level," to be sent into Vietnam to conduct psychological warfare operations. Godel believed that ARPA should begin providing local villagers with weapons to use, so as to turn them into counterinsurgency fighters for the Pentagon. "These forces should be provided not with conventional arms and equipment requiring third- and fourth-level maintenance but with a capability to be farmers or taxi drivers during the day and anti-guerrilla forces at night." William Godel was suggesting that ARPA take on a role that until now had been the domain of the Special Operations Division of the CIA and U.S. Army Special Forces teams. Godel believed that ARPA should create its own army of ARPA-financed fighters who would appear to be civilians by day, but who would take on the role of paramilitary operators by night. A new chapter in ARPA history had begun.

Upon returning from Vietnam, Godel roamed the halls of the Pentagon, intent on garnering support for his counterinsurgency views. He was largely ignored. "Godel continued to press his views on people throughout the government, many of them well-placed via his remarkable network of contacts," said an ARPA colleague, Lee Huff, but the Eisenhower administration had little interest in his ideas, and he was vetoed at every turn. With the arrival of a new president, this would change.

When a new president takes office, he generally changes the guard. And the arrival of John Fitzgerald Kennedy meant the departure of

Herb York. "When John Kennedy won the 1960 election [I] became what politicians call lame ducks," York later observed, adding that he was not sorry to go. "I didn't have to spend all my time putting out fires" anymore. York was proud of the work he had accomplished while at ARPA, the "truly revolutionary changes" he had overseen at the Pentagon. At the top of the list was the arsenal of nuclear weapons he had helped build up. "By the end of the Eisenhower period, we had firm plans and commitments for the deployment of about 1,075 ICBMs (805 Minutemen plus 270 Atlas and Titans)," York noted with pride.

He also admitted that these accomplishments presented a paradox. As he put it, "Our nuclear strategy, and the objective situation underlying it, created an awful dilemma." After his years working on ARPA's Defender program, he had "concluded that a defense of the population was and very probably would remain impossible in the nuclear era."

At noon on January 20, 1960, John F. Kennedy became the thirty-fifth president of the United States. It would be more than a week before York would officially leave office. As the "senior holdover in the [Defense] Department," York explained, "I became the Secretary of Defense at the same moment" the president took office. Former Ford Motor Company president Robert McNamara had been nominated to serve as Kennedy's secretary of defense, but it was not known how long the confirmation hearings would take. In the meantime, someone had to be in charge of the nation's nuclear weapons. The practice of the president remaining in constant contact with the so-called nuclear football, the briefcase containing the codes and other data enabling a president to order a nuclear launch, was not yet in effect. In January 1961 it was the job of the secretary of defense to carry the case, to be responsible for, in York's words, "getting the nuclear machine ready to go into action when the president so ordered it." What this meant was that for now, Herb York was in charge of America's entire nuclear arsenal.

A special red telephone was installed in York's bedroom, at his home just outside Washington. It had a large red plastic light on top that would flash if York was being called. The red phone was connected to one place only, the War Room located beneath the Pentagon. The day after Kennedy's inauguration, York decided to venture over to the War Room to see what was going on down there.

"When I knocked at the door, a major opened it a crack," York recounted.

From behind the crack in the door, the man asked, "What do you want?"

"I'm the acting secretary of defense," York answered.

"Just a minute," said the man. He closed the door gently in York's face. A few moments later, the man, an Army major, returned and let Herb York inside, not without some fanfare. York looked around. Here, the Pentagon was keeping special "watch" on situations around the globe considered most critical to national security. One place was the Central African Republic of the Congo, not yet called Zaire, where a rebellion was under way in the mineral-rich province of Katanga. "The other was Laos," recalled York, Vietnam's turbulent neighbor. The next three presidents would have their presidencies defined by the Vietnam War. But at that time, as far as the rest of America was concerned, "nothing special was going on in either place, as far as our people knew. Vietnam was not yet in our sights."

The following week, Robert McNamara was confirmed as the new secretary of defense. No one bothered to go to York's house and retrieve the red telephone. "It remained there until I left Washington, permanently, some four months later," said York.

PART II

THE VIETNAM WAR

CHAPTER SEVEN

Techniques and Gadgets

The first two U.S. military advisors to die in the Vietnam War were ambushed. Major Dale Buis and Master Sergeant Chester Ovnand were sitting with six other Americans in the mess hall of a South Vietnamese army camp twenty-five miles north of Saigon when the attack came. The lights were off and the men were watching a Hollywood movie, a film noir thriller called *The Tattered Dress*. When it was time to change the reel, a U.S. Army technician flipped on the lights.

Outside, a group of communist guerrilla fighters had been surveilling the army post and waiting for the right moment to attack. With the place now illuminated, they pushed the muzzles of their semiautomatic weapons through the windows and opened fire. Major Buis and Master Sergeant Ovnand were killed instantly, as were two South Vietnamese army guards and an eight-year-old Vietnamese boy. In a defensive move, Major Jack Hellet turned the lights back off. The communist fighters fled, disappearing into the jungle from where they had come.

In his first two months in office, President Kennedy spent more time on Vietnam and neighboring Laos than on any other national security concern. Counterinsurgency warfare, all but ignored by President Eisenhower, was now a top priority for the new president. William Godel finally had an ear, and by winter, the Advanced Projects Research Agency made its bold first entry into the tactical arena. On the morning of his eighth day in office, the new president summoned his most senior advisors—the vice president, the secretary of state, the secretary of defense, the director of the CIA, the chairman of the Joint Chiefs of Staff, the assistant secretary of defense, and a few others—to the White House. The subject of their meeting was the "Viet-nam counter-insurgency plan," the location still so foreign and far away that it was hyphenated in the official memorandum. Two days after the meeting, President Kennedy authorized an increase of $41.1 million to expand and train the South Vietnamese army, roughly $325 million in 2015. Of far greater significance for ARPA, President Kennedy signed an official "Counter-insurgency Plan." This important meeting paved the way for the creation of two high-level groups to deal with the most classified aspects of fighting communist insurgents in Vietnam, the Vietnam Task Force and the Special Group. William Godel was made a member of both groups.

From the earliest days of his presidency, Kennedy worked to distance himself from a traditional, old school military mindset. President Eisenhower, age seventy-one when he left office, had been a five-star general and served as Supreme Commander of the Allied Forces in Europe during World War II. President Kennedy was a dashing young war hero, full of idealism and enthusiasm, and just forty-three years old. Kennedy sought a more adaptable, collegial style of policy making when it came to issues of national security. The Eisenhower doctrine was based on mutual assured destruction, or MAD. The Kennedy doctrine would become known as "flexible response." The new president believed that the U.S. military needed to be able to fight limited wars, quickly and with flexibility, anywhere around the world where communism threatened democracy. In describing his approach, Kennedy said that the nation must be ready "to deter all wars, general or limited, nuclear or conventional, large or small."

The new president reduced the number of National Security Council staff by more than twenty and eliminated the Operations Coordinating Board and the Planning Board. In their place, he created interagency task forces. These task forces were almost always chaired by men from his inner circle, Ivy League intellectuals on the White House staff or in the Pentagon. Kennedy's secretary of defense, Robert McNamara, was a Harvard Business School graduate whose deputy, Roswell Gilpatric, was a graduate of Yale Law School. The president's brother and attorney general, Robert Kennedy, was, like the president, a Harvard grad. National security advisor McGeorge Bundy graduated from Yale, as did deputy national security advisor Walt Rostow and Deputy Assistant Secretary of Defense for International Security Affairs William Bundy (brother of McGeorge Bundy), who also attended Harvard Law School. The staffs of many presidential administrations have been top-heavy with Ivy League graduates, but to many in Washington, it seemed as if President Kennedy was making a statement. That a man's intellectual prowess was to be valued above everything else. War was a thinking man's game, he seemed to be saying. Intellect won wars. The most powerful men in Secretary McNamara's Pentagon were defense intellectuals, including many former RAND Corporation employees. As a group, they would become known as McNamara's whiz kids.

"Viet-nam" had to be dealt with, the president's advisors agreed. On April 12, 1961, in a memo to the president, Walt Rostow suggested "Nine Proposals for Action" in Vietnam to fight the guerrillas there. "Action Proposal Number Five," written by William Godel, suggested "the sending to Viet-Nam of a research and development and military hardware team which would explore with General McGarr which of the various techniques and 'gadgets' now available or being explored that might be relevant and useful in the Viet-nam operation." General Lionel McGarr was the commander of the Military Assistance Advisory Group, Vietnam (MAAG-V), and the ongoing "Viet-nam operation," which involved training the South Vietnamese army in U.S. war-fighting skills. Godel's action proposal called for ARPA to augment MAAG-V efforts with a new assemblage of "techniques and 'gadgets.'"

President Kennedy liked Godel's proposal and personally requested more information. The following week, Deputy Secretary of Defense Roswell Gilpatric submitted to the president a memorandum that elaborated on "Action Proposal Number Five." This particular plan of action, according to Gilpatric, involved the use of cutting-edge technology to fight the communist insurgents. He proposed that ARPA establish its own research and development center in Saigon, a physical location where an ARPA field unit could develop new weapons specifically tailored to jungle-fighting needs. There would be other projects too, said Gilpatric—the "techniques" element of Godel's proposal. These would involve sociological research programs and psychological warfare campaigns. The ARPA facility, set up in buildings adjacent to the MAAG-V center, would be called the Combat Development and Test Center. It would be run jointly by ARPA, MAAG-V, and the South Vietnamese armed forces (ARVN). The ARPA program would be called Project Agile, as in flexible, capable, and quick-witted. Just like the president and his advisors.

The following month, President Kennedy sent Vice President Lyndon B. Johnson to meet personally with South Vietnamese president Ngo Dinh Diem and garner support for the "techniques and 'gadgets'" idea. Photographs of the two men dressed in matching white tuxedo jackets and posing for cameras at Diem's Independence Palace in Saigon were reprinted in newspapers around the world. Johnson, who was six foot four, towered over the diminutive Diem, whose head barely reached Johnson's shoulder. Both men smiled broadly, expressing commitment to their countries' ongoing partnership. Communism was a scourge, and together the governments of the United States and South Vietnam intended to eradicate it from the region.

President Diem, an avowed anticommunist and fluent English speaker, was Catholic, well educated, and enamored of modernity. These qualities made him a strong ally of the U.S. government but alienated him from many of his own people. In the early 1960s, the majority of Vietnamese were agrarian peasants—Buddhist and Taoist rice farmers who lived at the subsistence level in rural communities distant from Saigon. By the time President Diem met with Vice President Johnson to discuss fighting communist insurgents with techniques and gadgets, Diem had been in power for six years. Diem ruled with a heavy hand and was notoriously corrupt, but the Kennedy administration believed it could make the situation work.

During the meeting, Johnson asked Diem to agree to an official memo of understanding, to "consider jointly the establishment in [Saigon] of a facility to develop and test [weapons], using the tools of modern technology and new techniques, to help [both parties] in their joint campaign against the Communists." Diem agreed and the men shook hands, setting Project Agile in motion and giving ARPA the go-ahead to set up a weapons facility in Saigon.

"[Diem] is the Winston Churchill of Asia!" Johnson famously declared.

The following month, on June 8, 1961, William Godel traveled to Vietnam with Project Agile's first research and development team to set up ARPA's Combat Development and Test Center (CDTC). Project Agile was now a "Presidential issue," which gave Godel authority and momentum to act. The new R&D center was located in a group of one-story stone buildings facing the Navy Yard, near the Saigon River. Each building had heavy shutters on the windows and doors to keep out the intense Saigon heat. Ceiling fans were permanent fixtures inside all the buildings, as were potted palms and tiled floors. On the walls hung large maps of Vietnam and framed posters of the CDTC logo, an amalgamation of a helmet, wings, an anchor, and a star. Desks and tabletops were adorned with miniature freestanding U.S. flags, and there were large glass ashtrays on almost every surface. Some buildings housed ARPA administrators, while others functioned as laboratories where scientists and engineers worked. Photographs in the National Archives show "ARPA" stamped in bold stenciling on metal desks, tables, and folding chairs.

During the trip, Godel met three separate times with President Diem. On one visit Diem toured the CDTC, and in photographs he appears confident and pleased as he strolls down the pebble pathways, wearing his signature Western-style white suit and hat. Accompanying Diem is his ever-present entourage of military advisors, soldiers dressed in neat khaki uniforms, aviator sunglasses, and shiny shoes. In Godel's first field report he notes President's Diem insistence that U.S. military involvement in South Vietnam remain disguised. This, warned Diem, was the only way for the two countries to continue their successful partnership. The success of Project Agile rested on discretion and secrecy. Godel agreed, and a large open-sided workspace—similar to an airplane hangar but without walls—was constructed adjacent to the CDTC. Here, local Vietnamese laborers toiled away in plain sight, building components for Project Agile's various secret weapons programs.

By August, ARPA's Combat Development and Test Center was up and running with a staff of twenty-five Americans. Colonel William P. Brooks, U.S. Army, served as chief of the ARPA R&D field unit, while President Diem's assistant chief of staff, Colonel Bui Quang Trach, was officially "in charge," which was how he signed documents related to the CDTC. ARPA's first staffers included military officers, civilian scientists, engineers, and academics. Some had research and development experience and others had combat experience. The CDTC was connected by a secure telephone line to room 2B-261 at the Pentagon, where Project Agile had an office. Agile's budget for its first year was relatively modest, just $11.3 million, or one-tenth of the budget for ARPA's biggest program, Defender. By the following year, Project Agile's budget would double, transforming it into the third-largest ARPA program, after Defender and Vela.

Upon returning to Washington, D.C., from Saigon, Godel traveled across the nation's capital, giving briefings on Project Agile to members of the departments of State and Defense, and the CIA. On July 6, 1961, he gave a closed seminar at the Foreign Service Institute. There he discussed the first four military equipment programs to be discreetly introduced into the jungles of Vietnam—a boat, an airplane, guns, and dogs. At first glance, they hardly seem high-tech. Two of the four programs, the boats and the dogs, were as old as warfare itself. But ARPA's "swamp boat" was a uniquely designed paddlewheel boat with a steam engine that burned cane alcohol; it carried twenty to thirty men. What made it unusual was that it was engineered to float almost silently and could operate in as little as three inches of water. In 1961, the night in Vietnam was ruled by the Vietcong communist insurgents, which meant the boat had to be able to travel quietly down the Mekong Delta waterways so that U.S. Special Forces working with South Vietnamese soldiers could infiltrate enemy territory without being ambushed.

ARPA's canine program was far more ambitious than using dogs in the traditional role of sentinels. "One of the most provoking problems [in Vietnam] is the detection and identification of enemy personnel," ARPA chemists A. C. Peters and W. H. Allton Jr. stated in an official report, noting how Vietcong fighters were generally indistinguishable from local peasants in South Vietnam. ARPA's dog program sought to develop a chemical whose scent could be detected by Army-trained dogs but not by humans. As part of a tagging and tracking program, the plan was to have Diem's soldiers surreptitiously mark large groups of people with this chemical, then use dogs to track whoever turned up later in a suspicious place, like outside a military base.

ARPA's canine program was an enormous undertaking. The chemical had to work in a hot, wet climate, leave a sufficient "spoor" to enable tracking by dogs, and be suitable for spraying from an aircraft. The first chemical ARPA scientists focused their work on what was called squalene, a combination of shark and fish liver oil. German shepherds were trained in Fort Benning, Georgia, and then sent to the CDTC in Saigon. But an administrative oversight set the program back when Army handlers neglected to account for "temperatures reaching a level greater than 100 F." After forty-five minutes of work in the jungles of Vietnam, the ARPA dogs "seemed to lose interest in any further detection trials." The German shepherds' acute sense of smell could not be sustained in the intense jungle heat.

The first Project Agile aircraft introduced into the war theater was a power glider designed for audio stealth—light, highly maneuverable, and able to fly just above the jungle canopy for extended periods on a single tank of gasoline. Godel called it "an airborne Volkswagen." Because it flew so close to the treetops, guerrilla fighters found it nearly impossible to shoot down. ARPA's power glider would pave the way for an entirely new class of unconventional military aircraft, including drones.

The most significant weapon to emerge from the early days of Project Agile was the AR-15 semiautomatic rifle. In the summer of 1961, Diem's small-in-stature army was having difficulty handling the large semiautomatic weapons carried by U.S. military advisors. In the AR-15 Godel saw promise, "something the short, small Vietnamese can fire without bowling themselves over," he explained. Godel worked with legendary gun designer Eugene M. Stoner to create ten lightweight AR-15 prototypes, each weighing just 6.7 pounds. Vietnamese commanders at the CDTC expressed enthusiasm for this new weapon, Godel told Secretary McNamara, preferring it to the M1 Garand and Browning BARs they had been carrying.

Inside the Pentagon, the military services had been arguing about a service-wide infantry weapon—since Korea. With Agile's "Presidential issue" authority, Godel cut through years of red tape and oversaw the shipment of one thousand AR-15s to the CDTC without delay. U.S. Special Forces took the AR-15 into the battle zone for live-action tests. "At a distance of approximately fifteen meters, [a U.S. soldier] fired the weapon at two VC [Vietcong] armed with carbines, grenades, and mines," read an after-action report from 340 Ranger Company. "One round in the [VC's] head took it completely off. Another in the right arm took it completely off, too. One round hit him in the right side, causing a hole about five inches in diameter. It can be assumed that any one of the three wounds would have caused death," the company commander wrote.

In 1963 the AR-15 became the standard-issue rifle of the U.S. Army. In 1966 it was adapted for fully automatic fire and redesignated the M16 assault rifle. The weapon is still being used by U.S. soldiers. "The development of the M-16 would almost certainly not have come about without the existence of ARPA," noted an unpublished internal ARPA review, written in 1974.

The Combat Development and Test Center was up and running with four weapons programs, but dozens more were in the works. Project Agile "gadgets" would soon include shotguns, rifle grenades, shortened strip bullets, and high-powered sound canons. ARPA wanted a proximity fuse with an extra 75-millisecond delay so bombs dropped from aircraft could be detonated below the jungle canopy but just above the ground. Big projects and small projects, ARPA needed them all. Entire fleets of Army vehicles required retrofitting and redesign to handle rugged jungle trails. ARPA needed resupply aircraft with short takeoff and landing capability. It had plans to develop high-flying helicopters and low-flying drones. ARPA needed scientists to create disposable parachutes for aerial resupply, chemists to develop antivenom snakebite and leech repellent kits, technicians to create listening devices and seismic monitoring devices that looked like rocks but could track guerrilla fighters' movement down a jungle trail. ARPA needed teams of computer scientists to design and build data collection systems and storage systems, and to retrofit existing air, ground, and ocean systems so all the different military services involved in this fight against the Vietnamese communists could communicate better.

But there was one weapons program—highly classified—that commanded more of Godel's attention than the others. This particular program was unlike any other in the Project Agile arsenal in that it had the potential to act as a silver bullet—a single solution to the complex hydra-headed problem of counterinsurgency. It involved chemistry and crops, and its target was the jungle. Eventually the weapon would become known to the world as Agent Orange, and instead of being a silver bullet, Agent Orange was a hideous toxin. But in 1961, herbicidal warfare was still considered an acceptable idea and William Godel was in charge of running the program for ARPA.

At Fort Detrick, in Maryland, ARPA ran a toxicology branch where it worked on chemical weapons–related programs with Dr. James W. Brown, deputy chief of the crops division of the Army Chemical Corps Biological Laboratories. ARPA had Dr. Brown working on a wide variety of defoliants with the goal of finding a chemical compound that could perform two functions at once. ARPA wanted to strip the leaves off trees so as to deny Vietcong fighters protective cover from the jungle canopy. And they wanted to starve Vietcong fighters into submission by poisoning their primary food crop, a jungle root called manioc.

On July 17, 1961, Godel met with the Vietnam Task Force to

brief its members on what was then a highly classified defoliation program, and to discuss the next steps. "This is a costly operation which would require some three years for maximum effectiveness," Godel said. The use of biological and chemical weapons was prohibited by the Geneva Convention and from his experience in Korea, Godel knew how easily the international spotlight could turn its focus on claims of Geneva Convention violations. For this reason, anyone briefed on the defoliation campaign and all personnel working at the CDTC were advised to move forward, "subject to political-psychological restrictions (such as those imposed by Communist claims of U.S. biological warfare in Korea)." The classified program would be called "anticrop warfare research," as destroying enemy food supplies was not against the rules of war. In the field, operational activities were to be referred to as "CDTC Task Number 20," or "Task 20" for short.

While it is interesting to note ARPA's unity with the Vietnam Task Force on the question of allowing this controversial decision to proceed, the record indicates that the meeting was a formality and that Godel had already gotten the go-ahead. On the same day Godel met with the Vietnam Task Force, the first batch of crop-killing chemicals—a defoliant called Dinoxol—arrived at the Combat Development and Test Center in Saigon. A few days later, spray aircraft were shipped. And a week after that, Dr. James W. Brown, deputy chief of the crops division at Fort Detrick, arrived at the CDTC to oversee the first defoliation field tests.

The first mission to spray herbicides on the jungles of Vietnam occurred on August 10, 1961. The helicopter—an American-made H-34 painted in the colors of the South Vietnamese army and equipped with an American-made spray system called a HIDAL (Helicopter Insecticide Dispersal Apparatus, Liquid)—was flown by a South Vietnamese air force pilot. President Diem was an enthusiastic advocate of defoliation, and two weeks later he personally chose the second target. On August 24 a fixed-wing aircraft sprayed the poisonous herbicide Dinoxol over a stretch of jungle along Route 13, fifty miles north of Saigon.

The defoliation tests were closely watched at the Pentagon. R&D field units working out of the CDTC oversaw Vietnamese pilots as they continued to spray herbicides on manioc groves and mangrove swamps. Godel and his staff were working on a more ambitious follow-up plan. A portion of the Mekong Delta believed to contain one of the heaviest Vietcong populations, designated "Zone D," was chosen to be the target of a future multiphase campaign. Phase I set a goal of defoliating 20 percent of the manioc groves and mangrove swamps over a thirty-day period. This was to be followed by Phase II, with a goal of defoliating the remaining 80 percent of Zone D, meaning the entire border with North Vietnam. Together, the two-part operation would take ninety days to complete. After Phase I and Phase II were completed, Phase III called for the defoliation of another 31,250 square miles of jungle, which was roughly half of South Vietnam. Finally, ARPA's R&D field units would be dispatched to burn down all the resulting dead trees, turning the natural jungle into man-made farmland. This way, Godel's team explained, once the insurgency was extinguished, it would not be able to reignite. The projected cost for the Project Agile defoliation campaign was between $75 and $80 million, more than half a billion dollars in 2015. The only foreseeable problem, wrote the staff, was that the program's ambitious scope would require more chemicals than could realistically be manufactured in the United States.

In 1961, few Americans outside elite government circles knew what was happening in Vietnam. Inside Washington, the power struggles over how best to handle the communist insurgency were becoming contentious as the rift between the White House and the Pentagon widened. Just three months after taking office, Kennedy experienced the bitter low point of his presidency when a

CIA-sponsored, military-supported paramilitary invasion of the Bay of Pigs in Cuba failed. More than a hundred men were killed and twelve hundred were captured. The fiasco damaged the president's relationship not only with the CIA but also with the Joint Chiefs of Staff. Publicly, President Kennedy assumed full blame. "I'm the responsible official of the government," he famously said. But to his closest White House advisors, he said that the Joint Chiefs of Staff had failed him.

"The first advice I'm going to give my successor," Kennedy told *Washington Post* editor Ben Bradlee, "is to watch the generals and to avoid feeling that just because they were military men their opinion[s] on military matters were worth a damn." The situation seemed to strengthen his perception that his group of intellectually minded White House advisors and civilian Pentagon advisors, the so-called McNamara whiz kids, not only were more trustworthy but also had better ideas on military matters than did the military men themselves.

After the Bay of Pigs, in the summer of 1961 President Kennedy created a new position on his White House staff called military representative of the president. The post was created specifically for General Maxwell Taylor, a dashing multilingual World War II hero who had written a book critical of the Eisenhower administration. According to a memo that outlined General Taylor's duties as military representative of the president, he was to "advise and assist the President with regard to those military matters that reach him as Commander in Chief of the Armed Forces." General Taylor was also to "give his personal views to assist the President in reaching decisions," and he was to have a role in offering "advice and assistance in the field of intelligence." It was a position of enormous influence, particularly in light of the coming war in Vietnam. General Taylor was to advise the president on all military matters, and yet he was part of the White House staff, not the Pentagon.

General Taylor was dispatched to Vietnam as head of a delegation that would become known as the Taylor-Rostow mission. The purpose of the mission was to investigate what future political and military actions were necessary there. Accompanying Taylor on this trip was William Godel. The two men shared similar views on counterinsurgency programs; in fact, Godel would write major portions of Taylor's trip report. Godel took General Taylor to ARPA's new Combat Development and Test Center and showed him some of the gadgets and techniques being developed there. In Taylor's report to President Kennedy, he praised the CDTC's work, noting "the special talents of the U.S. scientific laboratories and industry" on display.

The Taylor-Rostow mission left Washington on Sunday, October 15, 1961, stopped for a briefing in Honolulu, and arrived in Saigon on October 18. Godel joined the party in Saigon. General Taylor wore civilian clothes and requested that there be no press briefings, no interviews, no social functions, and most of all no military formalities. To the president, General Taylor described the Vietnam situation as "the darkest since the early days of 1954," a reference to the year when the French lost Dien Bien Phu. Taylor warned how dangerous the terrain had become, noting that the "Vietcong strength had increased from an estimated 10,000 in January 1961 to 17,000 in October; they were clearly on the move in the delta, in the highlands, and along the plain on the north central coast." He painted the picture facing the government of South Vietnam in the bleakest of terms. President Diem and his generals "were watching with dismay the situation in neighboring Laos and the negotiations in Geneva, which convinced them that there would soon be a Communist-dominated government in Vientiane," the capital of Laos, Taylor wrote, and proposed that President Kennedy take "vigorous action" at once.

"If Vietnam goes, it will be exceedingly difficult if not impossible to hold Southeast Asia," Taylor warned. "What will be lost is not merely a crucial piece of real estate, but the faith that the U.S. has the will and the capacity to deal with the Communist offensive in that area." General Taylor's message was clear. The United States needed to expand its covert military action in Vietnam. In his report to President Kennedy, Taylor suggested making use of ARPA's gadgets and techniques, most notably "a very few 'secret weapons' on the immediate horizon" at the CDTC. One such "secret weapon" was herbicide. As the program moved forward, however, there was a hitch.

In the fall of 1961, Radio Hanoi in North Vietnam made public ARPA's secret defoliation tests. The United States had "used poisonous gas to kill crops and human[s]," Radio Hanoi declared in a condemnatory broadcast. The revelatory radio program was then rebroadcast on Radio Moscow and Radio Peking, but surprisingly, it did not produce the kind of international uproar that the Vietnam Task Force had cautioned against in the July 17 meeting. But the president's advisors agreed that a formal decision had to be made about whether to proceed with ARPA's defoliation program or to halt it. The Vietnam Task Force asked the Joint Chiefs of Staff to weigh in.

On November 3, they expressed their opposition. Mindful of the Geneva Protocols, they wrote, "the Joint Chiefs of Staff are of the opinion that in conducting aerial defoliant operations [against] food growing areas, care must be taken to assure that the United States does not become the target for charges of employing chemical or biological warfare." Echoing earlier concerns from the Vietnam Task Force, the Joint Chiefs warned that the world could react with solemn condemnation, and that "international repercussions against the United States could be most serious."

Even deputy national security advisor Walt Rostow, just back from the trip to Vietnam with General Taylor and William Godel, felt compelled to point out to the president the reality behind spraying defoliants. In a memorandum with the subject line "Weed Killer," Rostow told President Kennedy, "Your decision is required because this is a kind of chemical warfare." There was no uncertainty in Walt Rostow's words.

On November 30, 1961, President Kennedy approved the chemical defoliation program in Vietnam. The program, said Kennedy, was to be considerably smaller than the Advanced Research Projects Agency had originally devised, and it should instead have a budget between $4 million and $6.5 million. With President Kennedy's blessing, the genie was out of the bottle. By war's end, roughly 19 million gallons of herbicide would be sprayed on the jungles of Vietnam. A 2012 congressional report determined that over the course of the war, between 2.1 million and 4.8 million Vietnamese were directly exposed to Agent Orange.

From his ARPA office at the Pentagon, William Godel sent a memo, marked "Secret," to Dr. James Brown, the Army scientist at Fort Detrick, asking Brown to come see him at once. During the meeting, Dr. Brown was informed that he was now officially the person in charge of defoliation operations in Vietnam and that he was a representative of the secretary of defense. "He was advised to be ignorant of all other technical matters," notes a declassified memo. "If friendly authorities requested information on biological anticrop or antipersonnel agents or chemical agents or protective measures or detection kits, etc., etc. he [Dr. Brown] was to state he knew nothing about them and suggest that they direct their inquiries to Chief MAAG [Military Assistance Advisory Group]."

Like much of ARPA's Project Agile, the defoliation campaign was a "Presidential issue." Details about the program, what it involved, and what it sought to accomplish were matters of national security, and the narrative around this story needed to be tightly controlled. In the words of Walt Rostow, the Agent Orange campaign was "a kind of chemical warfare." But it was also a "secret weapon," and had the potential of serving as a magic bullet against communist insurgents in Vietnam.

CHAPTER EIGHT

RAND and COIN

At the RAND Corporation in sunny Santa Monica, California, by 1961 war game playing had expanded considerably since the days of John von Neumann and the lunchtime matches of *Kriegspiel.* For several years now, RAND had been simulating counterinsurgency war games played out between U.S. forces and guerrilla fighters in Vietnam. These counterinsurgency games were the brainchild of Ed Paxson, an engineer from the mathematics department, who called the game series Project Sierra. Unlike the old lunchtime matches, the Sierra games lasted months, sometimes more than a year, and involved various scenarios, including ones in which U.S. forces used nuclear weapons against communist insurgents. One day back in the mid-1950s, while observing one of the Sierra war games, an analyst named George Tanham made an astute observation. He mentioned that the entire Sierra series was unrealistic because the RAND analysts were assuming Vietnamese communist fighters fought like American soldiers, which they did not.

In the mid-1950s it was generally agreed that Tanham knew

more about counterinsurgency than anyone else at RAND. A Princeton University graduate and former U.S. Air Force officer, Tanham was a highly decorated veteran of World War II. After the war he earned a Ph.D. from Stanford in unconventional warfare and joined RAND in 1955. Tanham's observations about the Sierra war games impressed RAND president Frank Collbohm, who sent Tanham to Paris to study counterinsurgency tactics, and to learn how and why the French army lost Vietnam at Dien Bien Phu in 1954. Tanham's study was paid for by the Pentagon and was classified secret. When a sanitized version appeared in 1961, George Tanham became the first American author to publish a book about communist revolutionary warfare.

At the Pentagon, Tanham's book caught Harold Brown's eye. Brown, who had taken over Herb York's job as director of Defense Department Research and Engineering (DDR&E), was the man to whom ARPA directors reported. Like Herb York, Harold Brown had served as chief scientist at Livermore laboratory before coming to Washington, D.C. Harold Brown reached out to Tanham and asked him to pay a visit to ARPA's Combat Development Test Center in Saigon and write up his assessment of CDTC progress there. Tanham's 1961 report remains classified, but he referred to some of his observations in a report three years later, since declassified. ARPA's weapons programs in Vietnam—CDTC's "gadgets"—needed to expand, said Tanham. And so did psychological warfare efforts—CDTC's "techniques." But equally important, said Tanham, was the war's presentation back home. He suggested that the conflict be presented to the American people as a "war without guns being waged by men of good will, half a world away from their native land."

When Tanham returned from Saigon, he met with the Vietnam Task Force, the Special Group, and the CIA. The following month Harold Brown sent a classified letter to Frank Collbohm asking the RAND Corporation to come on board and work on

Project Agile in Vietnam. RAND was needed to work on "persuasion and motivation" techniques, programs designed to win the hearts and minds of the Vietnamese people.

In its "persuasion and motivation" campaign, ARPA began pursuing a less traditional defense science program involving social science research. Accepted as an offshoot of anthropology, and generally looked down upon by nuclear physicists like those in the Jason advisory group, social science concerned itself with societies and the relationships among the people who live in groups and communities. Harold Brown told Frank Collbohm that ARPA needed studies performed that could answer questions that were confounding defense officials at the Pentagon. Who were these people, the Vietnamese? What made one Vietnamese peasant become a communist and another remain loyal to President Diem? How did these foreign people live, work, strategize, organize, and think? The idea was that if only ARPA could understand what motivated Vietnamese people, the Pentagon might be able to persuade them to see democracy as a form of government superior to communism.

It was an enticing proposal for RAND. Social science research was far afield from the RAND Corporation's brand of nuclear war analysis and strategy, and of game theory. But defense contractors need to stay relevant in order to survive, and Frank Collbohm recognized that with President Kennedy in office, there was much new business to be had in counterinsurgency studies and strategy. Here was an opportunity for RAND to expand its Defense Department contracts beyond what it had become famous for.

RAND formed two counterinsurgency committees to strategize how best to handle Harold Brown's requests. One committee was called the Third Area Conflict board and was run by Albert Wohlstetter, the man behind RAND's legendary "second strike" nuclear strategy, also known as NUTS. The second committee was run jointly by RAND vice president George H. Clement, an expert on missiles, satellites, and "weapons systems philosophy," and Bob Bucheim, head of the aero-astronautics department. Proposals were written, and in a matter of months, ARPA and RAND entered into an initial Project Agile contract for $4 million (roughly $32 million in 2015), to be paid out over a period of four years. With funding secure, RAND was given its own office inside the Combat Development Test Center in Saigon, where a secretary answered telephones, typed letters, and received mail. RAND analysts could reside in a French colonial villa down the street from the MAAG-V headquarters at 176 Rue Pasteur, or they could have their own apartments. In early 1962, RAND began sending academics, analysts, and anthropologists to Saigon. Soon the number of RAND staff working out of the CDTC would more than double the number of Pentagon employees there.

The first two RAND analysts to arrive in Saigon, in January 1962, were Gerald Hickey and John Donnell. Both men were eminently qualified anthropologists and spoke fluent Vietnamese. Hickey had been a professor at Yale University, where he specialized in Vietnamese culture. Donnell taught social sciences at Dartmouth College. Both had spent time working in Vietnam as government consultants. Before working for RAND, Hickey was part of the Michigan State University Group, whose members, at the behest of the State Department, counseled President Diem's government in how to be better administrators. Donnell, who also spoke Chinese, consulted for the State Department on Asian affairs.

Saigon in January 1962 was a beautiful city, resplendent with French colonial architecture and still called the Paris of the Orient. Its broad boulevards were lined with leafy trees, and the streets were filled with bicycles, rickshaws, and cars. Locals relaxed outside in parks or in European-style cafés. Vendors sold flowers, and President Diem's police forces patrolled the streets. But for Hickey and Donnell, there was a not so subtle indication that things had changed in Saigon since their last visits in the late fifties. "Signs of conflict had replaced the feeling of peace," Hickey later wrote. "Everyone was concerned with security."

The road from the airport to RAND's office at the CDTC was crowded with military vehicles. During dinner their first night in Saigon under the ARPA contract, Hickey and Donnell sat in a rooftop café at the Caravelle Hotel listening to mortar explosions in the distance and watching flares light up the edges of the city. "Both John and I were somewhat astonished how the advent of the insurgency had changed the atmosphere of Saigon," Hickey recalled.

The plan was for the two anthropologists to travel into the central highlands and study the mountain people who lived there, the Montagnards. President Diem told his American counterparts that he doubted the loyalty of the mountain dwellers, and Hickey and Donnell were being sent to assess the situation. Before leaving for the mountains, they checked in with ARPA's Combat Development and Test Center, where they were met by a CIA officer named Gilbert Layton, who told them there had been a change of plans. The CIA was working on its own project with the Montagnards, Layton said, and there was not room for both programs. Hickey and Donnell would have to find another group of people to study.

Hickey and Donnell discussed the situation, consulted with RAND headquarters back in Santa Monica, and agreed on a different study to pursue. There was another important program that the Defense Department and the CIA had been working on with President Diem called the Strategic Hamlet Program, or "rural pacification." The plan was for the South Vietnamese army to move peasants away from the "Vietcong-infested" countryside and into new villages, or hamlets, where they would allegedly be safe. The Strategic Hamlet Program offered financial incentives to get the villagers to move. Using Defense Department funds, Diem's army would pay the villagers to build tall, fortress-like walls around their new jungle settlements.

Building these fences required weeks of intense labor. First, a deep ditch had to be dug around each new hamlet. Next, concrete posts needed to be sunk down into the ditch at intervals of roughly ten feet. Finally, villagers were to venture out into the jungle forests, cut down hundreds of thick stalks of bamboo, and make spears, which would then be used to build the fence. The South Vietnamese army would provide the villagers with the concrete posts and also with large rolls of barbed wire, courtesy of the Pentagon. The rest of the labor was for the villagers to do.

Defense Department officials saw U.S. investment in the Strategic Hamlet Program as an effective means of pacification and a way to help President Diem gain control over the region. The idea was that in exchange for their safety, the Vietnamese farmers would develop a sense of loyalty toward President Diem. But there was also a far more ambitious plan in place whereby ARPA would collect enough information on strategic hamlets to be able to "monitor" their activity in the future.

After the CIA canceled Hickey and Donnell's Montagnard project, the men decided to study the Strategic Hamlet Program. It is unlikely they knew about ARPA's future monitoring plans. Hickey and Donnell rented a Citroën and set off for a village northwest of Saigon called Cu Chi.

In Cu Chi, at a small shop, they came across a group of village farmers drinking tea. At first they found the villagers to be reticent, but after they spent a few days talking with them in their own language, tongues loosened up. As anthropologists, Hickey and Donnell were familiar with local farming techniques, and they also understood the villagers' deeply held beliefs in spirit culture, or animism, the idea that a supernatural power organizes and animates the material world. After a few more afternoon visits, the villagers began offering information to Hickey and Donnell about what had been going on in their village as far as the Strategic Hamlet Program was concerned.

"Without our asking, the Cu Chi villagers complained about the strategic hamlet," Hickey wrote in his report. The program had required villagers to move away from where they had been living, deep in the jungle, to this new village they did not consider their own. The mandatory relocation was having a devastating effect. People were distraught over having been forced to leave their ancestral homes and their ancestors' graves. Here, in this new village, farmers now faced a new challenge as they struggled to plant crops on unfamiliar land. Villagers were angry with the Diem government because they had been told that in exchange for digging ditches and building walls, they would be paid ten piasters a day and given lunch. President Diem's forces were supposed to have provided them with concrete posts and barbed-wire fence. Instead, the villagers said, Diem's soldiers had rounded up groups of men, forced them to work, refused to feed them, and charged them money for building supplies. The forced labor lasted roughly three months, with only one five-day break for the New Year festival. The labor program coincided with the most important planting time of the year, which meant that many farmers had been unable to plant their own crops. As a result, they would likely end up producing only one-tenth of their usual annual yield. "One bad crop year can put a Vietnamese farmer in debt for several years afterwards because [farmers] live on a very narrow subsistence margin," Hickey wrote. Subsistence farmers live season to season, producing just enough food to feed their families, meaning they rarely have anything left over to spare or save.

In one interview after another, Hickey and Donnell found widespread dissatisfaction with the Strategic Hamlet Program. Most villagers had never wanted to leave their original homes in the first place. The "compulsory regrouping" and "protracted forced-labor" had caused villagers undue emotional suffering. President Diem promised political and economic reforms, but nothing had materialized. Even on a practical level, the program was failing. A group of villagers showed Hickey and Donnell a deep underground tunnel that had been dug by the Vietcong. It ran directly under the perimeter defense wall and up into the center of the village. Vietcong could come and go as they wished, the villagers said. And they did.

Hickey and Donnell spent three months interviewing villagers in Cu Chi. The conclusion they drew cast the Strategic Hamlet Program in a very grim light. In the winter of 1962, strategic hamlets were being erected at a rate of more than two hundred per month. The Defense Department had set a goal of establishing between ten thousand and twelve thousand hamlets across South Vietnam over the next year.

Hickey and Donnell presented their findings to General Paul Harkins, the new commander of the recently renamed Military Assistance Command, Vietnam, or MACV. The anthropologists believed that General Harkins would be unhappy with the news but that he would take seriously the villagers' legitimate concerns. Years later, when the ARPA report was finally declassified, Hickey recalled the meeting. "I said, in essence, that strategic hamlets had the potential of bringing security to the rural population but they would not work if they imposed economic and social burdens on the population," he said. If President Diem wanted villager support, he had to hold up his end of the bargain and pay the workers, as agreed. "General Harkins replied that everyone wanted protection from the Viet Cong, so they would welcome the strategic hamlets." The discussion was over, General Harkins told Hickey and Donnell, and the anthropologists left Harkins's office in Saigon.

Hickey and Donnell were flown to the Pentagon, where they were scheduled to brief Harold Brown and Walt Rostow, the president's national security advisor, on the Strategic Hamlet Program. The Pentagon was a world away from Saigon and from Cu Chi, and yet the anthropologists knew firsthand what an impact the Defense Department's work was having on the villagers living there. They made their way through security, into the mezzanine, past the food shops and the gift shops and the employee banks. They walked up stairs, down corridors, and into Harold Brown's office in the E-Ring, not far from the secretary of defense and the Joint Chiefs of Staff. Brown's office was spacious and well decorated, with large leather chairs and couches, and a view of the Potomac River.

Hickey recalled paraphrasing from their written ARPA report. "In the present war," he said, "the Vietnamese peasant is likely to support the side that has control of the area in which he lives, and he is more favorably disposed to the side which offers him the possibility of a better life." Hickey and Donnell told Brown and Rostow that Diem's army was simply not holding up its end of the bargain. As a result, and despite the well-intended efforts of the Strategic Hamlet Program, local Vietnamese peasants were more likely to side with the Vietcong.

Then something strange happened. "As we began our first debriefing at the Pentagon with Harold Brown," Hickey noted, "[he] swung his heavy chair around and looked out the window, leaving us to talk to the back of his chair." Hickey and Donnell kept talking. Perhaps Brown was simply contemplating the severity of the situation.

"Farmers were unwilling to express enthusiasm for the program and appeared to harbor strong doubts that the sacrifices of labor and materials imposed on them could yield any commensurate satisfaction," the anthropologists explained. If something wasn't done, the entire Strategic Hamlet Program was at risk of collapse. Hickey and Donnell suggested that the Pentagon put pressure on Diem's forces to pay the farmers a small amount of compensation, immediately.

Harold Brown did not respond. Throughout most of the meeting, he kept his back turned on the two men, and though now they had finished their briefing, Brown still didn't turn around to face them. National security advisor Walt Rostow, who had been paying attention, looked away. An aide walked into the room, and Hickey and Donnell were shown the door.

Escorted out of Harold Brown's office, the two men were led down the corridor to where they were scheduled to brief Marine Corps lieutenant general Victor "Brute" Krulak, now serving as special assistant for counterinsurgency and special activities. Krulak was a hard-charging militarist. During World War II he had masterminded the invasion of Okinawa, the largest amphibious assault in the Pacific theater and the last battle of the war. In the Korean War, Krulak had pioneered the use of helicopters in battle. Krulak was not happy with what Hickey and Donnell had to say, and he was demonstrative in his disapproval. He told them that he wasn't going to pay a bunch of Vietnamese peasants for their support. "He pounded his fist on the desk [and said] that 'we' were going to make the peasant do what's necessary for the strategic hamlets to succeed," Hickey recalled.

The anthropologists from RAND were shown the door. Their thirty-page report, originally prepared for ARPA as an unclassified report, was now given a classification of secret, which meant it could not be read by anyone without an appropriate government clearance. Harold Brown told RAND president Frank Collbohm about his dissatisfaction with what he saw as Hickey and Donnell's overly pessimistic analysis of the Strategic Hamlet Program. The anthropologists' findings were "too negative," ARPA officials complained, and they prepared an official rebuttal to be attached to each copy distributed around the White House and the Pentagon.

Determined to repair any damage that Hickey and Donnell might have done, Collbohm sent a new set of RAND researchers to Saigon with specific instructions to reevaluate the Strategic Hamlet Program. This included Fulbright scholar Joe Carrier, who worked in cost analysis at RAND, and Vic Sturdevant, from systems analysis. With no previous knowledge of Southeast Asia, and with no local language skills, the two men studied incidents in strategic hamlets initiated by the Vietcong over a nine-month period, from December 1962 to September 1963. Their findings were markedly different from Hickey and Donnell's. In this new ARPA report on the Strategic Hamlet Program, Carrier and Sturdevant concluded that it would likely prove promising in the long run, if only the Defense Department would take a "more patient approach."

Another RAND analyst dispatched to Vietnam to write a similarly themed report was George B. Young, an expert in missile design, aerodynamics, and nuclear propulsion. Young, who was Chinese American, became the first RAND employee assigned full-time to the Combat Development Test Center in Saigon. His analysis of the Strategic Hamlet Program was enthusiastic. Young said the villagers were committed to participating. In his ARPA report, called "Notes on Vietnam," Young wrote about the fluid "delivery of intelligence" information that was taking place. Locals in the program had been taught to make written notes on any Vietcong activity they observed, Young reported. In turn, that information was taken to village elders, who wrote up reports for the Diem government. Soon, Young declared, the Vietcong forces would be "ground to a pulp."

George Tanham returned to the CDTC in Saigon in 1963, now under a long-term ARPA contract. Much had changed since Tanham's first trip, at Harold Brown's behest, in the summer of 1961. In his "Trip Report: Vietnam, 1963," Tanham showed great optimism about how things were shaping up in Vietnam. An Air Force officer from the Combat Development and Test Center took Tanham in an airplane ride over the strategic hamlet regions, just outside Saigon—some of the very same hamlets that Gerald Hickey and John Donnell had written so pessimistically about in their report, the one that caused Harold Brown to turn his back on them. Tanham marveled at the little villages down below. He said he could see the bamboo huts, the barbed-wire fences, even the distinct perimeter ditches, and that it all looked wonderful. In Tanham's estimation, the Defense Department could look ahead to "successfully concluding the war in two or three years or even less." He included in his report an interview with an officer from the U.S. Air Force who said that the Air Force was "proud of its contribution to the war in Vietnam" and that it planned to "leave behind helicopters and airplanes when it left, ideally sometime in 1964." Things were looking very positive, Tanham wrote. He quoted a high-ranking general as telling him, "Given a little luck we can wind this one up in a year."

CHAPTER NINE

Command and Control

In October 1962, a quiet forty-seven-year-old civilian scientist from Missouri arrived at the Pentagon to begin a new job with the Advanced Research Projects Agency. His work would change the world. By 2015, 3 billion of the 7 billion people on the planet would regularly use technology conceived of by him. The man, J. C. R. Licklider, invented the concept of the Internet, which was originally called the ARPANET.

Licklider did not arrive at the Pentagon with the intent of creating the Internet. He was hired to research and develop command and control systems, most of which were related to nuclear weapons at the time. The idea that a bright red telephone, like the one installed in Herb York's bedroom in the first week of the Kennedy presidency, was the only way for heads of state to communicate the dreaded "go or no-go" decision in a potential nuclear launch scenario was absurd. In the world of push-button warfare, fractions of seconds mattered. World leaders could not afford the extra seconds it would take to dial a 1962 telephone.

The mandate to update the command and control system,

which would become known as C2, came from the president. Within months of taking office, Kennedy ordered Congress to allocate funds to rapidly modernize the U.S. military command and control system, specifically to make it "more flexible, more selective, more deliberate, better protected, and under ultimate civilian authority at all times." The directive for "new equipment and facilities" was sent to the Pentagon, where it was tasked to ARPA. Harold Brown recruited J. C. R. Licklider for the job.

Licklider was a trained psychologist with a rare specialization in psychoacoustics, the scientific study of sound perception. Psychoacoustics concerns itself with questions such as, when a person across a room claps his hands, how does the brain know where that sound is coming from? It involves elements of both psychology and physiology, because sound arrives at the ear as a mechanical sound wave, but it is also a perceptual event. People hear differently in different situations, and those "conditions have consequences," Licklider liked to say. During World War II, while working at Harvard University's Psycho-Acoustic Laboratory, Licklider conducted experiments with military pilots in all kinds of flight scenarios, with the goal of developing better communication systems for the military. Aircraft were not yet pressurized, and at altitudes of 35,000 feet, cockpit temperatures descended below freezing, which profoundly affected how pilots heard sound and how they responded through speech. Licklider conducted hundreds of experiments with B-17 and B-24 bomber pilots, analyzed data, and published papers on his findings. By war's end, he was considered one of the world's authorities on the human auditory nervous system.

After the war, Licklider left Harvard for the Lincoln Laboratory at MIT, where he became interested in how computers could help people communicate better. Engineers at the Lincoln Laboratory were working on an IBM-based computer system for the Air Force called the Semi-Automatic Ground Environment, or SAGE, which was being built to serve as the backbone of the North American Air Defense Command (NORAD) air defense system. SAGE was the first computer to integrate radar with computer technologies, and to perform three key functions simultaneously: receive, interpret, and respond. The SAGE system received information from tracking radar; it interpreted data as it came in; and in response, it pointed America's defensive missile systems at incoming threats. It was a gargantuan machine, so large that technicians walked inside it to work on it. SAGE system operators were among the first computer users in the world required to multitask. While sitting at a console, they watched display monitors, typed on keyboards, and flipped switches as new information constantly flowed into the SAGE system through telephone lines.

Licklider was inspired by the SAGE system. To him, it exemplified how computers could do more than just collect data and perform calculations. He imagined a time in the future when man and machine might interact and problem-solve to an even greater degree. He wrote a paper outlining this concept, called "Man-Computer Symbiosis," in which he described a partnership between humans and "the electronic members of the partnership," the computers. Licklider envisioned a day when a computer would serve as a human's "assistant." The machine would "answer questions, perform simulation modeling, graphically display results, and extrapolate solutions for new situations from past experience." Like John von Neumann, Licklider saw similarities between the computer and the brain, and he saw a symbiotic relationship between man and machine, one in which man's burdens, or "rote work," could be eased by the machine. Humans could then devote their time to making important decisions, Licklider said.

Licklider believed that computers could one day change the world for the better. He envisioned "home computer consoles," with people sitting in front of them, learning just about anything they wanted to. He wrote a book, *Libraries of the Future,* in which he described a world where library resources would be available to remote users through a single database. This was radical thinking in 1960 yet is almost taken for granted today by the billions of people who have the library of the Internet at their fingertips twenty-four hours a day. Computers would make man a better-informed being, Licklider wrote, and one day, "in not too many years, human brains and computing machines will be coupled... [and] the resulting partnership will think as no human brain has ever thought."

It was exactly this kind of revolutionary thinking that interested the Advanced Research Projects Agency and why the work of J. C. R. Licklider caught ARPA's attention. Computing power needed to be leveraged beyond its present capabilities in order to advance command and control systems, and J. C. R. Licklider was the man for the job. ARPA director Jack Ruina telephoned Licklider and asked him to come to Washington and give a series of seminars on computers to Defense Department officials. Then he offered Licklider a job. When Licklider arrived at the Pentagon just a few months later for his first day of work, the sign on his door read "Advanced Research Projects Agency, Command and Control Research, J. C. R. Licklider, Director." It was a small office, in both physical size and relative importance. At the time, it was impossible to imagine just how colossal a program command and control would become. In 1962, it was just an idea.

When Licklider arrived at the Pentagon in the fall of 1962, the Department of Defense purchased more computers than any other organization in the world, and ARPA had just entered the world of advanced computer research. The agency inherited four computers from the Air Force, old dinosaurs called Q-32 machines. Each was the size of a small house. These were the computers that the SAGE program had run on at the MIT Lincoln Laboratory, starting in 1954; there was no way the Pentagon was going to throw them away. The Q-32s, built by Systems Development Corporation, a subdivision of RAND, had been incredibly expensive to construct, each costing $6 million (roughly $50 million in 2015). ARPA had inherited them, and Licklider was given the job of making sure they got used.

Fifteen days after Licklider's arrival at the Pentagon, the most harrowing of conflicts set the world on a razor's edge. Photographs taken by a U-2 spy plane revealed that the Soviets had covertly placed nuclear-armed missiles in Cuba, ninety miles off the coast of Florida. President Kennedy demanded that the missiles be removed, but Premier Nikita Khrushchev refused. For thirteen days, starting on October 16, the United States and the Soviet Union played a game of nuclear chicken. At the height of the crisis, on October 24, the United States set up a military blockade off the island and a standoff in the ocean ensued. By all accounts, this thirteen-day period was the closest the world has ever come to nuclear war, before or since. The president raised the defense condition to DEFCON 2 for the first and only time in history. And yet new information from ARPA's history has recently come to light that paints an even more dramatic Cuban Missile Crisis than was previously understood.

"Guess how many nuclear missiles were detonated during the Cuban Missile Crisis?" asks Paul Kozemchak, special assistant to DARPA director Arati Prabhakar, during an interview for this book. Kozemchak is a thirty-year veteran of DARPA, which makes him the longest-serving employee in its history. "I can tell you that the answer is not 'none,'" said Kozemchak. "The answer is 'several.'" In this case, "several" refers to four.

By the time of the Cuban Missile Crisis, Eisenhower's test ban had failed, and the United States and the Soviet Union had both returned to nuclear weapons testing. Twice during the height of the Cuban Missile Crisis, on October 20 and October 26, 1962, the United States detonated two nuclear weapons—code-named Checkmate and Bluegill Triple Prime—in space. These tests, which sought to advance knowledge in ARPA's pursuit of the Christofilos effect, are on the record and are known. What is not known outside Defense Department circles is that in response, on October 22 and October 28, 1962, the Soviets also detonated two nuclear weapons in space, also in pursuit of the Christofilos effect. In recently declassified film footage of an emergency meeting at the White House, Secretary of Defense McNamara can be heard discussing one of these two Soviet nuclear bomb tests with the president and his closest advisors. "The Soviets fired three eleven-hundred-mile missiles yesterday at Kapustin Yar," McNamara tells them, one of which contained a 300-kiloton nuclear warhead. "They were testing elements of an antimissile system in a nuclear burst environment."

It is hard to determine what is more shocking, that this information, which was made public by Russian scientists in the early 1990s, is not generally known, or that four nuclear weapons were detonated in space, in a DEFCON 2 environment, during the Cuban Missile Crisis. Firing off nuclear weapons in the middle of a nuclear standoff is tempting fate. The BMEWS system, at J-Site in Thule, could easily have misidentified the Soviet missile launches as a nuclear first strike. "The danger of the situation simply getting out of control, from developments or accidents or incidents that neither side—leaders on either side—were even aware of, much less in control of, could have led to war," says the former CIA officer Dr. Raymond Garthoff, an expert in Soviet missile launches.

The information about the Soviet high-altitude nuclear tests remained classified until after the Berlin Wall came down. The Soviet nuclear weapon detonated on October 28, 1962, over Zhezqazghan in Kazakhstan at an altitude of ninety-three miles had a consequential effect. According to Russian scientists, "the nuclear detonation caused an electromagnetic pulse [EMP] that covered all of Kazakhstan," including "electrical cables buried underground."

The Cuban Missile Crisis made clear that command and control systems not only needed to be upgraded but also needed to be reimagined. It was J. C. R. Licklider who first challenged his

ARPA colleagues to rethink old ideas about what computers could do beyond mathematical tasks like payroll and accounting. Licklider proposed the development of a vast multiuser system, a "network" of computers that could collect information across multiple platforms—from radar and satellites to intelligence reports, communication cables, even weather reports—and to integrate them. What was needed, said Licklider, was a partnership between man and machine, and between the military and the rest of the world.

Of his ARPA bosses, Licklider wrote, "I kept trying to convince them of my philosophy that what the military needs is what the business man needs, is what the scientist needs." Six months after arriving at ARPA, he sent out a memo calling this network the "Intergalactic Computer Network." At the time, different computers spoke different programming languages, something Licklider saw as a hurdle that needed to be immediately overcome. It was an extreme problem, he wrote, one "discussed by science fiction writers: How do you get communications started among totally uncorrelated sapient beings?" Finding the answer would take decades, but it began at ARPA in 1962.

J. C. R. Licklider is sometimes called modern computing's "Johnny Appleseed" for planting the first seeds of the digital revolution. What is not generally known about Licklider is that he ran a second office at the Pentagon called the Behavioral Sciences Program, an office that would eventually take on much more Orwellian tasks related to surveillance programs. This office grew out of a study originally commissioned by Herb York, titled "Toward a Technology of Human Behavior for Defense Use." This study examined how computers, or "man-machine systems," could best be used in conflict zones. The results, today, are far-reaching.

In its Behavioral Sciences Program, ARPA wanted to "build a bridge from psychology into the other social sciences" using computers, according to an early ARPA report. Because Licklider was trained as a psychologist, ARPA director Jack Ruina believed he was the right man for this job, too.

One task of the Behavioral Sciences Program was to imagine a future world where computers could be used by the Defense Department as teaching tools. This was visionary thinking in 1962, when computers still took up entire rooms and cost millions of dollars to build and operate. "Computer assisted teaching systems and computer assisted gaming and simulation studies are examples of work chosen [for] human performance research believed to be defense relevant," read an internal ARPA report. Training President Diem's South Vietnamese army was a solid example. ARPA sought ways in which to teach Vietnamese recruits to be better soldiers and more efficient administrators so they could defeat communism. This was arduous, labor-intensive work. Language and culture barriers added an extra layer of toil. One idea behind the Behavioral Sciences Program was that computers could one day shoulder the burden of this kind of work.

The Behavioral Sciences Program initiated a number of projects. These were programs that had a public face but also had highly classified components. ARPA secretly opened a second Combat Development Test Center, this one on the outskirts of Bangkok, five hundred miles to the northwest of Saigon. Like its Vietnamese counterpart, this new CDTC would also research and develop techniques and gadgets but with a focus on longer-term counterinsurgency goals, including Licklider's plans for computer-assisted teaching, gaming, and simulation studies. Congress was not told about the new Combat Development Test Center in Bangkok, nor was the House Committee on Appropriations, though the Defense Department was legally required to notify it before constructing new facilities.

"Thailand was the laboratory for the soft side and Vietnam was the laboratory for the hard side, or things that go boom," explained

James L. Woods, an ARPA officer who worked at the CDTC in Thailand.

There was a bigger plan in play, until now unreported. Secretary McNamara was eager to have ARPA create additional Combat Development Test Centers around the world, something he considered an important part of the president's national security policy of flexible response. Insurgent groups, also called terrorist organizations, were on the rise across Southeast Asia, Latin America, Africa, and the Middle East. "The U.S. would need to support Limited Wars in these remote areas," one Project Agile report declared, adding that "similar representation is being considered by OSD [Office of the Secretary of Defense] in other areas of the world." ARPA called its worldwide program "Remote Area Conflict" and hired the defense contractor Battelle Memorial Institute to open and operate two "Remote Area Conflict Information Centers," one in Washington, D.C., and the other in Columbus, Ohio, to keep track of programs at the Combat Development Test Centers in Saigon and Bangkok and all future CDTCs, and to write summary reports and produce analyses of progress made. As early as 1962, ARPA drew up plans for CDTCs in Beirut and Tehran under this new "Remote Area Conflict" banner. The declassified CDTC files housed at the National Archives have been miscataloged and are lost. The only known copies remain with Battelle. Though the copies are more than fifty years old, Battelle declined to release them, stating that "unfortunately, it is Battelle policy not to release copies of Battelle reports."

In Thailand, the new CDTC flourished. ARPA engineers in Licklider's Behavioral Sciences Program office believed that computers could be used to model social behavior. Data could be collected and algorithms could be designed to analyze the data and to build models. This led Licklider to another seminal idea. What if, based on the data collected, you could get the computer to predict human behavior? If man can predict, he can control. "Much of the work is theoretical and experimental," stated T. W. Brundage, the first director of the CDTC in Bangkok, "and for the time being is mainly non-hardware oriented." Brundage was referring to one of the first tests of Licklider's theory to be conducted at the new center. It was called "Anthropometric Survey of the Royal Thai Armed Forces," and involved 2,950 Thai soldiers, sailors, and pilots. It was an example of a CDTC program with a public face but a classified motive. The Thai government was told that the purpose of the program was "to provide information on the body size of Thai military personnel," which could then be used for "design and sizing of clothing and equipment" of the Thai armed forces in the future. ARPA technicians took fifty-two sets of measurements from each of the 2,950 Thai participants, things like eye height, seated height, forearm-to-hand length, and ankle circumference. But the Thai participants were also asked a bevy of personal questions—not just where and when they were born, but who their ancestors were, what their religion was, and what they thought of the king of Thailand.

The true purpose of the "Anthropometric Survey of the Royal Thai Armed Forces," and dozens of other surveys like it, was "data collection and data processing." The information was sent back to the Computer Branch of the U.S. Army Natick Laboratories in Natick, Massachusetts. "After coding the background information, all of the data were transferred from the data sheets to punched cards," reads a declassified report. A digital profile was then made "on each of the men in the series." ARPA wanted to create a prototype showing how it could monitor third world armies for future use. The information would be saved in computers stored in a secure military facility. In 1962 Thailand was a relatively stable country, but it was surrounded by insurgency and unrest on all sides. If Thailand were to become a battle zone, ARPA would have information on Thai soldiers, each of whom could be tracked.

Information—like who deserted the Thai army and became an enemy combatant—could be ascertained. Using computer models, ARPA could create algorithms describing human behavior in remote areas. Eventually these patterns could lead to predictive computer modeling, Licklider believed.

There were other individuals working with and for Licklider in his predictive modeling programs. One was Ithiel de Sola Pool, a left-leaning revolutionary in the field of social science. Doing contract work for ARPA, Pool became one of the first social scientists to use computers to create models for analyzing human behavior. He would become the world's first authority on the social impact of mass media. J. C. R. Licklider and Ithiel de Sola Pool put together a series of proposals for ARPA to consider. Computer models could be used to answer important questions, the men said. They proposed that studies be done on "peasant attitudes and behavior," "'stability and disorder' in several countries," and "cultural patterns."

Pool and Licklider both served on ARPA's Behavioral Sciences Panel, and in that capacity they examined Hickey and Donnell's study of the Strategic Hamlet Program. "They [Hickey and Donnell] have yielded much useful information and opened up promising areas for investigation," Licklider and Pool wrote, "but with regard to the solution of these important, complex problems, they have barely scratched the surface." The two behavioral scientists recognized that the information Hickey and Donnell had collected on the villagers could also be used to create computer models and to predict how these kinds of individuals might act in future conflicts. "These are important tools," said Licklider, for they can lead to a better understanding of the "inexorable flow from conditions to consequences." With baseline data in a Defense Department computer system, the behavior of the villagers could be covertly monitored, analyzed, and modeled. This was an effective means of command and control.

But as with the history of warfare, the desire to control and the ability to control are often at odds. Despite inventive government efforts to influence a population, events occur that are beyond military control. What happened next in Vietnam had consequences that could not be undone.

May 8, 1963, marked the 2,527th birthday of the Buddha, and a group of religious followers gathered in the village of Hue to celebrate. Protest was in the air. Buddhists were being repressed by President Diem's autocratic Catholic regime. The villagers of Hue had been told not to fly Buddhist flags, but they did anyway. The mood was festive, and a large crowd of nearly ten thousand people had assembled near the Hue radio station when eight armored vehicles and several police cars arrived on the scene in a show of force. Police ordered revelers to disperse, but they refused. Police used fire hoses and tear gas, still with no effect. Someone threw a grenade onto the porch of the radio station, killing nine people, including four children. Fourteen others were severely injured. A huge protest followed. The event became a catalyst for people across South Vietnam to express widespread resentment against President Diem and his brother, Ngo Dinh Nhu, who was head of the secret police. The Buddhists demanded the right to fly their own flags and to have the same religious freedoms accorded to members of the Catholic Church. When the government refused, more than three hundred monks and nuns convened in Saigon for a protest march, including an elderly monk named Thich Quang Duc. The group made its way silently down one of Saigon's busiest boulevards to a crossroads, where everyone stopped and waited. Thich Quang Duc sat down on a cushion in the middle of the street and assumed the lotus position. A crowd gathered around him, including *New York Times* reporter David Halberstam. Two other monks, each carrying a five-gallon can of gasoline, walked up to Thich Quang Duc and poured gasoline on him. One of them handed Thich Quang Duc a single match. He struck the match, touched it to his robe, and set himself on fire.

David Halberstam described the devastation he felt watching the monk catch fire and burn to death right in front of him on the Saigon street. "Flames were coming from a human being; his body was slowly withering and shriveling up, his head blackening and charring," Halberstam wrote. "In the air was the smell of burning flesh; human beings burn surprisingly quickly. Behind me I could hear the sobbing of the Vietnamese who were now gathering. I was too shocked to cry, too confused to take notes or ask questions, too bewildered even to think.... As he burned he never moved a muscle, never uttered a sound, his outward composure in sharp contrast to the wailing people around him."

During the self-immolation, somehow the monk was able to remain perfectly still. He did not writhe or scream or show any indication of pain. Even as he was consumed by fire, Thich Quang Duc sat upright with his legs folded in the lotus position. His body burned for about ten minutes until finally the charred remains toppled over backwards.

Journalist Malcolm Brown, the Saigon bureau chief for the Associated Press, took a photograph of the burning monk, and this image was printed in newspapers around the world. People everywhere expressed outrage, and overnight President Diem became an international pariah.

But instead of showing empathy or capitulating to the Buddhists' wishes, President Diem, together with his brother Ngo Dinh Nhu and Nhu's wife, the glamorous Madame Nhu, began to slander the Buddhists. Madame Nhu went on national TV in pearls and a black dress, fanning herself with a folding fan, to say that Buddhist leaders had gotten Thich Quang Duc drunk and set him up for suicide as a political ploy.

"What have the Buddhist leaders done?" asked Madame Nhu on television. "The only thing they have done, they have barbecued one of their monks whom they have intoxicated.... Even that barbecuing was done, not even with self-sufficient means because they used imported gasoline." By the end of summer, the crisis was full-blown. The White House advised President Diem to make peace with the Buddhists immediately. Diem ignored the request and instead, in August 1963, declared martial law.

In late October, the U.S. ambassador to South Vietnam, Henry Cabot Lodge Jr., told President Kennedy that a coup d'état was being organized against President Diem by a group of Diem's own army generals. In the now famous "Hillman cable," the president, the ambassador, and diplomats Averell Harriman and Roger Hillman agreed not to interfere with the overthrow of Diem by his own military. In the cable, Ambassador Lodge gave secret assurances to the South Vietnamese generals that it was fine with the White House for them to proceed with the coup.

On November 1, 1963, a group of Diem's generals overthrew the government of South Vietnam. President Diem and his brother escaped to the Saigon district of Cholon, where they hid inside a Catholic church. The following morning, November 2, the brothers were discovered. Diem and Nhu were thrown into the back of an American-made armored personnel carrier and driven away. Sometime shortly thereafter, President Diem and his brother were executed. Their bullet-riddled bodies were photographed, then buried in an unmarked grave in a plot of land adjacent to Ambassador Lodge's house.

When the leader of the Vietnamese communist movement, Ho Chi Minh, learned of the assassination, even he was surprised. "I can scarcely believe the Americans would be so stupid," he said.

Out in the countryside across South Vietnam, the garrison state constructed by President Diem and the U.S. Department of Defense began to crumble. The local people, be they paddy rice farmers or committed Vietcong, began tearing down the fabricated enclaves the Diem regime had forced them to build as part of the Strategic Hamlet Program. News footage seen around the world showed farmers smashing the fortifications' bamboo walls with sledgehammers, shovels, and sticks, as the strategic hamlets disappeared. Seizing the opportunity, the communists began sending thousands of Vietcong fighters to infiltrate the villages of South Vietnam. They came down from the North by way of a series of footpaths and jungle trails, which would become known as the Ho Chi Minh Trail. Soon it would be impossible to tell a neutral farmer from a committed communist insurgent.

Command and control was an illusion in Vietnam. Despite millions of dollars, hundreds of men, and the use of lethal chemicals as part of a herbicide warfare campaign, ARPA's Project Agile—with its cutting-edge gadgets and counterinsurgency techniques—was having little to no effect on the growing communist insurgency spreading across South Vietnam. Perhaps Americans in Saigon might have been able to foresee the fall of President Ngo Dinh Diem, but it is unlikely that anyone could have predicted what happened shortly thereafter, halfway around the world in Texas. Twenty days after the execution of Diem and his brother, while riding in an open car through Dealey Plaza in Dallas, President John Kennedy was shot dead by an assassin.

Another president, Lyndon Baines Johnson, would inherit the hornet's nest that was Vietnam.

CHAPTER TEN

Motivation and Morale

The anthropologist Gerald Hickey leaned out the side of a low-flying military aircraft watching the sea snakes swimming below. The weather was warm, the sea calm, and as the aircraft he shared with a team of ARPA officials approached Phu Quoc Island in the Gulf of Siam, the water was robin's egg blue. It was the winter of 1964, and Hickey was back in Vietnam, working for the RAND Corporation on another ARPA contract, this time studying how U.S. military advisors got along with their Vietnamese counterparts. The war that did not officially exist marched on.

The ARPA officers were heading out to the island to test weapons and gear which they would then turn over to their junk fleet commander counterparts, local Vietnamese fishermen paid by the Pentagon to patrol the coasts and keep an eye out for Vietcong. Hickey was here to interview participants on both sides. "En route, the ARPA officers tested the new AR-15, an early version of the M-16, by shooting at long sea snakes, which when hit, flew into the air," Hickey recalled.

Once on the island the group set up a beachfront camp, stringing ARPA-engineered hammocks between palm trees and setting up ARPA-engineered tents before heading over to the steep sea cliffs, where they tested the ruggedness of ARPA-designed military boots. Hickey tagged along, notebook in hand, taking notes and asking questions, as he always did. After the day's work, the men sat around a fire pit eating grilled shark and giant sea turtle, washing it down with rice and La Rue beer.

After the Phu Quoc Island trip, Hickey headed back to Saigon and then up to the U.S. military facility at Da Nang, conducting dozens of interviews along the way. On July 4, 1964, he caught a ride in an H-34 Marine helicopter and headed into the Ta Rau Valley to a Special Forces camp located at Nam Dong.

"Known as deep VC territory," Hickey noted in his journal.

Captain Roger Donlon, commander of the unit at Nam Dong, met Hickey at the dirt landing pad when his helicopter touched down. Hickey noted how heavily fortified the camp was, its perimeter ringed with anti-sniper sandbags, machine gun posts, mortar pits, and concrete bunkers. Hickey was here at Nam Dong to interview each member of the twelve-man Special Forces team as well as their Vietnamese counterparts, young men who were mostly Nung people, an ethnic minority of Chinese descent.

The team at Nam Dong was here in the Ta Rau Valley to protect five thousand Vietnamese who lived in the surrounding area. In addition to patrolling the jungle, the Special Forces team organized locals' efforts to dig wells and build schools. There was little else to do here, and Hickey recalled that "the A-team members were happy to have an anthropologist in town."

His first day in Nam Dong, Hickey accompanied Captain Donlon out to one of the villages where there had been reports of chemicals being sprayed out of aircraft. "Rice crops had been destroyed and villagers were sick," Hickey noted. Captain Donlon told the sick villagers that he would send their complaints up the chain of command. Hickey had no way of knowing that the organization paying for his report, ARPA, was the same organization behind the science program that had sprayed the chemicals on the villagers and their rice crops.

The men drove back to the base in an Army jeep, careful to get to the camp before nightfall. Once the sun disappeared behind the mountains, the valley was plunged into darkness, making travel dangerous and difficult. Back at Nam Dong, Hickey filled out a timesheet, required by RAND to be submitted each week, and dropped it in the command center's U.S. mailbox. He ate dinner with the Nung soldiers, interviewing them in their native language. The Nung soldiers told Hickey they believed a Vietcong attack was imminent, and he took the news to Captain Donlon. A team meeting was organized, and Donlon ordered the Vietnamese strike force to double its outer perimeter security and also ordered the helicopter landing zone to be fortified. Donlon gave Hickey an AR-15 and told him to sleep with it close by his bed.

In the middle of the night, at 2:26 a.m., a massive explosion knocked Hickey out of bed. More explosions followed, and suddenly the camp was filled with white phosphorus smoke. With the sound of automatic weapons fire coming from every direction, Hickey grabbed his eyeglasses and his AR-15 and started to run. "Suddenly bullets were piercing the bamboo walls," he later recalled.

Outside his bunkroom, the mess hall and supply room were on fire. "Mortar rounds landed everywhere, grenades exploded, and gunfire filled the air. In a matter of minutes," Hickey recounted, "the camp had become a battlefield." For a moment, he felt all was lost. That he would die here in Nam Dong. Instead, the anthropologist raised his AR-15 and assumed the role of a soldier, fighting alongside the Green Berets and the Nung commandos through the night.

When light dawned and the Vietcong retreated back into the jungle, Hickey surveyed the carnage. Sixty Nung, two Americans, and one Australian had been killed. "There were bodies and pieces of bodies everywhere—on the cluttered parade ground, in the grasses, and on the [perimeter] wires." One of the Nung soldiers he had eaten dinner with the night before was dead, recognizable only by the insignia on his shirt. "The smoky air was heavy with the odor of death," Hickey recalled. Overcome by a wave of nausea, he threw up.

"The July 1964 Nam Dong battle foreshadowed the fury of the struggle that would become known as the Vietnam War," wrote Hickey. "As that war, with its modern technology and armaments and large armies, drew all of South Vietnam into its vortex and captured the world's attention, the battle of Nam Dong faded into obscurity." Americans still did not know they were fighting a war in Vietnam. Captain Roger Donlon was awarded the Congressional Medal of Honor, the first of the Vietnam War, and Gerald Hickey would continue his work as an anthropologist, writing more than a dozen reports for ARPA, on subjects including the role of the AR-15 in battle and the effects of Agent Orange on the Vietnamese.

Back in America, RAND Corporation president Frank Collbohm had set his focus on securing a lucrative new contract with the Advanced Research Projects Agency. Collbohm and analyst Guy Pauker flew to Washington, D.C., to meet with ARPA officials. RAND's Third Area Conflict Board believed that the firm's social scientists could help stop the Vietcong insurgency by researching and analyzing for the Pentagon the "human problems" connected to insurgent groups. The broad-themed contract they sought had enormous potential value and would turn out to be RAND's single-biggest contract during twelve years of war in Vietnam. It was called the Viet Cong Motivation and Morale Project, and it was secured in a single meeting in Washington, D.C.

In Washington, Collbohm and Pauker met with Seymour

Deitchman, Harold Brown's new special assistant for counterinsurgency at ARPA. Before Deitchman took over the counterinsurgency reins, ARPA's Project Agile programs had been overseen by William Godel. But the situation with Godel had taken a bizarre turn. For eighteen months, Godel had received high praise from the White House and the Pentagon for his counterinsurgency work, winning the prestigious National Civil Service League award and being named one of the nation's ten top government administrators in 1962. But suddenly and mysteriously, financial incongruities within Project Agile's overseas expense accounts were brought to the attention of Secretary of Defense McNamara, and the FBI was brought in to investigate. Godel was at the very center of the investigation. Counterinsurgency was too significant a program to leave in the hands of a man under suspicion, and Deitchman, an aeronautical and mechanical engineer working at the Institute for Defense Analyses, or IDA, was chosen to replace Godel.

Also present during the meeting was the powerful William H. Sullivan, a career State Department official and the head of President Johnson's new Interagency Task Force on Vietnam. In a few months' time, Sullivan would become ambassador to Laos. Between Sullivan and Deitchman, the officials in the room had the power to award a significant counterinsurgency contract to whomever they saw fit, in this case RAND. Which is exactly what the record shows happened next.

William Sullivan pulled out a sheet of paper and set it in front of Collbohm and Pauker. On the paper was a list of twenty-five topics that the Interagency Task Force and the Pentagon wanted researched. Down at the bottom, near the end, one topic leaped out at Guy Pauker. It read:

"Who are the Vietcong? What makes them tick?"

Pauker was electrified. "Where did this question come from?" he asked.

"That question came directly from Secretary of Defense Robert McNamara," Sullivan said, "who keeps asking the question."

"Frank and I agreed on the spot that RAND would try to answer the Defense Secretary's question," Pauker recalled.

Guy Pauker, born in Romania, was a staunch anticommunist. He had a Ph.D. from Harvard in Southeast Asian studies, and was an expert on how Stone Age cultures, such as the Navajo, do or do not adapt to the modern world. He felt excited by this counterinsurgency challenge. The Vietcong were like a Stone Age people, Pauker believed, and he welcomed the opportunity to determine what it was that made them tick. Collbohm and Pauker returned to RAND headquarters in Santa Monica, where they put together an outline for the new project and a bid.

Over at the Pentagon, the question "What makes the Viet Cong tick?" had also been confounding the Advanced Research Projects Agency. "The original intent" of the RAND program, as Seymour Deitchman later explained it, was to understand the nature of the Vietcong revolutionary movement by finding answers "to such questions as, what strata of society its adherents came from; why they were adherents; how group cohesiveness was built into their ranks; and how they interacted with the populace." By the summer of 1964, the secretary of defense had grown frustrated by the lack of progress being made in the "techniques" area of Project Agile. Three years into the conflict and still no one seemed to have a handle on who these Vietcong insurgents really were. ARPA needed quality information on the enemy combatant, said Deitchman, and for this, to help facilitate the new RAND Corporation study, the secretary of defense made a deal with the CIA.

Joseph Zasloff was the lead social scientist on the original Viet Cong Motivation and Morale Project, and in 2014 he recalled the premise of the RAND study. "The CIA had detention centers and prisons in South Vietnam," Zasloff said, facilities that were not supposed to exist. It was in these secret detention centers that the CIA kept captured communist POWs, from whom various case officers tried to extract information. "We interviewed these prisoners for our study," explained Zasloff. "We learned a lot from them about what had been going on. Some were old and had fought at Dien Bien Phu. Some were just teenagers. They were all very dedicated. Had great discipline and commitment. They were indoctrinated into the communist way of thinking."

Joe Zasloff and his wife, Tela, arrived in Saigon for the Motivation and Morale Project in the summer of 1964. Zasloff, an expert on Southeast Asian studies, had spent the previous year at RAND working on a report for the U.S. Air Force called *The Role of North Vietnam in the Southern Insurgency.* In this report, which he produced from his office in Santa Monica, Zasloff concluded that the North Vietnamese were responsible for fueling the insurgency in the South. Through the lens of history this is hardly news, but in 1964 Zasloff's findings were considered original. He was sent to Saigon to lead this new RAND study. Zasloff did not have the kind of hands-on social science research experience that Gerald Hickey and John Donnell had, but he had been to Vietnam, in the late 1950s, as a university professor teaching social science at the Faculty of Law in downtown Saigon.

Because Zasloff would be working directly with the highest-ranking members of the MACV, he was given a civilian rank equal to the rank of general, as well as accommodations fit for a general. The Zasloffs settled into ARPA's elegant two-story villa at 176 Rue Pasteur, just down the street from the Combat Development Test Center. Their front yard had trees and a grassy lawn. A wide wooden veranda and second-story balconies added to the French colonial feel, as did the staff of servants who took care of housekeeping needs. Tela Zasloff had the maids string white lights throughout the garden, said to be inhabited by ghosts. A ten-foot-tall concrete wall had been constructed around the villa's perimeter as an added security precaution.

The villa's first-floor interior was grand, laid out like a posh hotel lobby, with rattan furniture and potted palm trees. The downstairs served as a work area for the RAND researchers who came and went. At night, the Zasloffs frequently hosted dinner parties.

One month after the Zasloffs got the place up and running, John Donnell, the author with Hickey of the unfavorable Strategic Hamlet Program report, arrived. Donnell was to be Zasloff's partner on the new ARPA project, examining communist motivation and morale. The success of the program relied on getting accurate information from POWs, and Donnell spoke Vietnamese. Zasloff also hired local academics to act as interpreters, French-speaking Vietnamese intellectuals who were considered wealthy by national standards. The Vietnamese interpreters were often invited to the Zasloffs' dinner parties and were asked to share their thoughts and perceptions. The interpreters were candid and open, admitting freely that they knew almost nothing about Vietnamese peasants who lived in villages outside Saigon. They were all citizens of the same country, but with very little in common. Most farmers, the interpreters said, lacked dreams and aspirations and were generally content. Most had no ambition to do anything but farm. All the peasants wanted out of this life, the interpreters said, was to live with their families in peace, in rural villages, without being harassed or disturbed.

The interpreters set out with Zasloff and Donnell to interview prisoners of war in the secret CIA prisons across the South. The group interviewed prisoners inside the notorious Chi Hoa prison in Saigon as well as in many smaller detention centers out in the provinces. Most of the POW interviews were done with either Zasloff or Donnell and one Vietnamese interpreter, who also acted as a stenographer or note taker. There were no uniformed officials present, which meant the prisoners often loosened up and spoke freely.

"We interviewed all kinds of prisoners," Zasloff recalled. "Some from the North and some from the South." Most of the northern-born fighters had made their way to the South along the Ho Chi Minh Trail. While their histories unfolded, the initial assumptions of the interpreters from Saigon began to change, including the preconception that all a Vietnamese farmer wanted was to own a small plot of land and be left in peace. As work progressed, the RAND researchers started to learn more about what was actually fueling the insurgency. It was a relatively simple answer that was echoed among the prisoners. What motivated Vietcong fighters, the prisoners said, was injustice, "grievances the peasants held against the Saigon government." The prisoners told Zasloff and Donnell they believed that through communism, they could have a better life, one that was not based on corruption. The prisoners expressed "ardent aspirations they had for education, economic opportunity, equality and justice for themselves and their descendants," Zasloff and Donnell wrote.

The POWs also talked of being tortured by the government of South Vietnam. Some prisoners showed the RAND analysts scars they claimed were the results of incessant torture by prison guards. They spoke of being forced to watch summary executions of fellow prisoners, without explanation or trial. There was no way to verify the veracity of what they were told, but Zasloff and Donnell felt compelled to report these Geneva Convention violations to Guy Pauker at RAND. When Pauker forwarded the information on to the Pentagon in a memo titled "Treatment of POWs, Defectors and Suspects in South Vietnam," Seymour Deitchman got involved.

He asked questions: How did Zasloff and Donnell know that the prisoners were not lying? Why believe a prisoner in the first place? Instead of looking into Zasloff and Donnell's claims, Deitchman later commissioned a RAND study on how to detect when a

Vietcong prisoner was telling a lie. In "Estimating from Misclassified Data," RAND analyst S. James Press used a probability theorem called Bayes' theorem to refute the idea that POW interviews could always be trusted. "The motivation for the work had its genesis in a desire to compensate for incorrect answers that might be found in prisoner-of-war interviews," Press wrote. After forty-eight pages of mathematical calculations that placed Vietcong POWs' answers in hypothetical categories, Press concluded, "It is clear that if hostile subjects were aiming at an optimal strategy, they would lie independently of all the categories."

The same summer that Zasloff and Donnell presented their concerns to Seymour Deitchman, something totally unexpected happened at the Pentagon, a situation that still confounded Joseph Zasloff after more than fifty years. His earlier RAND monograph, *The Role of North Vietnam in the Southern Insurgency,* began making its way around the upper echelons of the Pentagon. In this report Zasloff had concluded that the North Vietnamese were responsible for most insurgent activity in the South. "Much of the strength and sophistication of the insurgent organization in South Vietnam today is attributable to the fact that North Vietnam plans, directs, and coordinates the over-all campaign and lends material aid, spiritual leadership and moral justification to the rebellion," Zasloff had written. A copy went to the Air Force chief of staff, General Curtis LeMay. The overall war policy at the time called for "graduated pressure," a strategy that Robert McNamara had developed for President Johnson to avoid making the war in Vietnam official. Only a few months remained until the November presidential election; Johnson desperately wanted to maintain what was known at the Pentagon as his "hold until November" policy. This strategy allowed for so-called tit-for-tat bombing raids, small-scale U.S. Air Force attacks against communist activity. Up to this point in the conflict, Hanoi, the capital of the North, had not been targeted.

Reading Zasloff's *The Role of North Vietnam in the Southern*

Insurgency, General LeMay decided the paper was the perfect report on which to base his argument to bomb North Vietnam. Unknown to Zasloff, his RAND report would now become the centerpiece of LeMay's new strategy for the secretary of defense. In this unconventional war, which America was still not officially fighting, the role of bombing had been fraught with contention. In the summer of 1964, the U.S. Air Force was playing a subordinate role to the U.S. Army, which led efforts on the ground. General LeMay had been arguing that airpower was the way to quell the insurgency, but his arguments had been falling on deaf ears. As LeMay geared up to use Zasloff's RAND study in a new push with Secretary McNamara, a major incident and turning point in the war occurred.

In the first week of August 1964, U.S. naval forces clashed with North Vietnamese torpedo boats in the Gulf of Tonkin. It served as a casus belli, an act or event used to justify war. President Johnson went on national television, interrupting regular programming across the country to announce North Vietnamese aggression and request from Congress the authority to take military action. This was the official beginning of the Vietnam War. In a matter of days, Congress passed the Tonkin Gulf Resolution, giving President Johnson the authority to take whatever actions he saw necessary, including the use of force. At the Pentagon, Zasloff's study was now at the center of a perfect storm. On August 17, 1964, General LeMay sent a memorandum to General Earle "Bus" Wheeler, the chairman of the Joint Chiefs of Staff. "The best chance" for winning the war in Vietnam, LeMay wrote, was to choose ninety-four targets in North Vietnam already identified by the Pentagon as "crucial" to the communists and therefore necessary to destroy. Zasloff's study, also sent to General Wheeler, was the centerpiece of LeMay's argument. At the time, Zasloff had no idea.

In Saigon, Zasloff and Donnell were getting close to the end of their prisoner of war study, the first of the Viet Cong Motivation and Morale Project reports for ARPA. The men had conducted 145 interviews over five months, in multiple CIA prisoner facilities. In December 1964, Guy Pauker flew to Saigon to help compile the information. In the downstairs mezzanine of the ARPA villa on Rue Pasteur, the three men labored for weeks to put together Zasloff and Donnell's final report, which was fifty-four pages long.

Once it was completed, the RAND analysts briefed General William Westmoreland, at MACV headquarters just down the street. The Vietcong insurgents, Zasloff and Donnell said, saw the Americans as invaders and would do anything they could to make them give up and leave. Ten years earlier, participants from the same movement had fought to kick the French out, and had succeeded. Now they were fighting for the same cause. The insurgency was not an insurgency to the locals, Zasloff and Donnell said. It was a nationalist struggle on behalf of the people of Vietnam. The insurgents saw themselves as being "for the poor," the analysts said, and they saw the Americans as the villains, specifically "American imperialists and their lackeys, the GVN [Government of Vietnam]." Zasloff and Donnell said that in their POW interviews they had learned that very few fighters understood what communism meant, what it stood for. Hardly any of the Vietcong had even heard of Karl Marx. It was a fact that the Vietcong had patrons among the Chinese communists and that the same patrons had been helping the North Vietnamese, giving them weapons and teaching war-fighting techniques. But what the local people were after was independence. South Vietnamese peasants had aspirations, too. They wanted social justice, economic opportunity. And they wanted their land back—land that had been taken from them during dubious security operations like the Strategic Hamlet Program. That was what made the Vietcong tick, Zasloff and Donnell told General Westmoreland.

Next, the men briefed General Maxwell Taylor, whom Johnson had made U.S. ambassador to Vietnam. After that, it was back to MACV headquarters to brief the senior staff, as well as the ARPA officials at the Combat and Development Test Center. In each facility, to each person or group of people, they said the same thing. The Vietcong were a formidable foe. They "could only be defeated at enormous costs," Zasloff and Donnell said, "if at all."

Under the aegis of the Viet Cong Motivation and Morale Project, the Advanced Research Projects Agency sought to determine what made the Vietcong tick. But the agency did not want to hear that the Vietcong could not be defeated. Seymour Deitchman took the position that Zasloff and Donnell had gone off the rails, same as Hickey and Donnell had done with the Strategic Hamlet Program report a few years before. According to other RAND officers, Deitchman perceived the POW report as unhelpful. RAND needed to send researchers into the field whose reports were better aligned with the conviction of the Pentagon that the Vietcong could and would be defeated. Frank Collbohm took to the hallways of the RAND headquarters he was in charge of in Santa Monica. "I am looking for three senior, imaginative fellows to go over to Vietnam," he said, and to get a handle on the chaos in Southeast Asia. He needed to replace Zasloff and was looking for a quality analyst to take over the Viet Cong Motivation and Morale Project. Collbohm found what he was looking for in a controversial nuclear strategist named Leon Gouré.

Leon Gouré, born in Moscow in 1922, was a Sovietologist who loathed Soviet communism. He was born into a family of Jewish socialist intellectuals who were part of a faction called the Mensheviks, who came to be violently persecuted by the Leninists. When Gouré was one year old, the family went into exile in Berlin, only to flee again a decade later when Hitler became chancellor of Germany. The Gourés moved to Paris but in 1940 were again forced to flee. Gouré once told the *Washington Post* that his family left Paris on the last train out, and that only when he arrived in America did he finally feel he had a home. Gouré enlisted in the U.S. Army, became a citizen, and was sent back to Germany to fight the Nazis in the Battle of the Bulge. As a member of the Counterintelligence Corps, America's Army intelligence group, he became fluent in German and French. He also became a valuable interrogator, learning how to draw information out of captured prisoners, and to write intelligence reports.

After the war, Gouré earned an undergraduate degree from New York University and a master's degree from Columbia. In 1951 he became an analyst with RAND, and in no time he was working on post–nuclear war scenarios with the firm's elite defense intellectuals, including Albert Wohlstetter and Herman Kahn. Gouré's particular area of expertise was post-apocalypse civil defense, and in 1960 he traveled to Moscow on a civil defense research trip for RAND. In 1961 his findings were published as a book that caused a national outcry.

Gouré claimed that during his trip to Moscow, he had seen firsthand evidence indicating that the Soviet Union had built a vast network of underground bunkers, which would protect the Russian people after a nuclear first strike against the United States. The Soviet action would inevitably be followed by a U.S. nuclear response. The concept of mutual assured destruction was based on the idea that the superpowers would not attack each other, provided they remained equally vulnerable to a nuclear strike. Gouré's frightening premise suggested that the Soviet Politburo believed they could survive a nuclear war and protect the majority of their population as well. Like Albert Wohlstetter's second-strike theory, Gouré's findings suggested that since the Soviets believed they could survive, they might attempt a decapitating first strike.

Gouré's critics said his work was unreliable. That he hated Soviet communism with such passion that he was biased to the point of being blind. In December 1961 an article attacking Gouré's work appeared in the *New York Times* under a headline that read "Soviet Shelters: A Myth or Fact?" Reporter Harrison E. Salisbury had taken a month-long trip across the Soviet Union, covering roughly twelve thousand miles. He said that he "failed to turn up evidence of a single Soviet bomb shelter," and that the underground bomb shelters purported to have been built across Moscow were nothing more sinister than subway tunnels. He singled out "Leon Gouré, research specialist of the Rand Corporation," who, Salisbury wrote, "has presented several studies contending that the Russians have a wide program for sheltering population and industry from atomic attack." Salisbury had interviewed scores of Russians for his article and learned that Gouré's reports had been "vigorously challenged by observers on the scene." Close scrutiny of the alleged facts, wrote Salisbury, revealed that no shelters had been constructed. "Diplomats, foreign military attaches and correspondents who have traveled widely in the Soviet Union report that there is no visible evidence of a widespread shelter program." The Gouré report, Salisbury suggested, served only one master, RAND's single largest customer, the U.S. Air Force, in its quest for tens of millions more dollars from the Pentagon for its ever-growing bomber fleets.

The acrimonious debate over the legitimacy of Gouré's civil defense report raged for months and then subsided. Gouré disappeared from the headlines but continued to write reports for RAND. Now, as 1964 drew to a close, Frank Collbohm tapped Leon Gouré to replace Joseph Zasloff as the lead social scientist on the ARPA Viet Cong Motivation and Morale Project in Saigon. Zasloff saw this appointment as a disaster waiting to unfold.

"Still, after fifty years, I get red in the face just thinking of what Leon Gouré did," Zasloff said in 2014. Within a matter of weeks Gouré was in Saigon. And he was ready to take charge.

In Saigon, stability and security were quickly deteriorating as chaos enveloped the city. On Christmas Eve, 1964, two Vietcong fighters drove a car packed with two hundred pounds of explosives into the underground parking garage beneath the Brink Bachelor Officers

Quarters, a seven-story hotel leased by the Defense Department to provide housing for its officers in Saigon. The bomb demolished three floors of the building, killing two U.S. servicemen and injuring sixty-three Americans, an Australian Army officer, and forty-three Vietnamese civilians.

Suddenly faced with the possibility that Saigon could fall to the Vietcong, Secretary of Defense McNamara pressured President Johnson to take action. On February 7, 1965, a limited bombing campaign called Operation Flaming Dart began. Eleven days later, Johnson ordered the Joint Chiefs of Staff to initiate Rolling Thunder I, the air campaign that General LeMay had been arguing for. On March 8, the Marines landed in the city of Da Nang. It was war. Officially now.

Leon Gouré settled into the RAND Saigon villa previously occupied by the Zasloffs and got to work. His first report for the Viet Cong Motivation and Morale Project drew conclusions that were diametrically opposed to what Zasloff and Donnell had found.

"By and large," wrote Gouré, "Vietnamese farmers hold no strong political views." Indeed, it was "the ideological apathy of the peasant" that allowed most Vietnamese to concentrate on "personal survival," not political aspirations, Gouré wrote. The majority of the Vietnamese were neutral, he said, and unlike people from the West, they did not adhere to the democratic notion that "they have a real freedom of choice." Gouré argued that bombing was the pathway to victory in Vietnam. Bombing weakened the morale of the Vietcong, he said.

"Gouré gave the Pentagon exactly what the Air Force wanted to hear, about bombing [Vietnam]," Zasloff said. But to Zasloff, what was particularly egregious was that Gouré used the transcripts of Zasloff and Donnell's prisoner interviews to draw his own conclusions. These conclusions, said Zasloff, "simply were not there." Gouré did not interview any Vietcong prisoners on his own for his original report.

In the winter of 1965, RAND's Guy Pauker flew to Washington to meet with the Joint Chiefs of Staff and to sell an expanded idea for the Viet Cong Motivation and Morale Project, now being run by Leon Gouré. The premise, Pauker said, was to determine how best to "break the backbone of the VC [Vietcong] hard core." In this new study, Gouré would interview Vietcong prisoners himself, and by doing so, he would best be able to determine the psychological effect that airpower and heavy weapons were having on the Vietcong. "Judicious exploration" of this concept, Pauker said, "offered considerable promise" about the way to win this war. The Joint Chiefs of Staff agreed, and the ARPA project was expanded. With no previous experience studying Southeast Asia, Leon Gouré, RAND's leading Sovietologist and civil defense expert, was put in charge of the expanded Viet Cong Motivation and Morale Project.

The villa at Rue Pasteur was now a regular meeting place for RAND anthropologists and social scientists working on various ARPA projects over the course of the long war. This group included Gerald Hickey, now back in Saigon to work on studies about how Special Forces worked with Montagnards and how Vietnamese beliefs in "cosmic forces" factored into the war. In his memoir, Hickey recalled how a rising star at the Pentagon named Dan Ellsberg regularly came around the RAND villa. Hickey had met Ellsberg the previous summer and was aware of his reputation as a brilliant Harvard economist who had written a fascinating paper on how diplomacy was similar to blackmail. Ellsberg was now working in Vietnam for the Defense Department, with the mysterious title of "special liaison" to the Pentagon. One particular evening with Daniel Ellsberg stuck in Hickey's mind.

"In November 1965, I was invited to have an informal dinner with Dan Ellsberg at his Saigon villa next to the heavily guarded villa of General Westmoreland," Hickey recalled. "Dan was affable as we talked about many subjects relating to Vietnam, and then he produced a packet of photos taken on trips into the countryside with [Lieutenant Colonel] John Paul Vann. In the photographs he carried an automatic weapon, which he said he often fired into the thick foliage along the road where the Vietcong might be hiding. Talking about these trips," recalled Hickey, "Dan became more excited by the bravado, the adventure, something I had seen in other such men (*combattant manqué* [frustrated fighter], the French called them) who came to Vietnam for reasons I could never understand."

Vietnam was a complicated, labyrinthine place to work and to live, with professionals serving many masters on many projects about whose real meaning they had no idea. This was the nature of classified defense work, with individual scientists and soldiers given but a sliver of the truth, just enough to be able to do the job without always knowing the reason behind it. Ellsberg's bravado may not have made much sense to Hickey in 1965. In the fall of 1972, things would become illuminated when Ellsberg took actions against the Pentagon that would force him to go underground as, for a time, the most wanted man in America.

Leon Gouré continued to produce reports for ARPA, almost all of which promised the Pentagon that Vietcong fighters were rapidly losing motivation and morale. In "Some Impressions of Viet Cong Vulnerabilities: An Interim Report," Gouré and co-author C. A. H. Thomson declared that Vietcong soldiers had become "discouraged and exhausted," and that "life in the Viet Cong has become more dangerous and that the hardships are greater than in 1964." These findings, Gouré said, drew upon a record of 450 interviews with Vietcong captives, "a body of evidence yielding more or less reliable impressions . . . of the Viet Cong's current vulnerabilities." Furthermore, wrote Gouré, Vietcong cadres had confided in him that they had lost hope. In recent months, as he put it, Vietcong "soldiers have spoken more often of their probable death in the next battle, of never seeing their families again." There is no mention in these reports that Vietcong fighters also expressed a willingness to die for their nationalist cause. Instead, Gouré's reports served as pithy endorsements for continued U.S. Air Force bombing campaigns. "Fear of air power," Gouré promised, would "bring the VC to their knees."

In 1965 Leon Gouré became an advisor to Secretary McNamara. It was not unusual for him to be picked up at the RAND villa on Rue Pasteur and helicoptered to an aircraft carrier stationed off the coast of Vietnam, where he would brief field commanders on the studies that RAND was doing for ARPA and the Pentagon. When summoned to Washington, Gouré was treated with equal fanfare. The word among defense intellectuals was that President Johnson walked around the White House with a copy of Gouré's findings in his back pocket.

"When Gouré would return from Vietnam to [RAND headquarters in] Santa Monica, he would stay long enough to change shirts, then fly off to Washington to brief McNamara," recalled Guy Pauker, who had begun to sour on the truthfulness of Gouré's findings. For as much as Gouré was respected by the Pentagon and the White House, he was creating enemies inside RAND. Gouré's undoing began in late 1965, when RAND's work on the Viet Cong Motivation and Moral Project came under scrutiny by Congress. During a hearing before the Subcommittee on International Organizations and Movements, Congressman Peter H. B. Frelinghuysen demanded to know why the RAND Corporation had been hired to do so much work on the Vietcong when it seemed that what they were gathering was "straight military intelligence." That work "should be done by the military," Frelinghuysen said, not "highly-paid consultants like Rand."

"As a matter of convenience, [we] gave the contract to the Rand Corporation, as an instrument of the military systems, to perform the study," ARPA's Seymour Deitchman said. ARPA did not want to send its own people into the field—people like Deitchman—because they were "heavily occupied with operational problems associated with the war, and would not have time to spend several months on these detailed questions—important as they were," Deitchman explained. A think tank like Rand had the manpower, the expertise, and the time.

Congressman Frelinghuysen did not agree. Not only was the work expensive, but also its conclusions were puerile, he said. He quoted from one of Gouré's reports, calling the work so banal "it was something a child could have come up with."

Frelinghuysen's accusations caught the attention of Senator J. William Fulbright, who in turn made himself familiar with Gouré's reports and was appalled by what he saw as Gouré's manipulation of prisoner of war interviews. "[We have] received reports of recent surveys conducted by the RAND Corporation and others concerning the attitudes of the Viet Cong defectors and prisoners," Fulbright wrote to Secretary McNamara. It appeared to him that "those in charge of the project may have manipulated the results in such a way as to affect the results." Senator Fulbright demanded that the entire RAND effort be reviewed.

When McNamara assigned an Air Force officer to investigate, the Air Force found nothing wrong with the RAND work. But the national attention that Congress had directed at RAND made the corporation look bad. Despite RAND's initial support of Leon Gouré, the controversy surrounding him could no longer be ignored. Gouré needed to be removed. RAND president Frank Collbohm sent analyst Gus Shubert to Saigon to take over the ARPA contract. Gouré was relieved of his duties while the Viet Cong Motivation and Morale Project continued on. By 1968, RAND analysts had conducted more than 2,400 interviews related to Vietcong fighters, which were typed up into 62,000 pages of text and compiled into more than fifty ARPA reports.

Leon Gouré was not alone in his downfall. William Godel, the man responsible for Project Agile to begin with, was arrested by the FBI in August 1964 on charges that he had siphoned ARPA monies into his own personal bank account. On December 16, a federal grand jury indicted Godel and two former Pentagon colleagues for defrauding the U.S. government and embezzling a total of $57,000 in Defense Department funds. Godel and his attorney worked hard to clear Godel's name. Depositions were taken on his behalf from U.S. ambassador to Vietnam general Maxwell Taylor and others. A judge granted Godel permission to travel to Vietnam to take depositions from a Vietnamese general and Thai prince, but to no avail. At trial, the government produced 150 exhibits and a large number of eyewitnesses to testify against him. After eight days of testimony and ten hours of jury deliberation, William Godel was convicted on two counts of embezzlement and conspiracy to mishandle government funds. The judge ordered that he serve concurrent five-year prison terms on both counts.

William Godel, war hero, spy, diplomat, and the architect of many of ARPA's most controversial programs in Vietnam, including its counterinsurgency efforts and the Agent Orange defoliation campaign, was sent to a low-security federal correctional institution in Allenwood, Pennsylvania. His personal financial benefit from the embezzlement scheme was determined to have been $16,922, roughly $135,000 in 2015.

CHAPTER ELEVEN

The Jasons Enter Vietnam

During the Vietnam War, the RAND Corporation handled soft science programs for the Advanced Research Projects Agency. For hard science programs, in fields characterized by the use of quantifiable data and methodological rigor, ARPA looked to the Jason scientists. The Jasons were an elite, self-selected club mostly of physicists and mathematicians interested in solving problems that seemed unsolvable to the rest of the world. All throughout the 1960s, their only client was ARPA, which meant that all of their reports—the majority of which were classified secret, top secret, or secret restricted data (involving nuclear secrets)—wound up on the desk of the secretary of defense. The Jasons were quintessential defense scientists, following in the footsteps of John von Neumann, Ernest Lawrence, and Edward Teller. The core group, including Murph Goldberger, Murray Gell-Mann, John Wheeler, and William Nierenberg, had been closely intertwined, academically, since the Manhattan Project during World War II. In the early 1960s, the Jasons began expanding, bringing some of their

Ph.D. students on board, including a young geophysicist named Gordon MacDonald.

In the Jason scientists' first four years they had performed scientific studies for ARPA covering some of the most esoteric problems facing the Pentagon, including high-altitude nuclear explosions, electromagnetic pulse phenomena, and particle beam lasers. Their reports had titles like "The Eikonal Method in Magnetohydrodynamics" (1961), "Radar Analysis of Waves by Interferometer Techniques" (1963), and "The Hose Instability Dispersion Relation" (1964).

"We were interested in solving defense problems because they were the most challenging problems to solve," Murph Goldberger explained in 2013 in an interview for this book, and for the first several years this was generally the case. Then came Vietnam. "The high goals set by the originators of the Jason concept were being met when the Vietnam War intervened," said Gordon MacDonald, who joined the Jasons in the summer of 1963. "Murray Gell-Mann called to ask if I'd like to join Jason. I respected Murray a great deal," and said yes to joining. The first year as a Jason, MacDonald recalled, "my contribution was principally related to [nuclear effects]—what happens to the ionosphere when you set off nuclear explosions, things of that sort." But as individual Jasons became interested in Vietnam, so did the group. The first Jason to be very interested was Murray Gell-Mann.

Gell-Mann was one of the most respected thinkers in the Jason group, and one of the most esoteric. In 1969 he would win the Nobel Prize in physics for his discovery of quarks, a subatomic particle the nature of which is far beyond the grasp of most people. But Gell-Mann's areas of interest were also incredibly plebeian; he liked to think about things common to all men, including mythology, prehistory, and the evolution of human language. During the 1961 summer study in Maine, Gell-Mann led a seminar called "White Tiger." It addressed the growing counterinsurgency movement in Vietnam from the standpoint of "tribal warfare." This was well before any of the other Jason scientists were thinking about the Vietnam problem, Goldberger recalled.

Gell-Mann had unsuccessfully tried to get the California Institute of Technology, where he was a professor, to open a department of behavioral sciences. To Gell-Mann, guerrilla warfare was a topic well worth examining. "Because he was intrigued, the Jasons became intrigued," Goldberger recalled. "We thought, well, if the Jasons can understand the sociology behind counterinsurgency, perhaps the Vietnam problem" could be solved. And so in the summer of 1964, ARPA asked the Jasons to conduct a formal summer study on Vietnam. William Nierenberg, a former Manhattan Project scientist, was chosen to lead the study, which was conducted in La Jolla. This was not the first time the Jasons examined what Goldberger called "the Vietnam problem," but it was the first time they wrote a report about it.

Murray Gell-Mann invited the revered war correspondent and political scientist Bernard Fall to come and speak to the Jason scientists that summer in La Jolla. In 1964 Fall was considered one of the most knowledgeable experts on Southeast Asia. His book *Street Without Joy*, published in 1961, chronicled the brutal eight-year conflict between the French army and the Vietnamese communists, ending with the staggering defeat of the French at Dien Bien Phu. "Street Without Joy" was the name given by French troops to the communist-held stretch of road between the villages of Hue and Quang Tri.

Fall had personal experience with insurgency and counterinsurgency groups. A Jew born in Vienna in 1926, he fled with his parents to Paris after the Nazis annexed Austria. Fall's father joined the French resistance but was captured, tortured, and murdered by the Gestapo. Fall's mother was deported to Auschwitz, then murdered in the gas chamber there. An orphan by the age of sixteen, Fall joined the French resistance and learned firsthand what a resistance movement was about. After France was liberated in 1944 he joined the French army, and after the war he worked as an analyst for the Nuremberg war crimes tribunals. Fall won a Fulbright scholarship and moved to America, where he was initially known as a scholar and political scientist. But wanting to see the guerrilla war in Indochina up close, he became a war reporter. Still a French citizen in the 1950s, he was allowed to travel behind enemy lines with French soldiers and reported from the battlefield. Bernard Fall knew what it was like to be a soldier. Soldiers and scholars alike admired him. He became a U.S. citizen and was one of the few Americans ever invited to Hanoi to interview Ho Chi Minh.

Fall believed in and advocated for U.S. development of counterinsurgency tactics in Vietnam. Asymmetrical warfare was a formidable foe; Fall had seen it in person. At Dien Bien Phu, French forces had far more sophisticated weaponry, but the communist Viet Minh won the battle with the crafty use of shovels, a Stone Age tool. The communists literally dug a trench around French forces and encircled them. Then they brought in the heavy artillery and bombarded the French soldiers trapped inside. The battle of Dien Bien Phu marked the climactic end of the French occupation of Vietnam, and with the signing of the Geneva Accords, Vietnam was divided at the seventeenth parallel. Control of the North went to Ho Chi Minh, and control of the South went to Emperor Bao Dai, with Ngo Dinh Diem as prime minister.

Fall believed that unless the Americans wanted to repeat what had happened to the French in Vietnam, their efforts had to match guerrilla warfare tactics in ingenuity. After Fall's briefing, the Jasons wrote a report titled "Working Paper on Internal Warfare." It has never been declassified but is referred to in an unclassified report for the Naval Air Development Center as involving a "tactical sensor system program." The information in this report—the Jasons' seminal idea of using "tactical sensors" on the battlefield in a counterinsurgency war—would soon become central to the war effort. In 1964 this was considered just too long-term an idea and it was shelved.

Two and a half years after he participated in the Jason summer study in La Jolla, educating physicists and mathematicians about counterinsurgency warfare in Vietnam, Bernard Fall was killed by a land mine in Vietnam. With terrible irony, the place where Fall was killed was the same stretch of road that had given his book its title, *Street Without Joy.* Fall's book would become one of the most widely read books among U.S. officers during the Vietnam War. In 2012 General Colin Powell, now retired, told the *New York Times Book Review* that Fall's book was one that deeply influenced his thinking over the course of his career from a young soldier to chairman of the Joint Chiefs of Staff to secretary of state. "*Street Without Joy,* by Bernard Fall, was a textbook for those of us going to Vietnam in the first wave of President Kennedy's advisors," Powell said.

The Jason scientists were expanding their work and commitment to the Vietnam War, and in the process, there was growing discord among them about how to proceed, specifically in the scientific gray area called social science. Some, like Murray Gell-Mann, saw promise in understanding human motivation. Others believed that using advanced technology was the only way to win the war. In Gordon MacDonald's opinion, ingenuity needed to be applied across the board, including the use of weather as a weapon. Climate change is, and always has been, "a driver of wars," he believed. Drought, pestilence, flood, and famine push people to the limits of human survival, often resulting in war for control over what few resources remain. With war escalating in Vietnam, the Pentagon sought new ways to use weather as a weapon. As a Jason scientist, MacDonald had a rare front-row seat at these events. Most of what occurred remains classified; but some facts have emerged. They come from the story of Gordon MacDonald, one of the most influential and least remembered defense science advisors of the twentieth century.

Gordon MacDonald was born in Mexico in 1929. His father, a Scotsman, was an accountant at a Canadian bank in Mexico City. His mother, a secretary, worked in the American embassy down the street. His first passion was rocks, which he embraced as a child with the enthusiasm of a geologist until his childhood was shattered by illness. In the second grade, MacDonald contracted a mysterious disease that left him temporarily paralyzed in both legs and one arm. He had polio, an acute, virulent infectious disease that was not immediately diagnosable in Mexico in the 1930s. He was transported by railcar to Dallas, where, like so many child polio sufferers, he was left alone in a hospital, feeling abandoned. This was "not a pleasant experience," he confided to a fellow scientist in 1986, in a rare discussion about his childhood trauma. From tragedy springs inspiration. While recovering in the Texas hospital, MacDonald developed two skills that would shape his life: reading everything made available to him, then discussing and debating the contents with a person of equal or greater intellect.

"One very positive thing that came out of that [experience] was an uncle, Dudley Woodward," who lived not far away from the hospital, MacDonald recalled. "He made it a practice of virtually every day coming by to see me." Dudley Woodward was a man of many interests, an attorney who also served as chairman of the Board of Regents at the University of Texas. "He subscribed to the *Dallas Morning News* for me," said MacDonald. "I would read the paper and be ready to discuss world events with him every morning. We did this every single day." Gordon MacDonald was just nine years old.

The young boy returned home to Mexico, but with an acute physical disability. For seven long years he could not attend school. "There was a gap in my education," as he put it. "From second to ninth grade...I had taken my first years [of schooling] in a Mexican school, a church school, and then I had no formal education. I did a great deal of reading at home." What his uncle Dudley Woodward had taught him in the hospital in Texas had sharpened his ability to learn without formal teaching. His mother also helped, through tutoring. Finally he was well enough to attend school again and "made the leap into high school." In an understatement he added, "And I was able to do very well."

He left home for a military boarding school, San Marcos Baptist Academy, in rural Mexico, a day and a half away from Mexico City by train. School "was difficult with the disability." He explained, "I still continued to suffer from physical deficiency, [while] trying to maintain standing with the corps of cadets." San Marcos was a religious school, but it also had a football team. "My principal ambition was to overcome my physical defect, and so in the last year I was there, I played football, became a member of their starting team, and that I regarded as a very great achievement." During summer vacations he worked at the American Smelting and Refining Company plant in San Luis Potosí, by the sea, where it was his job to collect ore samples in the field to bring back for study in the lab. During this time, he refined his interest in rocks to specific minerals and crystals. To keep current with world events, he listened to shortwave radio while he worked. In his junior year in high school, he decided to apply to Harvard University, and was accepted—on a football scholarship.

The year was 1946, and Gordon MacDonald had never been out of Mexico, except when he was in the hospital in Texas. He took the train up from San Luis, stopping for a short stay with an aunt in New York City, never before having visited a city outside Mexico or ridden on a subway. Finally, he arrived at the Harvard University campus in Cambridge, Massachusetts. "By a very good fortune I had been placed in Massachusetts Hall, which is the oldest of the dormitories at Harvard, and my room was right over the room of Jim Conant, who was president [of Harvard]." Jim Conant was James Conant, the famous American chemist who had just returned from working on the Manhattan Project. "I got to know [Conant] very well later in life," MacDonald said, but their first meeting was far more commonplace. "He made a point of letting [me] know I was living over his office, and to be appropriately quiet during the daytime hours."

MacDonald chose physics as a course of study but soon decided that Harvard had "miserable" physics teachers. "I began to see the difference between memory and understanding when it comes to difficult subjects," he said, meaning that to learn facts by rote was one thing, but to understand concepts on a fundamental level required serious intellectual discipline. After six months of physics, he decided to shift his concentration to geology and math. Socially he struggled. Many students had matriculated from exclusive boarding schools—St. Paul's, Andover, and Exeter—and coming from a Bible school in Mexico, he felt outclassed. Playing on the football team proved almost impossible, but he refused to give up and instead persevered.

In his second year at Harvard, his interest in weather peaked during a confrontation with a visiting professor. The venerable Dr. Walter Munk, one of the world's greatest oceanographers, was giving a seminar on the variable rotation of the earth and, as Munk later recalled, "how that was associated with a seasonal change in the high-altitude jet stream that had just been discovered." So, "feeling reasonably secure that no one in the audience knew anything about this, I was surprised when a student in the first row interrupted [me] with rude comments about neglect of tides, variable ocean currents, and such like." Dr. Munk was not amused and dismissed the student's questions as inconsequential. The student was Gordon MacDonald. "Four years later I gave a much-improved account at MIT; there he was again sitting in the front row, complaining that I had not answered his questions of four years ago."

In 1950 MacDonald graduated summa cum laude from Harvard, the first ever to do so in the geology department. Despite his physical limitations, he managed to play football and row crew in intercollegiate scull racing. He was granted membership in Harvard's legendary Society of Fellows, making him one of twenty-four scholars from around the world who were given complete freedom to do what they wanted to do, all expenses paid, for three years. He was the youngest fellow on record, and remains so to date. MacDonald traveled around the country and the world, returning to Harvard for a master's degree in 1952 and a Ph.D. in geology and geophysics in 1954. Some of his fondest memories of that period in his life were the so-called Monday night sherry dinners hosted by the Society of Fellows. During them, he enjoyed long discussions with physics giants like Enrico Fermi, with whom he discussed the earth's rotation, its core, and its crust—still rather mysterious concepts in 1959. "And with Adlai Stevenson, who was a candidate for president, I talked about science policy," said MacDonald. "I became aware that there was this much larger world, other than the world of rocks, minerals, and thermodynamic relationships." Suddenly it all "sort of fitted together." He wanted to learn everything he could about the geophysical world, but also about how those who inhabited it used science for their own benefit.

His academic output was phenomenal. MacDonald was able to see, in ways other scientists before him had not, how elements of the earth were connected. "Paleontology is not distinct from astronomy," he said. In an award from the American Academy of Arts and Sciences in 1959, he was praised for his groundbreaking studies. His work, the academy declared, "brought together very distinct parts of geophysics: meteorology, oceanography, the interior of the earth, and astronomical observations about the earth's rotation." In 1958 he appeared on Walter Cronkite's program *The World Tomorrow*, in the first-ever public discussion on American television about how man would soon be able to explore the moon. Then he became a consultant for the Pentagon, for ARPA, and for NASA. "I was very enthusiastic," he said. "I felt we could learn a great deal about the earth by looking at the moon, and so I was eager to participate."

As passionate as MacDonald could become about earth sciences, he could also lose interest in a subject as quickly. By 1960, he said, "I was becoming more interested in the atmosphere, working on climate problems." The University of California, Los Angeles, was developing a program in atmospheric science, and he accepted a position there as director of the Atmospheric Research Laboratory. At UCLA he found himself working on weather and the ionosphere. This led him to become interested in climate control. In 1962 he was appointed to the National Academy of Sciences and its Committee on Atmospheric Sciences. In 1963 MacDonald was elected chairman of the Panel on Weather and Climate Modification, which was part of the National Academy of Sciences.

In 1963, weather modification was still legal. The job of the panel, MacDonald wrote, was "to take a deliberate and thoughtful review of the present status and activities in this field, and of its potential and limitations for the future." The public was told that the National Academy of Sciences was investigating weather modification for "benign purposes only," in areas that included making rain by seeding clouds. "There is increasing but somewhat ambiguous evidence that precipitation from some types of clouds and storm systems can be modestly increased and redistributed by seeding techniques," MacDonald wrote in a 1963 report.

At the same time, in his classified work, Gordon MacDonald was becoming deeply interested in weather modification. He told the *Journal of the American Statistical Association:* "I became increasingly convinced that scientists should be more actively engaged in questions of environmental modification, and that [the] federal government should have a more organized approach to the problem. While research could take place in both the public and the private sector, the government should take the lead in large-scale field experiments and monitoring, and in establishing appropriate legal frameworks for private initiatives."

At the Pentagon, where the uses of weather weapons were being explored, MacDonald had an additional job: serving as a scientific consultant. In the winter of 1965 there was a feeling of "hesitancy" at the Pentagon about how to proceed in Vietnam, and by late fall, the feeling was moving toward what he called "complexity." Secretary of Defense McNamara and his colleagues "were searching, almost desperately, for a means to contain the war," MacDonald told an audience of fellow Jasons in 1984. In December 1965, the Joint Chiefs of Staff and the secretary of defense authorized ARPA to research and develop "forest fire as a military weapon" in Vietnam.

The secret program, called Project EMOTE, was developed by ARPA, ostensibly to study the use of "environmental modification techniques." It was conducted in partnership with the Department of Agriculture's Forest Service, under ARPA Order 818. The central premise of the program was to determine how to destroy large areas of jungle growth by firestorm. Jungles are inherently damp and nonflammable. In order to modify the jungle's natural condition to "support combustion," ARPA scientists discovered that the lush jungle canopy had to be destroyed with chemicals before it would effectively burn to the ground. ARPA already had the arsenal of chemicals to do this, from its ongoing Project Agile defoliant campaign. The herbicides, varied in composition, were now being called Agent Orange, Agent Purple, Agent Pink, and other colors of the rainbow. Project EMOTE called for millions of gallons of Agent Orange to be sprayed in the forests as one element of the "weather modification campaign."

Since the earliest days of recorded history, forest fire has been used as a weapon, and the authors of the ARPA study quoted from the Bible to make this point. "The battle was fought in the forest of Ephraim; and the forest devoured more people that day than the sword," they wrote, citing 2 Samuel 18. In Vietnam, forests provided cover for the enemy, as they had since time immemorial. "Forests were a haven and refuge for bandits, insurgents and rebel bands," the report stated. Leaders from "Robin Hood [to] Tito to Castro had learned to conduct successful military operations from forest lairs." Chairman Mao boasted that insurgents were like "fish who swim in the sea of peasants," but to the ARPA scientists working on weather modification, the insurgents were more like jungle cats, hiding in the forest to prey on unsuspecting villagers. "A recent study of VC [Vietcong] bases showed that 83 percent were located in the dense forest," the report noted. Forests had served the enemy throughout history. Now, modern technology was working to put an end to that.

In late March 1965, the 315th Air Commando Group conducted a firebombing raid, code-named Operation Sherwood Forest, "against" the Boi Loi Forest, twenty-five miles west of Saigon. Aircraft loaded with 78,800 gallons of herbicide sprayed Agent Orange over the jungle, after which B-52 bombers dropped M35 incendiary bombs. But it had rained earlier in the day and the experiment did not result in "appreciable destruction of forest cover," as was hoped. ARPA postponed the next test until the height of the dry season, ten months later. Operation Hot Tip, on January 24, 1966, mimicked the earlier raid but with slightly better results, mostly because there was no rain.

The first full-scale operation occurred a year later, again at the height of the dry season, and was code-named Operation Pink Rose. This time, U.S. Air Force crews, flying specially modified UC-123B and UC-123K aircraft, sprayed defoliants on a first pass, then sprayed a chemical drying agent on a second pass. Next, the Air Force flew B-52 bombers that dropped cluster bombs to ignite the chemicals. Targets included "known enemy base areas" and also village power lines. Short of "killing" the jungle and an unknown number of its inhabitants, and starting localized fires, no "self-sustaining firestorm" occurred. There were simply too many environmental factors at issue, ARPA scientists concluded. Rain and humidity consistently got in the way.

One year later a secret operation, code-named Operation Inferno, was launched against the U Minh Forest, the Forest of Darkness. Instead of using defoliants, the Air Force flew fourteen C-130s low over the jungle canopy, pouring oil from fifty-five-gallon drums over each target area, four times. A forward air controller then ignited the fuel by sending white phosphorus rockets to each target. An intense inferno ignited and burned. But as soon as the fuel was consumed, the fire died down and went out.

ARPA's final 170-page report, originally classified secret, is kept in the Special Collections of the U.S. Department of Agriculture in Maryland. The report indicates that forest flammability depended primarily on two elements. One was weather, which could not be controlled. The other was "the amount of dead vegetation on or near the ground surface," which scientists determined could be controlled. "Forest flammability can be greatly increased by killing all shrub vegetation, selecting optimum weather conditions for burning, and igniting fires in a preselected pattern," ARPA scientists wrote. But to kill all shrub vegetation was too big a task even for ARPA, and the idea of using forest fire as a military weapon was shelved.

As war in Vietnam widened, the Jason scientists were continuously consulted for hard science ideas about how to defeat the communist insurgents. In 1965 they were asked to focus on the Ho Chi Minh Trail, the Pentagon's name for that system of 1,500 miles of roads and pathways that stretched from North Vietnam, through Laos and Cambodia, and down into South Vietnam. Some of the roads were wide enough for trucks and oxcarts; others were meant for bicycles and feet. The Defense Intelligence Agency (DIA) determined that each day some two hundred tons of weapons and supplies made their way down communist supply routes, from the North to the South, by way of the Ho Chi Minh Trail. The trail contained storage depots, supply bunkers, underground command and control facilities, even hospitals. A top secret report by the National Security Agency, declassified in 2007, described the trail as "one of the great achievements in military engineering of the twentieth century."

Cartographers, geographers, and map designers briefed the Jason scientists on the Ho Chi Minh Trail and its terrain. The Jasons read the RAND prisoner of war transcripts, originally compiled by Joe Zasloff and John Donnell, to learn more about how things worked on the trail. ARPA's Seymour Deitchman, still overseeing Project Agile at the Pentagon, sent the Jason scientists dozens of reports on the trail, classified and unclassified. To Jason scientist William Nierenberg, the trail seemed almost alive, "an anastomosed structure," he wrote, like a human body or a tree, a "network of interconnected channels," like blood vessels or branches, which depended on one another to flow. The Pentagon wanted the Jasons to figure out how to sever the trail's arteries.

ARPA doubled the Jasons' annual budget, from $250,000 to $500,000, roughly $3.7 million in 2015, and the scientists began working on tactical technologies they thought might be useful in obstructing movement along the trail. At least three studies the Jasons performed during this time period remain classified as of 2015; they are believed to be titled "Working Paper on Internal Warfare, Vietnam," "Night Vision for Counterinsurgents," and "A Study of Data Related to Viet Cong/North Vietnamese Army Logistics and Manpower." Because the contents are still classified, it is not known how they were received by Secretary McNamara. But according to Murph Goldberger, McNamara felt the ideas the

Jasons were proposing would take too long to implement. "We did our studies based on the assumption of a relatively long war lasting several years," he said, and the secretary of defense wanted more immediate results. So McNamara asked the Jason scientists to determine if it would be effective to use nuclear weapons to destroy the Ho Chi Minh Trail.

The Jasons' top secret restricted data report "Tactical Nuclear Weapons in Southeast Asia" remained classified until 2003, when the Nautilus Institute in Berkeley, California, obtained a copy under the Freedom of Information Act. "The idea had been discussed at the Pentagon," said Seymour Deitchman in 2003, in response to the outrage the report created. Deitchman recalled that Secretary McNamara believed the Jason scientists were best equipped to decide if using nuclear weapons was a wise idea. "Mr. McNamara would have said, 'There has been some talk about using tactical nuclear weapons to close the passes into Laos; tell me what you think of the idea,'" according to Deitchman, who says the Jasons were asked to determine "whether it made sense to think about using nuclear weapons to close off the supply routes [along] the Ho Chi Minh trail through Laos over which the supplies and people moved."

For a possible nuclear target, the Jasons focused on the Mu Gia Pass, a steep mountain roadway between Vietnam and Laos. Thousands of Vietcong, as well as weapons and supplies, moved through this pass, which the Jasons described as "a roadway carved out of a steep hillside, much like the road through Independence Pass southeast of Aspen, Colorado." If nuclear weapons were to be used against the Ho Chi Minh Trail, the Jasons concluded, they should be tactical nuclear weapons, lightweight and portable like the Davy Crockett nuclear weapon, a mockup of which Herb York had transported from California to Washington, D.C., in his carry-on luggage aboard a commercial flight in 1959.

But the Jason scientists calculated that use of nuclear weapons to destroy the Ho Chi Minh Trail would not be as easy as one might think. Indeed, "the numbers of TNW [tactical nuclear weapons] required will be very large over a period of time," the Jason scientists wrote. "At least one TNW is required for each target, and the targets are mostly small and fleeting. A reasonable guess at the order of magnitude of weapons requirements . . . would be ten per day or 3000 per year." The Vietcong were tenacious, the Jasons said, and it was likely that even if the pass were destroyed in a nuclear strike, the battle-hardened communist fighters would simply create a new pass and new supply trails. As an alternative, the Jason scientists proposed dropping radioactive waste at certain key choke points along the trail, thereby rendering it impassable. But radioactivity decays, they explained, and the window of impassability would also pass. In the end, the Jasons argued against using tactical nuclear weapons in Vietnam and Laos. They warned that if the United States were to use them, China and the Soviet Union would be more likely to provide similar tactical nuclear weapons from their own arsenals to the Vietcong and to the government of North Vietnam. "A very serious long-range problem would arise," the Jasons warned, namely, "Insurgent groups everywhere in the world would take note and would try by all means available to acquire TNW [tactical nuclear weapons] for themselves."

The study was read by many at the Pentagon. Dropping a few thousand nuclear bombs was not an option, and the Jasons were told to come up with another idea to solve the Ho Chi Minh Trail problem. "We put our thinking caps on," recalled Murph Goldberger, and got to work. Their next idea would totally revolutionize the way the U.S. military conducts wars.

CHAPTER TWELVE

The Electronic Fence

Lieutenant Richard "Rip" Jacobs had a terrible nickname for someone who flew on combat missions in a war zone. "Rip" made many of the other fliers and crewmembers in VO-67 Navy squadron think of RIP, "Rest in peace," a phrase used after a person is dead.

The real reason Jacobs was called Rip was because of a mishap in high school, just a few years before, in Georgia. "I stepped on this girl's dress at a high school dance and I accidentally tore it," Rip Jacobs explains. "Then I kind of got the nickname."

Now it was February 27, 1968, and Rip Jacobs, age twenty-four, stood on the tarmac of the Nakhon Phanom Royal Thai Air Base in Thailand, eighteen miles from the border with Vietnam. Jacobs was preparing for a highly classified mission he knew very little about, other than that it involved dropping high-technology sensors mounted on racks beneath an OP-2E Neptune armed reconnaissance aircraft onto the Ho Chi Minh Trail. He was part of Lucky Crew Seven, and today's assigned target was in Khammouane Province, in Laos, about fifteen miles southwest of the

Ban Karai Pass. This was deeply held enemy territory. Jacobs had been on twelve missions like this, but recently things had gotten bad.

Six weeks before, on January 11, 1968, Crew Two was lost. Nine men KIA. Killed in action. Bodies not recovered. They had left early in the morning on a sensor-dropping mission. Their aircraft lost radio and radar contact at 9:57 a.m., and they never returned to base. "It didn't cross my mind they wouldn't come back," Jacobs remembered in 2013. The men had left on an ordinary mission that morning, same as they always did. They even had the Crew Two mascot with them, a black-and-white puppy everyone called Airman Snoopy Seagrams. "It got somewhat routine. Then word spread. 'Crew Two down.' No parachutes, no beeper. No Jolly Greens," meaning search and rescue crews.

On February 17, a similar thing had happened. Crew Five was lost. They had completed the first target run. During the second run, one of the escort aircraft reported the OP-2E Neptune's starboard engine had been hit and was on fire. During the last radio transmission, one of the Neptune pilots was heard saying, "We're beat up pretty bad." Then nothing after that. Nine men KIA. Bodies not recovered. No beepers, no parachutes, no Jolly Greens. The area was filled with Vietcong.

On this morning, February 27, 1968, Crew Seven consisted of nine men—eight crew and a commander. Navy captain Paul L. Milius would be flying the aircraft. Navy airmen like Rip Jacobs knew well enough to stay focused and cheerful, but at times a foreboding crept in. This was mission number thirteen. Jacobs checked his flight suit. Checked his gear. Checked the rack of technology that was the centerpiece of the mission.

Each mission was different, depending on the technology. Sometimes the OP-2E Neptunes had to fly in low and level over the trail, as was the case when crews were dropping listening devices called acoubuoys. Each sensor was jettisoned from the aircraft with its own small parachute attached. Aircraft needed to fly low on these missions because too much altitude raised the likelihood that the parachute lanyards would get tangled up in too much air and fail to emplace themselves in the canopy of trees. But flying low and level made them an easy target for the Vietcong antiaircraft guns that were so prevalent along the trail.

Other missions involved sensors that had to be dropped from a higher altitude, around five thousand feet. This was the case with Crew Seven's mission today. They would be dropping Air Delivered Seismic Intrusion Detectors, or ADSIDs. The seismic devices were made by Sandia weapons laboratory for ARPA and were based on technology developed for an earlier ARPA program, Vela Hotel, which involved ground sensors for detecting nuclear tests. The ADSID sensors were approximately two and a half feet long and five inches in diameter. Each one looked like a miniature missile, or a large dart, with tail spikes that were released outward once the ADSID was lodged firmly in the ground. ADSIDs were designed to penetrate the earth from a high speed and to be deployed from the OP-2E without a parachute.

Standing on the tarmac preparing for the mission, Rip Jacobs was ready. He double-checked his parachute. Then he climbed aboard the aircraft.

Crew Seven left the tarmac on time. Roughly an hour into the mission, Captain Milius reported his position not far from the Ban Karai Pass. Rip Jacobs was standing near the deck hatch, observing ordnance drops. Ensign Tom Wells was seated in a well-armored chair, with his face in the Norton bombsite, calling out coordinates when suddenly the aircraft was engulfed in flames. "That's how it happens," Wells explained in 2013. "You're flying fine, then *wham,* you're hit."

An antiaircraft projectile fired by the Vietcong had come up through the bottom skin of the airplane and exploded in the radar well. "Now everything was on fire," Wells recalled. "I grabbed the fire extinguisher next to the hydraulic panel, but it was on fire. It burned the skin off my hands." In a matter of seconds the flight deck area was filled with dense, dark smoke.

Lieutenant Barney Walsh, the co-pilot, climbed out of his seat and started to make his way to the back. "We couldn't control anything" in the cockpit, he says. "I'm yelling 'Get out!' That was the only choice. That was it." Someone else hollered, "Hatch open, parachutes ready to go!"

There was blood everywhere. In the chaos, Rip Jacobs tried to ascertain what was going on. Then he realized Petty Officer John F. Hartzheim, an avionics technician, had been hit badly.

"He wasn't wearing his parachute," Wells says.

"He had taken it off because it was so hot," Jacobs explains. "He was bleeding badly. Mortally wounded. I thought about trying to get a parachute on him. The smoke and flames were so intense. The G-forces. I was standing in a pool of [Hartzheim's] blood and I slipped and fell down on the floor. The plane was going down. In your mind you're saying, 'With the last crew, nobody got out.' "

Someone hollered again. "Parachutes, get ready. Go!"

Rip Jacobs turned to the deck hatch. He jumped out of the burning airplane and began to fall. He pulled his ripcord. The chute opened. What happened after that he can't get his memory to recall. Time passed. Was he dead? After a while he realized he had landed in a tree.

"I was alive. Everything hurt. Back. Legs. I looked down and I was covered in blood." The way he had landed in the tree canopy, his body was parallel to the ground. The parachute lanyards had wrapped around him in a way that made it impossible for him to wriggle free. "Did I remember to hit my locator button when I was falling through the air?" He asked himself this question again and again.

He tried to reach the button with his chin. It was out of reach.

"I was pretty sure I'd set off my locator button," Jacobs recalls. "But what if I didn't? What if I hadn't activated the locator? I'd die up here. What if no one knows where I am?"

Then a worse thought. He heard sounds. The unmistakable sound of gunfire. Single shots. One after the next. Getting closer. There were Vietcong on the ground looking for VO-67 crewmembers who had made it out of the burning airplane they had just shot down. More gunfire. What if the Vietcong spotted him up here in this tree?

"I had to be real quiet," Jacobs recalls. "Every time I tried to move at all, all the dead stuff around me fell to the ground." During missions, there were F-4 Phantom fighter jets that protected the OP-2E Neptunes from any approaching enemy MiGs. "One [F-4] flew over the top of my head. Did he see me?" Three, maybe four hours passed. "It felt like eternity."

Suddenly, Rip Jacobs heard the faint sound of a helicopter. Or was he imagining things? Then he was certain. He was hearing the unmistakable sound of helicopter blades. A Jolly Green. He saw it in the distance. A rescue team. Then a crushing thought. "What if it didn't see me? What if it was out searching a wide area?" If he hadn't hit his locator button, no one would know he was here in this tree.

And then, out of the corner of his eye, he saw the helicopter slow down. Slower. Closer. The Jolly Green was hovering overhead.

Out of the helicopter came a Pararescue crewman. The man was sitting on a little seat attached to a metal cable. The cable got longer and the man got closer as he was lowered down to where Rip Jacobs was tangled up in the tree.

"He reached out to me. I saw his two arms. Then he folded down this little seat next to his seat. He pulled out a knife and cut me from the shroud lines."

Rip Jacobs climbed onto the seat beside the Pararescue crewman. "I never talked to him. The helicopter was deafening. We were extremely high up. Adrenaline was pumping through my body. I was covered in blood." Jacobs was pulled into the Jolly Green. "There were medical people inside. They told me I was bleeding badly, but mostly I was covered in Hartzheim's blood."

The Jolly Green made its way back to Nakhon Phanom Air Base. Once the helicopter touched down, hundreds of people swarmed out onto the tarmac. It seemed like everyone from the VO-67 Navy squadron was there. It was overwhelming, Jacobs recalled. "To go from that terrified to that relieved." He was taken into a room for a debriefing. Hartzheim had died in the aircraft. Captain Milius was MIA, missing in action. Everyone else made it out alive and was rescued by now. "An Air Force officer started asking me a lot of questions. It took a moment to register that he was asking about the sensor devices. The devices were laid out in a string, with timing. He kept asking about the devices. I kept thinking I could care less about where those things went right now. But he kept talking about the devices. It was absurd."

At the time, Rip Jacobs had no idea that the sensor technology program he was part of was the highest-priority program of the war. He had no idea that the top secret program had cost well over $1 billion to bring from conception to fruition. Or that it was the brainchild of the Jason scientists—an idea they had come up with less than two years before, during a Jason summer study in Santa Barbara in 1966.

The Jasons called their idea the "Anti-Infiltration Barrier." The Pentagon gave it a series of code names as it transitioned from theory to reality. First it was called Project Practice Nine, then Illinois City, then Dyer Marker, then Igloo White and Muscle Shoals. After the war was over and parts of the program were made public, it would become known—and often ridiculed—as McNamara's electronic fence.

The electronic fence idea was born in the summer of 1966, shortly after the Jason scientists completed the study about whether or not the Pentagon should use nuclear weapons to cut off weapons traffic along the Ho Chi Minh Trail. The Defense Department was desperately seeking new ways to win the Vietnam War. The bombing campaigns were failing. ARPA's Project Agile was having no effect on the communist insurgency. Weather warfare wasn't working. Nuclear weapons were not an option. Soon there would be 385,000 U.S. military personnel in South Vietnam. And yet despite these numbers and the efforts of so many involved, Ho Chi Minh's men and matériel kept pouring down the Ho Chi Minh Trail in a steady, unrelenting stream.

Secretary McNamara wanted an unassailable solution, and he looked to the Jason scientists to help figure out a way to sever the trail's arteries. Their idea involved creating a series of electronic barriers across major access routes along the Ho Chi Minh Trail, so-called "denial fields," running through central and eastern Laos, into Vietnam. The Jasons proposed to bug the battlefield so as to be able to "hear" what was happening on the trail, then send in strike aircraft to bomb Vietcong troops and truck convoys on the move.

As ARPA's head of counterinsurgency, Seymour Deitchman organized the Jason summer study and then flew out to Santa Barbara to oversee efforts. Secretary McNamara personally made sure that General Maxwell Taylor and William Sullivan, the U.S. ambassadors to Vietnam and Laos, traveled to Santa Barbara to brief the Jasons on the Pentagon's electronic barrier idea. The ambassadors' presence that summer underscored just how badly the Pentagon needed the concept to work, even if the diplomats thought privately that the fence was a foolish idea. "Secretary McNamara asked me if I would go out with General Taylor, to talk to the Jason group out at Santa Barbara, where they were working on some electronics," Ambassador Sullivan later recalled. "Neither Taylor nor I thought very much of it. My expectations of it were never very high."

The electronic fence had two faces, one public and one classified. The program that the public would be told about was a physical fence or barrier that was being constructed by the Pentagon to disrupt traffic on the Ho Chi Minh Trail. This fence would be built by Army engineers and guarded by Army soldiers. "A mechanical barrier built of chain link fencing, barbed wire, guard towers, and a no-man's land," as Jason scientist William Nierenberg later described it. But the secret fence the Jason scientists were to design required no soldiers to keep guard. Instead, high-technology sensors would be covertly implanted along the trail.

Since their creation in 1960, the Jason scientists had been involved in many of the most classified sensor programs ARPA initiated, including the Navy's development of sonobuoys and magnetic detectors, Sandia's development of seismic sensors, and the Army's development of infrared sensors. Now, during the 1966 summer study, the Jason scientists developed a plan to fuse, or merge, various sensor technologies and to make them work together as a system, borrowing anti-submarine warfare tactics used by the Navy. Except instead of listening for Soviet submarines in a vast ocean expanse, the anti-infiltration barrier would listen for Vietcong fighters in a sea of jungle trails.

The prototype for the Santa Barbara summer study was ARPA Study No. 1, also called Project 137, which had taken place at the National War College at Fort McNair in Washington, D.C., in the summer of 1958. This time, in Santa Barbara, the scientists lived in University of California dormitories looking out over the Pacific Ocean. In the mornings, they gathered in a university lecture hall for daily briefings. They wrote reports in the afternoon and gathered together again in the evening for dinner and to share ideas. They studied history's great barriers and walls built over the previous two thousand years, from the walls around Jerusalem, to the Great Wall of China, to the Nazis' Siegfried Line. During breaks, Murph Goldberger recalled playing tennis. The particle physicist Henry Kendall surfed in the Pacific waves. The nuclear physicist Val Fitch and the experimental physicist Leon Lederman took long walks around the campus grounds. It was an interesting idea, this electronic fence. But could it be done?

The Jasons produced a classified study called *Air-Supported Anti-Infiltration Barrier.* In it, they concluded that an electronic fence could in fact be built across and along the Ho Chi Minh Trail. The barrier would be constructed of the most advanced sensors available in the United States, including audio and seismic sensors, but also thermal, electromagnetic, and chemical sensors designed to detect fluctuations in body heat, engine heat, and even scent. Initially, these sensors would be implanted along the trail by being dropped out of aircraft, like the OP-2E Neptune, flying low over the trail. Some of the small, camouflaged sensor packages would be carried down to the ground by small parachutes, while others would be jettisoned into the earth like spears. The idea was that enemy troops moving down the trail would trigger these sensors with movement or sound. The sensors would in turn relay the information to overhead reconnaissance and surveillance aircraft, which would in turn relay the information to the "brain" of the program—a room full of computers inside a highly classified Infiltration Surveillance Center, most likely at a U.S. air base in Thailand.

Computers would play a key role, the Jason scientists imagined. The machines would analyze and interpret the sensor data. Technicians would then use the information to pinpoint the exact locations of communist fighters, trucks, and other transport vehicles, including bicycles and oxen carts. Military commanders would then dispatch aircraft to drop SADEYE cluster bombs on jungle fighters moving down the trails. These unguided, or "dumb," bombs each carried a payload of 665 one-pound tennis-ball-sized BLU-26B fragmentation, or "frag," bombs, each with a delay fuse that allowed the submunitions to blow up just above the ground, spraying razor-sharp steel shards in a kill radius of roughly eight hundred feet. Jason scientist Richard Garwin, a nuclear physicist and ordnance expert who, years before, helped design the Castle Bravo hydrogen bomb, held a seminar on the SADEYE cluster bomb and other munitions that would be most effective when accompanying the sensors on the trail. The Jason scientists determined that the trail should be seeded with button bomblets, small, "aspirin-size" mini-bombs designed to make a firecracker-like noise when stepped on, thereby triggering the air-dropped acoustic sensors. Two anti-truck bombs were also included in the design, coin-sized "Gravel mines," and larger land mines called Dragontooth mines, so named because they looked like giant teeth. These anti-truck bombs were designed to damage vehicle tires, which would slow convoys down and give strike aircraft more time to hit their targets. When stepped on they were powerful enough to remove a person's foot.

The electronic fence concept was a colossal undertaking with many moving parts. The Jason scientists were very specific regarding the numbers of bombs it required: "20 million Gravel mines per month; possibly 25 million button bomblets per month; 10,000 SADEYE-BLU-26B clusters per month," the sum total of which made up "by far the major fraction [of what] has been estimated to be about $800 million per year" in operational costs alone. "It is difficult to assess the likely effectiveness of an air-supported barrier of this type," the Jasons concluded in their written report. "We are not sure the system will make the [trail] nearly impenetrable, but we feel it has a good claim of being the foundation of a system that will, over the years." Finally, a prescient warning: "We see the possibility of a long war."

With the work complete, the summer study came to an end. On September 1, 1966, Goldberger, Deitchman, and several other Jasons flew to the Pentagon to brief Secretary McNamara on their final proposal for an electronic fence. The projected costs had risen to roughly one billion to get the fence up and running, they said, and it could be constructed in about a year and a half. McNamara was impressed.

Meanwhile, that same summer, Secretary McNamara had assembled a second group of scientists on the east coast—made up of Jason scientists and non-Jason scientists from Harvard and MIT—also working on the electronic fence idea. This group, called Jason East, conducted its work on the campus of Dana Hall, a girls' school in Wellesley, Massachusetts. The two study groups were given similar information, classified and unclassified, and came up with like-minded ideas about what would work best on this fence project and why. Pleased with both sets of results, McNamara merged the two studies into one.

A second briefing took place on September 6, 1966, this time at the Cape Cod summer home of Jason East member Jerrod Zacharias. Secretary McNamara, Assistant Secretary of Defense John McNaughton, and Director of Defense Department Research and Engineering John Foster (who, like his predecessors Herb York and Harold Brown, had served as director of the Livermore laboratory before working at the Pentagon as the liaison between ARPA and the secretary of defense) helicoptered in to the meeting on Cape Cod. Gordon MacDonald represented the Jason group at the secret briefing. "The occasion was highly informal," he remembered, in one of the only known written recollections of the meeting. "Maps were spread out on the floor, drinks were served, a dog kept crossing the demilitarized zone as top secret matters were discussed. Even though the subject was the Jason study, I was the only Jason present." Seymour Deitchman did most of the talking. "It was, you know, a typical social occasion," MacDonald recalled, except the participants were "just... deciding the next years of the Vietnam War."

But at the Pentagon, McNamara's electronic fence idea was belittled by most of the generals. When McNamara sent the final Jason study to General Earle Wheeler and the Joint Chiefs of Staff for review, they rejected the idea. General Wheeler thought it was too expensive and feared it would pull valuable resources away from the front lines. "The very substantial funds required for the barrier system would be obtained from current Service resources thereby affecting adversely important current programs," General Wheeler wrote in his response. Admiral Ulysses Sharp, commander in chief of the Pacific Command (CINCPAC), saw the entire construction effort as "impractical." The Joint Chiefs felt that McNamara's electronic fence idea would require too much time and treasure, and relied too heavily on technology, some of which did not yet exist. "It [is] CINCPAC's opinion that maintenance of an air supported barrier might result in a dynamic 'battle of the barrier,' and that the introduction of new components into the barrier system would depend not only on R&D and production capability, but would also depend on the capability to place the companions in the right place at the right time." It was simply too complicated—not just to implement but to create. "CINCPAC concluded that even if the US were to invest a great deal of time, effort, and resources into a barrier project, it was doubtful that such a barrier would improve appreciably the US position in RVN [the Republic of Vietnam]." The commander of Military Assistance Command, Vietnam, kept his opinion succinct: "It is necessary to point out that I strongly oppose commitment to create and man a barrier."

On September 15, 1966, McNamara reviewed the negative opinions from the Joint Chiefs of Staff, the commander in chief of the Pacific, and others, and overruled them. The secretary of defense had the authority to move ahead with the electronic fence with or without the support of his military commanders, and he did, with the classification of top secret. That same day McNamara appointed Lieutenant General Alfred D. Starbird head of Joint Task Force 728. Starbird, an Army officer, was a favorite of the secretary of defense. He knew how to handle highly classified, highly sensitive military projects that involved thousands of people and billions of dollars. Starbird had overseen the nuclear detonations in space, code-named Checkmate and Bluegill Triple Prime, during the height of the Cuban Missile Crisis. Now he was in charge of developing the barrier and overseeing its deployment in the war theater. He had an impossible deadline of one year.

General Starbird was a master bureaucrat, soldier, government advisor, and engineer. Fast and thorough, he was a consummate athlete with a brilliant mind. He'd competed in Hitler's Olympics in 1936, in the pentathlon. After serving in World War II, Starbird had served in Europe as director of the Army's Office of the Chief of Engineers. During the development of the hydrogen bomb, he served as director of Military Applications for the Atomic Energy Commission, acting as liaison between the Defense Department and the AEC. He had a photographic memory and never lost his cool.

Joint Task Force 728, also called the Defense Communications Planning Group, was in charge of planning, preparing, and executing the electronic fence. Starbird got to work immediately, acquiring space at the U.S. Naval Observatory in Washington, D.C., as his headquarters in the United States. He began outlining projects, designating assignments, and creating schedules. For his Scientific Advisory Committee, Starbird hired seven of the fifteen Jason scientists who had worked on the original Santa Barbara summer study, including Murph Goldberger and Gordon MacDonald. A skillful diplomat, Starbird pulled together leaders from the four services. He had an enormous task in front of him, just the kind of operation he was used to. Technology, munitions, aircraft, ground systems, and "high-speed" computers. In October, McNamara and Starbird traveled to Vietnam to meet with field commanders. When McNamara returned, he briefed President Johnson on the barrier program, officially, for the first time. On January 12, 1967, the classified National Security Action Memorandum No. 358

gave the top secret electronic fence, then code-named Project Practice Nine, the "highest national priority" for expenditures and authorization. For reasons not explained, Walt Rostow signed for the president of the United States. Starbird had a billion dollars at his disposal and the authority to get the electronic fence up in one year's time. The program was the single most expensive high-technology project of the Vietnam War. It is nothing short of astonishing that the VO-67 Navy squadron was actually flying combat missions one year later, in January 1968.

A few months before the sensor-dropping missions began, General Starbird decided that he needed a liaison in Saigon, someone who could keep an ear to the ground inside CIA prisons and detention facilities to determine if the Vietcong had gotten word about what the U.S. military was planning on the Ho Chi Minh Trail. It was hard to find a qualified person. Starbird asked around at ARPA and was referred to RAND's George Tanham, who in turn referred Starbird to Leon Gouré. After having been embarrassed during congressional hearings on the spurious nature of ARPA's Viet Cong Motivation and Morale Project, Gouré had been keeping a low profile at RAND. Now General Starbird wanted Gouré to take the lead on an important new ARPA study for the Defense Communications Planning Group, this time related to the highly classified electronic fence project. With a new contract in place, in August 1967 Gouré returned to Saigon to conduct interviews with Vietcong prisoners being held in secret CIA prisons. According to Gouré, the enemy had not heard a thing about Americans building a high-technology fence.

McNamara's electronic fence, which the Jasons called an "anti-infiltration barrier," was constructed along the Ho Chi Minh Trail, at a cost of $1.8 billion, roughly $12 billion in 2015. It had very little effect on the outcome of the Vietnam War and did not help the

United States achieve its aim of cutting off enemy supplies. Most of the failures were technology-based. Sensors were temperature sensitive, and in the extreme heat of the jungle, batteries drained quickly and sensors went dead. The V0-67 aircrews were often unable to place sensors accurately along the trail. In 1968 there was no such thing as advanced laser-guided technology. Rip Jacobs and his fellow Navy airmen relied on an electrical device called a "pickle switch" to release sensors from the OP-2E Neptunes, hoping they would land where they were supposed to along the trail. Instead, many sensors landed hundreds, sometimes thousands, of feet away. But far-reaching seeds were sown.

Gradually, commanders changed their opinions about McNamara's electronic fence. In 1969, speaking to members of the Association of the U.S. Army at a luncheon at the Sheraton Park Hotel in Washington, D.C., retired four-star general William Westmoreland, former commander of U.S. military operations in Vietnam, spoke of the power of the electronic fence. "We are on the threshold of an entirely new battlefield concept," Westmoreland told his audience of former soldiers. "I see battlefields on which we can destroy anything we locate through instant communications and the almost instantaneous application of a lethal firepower."

In 1985, during a banquet to celebrate the twenty-five-year anniversary of the Jason program, Gordon MacDonald discussed how profound a moment in history the development of the barrier concept had been. "The most important element of the barrier study was its definition of a system concept," he said. Tiny sensors covertly placed in a war zone acted like eyes, ears, and fingertips on the ground, then relayed information back to a computer system far away, which filtered and analyzed it for a commander who would in turn decide what tactical action to take next. This was the first time anyone thought of creating a "system of systems," MacDonald observed. It gave birth to the "basic concept of unmanned sensors gathering tactical intelligence to be used for managing the delivery of munitions." As John von Neumann first imagined, and J. C. R. Licklider later discussed, this was the first truly symbiotic relationship between man and machine and the battlefield.

The electronic fence had initially been dismissed by a majority of defense officials, who saw it as newfangled gadgetry. But by the 1980s, the concept of the fence would be reinterpreted as visionary. And by the 1990s, the electronic battlefield concept would begin its transformation into the most revolutionary piece of military technology of the twentieth century, after the hydrogen bomb.

In a summary of the work performed by VO-67 Navy squadron, whose crewmembers dropped electronic sensors along the Ho Chi Minh Trail, U.S. Air Force colonel Warren H. Peterson wrote a top secret cable and a sixty-four-page report for the commander in chief. "It is worth observing that the program itself was visionary," Colonel Peterson said. "From its outset, [the electronic battlefield concept] combined extremes of the technically sophisticated with the amazingly primitive. How would an ordinary, reasonably educated layman, for instance, be likely to react when told of a system that proposed to detect enemy troops moving along jungle trails, but using modern electric acoustic detectors, which had to be activated by the detonations of firecrackers which the troops were expected to step on? Yet it must be remembered that this report covers only the stone age of what may be a long era of development."

Colonel Peterson could have been speaking about ARPA as a whole, about what it was doing and what it would do. The agency was growing used to taking old technologies and accelerating them into future ways of fighting wars. By the twenty-first century the electronic battlefield concept would be ubiquitous.

CHAPTER THIRTEEN

The End of Vietnam

The downfall of the Jason scientists during the Vietnam War began with a rumor and an anonymous phone call to Congress. On February 12, 1968, Carl Macy, the staff director of the Senate Foreign Relations Committee, received a tip saying that the committee should look into why the Pentagon had sent a nuclear weapons expert, Dr. Richard Garwin of Columbia University, to Vietnam. The battle of Khe Sanh was raging, the tipster said, and rumor had it that the Pentagon was considering the use of nuclear weapons against the Vietcong.

"Within a week the rumor had gone around the world and involved the President of the United States, the Prime Minister of Britain and leaders of Congress in a discussion over whether or not the United States was considering using tactical nuclear weapons in Vietnam," reported the *New York Times.* The White House expressed outrage, calling the accusations "false," "irresponsible," and "unfair to the armed services." But there was truth behind the allegation. The tipster was likely alluding to the highly classified Jason report "Tactical Nuclear Weapons in Southeast Asia," in which the Jason scientists advised *against* such use. The Senate Foreign Relations Committee was not convinced and convened a closed-door meeting where senators echoed similar concerns. The *New York Times* reported that one senator "said he had also picked up rumors that the Administration was considering the use of tactical nuclear weapons in Vietnam, perhaps in defense of Khesanh if necessary to save the Marine Corps garrison there."

The Pentagon issued a statement saying that Dr. Garwin and other scientists had been sent to Vietnam to oversee "the effectiveness of new weapons," ones that "have no relationship whatsoever to atomic or nuclear systems of any kind." This was true. Although the statement did not reveal the classified program itself, the "new weapons" the Pentagon was referring to were essential to McNamara's electronic fence.

Jason scientists Richard Garwin, Henry Kendall, and Gordon MacDonald were in Vietnam to problem-solve issues related to the sensor technology. The Tet Offensive was under way, and the Vietcong were in the process of cutting off access to the Marine base at Khe Sanh. There were fears at the Pentagon that what had happened to the French at Dien Bien Phu in 1954 could now happen to the Marines at Khe Sanh. The similarities were striking, including the fact that the Vietnamese general who had led the communists to victory at Dien Bien Phu, General Vo Nguyen Giap, was again leading communist fighters in the battle for Khe Sanh.

VO-67 Navy squadron crewmembers were called upon to assist. More than 250 sensors were dropped in a ring around the Marine outpost at Khe Sanh in an effort to help identify when and where the Vietcong were closing in. The target information officer at Khe Sanh, Captain Harry Baig, was having trouble with the technology, and so Richard Garwin, Henry Kendall, and Gordon MacDonald were flown to the classified Information Surveillance Center at Nakhon Phanom, Thailand, to help. Unable to solve the problem from Thailand, MacDonald offered to be helicoptered in to the dangerous Marine outpost at Khe Sanh.

"It was a scary place," MacDonald later recalled, "because you knew you were isolated. There were something on the order of four thousand Marines and to many [it seemed as if] there was little hope of getting them out. It was a dreadful situation." What was remarkable was that MacDonald offered to be inserted into the middle of the battle in the first place. A polio survivor and now a presidential advisor, he could easily have chosen to stay in the safety of neighboring Thailand with Kendall and Garwin.

The nuclear physicist and ordnance expert Richard Garwin later stated that he was likely the source of the information leak that set off the downfall of the Jasons. "I had probably told people I was going to Vietnam, which I shouldn't have," Garwin told Finn Aaserud, director of the Niels Bohr Archive, in 1991. "Colleagues with overheated imaginations and a sense of mission thought some-one should know about this," he surmised.

As reporters began digging into Garwin's backstory, the connection with the Jason scientists and the Advanced Research Projects Agency emerged. The classified report on barrier technology did not surface at this time, but the title of the Jasons' report, "Tactical Nuclear Weapons in Southeast Asia," did. For antiwar protesters, this information—that the Pentagon had actually considered using nuclear weapons—led to outrage. Many of the Jason scientists held positions at universities, and they were now targeted by antiwar protesters for investigation and denunciation.

A powerful antiwar coalition called the Mobilization Committee to End the War in Vietnam, or "the Mobe," had been organizing massive demonstrations across the country. The previous spring, hundreds of thousands of people had attended an antiwar march in New York City, walking from Central Park to the United Nations building, where they burned draft cards. The march, which was led by Dr. Martin Luther King Jr., made news around the world.

The Mobe's March on the Pentagon, in the fall of 1967, had turned violent when protesters clashed with U.S. marshals and heavily armed military police assigned to protect the building. Six hundred and eighty-two people were arrested, including the author Norman Mailer and two United Press International reporters. Now, after it was revealed that many university professors were discreetly working on classified weapons projects as defense scientists, the Mobe's underground newspaper, the *Student Mobilizer,* began an investigation that culminated in a report called "Counterinsurgency Research on Campus, Exposed." The article contained excerpts from the minutes of a Jason summer study, reportedly stolen from a professor's unlocked cabinet. It contained additional excerpts from classified documents written for ARPA's Combat Development and Test Center in Bangkok, Thailand, also allegedly stolen.

In March 1968, students at Princeton University learned that the Jasons' advisory board was the Institute of Defense Analyses, or IDA, the federally funded think tank that served the Department of Defense—and that IDA maintained an "ultra secret think-tank" on the Princeton campus, inside Von Neumann Hall (named in honor of John von Neumann). Further investigation by student journalists revealed that the windows of this building were made of bulletproof glass. Student journalists broke the story in the *Daily Princetonian*, reporting that inside this Defense Department–funded building, and using state-of-the-art computers, "mathematicians worked out problems in advanced cryptology for the National Security Agency" and did other "war research work." University records showed that the computer being used was a 1.5-ton CDC-1604, the "first fully transistorized supercomputer" in the world. When it arrived at the university in 1960, the supercomputer had a "staggering 32K of memory." The journalists also revealed that at Princeton, IDA was working on "long range projects with ARPA—The Defense Department's Advanced Research Projects Agency... in the field of communication."

The student journalists discovered, too, that Princeton University president Robert F. Goheen was also a member of IDA's twenty-two-man board of trustees and that numerous current and former Princeton physics professors, including John Wheeler, Murph Goldberger, Sam Treiman, and Eugene Wigner, had worked on IDA-ARPA projects related to war and weapons. As a result of these revelations, the antiwar group Students for a Democratic Society staged a sit-in, demanding that IDA be kicked off campus. The faculty voted that Princeton should terminate its association with IDA, and when university trustees overruled the demand, students chained the front doors of Von Neumann Hall shut, preventing anyone from getting in or out for several days. The issue died down until the following year. When students learned IDA was still operating on campus, protestors initiated a five-day siege of Von Neumann Hall, spray painting anti-Nixon graffiti across the front of the building, engaging with police officers, and chanting, "Kill the computer!"

Still, there was very little public mention of the Jason scientists and their position as the elite advisory group to the Pentagon, or that all their consulting fees were paid for by ARPA. But what happened at Princeton and elsewhere, as links between university professors and the Department of Defense became known, was just the tip of a very large iceberg that would take until June 13, 1971, to be fully revealed.

For the Pentagon, the antiwar protests were a command and control nightmare. For ARPA it meant the acceleration of a "nonlethal weapons" program to research and develop ways to stop demonstrators through the use of painful but not deadly force. There was a sense of urgency at hand. Not only were the protesters gaining support and momentum in their efforts, but also they were now controlling the narrative of the Vietnam War. "The whole world is watching!" chanted activists at an antiwar rally outside the Democratic National Convention in Chicago in August 1968. The phrase spread like wildfire and drew attention to National Guardsmen, in Chicago and elsewhere, as protesters were threatened with guns and fixed bayonets. In these antiwar protests, and also in civil rights protests across the nation, state police, military police, and the National Guard used water cannons, riot batons, electric prods, horses, and dogs to control and intimidate crowds.

ARPA's research into nonlethal weapons was classified and highly controversial. To keep this research secret, laboratories were set up abroad under an innocuous program name, Overseas Defense Research. This research took place at the Combat Development and Test Center (CDTC) in Bangkok, which had been renamed the Military Research and Development Center. Progress reports were delivered to ARPA program managers with a cover letter that stated, "This document contains information affecting the National Defense of the United States within the means of the Espionage Laws." The program was overseen by defense contractor Battelle Memorial Institute, in Columbus, Ohio, and was considered part of Project Agile's Remote Area Conflict program. A rare declassified copy of one such report, from April 1971, was obtained through the Freedom of Information Act.

"Nonlethal weapons are generally intended to prevent an individual from engaging in undesirable acts," wrote E. E. Westbrook and L. W. Williams, the authors of the report. "Apart from the moral arguments in the present and future use of nonlethal weapons, public officials find it prudent to examine nonlethal force using a framework that it was keeping 'innocent bystanders' from being hurt." At the overseas CDTCs, ARPA chemists examined a variety of incapacitating agents for future use against protesters, including dangerous chemical agents with a wide range of effects, from vomiting to skin injury to temporary paralysis.

Possible irritants for use against demonstrators included "CN (tear gas)... CS (riot control agent)... CX (blister agent)," also called phosgene oxide—a potent chemical weapon that causes temporary blindness, lesions on the lungs, and rapid local tissue death. CS was seen as a viable option: more than 15 million pounds of CS had already been used in Vietnam to flush Vietcong out of underground tunnels on the Ho Chi Minh Trail. CX was also recommended for crowd control. It "produced a corrosive injury to the skin, including tissue injury," but because the worst damage was inside the lungs, the harm would be disguised. Anticholinergics were considered, chemicals that cause physical collapse. "Probably the most promising of the anticholinergics (agents which block passage of impulses through parasympathetic nerves)," wrote the chemists, were compounds that produced "rapid heart rate, incoordination, blurred vision, delirium, vomiting, and in cases of higher doses, coma." Emetic agents, chemicals that induce vomiting, were also recommended.

A second program involved delivery systems. Mechanisms for delivery included liquid stream projectors, able to shoot a twelve-inch-diameter stream of liquid across a distance of up to forty feet, as well as grenades thrown by hand or discharged from a small rocket. A more powerful option was the E8-CS man-portable tactical launcher and cartridge, which could be fired electrically or manually into rioting crowds at a distance of up to 750 feet. "It is nonlethal in the impact area, but its high muzzle velocity creates a lethal hazard at the muzzle during firing," the scientists wrote.

Poison darts were discussed as a possible "means for injecting an enemy [i.e., a protester] with an incapacitating agent." Also recommended were tranquilizing darts, historically effective in subduing wild or frightened animals. The problem, the ARPA chemists cautioned, was that "using these kinds of darts was not entirely safe as accurate dosage was based on the weight of the animal." One advantage was that the "use of a dart allows selection of an individual target, perhaps the leader of a group or a particularly destructive person, without injuring others around him." Further, the darts "possess a psychological advantage not shared by many other systems," noted the scientists. "The victim may wonder what he has been hit with and whether or not it is essential that he find an antidote." This benefit needed to be weighed against another danger, however, which was that if someone was hit in the head or neck, it could be fatal. "Darts are not regarded by many as an 'acceptable' weapon," the scientists wrote. Following the dart discussion was a long treatise on whether or not the use of the electric cattle prod against human protesters would be defensible.

The 130-page report offered hundreds of additional development ideas about how to incapacitate demonstrators without killing them, programs that were currently being researched for battlefield use but had not yet been deployed in Vietnam. "Photic driving" was a phenomenon whereby the application of stroboscopic light within a certain frequency range could cause a person's brain waves "to become entrained to the same frequency as the flashing light." But early studies showed that this kind of flickering light was effective in only about 30 percent of the population. Laser radiation was suggested as a potential way of temporarily blinding people, also called flash blindness. One drawback, the ARPA scientists noted, was that "the laser must be aimed directly at the eye," which "diminishes its practicality in a confrontation situation." Microwaves could potentially be used to incapacitate individuals by burning their skin, but the science had not yet been adequately advanced. "Surface skin burns using microwaves would not form soon enough to create tactical advantage," the scientists wrote. Also, trying to burn someone with a microwave beam would be "ineffective against a person who is wearing heavy clothing or who is behind an object," the scientists wrote.

Another series of tests researched "the use of loud noises to scare people or to interfere with communications." But the ARPA scientists cautioned that sound would have to be "so offensive and repugnant that hearers leave the scene," meaning a volume so high that it presented the danger of permanent hearing loss. "Most subjects experience pain at about 140 db [decibels], and at about 160 db, the eardrum is torn."

Tagging was an option, to help police make arrests after a demonstration. "The marking of people for later apprehension is another technique which has been tried in some situations," the scientists wrote, suggesting specific materials including "invisible markings which were sensitive to ultraviolet light" and "odor identifying markings, sensed by dogs or gas chromatographs."

Crowd control had long been an engineering challenge at the Pentagon. To be effective, nonlethal weapons need to deliver enough power to produce a dispersal effect but not enough power to cause serious injury or harm. Most historical accounts of the use of nonlethal weapons in the United States cite the Omnibus Crime Control and Safe Streets Act of 1968 as a turning point. The act established the Law Enforcement Assistance Administration (LEAA), a federal agency within the U.S. Department of Justice designed to assist state police forces across the nation in upgrading their riot control hardware and officer-training programs. The act also provided $12 billion in funding over a period of ten years. Police forces across America began upgrading their military-style equipment to include riot control systems, helicopters, grenade launchers, and machine guns. The LEAA famously gave birth to the special weapons and tactics concept, or SWAT, with the first units created in Los Angeles in the late 1960s. "These units," says an LAPD historian, "provided security for police facilities during civil unrest." But what has not been established before this book is that much of this equipment was researched and developed by ARPA in the jungles of Vietnam and Thailand during the Vietnam War.

In America, antiwar protests raged on. Not even computers could escape the hostility between the Pentagon and the antiwar establishment. In early 1970, a Defense Department computer at the

University of Illinois at Urbana-Champaign, called the ILLIAC IV, came under fire. ILLIAC IV was the fastest computer on earth at the time. The scientist in charge of the project for ARPA was Professor Daniel L. Slotnick, a mathematician and computer architect. A former student of John von Neumann, Slotnick had worked with von Neumann on MANIAC, at the Institute for Advanced Study at Princeton, starting in 1952. It was there that Slotnick developed his first thoughts about centrally controlled parallel computers. A pioneer in his field, Slotnick was one of the first to develop the concept of parallel computing, a form of computation in which multiple calculations are carried out simultaneously by separate computers and solved concurrently. Slotnick co-authored the first paper on the subject, in 1958. His goal with ILLIAC IV was to build a machine that could perform a billion instructions per second. Although it used the same architecture conceived by John von Neumann, ILLIAC IV was a far cry from MANIAC in terms of computing power.

ILLIAC IV was fifty feet long, ten feet tall, and eight feet wide. The machine's power supply units were so massive they had to be moved with a specially designed forklift. The supercomputer was made up of a group of sixty-four processor elements, with a potential for up to 256—a groundbreaking number of processing units at the time. The machine was designed to cut down exponentially on the time it took to complete basic computational science and engineering tasks. Approximately two-thirds of the computer's time was designated for work on Department of Defense weapons programs, including "computational requirements for ballistic missile defense." Specifically, the calculations sought to differentiate a missile from the background noise, the problem that had been plaguing the Jason scientists since they first began studying the topic in 1960. ILLIAC IV was also used for climate modeling, and for weather modification schemes, as part of a still-classified ARPA program called Nile Blue. Not until July 1972 would the U.S. government renounce the use of climate modification techniques for hostile purposes. In May 1977 an international treaty, the Convention on the Prohibition of Military or Any Other Hostile Use of Environmental Modification Techniques, would be signed, in Geneva, by forty-eight nations. Until then, weather modification schemes were pursued.

Slotnick and his team called the ILLIAC IV "the ultimate number cruncher." ARPA officials believed that if they had two of these computers, their capability would cover "all the computational requirements on planet earth." The building of ILLIAC IV, most of which was done by graduate students, was the largest and most lucrative Defense Department contract in the history of the University of Illinois. By late 1969, the university had received more than $24 million in funds, roughly $155 million in 2015. Plans for a fancy new facility to house the machine were in place, with groundbreaking ceremonies to begin sometime during the following year. The specifics of the arrangement between Slotnick and ARPA were classified, but it was not a secret that a supercomputer was being built at the university.

What it would be used for was obscure until January 5, 1970, when the Illinois Board of Higher Education met for a budget review and a student reporter managed to attend. The following day, on January 6, 1970, a headline in the *Daily Illini* declared, "Department of Defense to employ UI [University of Illinois] computer for nuclear weaponry."

The revelation that the university was working with the Defense Department on nuclear weapons work had an explosive effect on an already charged student body. "The University has proven that it is not a neutral institution," declared the antiwar group Radical Union, "but is actively supporting the efforts of the military-industrial complex." One article after the next alleged malevolent intentions on the part of Professor Slotnick and the dean of the Graduate College, Daniel Alpert, in having tried to conceal from the student body the true nature of the computer. "The horrors ILLIAC IV may loose on the world through [the] hands of military leaders of this nation" could not be underestimated, the *Daily Illini* editorialized. "We fear the military... will use the computer to develop more ways to kill people and spend the people's money." In another article, a group of concerned students wrote, "Considering the evil demonstrated by our military in recent years, we would rather have seen the University resistant to the evil... than complicit with it."

Professor Slotnick tried to justify the Pentagon funding by pointing out that other institutions were unwilling to fund such an important but far-sighted program as building this supercomputer. "If I could have gotten $30 million from the Red Cross, I would not have messed with the DoD," Slotnick said. ARPA took offense, calling Slotnick a "volatile visionary." The board tried to throw a blanket over the fire by declaring the "more important" parts of the computer "non-military." Despite attempts to humanize the machine, the debate only grew. A teach-in was organized against ILLIAC IV. Students wanted the machine gone.

On February 23, 1970, the protests took a violent turn when unknown persons firebombed the campus armory, causing $2,000 worth of damage. Then on March 2, five hundred protesters disrupted a job-recruiting session with General Electric, the defense contractor that helped build ILLIAC IV. Windows were broken and three people were injured. Officers who tried to arrest people were pummeled with mud balls. The crowd grew to as many as three thousand. When antiwar demonstrators broke windows in the chancellor's office, state police wearing full riot gear appeared on the scene. Not until late that night was peace restored. Twenty-one students were arrested, eight seriously injured. On March 9, the university's faculty senate took a vote to oppose ILLIAC IV; it failed. Two days later, the Air Force recruiting station in Urbana was firebombed, the sixth local arson attack of the month.

The spring of 1970 was a tempestuous time on college campuses across America. On April 30, 1970, President Nixon went on national television to announce the U.S. invasion of Cambodia, yet another expansion of the Vietnam War. Nixon's disclosure that 150,000 more soldiers would now be drafted sparked major protests across the nation. Four days later, on May 4, four students at Kent State University in Ohio were shot dead by the National Guard.

The following day, the ILLIAC IV protests at the University of Illinois ratcheted up even further when two thousand demonstrators stoned police vehicles parked on campus. On the morning of May 6 the National Guard moved in, and on May 7, ten thousand students and faculty held a peace rally. When the university refused to fly flags at half-mast for the victims of the Kent State shootings, students pulled down the American flag that had been flying on the university fire station flagpole and set it on fire. On May 9, demonstrators staged a sit-in in front of the building that housed the ILLIAC IV. Protests and arrests continued until May 12.

In June, university officials told ARPA that they could no longer guarantee the safety of its supercomputer. ARPA began looking for a new facility to house the ILLIAC IV and in 1971 entered into a new contract with a federal research facility in California. Each side—the protesters and the government—believed strongly in the legitimacy of its position. Students at the University of Illinois and elsewhere across the nation continued to protest against war; the Department of Defense continued its weapons research and its war in Vietnam.

The supercomputer was packed up and taken to California. By the spring of 1972, ILLIAC IV was up and running at NASA's Institute for Advanced Computation at the Ames Research Center. This was adjacent to the U.S. Navy's west coast facility where highly classified antisubmarine warfare work was taking place. ILLIAC IV began making calculations for the Navy's Project Seaguard, a classified program to track submarines using acoustics, another ARPA program, with research taking place at ARPA's classified Acoustic Research Center, deep underwater in a lake in northern Idaho.

The submarine research facility was one of ARPA's best-kept secrets, an underwater test site located at the south end of a small resort community on Lake Pend Oreille in Bayview, Idaho. The forty-three-mile-long lake is 1,150 feet deep in places, making it the perfect locale to conduct secret submarine research. Acoustic sensors placed on the floor of the lake recorded and processed data which were then fed into ILLIAC IV, allowing for major Cold War advances in antisubmarine warfare.

The ILLIAC IV controversy coincided with a major turning point in the history of the Advanced Research Projects Agency. Public opposition to the Vietnam War, coupled with rising inflation, put an unwelcome spotlight on ARPA when Senator Mike Mansfield, an antiwar Democrat from Montana, introduced a bill that barred the Defense Department from using funds "to carry out any research project or study unless the project or study had a direct relationship to [a] specific military function." The Mansfield Amendment, introduced in late 1969 as an amendment to the Military Authorization Act, focused "the public's desire for practical outcomes" against the idea that not only was the Pentagon failing to end the war in Vietnam, but also its spending was out of control. The amendment put military research and development under intense scrutiny and had a direct impact on ARPA. Because most of its work was speculative, looking ten to twenty-five years into the future, directors of the agency would now have to present much more detailed information to Congress before their budgets could be passed.

Then in February 1970 came another devastating blow for ARPA. The secretary of defense authorized a decision that the entire agency was to be removed from its coveted office space inside the Pentagon to a lackluster office building in the Rosslyn district of Arlington, Virginia, two and a half miles away. Desks, chairs, file cabinets, and furniture were all boxed up and moved.

The Pentagon was the seat of military might, the locus of power. Moving even a short distance away was, as one insider put it, "the epitome of the Agency's downgrading." The underlying message being sent to staff was that the Advanced Research Projects Agency might just fold. Even the ARPA director at the time, the electrical engineer and telecommunications expert Eberhardt Rechtin, appeared to have lost confidence in the agency he was in charge of. Rechtin confided to a colleague, "It wouldn't surprise me that all of a sudden [a secretary of defense] would decide to kill ARPA." Since its inception in 1958, ARPA had been a place where there was always more money than ideas. Suddenly, "the dollar situation was so bad, [the agency] had far more ideas than money," Rechtin said. Without money, there was less power, and without power, there was greater tension.

To many on the ARPA staff, it seemed as if Rechtin did not particularly care whether the agency survived. "The staff just didn't know what was going to happen next," one program manager told a government historian in 1974. "They didn't know who was boss. They didn't know who to follow. They didn't know whether anyone cared." The staffer continued: "At least if you kill something[,] you know. You line it up against the wall, you take aim, you spend five minutes at the job and you kill it right. But to let it wither away by not even allowing it to have a Director [who cared] is almost [worse]. The feeling was: he [Rechtin] doesn't care anymore... he is selling us down the river... we've become the pawn, and we are moving away from the center." An "apocalyptic feeling" overwhelmed the ARPA staff. "We had terrible feelings that this [was] the end," said another unidentified staffer.

As ARPA director, Rechtin believed he knew why the agency had run into so many difficulties during the Vietnam War. He called it the "chicken-and-egg problem" in congressional testimony related to the Mansfield Amendment. When asked by a committee member if it was appropriate to describe the Advanced Research Projects Agency as a "premilitary research organization within the Defense Department," Rechtin said that if the word "military" were replaced with the word "requirement," then that assessment would be correct. Unlike the regular military services, Rechtin said, ARPA was a "pre-requirement" organization in that it conducted research in advance of specific needs. "By this I mean that the military services, in order to do their work, must have a very formal requirement based on specific needs," Rechtin said, "and usually upon technologies that are understood." ARPA existed to make sure that the military establishment was not ever again caught off guard by a *Sputnik*-like technological surprise. The enemy was always eyeing the future, he said, pursuing advanced technology in order to take more ground. And ARPA was set up to provide the Defense Department with its pre-requirement needs.

"There is a kind of chicken-and-egg problem in other words, in requirements and technology," Rechtin explained. "The difficulty is that it is hard to write formal requirements if you do not have the technology with which to solve them, but you cannot do the technology unless you have the requirements." The agency's dilemma, said Rechtin, was this: if you can't do the research before a need arises, by the time the need is there, it's clear that the research should already have been done.

Rechtin had defended ARPA's mission but wasn't long for the job and would soon move on to a more powerful position higher up the ladder at the Department of Defense. In December 1970 he resigned his post at ARPA and returned to the Pentagon, to take over as principal acting deputy of Defense Department Research and Engineering

(DDR&E), the person to whom the ARPA director reports. The rest of the agency employees waited for the other shoe to drop.

Drop it did. On June 13, 1971, the first installment of the Pentagon Papers appeared on the front page of the *New York Times.* The classified documents had been leaked to the newspaper by former Pentagon employee and RAND Corporation analyst Daniel Ellsberg. The papers unveiled a secret history of the war in Vietnam—three thousand narrative pages of war secrets accompanied by four thousand pages of classified memos and supporting documents, organized into forty-seven volumes. Back in 1967, when he was secretary of defense, Robert McNamara had commissioned the RAND Corporation to write a classified "encyclopedic history of the Vietnamese War," neglecting to tell the president he was undertaking such a project. The Pentagon Papers covered the U.S. involvement in Vietnam since the end of World War II. Revealed in the papers were specifics on how every president from Truman to Eisenhower, Kennedy, Johnson, and Nixon had misled the public about what was really going on in Vietnam. The classified documents were photocopied by Ellsberg, with the help of RAND colleague Anthony Russo, the individual who had worked extensively with Leon Gouré on the Viet Cong Motivation and Morale Project. Both Ellsberg and Russo had originally supported the war in Vietnam but later came to oppose it.

The papers revealed secret bombing campaigns, the role of the United States in the Diem assassination, the CIA's involvement with the Montagnards, and so much more. With respect to ARPA, the papers revealed the extensive role of the Jason scientists throughout the war—specifically that they had designed sensors, strike aircraft retrofits, and cluster bombs for the electronic fence. The scientists had first been brought into the spotlight back in February 1968 when the scandal broke over the possible use of tactical nuclear weapons against the Mu Gia Pass. Like so many controversies during the war, that scandal came and went. But now, with the revelations of the Pentagon Papers, the Jason scientists were caught in a much harsher spotlight. In the words of former ARPA director Jack Ruina, the Jason scientists were now portrayed as "the devil."

All across the country, and even overseas, the Jason scientists became targets for antiwar protesters. The words "war criminal" were painted on the pavement outside Kenneth Watson's house in Berkeley. Gordon MacDonald's Santa Barbara garage was set on fire. Herb York got a death threat. The Jasons' summer study office in Colorado was vandalized. In New York City, a consortium of professors at Columbia demanded that the scientists resign from Jason or resign from the university. In Paris, Murray Gell-Mann was booed off a stage. Riot police were called to a physics symposium in Trieste where Jason scientist Eugene Wigner was speaking as an honored guest. In New York City, Murph Goldberger was getting ready to deliver a lecture to the American Physical Society when a huge crowd interrupted his talk in a very public way. Goldberger had recently led the first-ever State Department–sanctioned delegation of American scientists to communist China, but as he began to speak, the demonstrators raised huge placards reading "War Criminal!" He tried to keep his composure and continue his talk about China, but the protesters kept interrupting him, shouting out questions about the Jason scientists and their role as weapons designers for the Vietnam War.

"Look, I'll talk about China or I won't talk about anything," Goldberger told the crowd, but his voice was drowned out by boos. He tried a different tactic and said that he would discuss Jason and Vietnam after his speech if the protesters were willing to secure a venue where they could have a conversation somewhere nearby after he was done. The protesters agreed. As soon as Goldberger finished giving his lecture about China, he walked over to the East Ballroom of the New York Hilton hotel and politely took questions from a crowd of what was now more than two hundred people, including lots of reporters.

"Jason made a terrible mistake," Goldberger said in a voice described by the *Philadelphia Inquirer* as "anguished" and fraught with moral guilt. We "should have told Mr. McNamara to go to hell and not become involved at all," said Goldberger.

No Jason scientist was spared defamation. A group of antiwar protesters learned the home address of Richard Garwin in upstate New York and showed up on his front lawn with hate signs. Another time, when Garwin was on an airplane, a woman sitting in the seat next to him recognized him, stood up, and declared, "This is Dick Garwin. He is a baby killer!"

An Italian physicist at the Institute of Theoretical Physics in Naples, Bruno Vitale, spearheaded an international anti-Jason movement. Vitale saw the revelations in the Pentagon Papers about the Jason scientists as a "perfect occasion to see bare the hypocrisy of the establishment physicists; their lust for power, prestige; their arrogance against the people." In a monograph titled "The War Physicists," he charged that the scientific world had become divided into insiders and outsiders. "Jason people are insiders," Vitale wrote. "They have access to secret information from many government offices." On the opposite side of the coin, "those who engage in criticism of government policies without the benefit of such inside access are termed outsiders." Vitale argued that scientists needed to stand together in their outrage and not accept what he called phony arguments. "When a debate arises between insiders and outsiders, invariably the argument is used that only the insiders know the true facts and that therefore the outsiders' positions should not be taken seriously."

Vitale's crusade garnered international support, and in December 1972 a group of European scientists, three of whom were Nobel Prize winners, wrote a very public letter to the Jason scientists, which was published in the *Bulletin of the Atomic Scientists.* The land mines that formed part of the electronic fence "have caused terrible wounds among Vietnamese civilians," they charged, and asked the

Jasons to respond. In the weeks that followed, in letters to the editor, other scientists demanded that the Jason researchers "explain how they could justify to their consciences" the work they had done designing land mines. Famed British physics professor E. H. S. Burhop wrote: "The scientists became, to some extent, prisoners of the group they had joined.... At what point should they have quit?" In *Science,* a reader wrote in to say that the Jasons "should be tried for war crimes." The Jasons did not collectively respond. Looking back in 2013, Goldberger said of the group he co-founded, "We should never have gotten involved in Vietnam."

By 1973, ARPA's new director, Stephen Lukasik, felt it was time for the agency to distance itself from the Jason scientists. For years the group had been at the "intellectual forefront of everything we were trying to do to prevent technological surprise," Lukasik later remarked. But he also felt that the Jason scientists suffered from an intellectual superiority complex. "The word 'arrogant' [was] associated with Jason," Lukasik acknowledged. He had worked with the Jasons for a decade, going back to the time when he was head of ARPA's Nuclear Test Detection Office, which handled the Vela program. On more than one occasion, Lukasik felt that the Jasons had displayed a "pattern of arrogance." That they were a self-congratulating group. "They picked their members. And so they had in 1969 the same members they had in 1959." Lukasik wanted new blood. The Jasons still "didn't have any computer scientists. They didn't have any materials scientists. They weren't bringing in new members." Lukasik notified the Jason scientists, through their oversight committee at IDA, that it was time for them to move on. "I probably was seen as an enemy of the Jasons," Lukasik admitted. In the winter of 1973, without any resistance, the Jasons departed IDA for the Stanford Research Institute, in California. "It was an agreeable move," Goldberger recalled. Before leaving IDA, the Jason scientists had had only one client, the Advanced Research

Projects Agency. Now, said Goldberger, the Jasons were free to work "for whomever we pleased."

Not all those affiliated with ARPA were feeling liberated. In their new office building away from the Pentagon, ARPA employees were at a crossroads. Feeling banished from the center of power and with budgets slashed, they feared that the future of ARPA was more uncertain than it had ever been. Who could have imagined this precarious time would give way to one of the most prosperous, most influential eras in the history of the Advanced Research Projects Agency?

PART III

OPERATIONS OTHER THAN WAR

CHAPTER FOURTEEN

Rise of the Machines

During the Korean War, when Allen Macy Dulles left the trench at Outpost Bunker Hill and headed down to check the fence, he was doing what soldiers have done for millennia. He was going out on patrol. The moment when Dulles saw someone had cut the fence, he likely sensed danger was near. But before he had time to notify anyone of the incursion, the twenty-two-year-old soldier took enemy shrapnel to the head, suffered a traumatic brain injury, and was rendered amnesic. Like millions and millions of soldiers before him, he became a war casualty. The Vietnam electronic fence, conceived and constructed hastily during the war, created the opportunity to change all that. Technology could do what humans had been doing all along: patrol and notify. The fence required no human guard. It guarded itself. From ARPA's research and development standpoint, the concept of the electronic fence was a sea change. It set in motion a fundamental transformation of the battlefield. This change did not happen overnight. By 2015 it would be irreversible.

By the winter of 1973, almost no one in America wanted anything more to do with the Vietnam War. On January 27, the Paris Peace Accords were signed and U.S. troops began fully withdrawing from Vietnam. On February 12, hundreds of long-held American prisoners of war began coming home. And in keeping with the Mansfield Amendment, which required the Pentagon to research and develop programs only with a "specific military function," the word "defense" was added to ARPA's name. From now on it would be called the Defense Advanced Research Projects Agency, or DARPA.

If the agency was going to survive and prosper, it needed to reinvent itself, beginning with the way it was perceived. Any program associated with the Vietnam War would be jettisoned. Project Agile became the scapegoat, the punching bag. In internal agency interviews, three former ARPA directors, each of whom had overseen Project Agile during the Vietnam War, spoke of it in the most disparaging terms. "We tried to work the counterinsurgency business," lamented Eberhardt Rechtin, "and found we couldn't. All the things we tried—radar systems and boats and whatever"—didn't work. "Agile was an abysmal failure; a glorious failure," said Charles Herzfeld. "When we fail, we fail big." Even William Godel, now freed from federal prison for good behavior, spoke candidly about failure. "We never learned how to fight guerrilla warfare and we never really learned how to help the other guy," Godel said in a rare recorded interview, in July 1975. "We didn't do it; we left no residue of good will; and we didn't even explain it right." Still, Godel insisted that the problem of counterinsurgency was real, was multiplying, and was not going to go away anytime soon. "We did a goddamn lousy job of solving those problems, and that did happen on my watch," he said.

But for DARPA, Vietnam was far from a failure; it could not be spoken of in any one way. The enormous sums of money, the volumes of classified programs, the thousands of scientists and technicians, academics, analysts, defense contractors, and businessmen, all of whom worked for months, years, some more than a decade, to apply their scientific and industrial acumen to countless programs, some tiny, some grand, some with oversight, others without—the results of these efforts could by no means be generalized as success or failure any more than they could be categorized as good or bad. Granted, the results of the Viet Cong Motivation and Morale Project, with its thousands of hours of interviews of prisoners, peasants, and village elders—allegedly to determine what made the Vietcong tick—amounted to zero, that mysterious number one arrives at when everything gained equals everything lost. The Strategic Hamlet Program, the Rural Security System Program, the COIN games, the Motivation and Morale studies: it is easy to discount these as foolhardy, wasteful, colonialist. But not all the ARPA Vietnam programs could or would be viewed by DARPA as failures. Among the hardware that was born and developed in those remote jungle environs, there was much to admire from a Defense Department point of view.

Testifying before Congress in 1973, director Stephen Lukasik said that DARPA's goal was to refocus itself as a neutral, non–military service organization, emphasizing what he called "high-risk projects of revolutionary impact." Only innovative, groundbreaking programs would be taken on, he said, programs that should be viewed as "pre-mission assignments" or "pre-requirement" research. The agency needed to apply itself to its original mandate, which was to keep the nation from being embarrassed by another *Sputnik*-like surprise. At DARPA, the emphasis was on hard science and hardware.

Project Agile was abolished, and in its place came a new office called Tactical Technology. Inside this office, components of the electronic fence were salvaged from the ruins of the war. The program, with its obvious applications in the intelligence world, was highly classified. When asked about the sensor program in an agency review in 1975, acting director Dr. Peter Franken told colleagues that even he was not cleared to know about it. "It was most difficult to understand the program," Franken told the interviewer, attributing the inscrutable nature of sensor research to the fact that "special clearance requirements inhibited even his access to the sensor program." In keeping with the mandate to develop advanced technology and then turn it over to the military for implementation, sensor programs were now being pursued by all of the services and the majority of the intelligence agencies. All born of the Vietnam War.

DARPA's early work, going back to 1958, had fostered at least six sensor technologies. Seismic sensors, developed for the Vela program, sense and record how the earth transmits seismic waves. In Vietnam, the seismic sensors could detect heavy truck and troop movement on the Ho Chi Minh Trail, but not bicycles or feet. For lighter loads, strain sensors were now being further developed to monitor stress on soil, notably that which results from a person on the move. Magnetic sensors detect residual magnetism from objects carried or worn by a person; infrared sensors detect intrusion by beam interruption. Electromagnetic sensors generate a radio frequency that also detects intrusion when interrupted. Acoustic sensors listen for noise. These were all programs that were now set to take off anew.

In the early 1970s, the Marine Corps took a lead in sensor work. The success of the seismic sensors placed on the ground during the battle for Khe Sanh had altered the opinions of military commanders about the use of sensors on the battlefield. Before Khe Sanh, the majority opposed sensor technology; after the battle, it was almost unanimously embraced. Before war's end, the Marines had their own sensor program, Project STEAM, or Sensor Technology as Applied to the Marine Corps. STEAM made room for sensor platoons, called SCAMPs, or Sensor Control and Management Platoons. Within SCAMP divisions there were now Sensor Employment Squad Sensors, called SES, and Sensor Employment

Teams, called SETs. The Marines saw enormous potential in sensor technology, not just for guard and patrol, but for surveillance and intelligence collection. These programs would develop, and from the fruits of these programs, new programs would grow.

Two other technologies that would greatly impact the way the United States would fight future wars also emerged from the wreckage of Vietnam. Night vision technology expanded into a broad multi-tiered program as each of the services found great strategic value in being able to see at night while the enemy remained in the dark. So did stealth technology, a radical innovation originally developed by the CIA for reconnaissance purposes, starting in 1957, when the agency first tried to lower the radar cross-section of the U-2 spy plane. ARPA's original work in audio stealth began in 1961 with William Godel's sailplane idea, one of the four original Project Agile gadgets, along with the AR-15, the riverboat, and the sniffer dogs. During the course of the Vietnam War, Project Agile's sailplane had developed successfully into the Lockheed QT-2 "quiet airplane," a single-engine propeller plane that flew just above the jungle canopy and was acoustically undetectable from the ground. Dedicated to surveillance and packed with sensor technology, the QT-2 would glide silently over Vietcong territory with its engine off. In 1968 ARPA turned the program over to the Army, which made modifications to the aircraft, now called the Lockheed YO-3 Quiet Star. After the war, DARPA sought to expand its stealth program from acoustically undetectable sailplanes to aircraft that were undetectable even by the most sophisticated enemy radar. In 1974 DARPA's Tactical Technology Office began work on a highly classified program to build "high-stealth aircraft." The following year, DARPA issued contracts to McDonnell Douglas and Northrop, considered by DARPA to be the two defense contractors most qualified for the stealth job.

There was a fascinating twist. By the mid-1970s, Lockheed had already achieved major milestones in stealth technology, having developed the highly classified A-12 Oxcart spy plane for the CIA. (The A-12 later became the unclassified SR-71 reconnaissance aircraft, flown by the Air Force.) Knowledge of the CIA's classified stealth program was so tightly controlled that even DARPA director George Heilmeier did not have a need to know about it. In 1974, when management at Lockheed Skunk Works learned of DARPA's "high-stealth aircraft" efforts—and that they had not been invited to participate—they asked the CIA to allow them to discuss the A-12 Oxcart with Heilmeier. After the discussion, Lockheed was invited to join the competition and eventually won the DARPA stealth contract.

The first on-paper incarnation of what would become the F-117 stealth fighter was called the Hopeless Diamond, so named because it resembled the Hope Diamond and because Lockheed engineers were not initially certain it would fly. "We designed flat, faceted panels and had them act like mirrors to scatter radar waves away from the plane," remembers Edward Lovick, who worked as a lead physicist on the program. After the Hopeless Diamond went through a number of drafts, the project became a classified DARPA program code-named Have Blue. Two aircraft were built at the Lockheed Skunk Works facility in Burbank, California, and test flown at Area 51 in Nevada in April 1977. Satisfied with the low observability of the aircraft, the U.S. Air Force took over the program in 1978. Stealth technology was a massive classified endeavor involving more than ten thousand military and civilian personnel. The power of this secret weapon rested in keeping it secret. To do so, the Air Force set up its own top secret facility to fly the F-117, just north of Area 51 outside Tonopah, Nevada. The base was nicknamed Area 52.

The 1970s were a formative time at DARPA from a historical perspective. Away from the Pentagon, DARPA came into its own. Congress remained averse to ARPA's former herd of social science programs, which it criticized in post-Vietnam oversight committees as having been egregiously wasteful, foolhardy, and without oversight. Any mention of the phrase "hearts and minds" in the Pentagon made people wince. To avoid the "red flag" reaction from Congress, ARPA programs that touched on behavioral sciences were renamed or rebranded.

ARPA's social science office (which actually existed during the Vietnam War) was called Human Resources Research Office, or HumRRO. But in the post-Vietnam era, HumRRO programs focused on improving human performance from a physiological and psychological standpoint. Two significant ideas emerged. The first was to research the psychological mechanisms of pain as related to military injuries on the battlefield. ARPA scientists sought to understand whether soldiers could suppress pain in combat, and if so, how. The second major project was a research program on "self-regulation" of bodily functions previously believed to be involuntary. The general, forward-thinking question was, how could a soldier maintain peak performance under the radically challenging conditions of warfare?

It was a transformative time at DARPA. The agency already had shifted from the 1950s space and ballistic missile defense agency to the 1960s agency responsible for some of the most controversial programs of the Vietnam War. And now, a number of events occurred that eased the agency's transition as it began to change course again. Under the direction of the physicist Stephen Lukasik, in the mid-1970s the agency would take a new turn—a new "thrust," as Lukasik grew fond of saying. In this mid-1970s period of acceleration and innovation, DARPA would plant certain seeds that would allow it to grow into one of the most powerful and most respected agencies inside the Department of Defense.

"The key to command and control is, in fact, communication," said Stephen Lukasik shortly after he took over the agency. Command and control, or C2, had now expanded into command, control, and communication, or C3, and this concept became the new centerpiece of the DARPA mission under Lukasik. The advancement of command, control, and communication technology relied heavily on computers. Since 1965 the power of microchips, then called integrated electronic circuits, had been doubling every year, a concept that a computer engineer named Gordon E. Moore picked up on and wrote about in *Electronics* magazine. In "Cramming More Components into Integrated Circuits," Moore predicted that this doubling trend would continue for the next ten years, a prescient notion that has since become known as Moore's law. Doubling is a powerful concept: 10 x 10 = 100; 100 x 100 = 10,000; 10,000 x 10,000 = 100 million. In 2014, Apple put 2 billion transistors into its iPhone 6.

In 1974, DARPA's supercomputer, ILLIAC IV, now up and running at the Ames Research Center in California, was the fastest computer in the world. Its parallel processing power allowed for the development of technologies like real-time video processing, noise reduction, image enhancement, and data compression—all technologies taken for granted in the twenty-first century but with origins in DARPA science. And Lukasik's C3 program also relied heavily on another emerging DARPA technology, the ARPANET.

It had been more than a decade since J. C. R. Licklider sent out his eccentric memo proposing the Pentagon create a linked computer network, which he called the "Intergalactic Computer Network." Licklider left the Pentagon in 1965 but hired two visionaries to take over the Command and Control (C2) Research office, since renamed the Information Processing Techniques Office. Ivan Sutherland, a computer graphics expert who had worked with Daniel Slotnick on ILLIAC IV, and Robert W. Taylor, an experimental psychologist, believed that computers would revolutionize the world and that a network of computers was the key to this revolution. Through networking, not only would individual computer users have access to other users' data, but also they would be able to communicate with one another in a radical new way. Licklider and Taylor co-wrote an essay in 1968 in which they predicted, "In a few years, men will be able to communicate more effectively through a machine than face to face." By 2009, more electronic text messages would be sent each day than there were people on the planet.

Sutherland and Taylor began asking DARPA contractors at various university research laboratories around the country what they thought about the networked computer idea. The feedback was unanimous in favor of it. In general, scientists and engineers were frustrated by how little access to computers they had. This got Sutherland and Taylor thinking. Why not try linking several of these university computers together so the DARPA contractors could share resources? To do so would require building a system of electronic links between different computers, located hundreds of miles apart. It was a radical undertaking, but Sutherland and Taylor believed it could be done.

Bob Taylor went to DARPA director Charles Herzfeld to request enough money to fund a networked connection linking four different university computers, or nodes. Herzfeld told Taylor he thought it sounded like a good idea but he was concerned about reliability. If all four computers were linked together, Herzfeld said, when there was a problem, it meant all four computers would be down at the same time. Thinking on his feet, Taylor said he intended to build a concept into the system called network redundancy. If one connection went down, the messages traveling between the computers would simply take another path. Herzfeld asked how much money Taylor thought be needed. Taylor said a million dollars.

Herzfeld asked, "Is it going to be hard to do?"

"Oh, no. We already know how to do it," Taylor said, when really he was guessing.

"Great idea," said Herzfeld. "You've got a million dollars more in your budget right now." Then he told Taylor to get to work.

Taylor left Herzfeld's office and headed back to his own. He later recalled the astonishment he felt when he looked at his watch. "Jesus Christ," he thought. "That only took twenty minutes." Even more consequential was the idea of network redundancy—making sure no single computer could take the system down—that emerged from that meeting. It is why in 2015, no one organization, corporation, or nation can own or completely control the global system of interconnected computer networks known as the Internet. To think it came out of that one meeting, on the fly.

The first four university sites chosen were Stanford Research Institute in northern California; the University of California, Los Angeles; the University of California, Santa Barbara; and the University of Utah in Salt Lake City. In 1969, ARPA contractor Bolt, Beranek and Newman became the first east coast node. By 1972 there were twenty-four nodes, including the Pentagon. The person largely responsible for connecting these nodes was an electrical engineer named Robert Kahn. At the time, Kahn called what he was working on an "internetwork." Soon it would be shortened to Internet.

This network of ARPA nodes was growing, and Kahn wanted to devise a common language, or protocol, so that all new nodes could communicate with the existing nodes in the same language. To do this, Kahn teamed up with another DARPA program manager named Vint Cerf, and together the men invented the concept of Transmission Control Protocol (TCP) and Internet Protocol (IP), which would allow new nodes seamless access to the ARPANET. Today, TCP/IP remains the core communications protocol of the Internet. By 1973 there were thirty-six ARPANET nodes connected via telephone lines, and a thirty-seventh, in Hawaii, connected by a satellite link. That same year the Norwegian Seismic Array became connected to the ARPANET, and J. C. R.

Licklider's vision for an "Intergalactic Computer Network" became an international reality.

In 1975 DARPA transferred its ARPANET system over to the Defense Communications Agency, and in 1982 standards for sending and receiving email were put in place. In 1983 the Pentagon split off a military-only network, called MILNET. Today the ARPANET is often referred to as "the most successful project ever undertaken by DARPA."

Between the advances in computer technology, networking power, and the ARPANET, DARPA was primed for the development of an entirely new C3-based weapons system. Sometime in 1974, DARPA commissioned several classified studies on how the Pentagon could best prepare itself for a Soviet invasion of western Europe. The strategist leading one analysis was the former RAND mathematician Albert Wohlstetter, author of the nuclear second-strike doctrine, or NUTS. Wohlstetter, now a professor at the University of Chicago, sought "to identify and characterize" new military technologies that would give the president a variety of "alternatives to massive nuclear destruction." Wohlstetter assembled a study group, called the Strategic Alternatives Group, to assist him in his analytic efforts. In February 1975 the group completed the generically titled "Summary Report of the Long Range Research and Development Planning Program."

In the report, Wohlstetter concluded that several Vietnam-era DARPA projects merited renewed attention. Topping the list was the effectiveness of laser-guided bombs and missiles. In the last year of the Vietnam War, the U.S. Air Force sent 10,500 laser-guided bombs into North Vietnam. Roughly one-half of these bombs, 5,100 in total, achieved a "direct hit," with another 4,000 achieving "a circular error probable (CEP) of 25 feet." Compared to the success rate of unguided "dumb" bombs of previous wars, including World War II, Korea, and most of Vietnam, these statistics were to be interpreted as "spectacularly good," wrote Wohlstetter. The best example was the bombing of the Thanh Hoa Bridge, a 540-foot steel span across the Song Ma River, roughly seventy miles south of Hanoi. The bridge was an important supply route for the North Vietnamese during the war, and they kept it defended with garrison-like strength. The bridge was surrounded by a ring of three hundred antiaircraft systems and eighty-five surface-to-air missile systems. A wing of Soviet-supplied MiG fighter jets was stationed nearby. For years in the late 1960s, the Air Force and the Navy tried to destroy the bridge but could not. By 1968, eleven U.S. aircraft had been shot down trying to bomb the bridge. Then, in May 1972, after a four-and-a-half-year bombing halt, fourteen F-4 fighter bombers equipped with newly developed laser-guided bombs were sent on a mission to bomb the bridge. With several direct hits, the bridge was destroyed. "It appears that non-nuclear weapons with near-zero miss may be feasibly and militarily effective," Wohlstetter wrote in praise of these new "smart" weapons.

Also of interest to Wohlstetter were DARPA's early efforts with mini-drones, which had played a major role in advancing laser-guided weapons technology—a fact largely underreported in military history books. DARPA's Vietnam drone program had grown out of DDR&E John Foster's love of model airplanes and remote control. Two of the mini-drones, called Praerie and Calere, caught Wohlstetter's eye. Praerie and Calere were exceptionally small at the time, each weighing seventy-five pounds, including a twenty-eight-pound payload that could be a camera, a small bomb, or an "electronic warfare payload." Each was powered by a lawn-mower engine and could fly for up to two hours. Praerie carried a TV camera and used laser target technology. It was the first drone to direct a cannon-launched guided projectile to a direct hit on a tank, a milestone achieved at Fort Huachuca, Arizona, during an undated field test. The Calere drone was equally groundbreaking. It carried forward-looking infrared, or FLIR, another Vietnam-era invention, which allowed the drone to "see" at low altitudes in the dark of night.

DARPA also developed another, much larger, "more complicated" drone that interested Wohlstetter, as revealed in an obscure 1974 internal DARPA review. Nite Panther and Nite Gazelle were helicopter drones, "equipped with a real time day-night battlefield reconnaissance capability including armor plate and self-sealing, extended-range fuel tanks." The drone helicopters were deployed into the battlefield, starting in March 1968, in response to an urgent operational request from the Marine Corps. To create the Nite Panther drone, DARPA modified a Navy QH-50 DASH antisubmarine helicopter—originally designed to fire torpedoes at submerged submarines—and added a remotely controlled television system, called a "reconnaissance-observation system," which could transmit real-time visuals back to a moving jeep, acting as a ground station. The jeep was loaded with racks of telemetry and television equipment, antennae, and a power supply. The drone operator sitting in the jeep was able to operate and monitor the drone helicopter from takeoff to touchdown. Images captured by the drone, flying over enemy territory, were recorded by the equipment on the jeep, then relayed back to a shipboard control station, where commanders could send high-performance strike aircraft to bomb targets identified by the drone. This was groundbreaking technology during the war. In 1974 Wohlstetter recognized its future potential. Conceivably, as computers got smaller and were able to process data faster, a drone could be sent deep behind enemy lines to photograph targets and send the images to commanders in real time.

Another significant DARPA technology that allowed these Vietnam-era systems to converge was a satellite-based navigation technology called Global Positioning Systems, or GPS. GPS began as a classified military program, the purpose of which was to direct weapons to precise targets. DARPA's pioneering GPS program was called TRANSIT. It began in 1959, when ARPA contracted with the Johns Hopkins Applied Physics Laboratory to create the first satellite positioning system, using six satellites, three for positioning and three as spares.

After several failed launches, TRANSIT finally took up residence in space in June 1963. To deny enemy access to this kind of precise targeting information, the system was originally designed with an offset feature built in, called selective availability (SA). If an individual were able to access the GPS system with a private receiver, the information would be offset by several hundred feet.

Over the next ten years, the Navy and the Air Force developed their own satellite-based navigational systems, but each system was incompatible with the other. In 1973 the Pentagon ordered DARPA to create a single system shared by all the military services, and a new DARPA program called NAVSTAR Global Positioning System emerged. It was a herculean effort filled with technical stumbling blocks and failed rocket launches. Finally, starting in 1989 a constellation of twenty-four satellites, each fitted with atomic clocks to keep them in sync, was sent aloft and began orbiting the earth. The U.S. military now had precise navigational coverage of the entire world, in all weather conditions, in real time.

During the 1990s, interest in satellite-based global positioning technology grew, and European companies began developing GPS-like systems for civilian use. In an effort to keep the United States at the forefront of the burgeoning new industry, in May 2000 President Clinton discontinued the selective availability feature on GPS, giving billions of people access to precise GPS technology, developed by DARPA.

To Albert Wohlstetter, working on the DARPA analysis in the mid-1970s, the fusion of various Vietnam-era technology systems—sensors, computers, laser-guided weapons, the ARPANET, drones—offered great promise and potential in the development of what he called a "system of systems." The following year, on the basis of suggestions made in the "Summary Report of the Long Range Research and Development Planning Program," DARPA initiated a new weapons program called Assault Breaker. A series of once disparate technologies could come together to fulfill Lukasik's vision to "command, control, and communicate." Using technologies that also included radar tracking and camera confirmation, Assault Breaker would one day allow commanders to precisely strike targets—even moving targets—deep behind enemy lines. Imagining a system in which this kind of weaponry and technology could work together was unprecedented. All of it had emerged from the Vietnam War.

In the 1970s, the Soviets were notorious for maintaining a network of spies in and around Washington, D.C., and it did not take long for the Russians to learn about DARPA's classified Assault Breaker plans. When they did, the Soviet military brass began studying the concept and planning countermeasures. In 1978 an article about Assault Breaker appeared in the classified Soviet military journal *Military Thought.* That the Soviets knew about DARPA's "system of systems" might have gone unnoticed had it not been for the sharp eyes of Andrew W. Marshall, a former RAND analyst and Wohlstetter protégé who now had his own office inside the Pentagon. Marshall served as director of the Office of Net Assessment, created by the Nixon White House in 1973 and dedicated to forecasting future wars. At RAND, Marshall had secured his reputation as a master game theorist, and at the Pentagon, his wizardry in prognosis and prediction earned him the nom de guerre Yoda, or the Jedi Master. It also put him in regular contact with DARPA directors and program managers, as he continued to be for over forty years.

Part of Andrew Marshall's job in the 1970s was to monitor what Soviet generals were writing in their classified journals. In reading *Military Thought,* Marshall learned that the Soviets felt so threatened by the prospects of an Assault Breaker–like system of systems that they were running exercises to practice countermeasures against one. Soviet fears of DARPA's Assault Breaker concept did not stop there but made their way to the top of the Soviet military chain of command. In 1984 Marshall Nikolai Ogarkov, chief of the general staff of the armed forces of the Soviet Union, worried in a classified memo that Assault Breaker gave the Americans the ability to conduct "automated reconnaissance-and-strike complexes," a capability that must be regarded as a "military-technical revolution." Marshall renamed the Russian pronouncement a "revolution in military affairs," which had since become a celebrated Pentagon maxim. The saying defines what happens when one country or fighting force creates a technology or tactic that makes everything else subordinate to it and makes many of the other side's earlier weapons systems obsolete.

Just a decade before, in the wake of the Vietnam War and with his agency's budget slashed, Stephen Lukasik had appealed to Congress to allow DARPA to pursue "high-risk projects of revolutionary impact." Lukasik told Congress that in the modern world, the country with the most powerful weapons would not necessarily have the leading edge. He argued that as the twenty-first century approached, the leading edge would belong to the country with the best information—with which it could quickly plan, coordinate, and attack. Eleven years later, his vision proved correct. The Soviets felt deeply threatened by DARPA's C3-based revolution in military affairs.

Technology continued to advance at a radical new pace. In 1977 Harold Brown became President Carter's secretary of defense, making Brown the first nuclear scientist to lead the Department of Defense. Brown believed that technological superiority was imperative to military dominance, and he also believed that advancing science was the key to economic prosperity. "Harold Brown turned technology leadership into a national strategy," remarks DARPA historian Richard Van Atta. Despite rising inflation and unemployment, DARPA's budget was doubled. Microprocessing technologies were making stunning advances. High-speed communication networks and Global Positioning System technologies were accelerating at whirlwind speeds. DARPA's highly classified, high-risk, high-payoff programs, including stealth, advanced sensors, laser-guided munitions, and drones, were being pursued, in the black. Soon, Assault Breaker technology would be battle ready. From all of this work, entire new industries were forming.

In the fall of 1978, Captain (later Colonel) Jack A. Thorpe, a thirty-four-year-old Air Force officer with a Ph.D. in psychology, was sitting inside a flight simulator at the Flying Training Division of Williams Air Force Base in Arizona when he got a radical idea. The flight simulator here at the Human Resources Laboratory was one of two of the most advanced simulators in the country—and the most expensive, having cost more than $25 million to build, roughly $100 million in 2015. The computer-driven simulator was mounted on a hydraulic motion system that moved like a carnival ride. The simulator Captain Thorpe was sitting inside was connected to a second computer, which made the pair state of the art and one of a kind.

"The other flyer's aircraft appeared in the corner of my screen like a small cartoonish icon," Thorpe remembers. "What this meant in 1978 was that this flight simulator was the only one in America where two pilots could engage in flight training research operations together, at the same time."

Thorpe was struck with an idea. What if an Air Force pilot could sit inside a small room like the one he was sitting in now, but instead of looking at cartoonish icons moving across a computer screen, he saw the world in front of him in three dimensions? What if it felt like he was actually inside the airplane, with his wingman flying alongside? Jack Thorpe had a name for what he imagined. It was a "high-fidelity simulator," a virtual world.

Back at Bolling Air Force Base in Washington, D.C., where he was stationed, Thorpe put his thoughts down on paper. In "Future Views: Aircrew Training, 1980–2000," Thorpe described a flight-training situation in which a whole squadron of pilots could prepare for combat readiness together, training on individual but networked flight simulators. Each airman would be flying a separate aircraft but in the same battle space. In this virtual reality, pilots would be in visual contact with one another and in audio contact with a commander, who would work from a remote information center, imagined as a real place, which Thorpe called a Tactical Development Center. Thorpe's Tactical Development Center would have "a three dimensional, holographic, electronic sand table," he wrote, "a place where tacticians and strategists could see what the pilots in their simulators were doing." In this computer-generated environment, a commander would be able to "see" what was happening in the battle space, in real time, thanks to an overhead satellite source delivering data. In this new virtual world, pilots would train and their commanders would strategize.

These simulators would allow for "real-time dress rehearsals," Thorpe wrote, teaching pilots how to train in groups, with the immediacy of real battle situations but without the lethal consequences. On the basis of the outcomes of various simulations, commanders could quickly decide what course of action each pilot should take. Without having access to any information about DARPA programs, and certainly not being privy to newly formulated classified details of the Assault Breaker program, Thorpe had envisioned almost the same thing that Wohlstetter saw. Only Thorpe's high-fidelity simulator was a training tool for war, played in a virtual world, and Assault Breaker was a billion-dollar weapons system to be developed and deployed in a real war.

Thorpe was invited to present his thoughts to a group of senior officials. "They were all command pilots, each with thousands of hours of flight time," Thorpe recalls. "Here I am, this clown with no wings, proposing to take away flight training time from air officers. I did not articulate myself very well. I got my lunch handed to me." The senior officials chuckled at his idea.

Thorpe figured he was missing a key piece of this puzzle he was designing, but he just did not know what it was yet. "There is nothing like getting yelled at to make you think harder, to really reflect," Thorpe says. "I figured out you can't take away flight training time. The simulator would be a better place to practice certain combat skills that can never be practiced except in battle," he says. "For example, you could practice with equipment like jammers, which you would never turn on in peacetime, [which] an opponent could [potentially] see. As soon as I had the 'ah-hah' moment, that the real value of the simulator was to teach and practice skills you could not practice until the first day of real combat, that's when the way to design the simulator became clear to me."

Thorpe ran the idea by a few senior officers, but it was just too difficult a concept for most people to visualize. Then, "by happenstance," says Thorpe, "I was offered the services of a graphic artist in the Pentagon, and he illustrated the key components of the proposed concept." Thorpe's paper, which now included elegant drawings, was reviewed by senior Pentagon staff. "Everyone said, 'Hey, that's cool,'" Thorpe recalls. "But they also said, 'The fact is, the technology isn't there yet.'" Most colleagues who looked at Thorpe's drawings said to him, "We don't even know how to start building something like that yet."

One of the greatest stumbling blocks to Thorpe's vision in 1978 was how these simulators could possibly be connected to one another. "The idea of networks connecting distant military installations was not yet imagined," says Thorpe. "The ARPANET experiments connecting a small number of computers between different universities were under way, but the results were not well known." Mostly they were still classified. With his vision for the future seeming more science fiction than science, Thorpe's paper was shelved.

Thorpe went back to school, to the Naval War College in Newport, Rhode Island, and in January 1981 he was assigned to DARPA, on loan from the Air Force. He was made a program manager in the Systems Science Division, next door to the Information Processing Technology Office that was being run by Bob Kahn, the man who, together with Vint Cerf, had invented the Transmission Control Protocol/Internet Protocol (TCP/IP). Thorpe recalls what an exciting time it was at DARPA, "the center of the universe for gadgets." DARPA was located at 1400 Wilson Boulevard in Arlington, Virginia, and the Systems Science Division had its own demonstration facility across the street, "a place to try out all the new gadgets, take them apart, put them back together again, or maybe integrate one with another system." Thorpe remembers one such example when one of the world's first compact disc players arrived in America, at DARPA, in 1981 or 1982. It had been sent from a small electronics company in Japan. "There were only a few CDs in the world at the time," Thorpe recalls, "and they had music on them. Our director wasn't interested in listening to music, but we were interested in thinking about using the technology for data storage." The CD player was the size of a suitcase.

In the DARPA building, down the hallway from Thorpe's office, was the Cybernetics Technology Office, where DARPA's artificial intelligence work was under way. One day Thorpe's boss, Craig Fields, the former program director of cybernetics technology, asked Thorpe if he had any bright ideas.

"I pulled out the old high-fidelity simulator drawings," recalls Thorpe. "Fields, a brilliant guy, and later the director of DARPA, says, 'I like that.' He suggested we go talk to the director, Larry Lynn." Thorpe explained his idea to Lynn, who said he liked it, too.

"How much to build this synthetic world?" Thorpe recalls Lynn asking.

"Seventeen million," Thorpe told him.

"Let's do it," Larry Lynn said.

"So we went ahead and started the program," says Thorpe.

Captain Jack Thorpe's paper was now a DARPA program called Simulator Networking, or SIMNET. Broadly speaking, the goal of SIMNET was to add a new element to command and control (C2), namely training. C2 would eventually become C2U, "with a 'U' for university," says Thorpe.

In April 1983, SIMNET was just another DARPA program. Nothing like it had ever been attempted before, and like other blue-sky science endeavors at DARPA, SIMNET was given room to succeed or to fail. "DARPA, unlike most agencies, is allowed to fail some fraction of the time," says Joe Mangano, a former DARPA program manager.

"In the early 1980s, most people in the defense community accepted the notion that building an affordable, large-scale, free-play, force-on-force worldwide networked war-fighting system was impossible," retired colonel Neale Cosby recalled in 2014. Cosby served as a SIMNET principal investigator for DARPA for five years. But SIMNET would astonish everybody, not only for its military application but for the multibillion-dollar industry it would help create. "William Gibson didn't invent cyberspace," *Wired* magazine reported in 1997, referring to the science fiction author who coined the term in 1982, "Air Force captain Jack Thorpe did." SIMNET was the first realization of cyberspace, and it was the world's first massively multiplayer online role-playing game, or MMORPG—more commonly known as an MMO.

MMOs first became popular in the gaming community in the late 1990s, and by 2003 they had entered the mainstream. MMOs are now able to support enormous numbers of game players simultaneously, with each individual gamer connected to the game by the Internet. One of the most popular MMOs is *World of Warcraft,* which sold more than $2.5 billion worth of subscriptions in its first ten years. Each month, some 10 million monthly *World of Warcraft* subscribers explore fantastic virtual landscapes, fight monsters, and complete quests using an avatar.

MMO users became so great in number that in 2008, the CIA, the NSA, and DARPA launched a covert data-mining effort, called Project Reynard, to track *World of Warcraft* subscribers and discern how they exist and interact in virtual worlds. To do so, CIA analysts created their own avatars and entered the virtual world of *World of Warcraft.* That the CIA was spying on MMO users was classified and remained unknown until 2013, when former National Security Agency contractor Edward J. Snowden disclosed top secret documents detailing the program, which also involved British intelligence agencies. "Although online gaming may seem like an innocuous form of entertainment, when the basic features and capabilities are examined, it could potentially become a target-rich communication network," reads one top secret report, "WoW [*World of Warcraft*] may be providing SIGINT [signals intelligence] targets a way to hide in plain sight."

But back in 1983, SIMNET was just getting started. MMOs were far in the future and still a figment of the imagination. SIMNET was about training warfighters for battle. And Jack Thorpe had more than a decade of work ahead of him.

CHAPTER FIFTEEN

Star Wars and Tank Wars

On the evening of March 23, 1983, a long black limousine pulled up to the south gate of Ronald Reagan's White House. In the back sat Edward Teller, now seventy-five years old. Teller was not exactly sure why he was here. He had just flown in from California, where he lived, because the aide who called him three days earlier said President Reagan thought it was important that he be at the White House on this night.

Walking with a limp and a cane, Teller made his way through the White House foyer, up the stairs, and into the Blue Room. There he was greeted by Admiral John Poindexter, the Military Assistant to the President for National Security Affairs. Poindexter suggested Teller have a seat. Thirty-six chairs had been set up in neat rows. Teller sat down and waited. In another seat was the Jason scientist and Nobel laureate Charles H. Townes, the principal inventor of the laser.

At 8:00 p.m., in a nationally televised address, President Reagan announced to the world his decision to launch a major new research and development program to intercept Soviet ICBMs in various stages of flight. The program, the Strategic Defense Initiative (SDI), would require numerous advanced technology systems, the majority of which were still in the development stage. DARPA would be the lead agency in charge until SDI had its own organization.

President Reagan said that the reason for this radical new initiative was simple. When he first became president, he was shocked to learn that in the event of a Soviet nuclear strike, his only option as commander in chief was to launch an all-out nuclear attack against the Soviets in response. Reagan said he was not willing to live in the shadow of nuclear Armageddon—mutual assured destruction. The United States needed the capability to strike down incoming Soviet missiles before they arrived. This bold new SDI program would allow for that.

For decades, defense scientists like the Jason scientists had been grappling with this conundrum of ballistic missile defense and had concluded that there was no way to defend against an onslaught of incoming ICBMs. Now, Reagan believed that technology had advanced to the point where this could be done sometime in the not-so-distant future.

The Strategic Defense Initiative involved huge mirrors in space, space-based surveillance and tracking systems, space-based battle stations, and more. But the element that got the most attention right away was the x-ray laser, which scientists at the Lawrence Livermore National Laboratory had been working on since the 1970s. Very few people outside the Livermore group understood the science behind an x-ray laser, and even fewer knew that x-ray lasers were powered by nuclear explosions.

Several days after Reagan's speech, Secretary of Defense Caspar Weinberger was leaving the Pentagon to brief Congress on SDI. Walking alongside him was Undersecretary Richard D. DeLauer, a ballistic missile expert. Secretary Weinberger was having trouble grasping the science behind SDI and DeLauer was trying to explain it to him.

"But is it a bomb?" Secretary Weinberger asked.

DeLauer was candid. As the former executive vice president of the missile company TRW, Inc., and with a Ph.D. in aeronautical engineering, DeLauer understood the science behind the x-ray laser. "You're going to have to detonate a nuclear bomb in space," he told the secretary of defense. "That's how you're going to get the x-ray."

This put Secretary Weinberger in an untenable position. President Reagan had assured the public that his new program would not involve nuclear weapons in space. "It's not a bomb, is it?" Weinberger asked a second time.

DeLauer chose his words carefully. He said that the x-ray laser didn't have to be called a bomb. It could be described as involving a "nuclear event."

In a 1985 interview for the *Los Angeles Times,* DeLauer relayed this story verbatim. He said that the secretary of defense "didn't understand the technology," adding, "Most people don't."

The laser was invented in the late 1950s by Charles Townes, who in 1964 was awarded the Nobel Prize in physics. In the most basic sense a laser is a device that emits light. But unlike with other light sources, such as a lightbulb, which emits light that dissipates, in a laser the photons all move in the same direction in lockstep, exactly parallel to one another, with no deviation. To many, the laser is something straight out of science fiction. In a 2014 interview for this book, Charles Townes, then age ninety-eight, confirmed that he had been inspired to create the laser after reading Alexei Tolstoi's 1926 science-fiction novel *The Garin Death Ray.* "This idea of a flashing death ray also has a mystique that catches human attention," said Townes, "and so we have Jove's bolts of lightning and the death rays of science fiction." A half century after

Tolstoi wrote about the Garin death ray, George Lucas modernized the concept with Luke Skywalker's light saber in the science-fiction film *Star Wars*.

One of the first sets of experiments involving lasers, mirrors, and space took place in 1969 and has been largely lost to the history books. The experiment began on July 21 of that year, said Townes, when, for the first time in history, two men walked on the moon. While on the lunar surface, "astronauts Neil Armstrong and Edwin [Buzz] Aldrin set up an array of small reflectors on the moon and faced them toward the Earth." Back here on earth—which is 240,000 miles from the moon—two teams of astrophysicists, one team working at the University of California's Lick Observatory, on Mount Hamilton, and the other at the University of Texas's McDonald Observatory, on Mount Locke, took careful notes regarding where, exactly, the astronauts were when they set down the mirrors. "About ten days later, the Lick team pointed the telescope at that precise location and sent a small pulse of power into the tiny piece of hardware they had added to the telescope," said Townes. Inside the telescope, a beam of "extraordinarily pure red light" emerged from a crystal of synthetic ruby, pierced the sky, and entered the near vacuum of space. A laser beam.

Traveling at the speed of light, 186,000 miles per second, the laser beam took less than two seconds to hit the mirrors left behind on the moon by Armstrong and Aldrin, and then the same amount of time to travel back to earth, where the Lick team "detected the faint reflection of its beam," explained Townes. The experiment delivered volumes of scientific data, but one set was truly phenomenal. "The interval between launch of the pulse of light and its return permitted calculation of the distance to the moon within an inch, a measurement of unprecedented precision," said Townes. The laser beam was able to measure what stargazers and astronomers have wondered since time immemorial: Exactly how far away from earth is the moon?

While the astrophysicists were using laser technology for peaceful purposes, the Defense Department was already looking at using lasers as directed-energy weapons (DEW). In 1968 ARPA had established a classified laser program called Eighth Card, which remains classified today, as do many other laser programs, the names of which are also classified. Directed-energy weapons have many advantages, none so great as speed. Traveling at the speed of light means a DEW could hit a target on the moon in less than two seconds.

After hearing Reagan's historic announcement from a front-row seat in the White House Blue Room, Edward Teller and Charles Townes had decidedly different reactions. Teller embraced the idea and would become a leading scientist on the Strategic Defense Initiative and the follow-up program, called Brilliant Pebbles. Charles Townes did not believe Reagan's SDI concept could work.

"For a president who doesn't know the technology one can see why [it] might be appealing," said Townes. "It doesn't really seem very attractive to me, or doable. But you can see how from a matter of principle it sounded good to Reagan. It's like an imaginary story of what might be done."

The day after the speech, Senator Edward Kennedy criticized the president's initiative, calling it a "reckless 'Star Wars' scheme." The name stuck. From then on, the president's program became known around the world as "Star Wars." Science fiction and science had crossed paths once again. For the general population, real-world lasers, death rays, and directed-energy weapons were scientifically impossible to grasp. Science fiction was not so hard.

Congress worried that SDI was not technically feasible and that it was politically irresponsible. That even if the technology were successful, it could trigger a dangerous new arms race with the Soviets. But after debating the issue, Congress gave the Reagan White House the go-ahead for the Strategic Defense Initiative, and over the next ten years, nearly $20 billion was spent. It is often said that the Clinton administration canceled the SDI program, when in fact it canceled only certain elements of the Strategic Defense Initiative. SDI never really went away. In 2012 the *Fiscal Times* reported that more than $100 billion had been spent on SDI technologies in the three decades since Reagan first proposed the idea, $80 billion of which had been spent in the past decade.

Space remains a domain where domination has long been sought but where all-out war has never been fought. For scientists and engineers working on DARPA's SIMNET program, the focus would remain on land. There had been steady progress with the SIMNET program in the year since director Larry Lynn gave it the go-ahead, including the fact that the Army was now involved. Which is how, in the spring of 1984, Jack Thorpe, now a major, found himself maneuvering a sixty-ton M1 Abrams tank up over a muddy hill deep in the pine-forested back lot of the legendary armor school at Fort Knox, Kentucky.

"When we started SIMNET, the threat was on Soviet armor warfare," says Thorpe, "meaning tanks." This meant that simulating tank warfare was SIMNET's first priority. The desired goal was to create a virtual reality that felt real. So Thorpe and the DARPA team were at Fort Knox, driving through the mud, attempting to "capture the sense of tankness," says Thorpe. DARPA had big plans for SIMNET, with a goal of building four SIMNET centers to house a total of 360 simulators, roughly 90 per site. At the time, Thorpe and the DARPA team were working on the first two simulators, which would be models of M1 Abrams tanks.

Because there would be no motion in these simulators, the emphasis was placed on sound. Science Applications International Corporation (SAIC) of La Jolla was in charge of working with field units at instrumented training ranges and collecting data. The defense contractor Perceptronics Corporation of California was hired to design the fiberglass and plywood simulators and wire them for sound. "For someone on the outside, the sound of the hundred-and-five-millimeter tank gun firing at a target downrange is incredibly loud, but for a person inside the tank the experience is totally different," says Thorpe. Because of the overpressure, there is almost no noise. "It's incredibly *quiet.*" What there is inside is movement, which, Thorpe says, "is a totally different kind of sound." The audio specialists with Perceptronics replicated the sound inside the tank by simulating the loose parts that vibrate when the gun fires. "Coins in the glove box," recalls Thorpe, "loose bolts, anything that's not tied down." Back in the laboratory, to convey that rattling sound, audio engineers filled a metal pie plate with nuts and bolts, then glued the pie plate to the top of a subwoofer which they hid behind the fiberglass in the tank simulator. Then Bolt, Beranek and Newman of Boston, which had been a principal contractor on ARPANET, developed the networking and graphics technology for the simulators.

The 1986 annual armor conference at Fort Knox was a milestone in SIMNET history, the first test run of two DARPA SIMNET simulators. General Frederic "Rick" Brown and another general would test the systems, and there was a lot resting on what they thought of a simulated war game. Thorpe recalls the first two simulators as being "about eighty percent [complete], made of fiberglass and plywood, with one hand control to control the turret." The two SIMNET tank simulators had been set up roughly twenty feet apart. The generals took their seats and the DARPA team piled inside.

"Neither general had any experience in the virtual world," says Thorpe. "Here's General Brown looking at a screen in front of him with an icon of the other tank. I say, 'There in that tank, that is the [opposing] general.' He doesn't get it. So I say, 'Turn the turret and point it toward the other tank.' The turret turns. General Brown got a little giddy. He gets it, I think," Thorpe recalls. "I tell him to load a sabot [round]. 'Sir,' I say, 'if you trigger here, you can shoot the general.'"

General Brown fired the virtual weapon. On the screen, General Brown watched the other general's tank blow up. "Everything went dark," Thorpe recalls, in the virtual world, "the general and his crew were 'dead.'" From the other tank, in the other fiberglass and plywood box, Thorpe heard the other general call out, "'Reinitialize!'" Inside his simulator, the second general's tank came back to life. He swung his turret around, put General Brown in his sights, and fired at him.

In that "reinitialize" moment, Thorpe says, he became convinced that both generals were sold on SIMNET. "The behavior in a virtual world is the same behavior as the behavior in the real world," Thorpe says.

After its initial trials, and with the endorsements from two U.S. Army generals, the SIMNET project had considerable momentum, and the DARPA teams went into production mode. In nine months, DARPA had constructed a building at Fort Knox the size of a small Costco. Inside there were roughly seventy tank simulators, each made of fiberglass, and each with the approximate dimensions of an M1 Abrams tank or a Bradley fighting vehicle. "The building was designed like a hockey rink," Thorpe says. Power and networking cables dropped from the ceiling. "Entire tank battalions would enter the SIMNET center and begin training together, as if they were in a real tank battle." Real-world problems had been built into the system. "If you left your virtual electricity on overnight, in the morning your battery would be dead," Thorpe recalls. "If you didn't pay attention to landmarks and disciplined map reading, you got lost in the virtual battle terrain. It was force on force. One group against another." Competition drove the training to a whole new level. "The desire to win forced people to invent new concepts about how to beat their opponents."

A second SIMNET center was built at Fort Benning, Georgia, then another at Fort Rucker, in Alabama, for attack helicopter training. In 1988 a fourth SIMNET center went up at the U.S. Army garrison in Grafenwoehr, Germany, also for armor vehicles. In DARPA's SIMNET, the U.S. Army saw a whole new way to prepare for war. Then an unexpected new center was requested by the Department of Defense.

"The high rankers at the Pentagon wanted a simulation center of their own," recalls Neale Cosby, who oversaw the engineering on this center. The facility chosen as the host was DARPA's longtime partner the Institute for Defense Analyses, just down the street from DARPA in Alexandria. The IDA offices were located in a collegiate-looking yellow-brick and glass building located at 1801 North Beauregard Street. In 1988, Cosby recalls, much of the ground floor, including the cafeteria, was taken over by DARPA so an IDA simulation center could be built there for Pentagon brass. Cosby recalls the production. "We covered all the windows with camouflage, laid down a virtual tarmac made of foam, set up fiberglass helicopters, tanks, and aircraft cockpits, then networked everything and wired it for sound." Finally, a mysterious feature was added, one that no other SIMNET center had. For reasons of discretion, Cosby and Thorpe called the feature a "flying carpet."

"It was a way for [participants] to put themselves into the virtual world not as a pilot or a tank driver or a gunner, but anywhere" in flight, says Cosby. "It was as if you were invisible." At the time, the details of the invisible component were classified because the flying carpet feature was a way for Pentagon officials with high clearances to experience what it would be like to fly through a virtual battle in a stealth fighter jet. These were the results of DARPA's "high-stealth aircraft" program, which began in 1974.

Over a ten-year period, DARPA and the Army spent $300 million developing simulation technology. In the summer of 1990 the SIMNET system was transferred over to the U.S. Army. Its first large-scale use was to simulate a war game exercise undertaken by U.S. Central Command (CENTCOM), in Tampa, Florida. For years CENTCOM had sponsored a biennial war game exercise called Operation Internal Look, based on a real-world contingency plan. The Internal Look war games trained CENTCOM's combatant commander and his staff in command, control, and communications techniques. The exercises involved a prescripted war game scenario in which U.S. forces would quickly deploy to a location to confront a hypothetical Soviet invasion of a specific territory. In the past, the war games had taken place in Cold War settings like the Zagros Mountains in Iran and the Fulda Gap in Germany.

In the summer of 1990 the Cold War climate had changed. The Berlin Wall had come down eight months before, and CENTCOM commander in chief General Norman Schwarzkopf decided that for Internal Look 90, U.S. forces would engage in a SIMNET-based war game against a different foe, other than the Soviet Union. A scripted narrative was drawn up involving Iraqi president Saddam Hussein and his military, the fourth largest in the world. In this narrative, Iraq, coming off its eight-year war with Iran, would attack the rich oil fields of Saudi Arabia. In response, U.S. armed forces would enter the conflict to help American ally Saudi Arabia. Because new SIMNET technology was involved, realistic data on Saudi Arabia, Iraq, and neighboring Kuwait were incorporated into the war game scenario, including geography, architecture, and urban populations, this for the first time in history. In playing the war game, CENTCOM battle staff drove tanks, flew aircraft, and moved men across computer-generated Middle Eastern cities and vast desert terrain with the astonishing accuracy and precision of SIMNET simulation.

"We played Internal Look in late July 1990, setting up a mock headquarters complete with computers and communications gear at Eglin Air Force Base," General Schwarzkopf wrote in his memoir. And then to everyone's surprise, on the last day of the simulated war game exercises, on August 4, 1990, Iraq invaded its small, oil-rich neighbor Kuwait—for real. It was a bizarre turn of events. Science and science fiction had crossed paths once again.

Months later, after the Gulf War began and ended, General Schwarzkopf commented on how strangely similar the real war and the simulated war game had been.

"As the exercise [i.e., the Gulf War] got under way," General Schwarzkopf said, "the movements of Iraq's real-world ground and air forces eerily paralleled the imaginary scenario of the game."

CHAPTER SIXTEEN

The Gulf War and Operations Other Than War

Secretary of Defense Dick Cheney sat in his office in the E-Ring of the Pentagon eating Chinese food. It was shortly after 6:00 p.m. on January 16, 1991. On the round table in front of him there were paper cartons of food: steamed vegetables, egg rolls, and rice. On a television set mounted on the wall, CNN war correspondents were reporting from Baghdad, Iraq, where it was the middle of the night. Secretary Cheney listened carefully as he ate his dinner. He would later say that what struck him as odd, even surreal, as he watched the news feed was just how ignorant the reporters and everyone else in Baghdad were regarding the reality that was about to unfold. Tomahawk land attack missiles, the engines of which were created by DARPA, and F-117A stealth fighter aircraft, also a DARPA-born program, were on their way to destroy parts of the city. The Tomahawks could not be recalled. War was less than an hour away.

Below the office of the secretary of defense, just one floor down, the chairman of the Joint Chiefs of Staff, General Colin Powell, sat reviewing target lists. The missiles and bombs were set to strike and destroy Saddam Hussein's military command centers, communication towers, electrical plants, radar sites, and more. The plan was to "give them the full load the first night," Cheney later observed. Any kind of gradual escalation carried the stench of Vietnam. It was an ambitious strategy. Baghdad had a sophisticated air defense network and was the second most heavily air-defended city in the world, after Moscow.

It was a little after 2:30 a.m. Baghdad time and the moonless sky over the city was dark as Major Greg "Beast" Feest prepared to drop the first bomb of the Persian Gulf War. Piloting his F-117A stealth fighter toward the target, Major Feest was overwhelmed by a wave of apprehension.

"Two thoughts crossed my mind," Feest later recalled. "First, would I be able to identify the target? Second, did the Air Force want me to drop this bomb?" But the doubts were fleeting and lasted only a few seconds. "As I approached the target area, my adrenaline was up and instinct took over. My bomb was armed."

Major Feest's target was the Information Operations Center at the Nukayb Airbase, southwest of Baghdad, a key link between Iraq's radar network and its air defense headquarters. Destroying this target would allow other, non-stealth aircraft to enter Iraq undetected. Feest looked down at the display panel in front of him. "My laser began to fire as I tracked the target," he said. "All I had to do was play, what I called, a highly sophisticated video game, and in 30 minutes I would be back in Saudi Arabia."

At precisely 2:51 a.m. local time, the weapons bay doors opened on Feest's F-117A and a two-thousand-pound laser-guided GBU-27 dropped from the fighter aircraft, headed for the target. On the display in front of him Feest watched what happened next. "I saw the bomb go through the cross-hairs and penetrate the bunker. The explosion came out of the hole the bomb had made and blew out the doors of the bunker." Feest's bomb hit and destroyed one-half of the Iraqi air defense center at Nukayb.

"The video game was over," Feest recalled thinking. Except this was not a video game. This was war, and Major Feest had just dropped the first bomb.

Precisely one minute later, a second laser-guided bomb from a second F-117A took out the remaining half of the building at Nukayb. As Feest headed back to the base in his stealth aircraft, he was stunned by what he saw. The sky was filled with a barrage of antiaircraft artillery shooting blindly at him. "I watched several SAMs [surface-to-air missiles] launch into the sky and fly through my altitude both in front [of] and behind me," as Feest later described it. But not a single missile was guided to hit him. The F-117A was invisible to radar. DARPA's stealth technology program had created a revolution in warfare.

Ten additional F-117As were on their way to drop bombs on targets in downtown Baghdad. In the first twenty-four hours of the war, a total of forty-two stealth fighters, which accounted for only 2.5 percent of the U.S. airpower used in the campaign, destroyed 31 percent of Iraqi targets. This was technology in action, and it gave the United States not only a tactical advantage but a psychological one as well. Stealth was like a silver bullet. It had allowed U.S. fighter jets to sneak into Iraqi airspace, destroy the country's air defense system, and leave without a loss. Still, Iraqi president Saddam Hussein declared, "The great showdown has begun! The mother of all battles is under way."

The U.S. air campaign against Baghdad devastated Saddam Hussein's Ba'ath Party military infrastructure. Between the laser-guided bombs, the infrared night-bombing equipment, and the stealth fighter aircraft, the Iraqi air force never had a chance to engage. In retaliation, the Iraqis launched Scud missiles at Israel and Saudi Arabia, but almost immediately, a U.S. Patriot missile shot down an Iraqi Scud missile, making the Patriot the first antimissile ballistic missile fired in combat. The Pentagon promoted the Patriot as having near-perfect performance. But in classified communications a different story was unfolding. There were twenty-seven Patriot missile batteries in Saudi Arabia and Israel, and each battery was shooting nearly ten missiles at each incoming Iraqi Scud. At first the numbers did not make any sense, certainly not to U.S. Army vice chief of staff General Gordon R. Sullivan. How could it take ten U.S. Patriot antimissile missiles to shoot a single Iraqi Scud out of the sky? A classified investigation revealed that because of poor-quality engineering, the Iraqi Scuds were breaking apart in their terminal phase, shattering into multiple pieces as they headed back down to earth. These multiple fragments were confusing Patriot missiles into thinking that each piece was an additional warhead. Shoddy workmanship had inadvertently created a poor man's version of the highly sophisticated MIRV—multiple independently targetable reentry vehicle—the deceptive penetration aid originally dreamed of by the Jason scientists thirty years before.

For the U.S. military, the Gulf War was an opportunity to demonstrate what its system of systems was capable of. While the stealth fighter aircraft received most of the attention, as far as high technology was concerned, there were other DARPA systems flying over Iraq that were equally revolutionary, just not as visible or as sleek. Drones played a prominent role in the system of systems, largely unreported. Remotely piloted vehicles, small and large, collected mapping information that helped steer Tomahawks to their targets. Some 522 drone sorties were flown, totaling 1,641 hours, many of them based on DARPA technology going back to the Vietnam War. Equipped with infrared sensors, the drones' cameras easily located ground troops and vehicles hidden behind sand berms or covered in camouflage. The drones relayed back the information, which was then used to take out the targets. In one instance, a group of Iraqi soldiers stepped out from a hiding place and waved the white flag of surrender at the eye of a television camera attached to a drone that was hovering nearby. This became the first time in history that a group of enemy soldiers was recorded surrendering to a machine.

Another DARPA technology workhorse was the four-engine Boeing 707-300 lumbering 42,000 feet above the battlefield. This was DARPA's JSTARS, or Joint Surveillance Target Attack Radar System, a command, control, and communication center flying overhead in racetrack formation, managing much of the action going on down below. JSTARS, run jointly by the Air Force and the Army, involved aircraft equipped with a forty-foot-long canoe-shaped radar dome mounted under the front of the fuselage. Inside the dome, a radar antenna the height of a two-story house was able to send precise target information to Army ground stations below. The radar could detect, locate, and track vehicles moving deep behind enemy lines, making JSTARS the first and only airborne platform in operation that could maintain "real time surveillance over a corps-sized area of the battlefield." The system software on board JSTARS was so complex it required almost 600,000 lines of code, roughly three times more than any other C3 system previously developed by the U.S. military. Sixteen years earlier, DARPA had begun developing this system of systems concept with Assault Breaker. Now it was in play in the war theater.

JSTARS was like an all-seeing commander in the sky. It could "see" some 19,305 square miles of terrain below, and it could detect moving targets 200 to 250 miles away. It could "see" in darkness and bad weather, including clouds and sandstorms. Two of these prototype JSTARS were flown in the Gulf War, providing what DARPA historical literature describes as a "real-time tactical view of the battlefield never seen before in the history of warfare." When, on February 1, a ten-mile-long column of Iraqi armored tanks headed into Saudi Arabia, JSTARS saw it and sent coalition aircraft to destroy the column. As bombing continued from the air, sorties passed the forty thousand mark—ten thousand more missions than the U.S. Army Air Force flew against Japan in the last fourteen months of World War II. The Pentagon began releasing mind-numbing statistics on what its system of systems had destroyed: 1,300 of Iraq's 4,280 tanks, 1,100 of Iraq's 3,110 artillery pieces, and 800 of Iraq's 2,870 armored tanks.

Next came the ground war, which began on Sunday, February 24, at 4:00 a.m. Saudi time. Saddam Hussein delivered a radio broadcast telling his troops to kill "with all your might." The decisive battle that ended the Gulf War two days later would become known as the Battle of 73 Easting, the last great tank battle of the twentieth century. But unlike so many of history's great tank battles, which were named after the cities in which they were fought, the Battle of 73 Easting was named after a GPS coordinate, or gridline.

On February 25, eight hundred M1A1 Abrams tanks lined up on Iraq's southern border with Saudi Arabia, and the following morning, the initial attack against Saddam Hussein's Republican Guard Tawakalna tank division began with an assault by the Second Armored Cavalry Division. Spearheading the attack were three troops: Ghost, Eagle, and Iron. The Second Armored Cavalry Division had been stationed in Grafenwoehr, Germany, and had trained on DARPA's SIMNET simulators before deploying to the Persian Gulf. The M1 Abrams tanks that Jack Thorpe and his DARPA team had driven around at Fort Knox had since been outfitted with a powerful new weapons system: night vision thermal imaging.

On the day of the battle that ended the Gulf War, there had been terrible weather all morning. After a night of rain, the flat, trackless desert remained encumbered by thick fog and clouds. Around 3:30 p.m. the sun briefly emerged, but then a sandstorm kicked in. Between the bad weather and the thick black smoke moving across the desert from the burning Kuwaiti oil fields, visibility was reduced to nil. The gunners in the Iraqi Tawakalna tank division were blind. Not so the Second Armored Cavalry. Equipped with thermal imaging systems, the M1A1 tanks made it possible for U.S. soldiers to see in the dark. Night vision was a science DARPA had been advancing since 1961, when ARPA wrote the first handbook on the subject, the *Handbook of Military Infrared Technology*. Infrared vision was developed in Vietnam to help soldiers see through dense jungle canopies. Now it was being used in the desert.

"We had thermal imagery," says Major Douglas Macgregor, who saw action in the Battle of 73 Easting as commander of Cougar Squadron, and "the Iraqis did not. Yes, our firepower was extremely accurate, pinpoint accurate, but we could see what we were firing at and they could not." When the Second Armored Cavalry's Eagle Troop launched its attack around 4:10 p.m., it caught the Iraqi Republican Guard unawares. In less than half an hour, Eagle Troop destroyed twenty-eight T-72 Iraqi tanks, sixteen armored personnel carriers, and thirty-nine trucks, with no losses of its own. "The battle took twenty-three minutes to win," retired four-star general Paul Gorman told Congress. "The U.S. alone enjoyed the advantage of satellite navigation and imagery, and of thermal-imaging fire control."

The Iraqi army was overpowered. Iraqi soldiers started to give up and abandon their posts en masse. During a vast exodus of Iraqi troops from Kuwait City, JSTARS pinpointed thousands of fleeing vehicles for coalition attack aircraft to bomb. The stark photographs of destroyed vehicles along Iraq's Highway 80 provided a striking visual image of how a system of systems worked. Between JSTARS, stealth aircraft, GPS satellite navigation, bomber aircraft, laser-guided bombs, and night vision, the United States and its technological firepower wrought mega-death. Between 1,500 and

2,000 charred and abandoned vehicles were left littering the road, including Iraqi tanks, Mercedes-Benz sedans, stolen Kuwaiti fire trucks, and minivans. There were charred bodies and loose flip-flops, suitcases, and fruit crates. Some of the victims had been flash-heated to death in crawling and stretching motions, like the famous bodies from Pompeii. The international press called the four-lane stretch of highway between Iraq and Kuwait the "Highway of Death."

Concerned about the negative narrative unfolding in the press, Colin Powell met with General Schwarzkopf to discuss the matter.

"The television coverage," said Powell, is "starting to make us look as if we engaged in slaughter for slaughter's sake."

"I've been thinking the same thing," Schwarzkopf told him.

Powell asked General Schwarzkopf what he wanted to do.

"One more day should do it," Schwarzkopf said, indicating he was authorizing one more day of bombing.

Late the following day, on February 27, President George H. W. Bush declared "suspension of offense combat" in the Persian Gulf and laid out conditions for a permanent cease-fire with Iraq. The Gulf War had lasted one month and twelve days.

One week after the cease-fire, back in Washington, D.C., DARPA director Victor Reis met with General Gordon Sullivan, vice chief of staff of the Army, for lunch. General Sullivan had formerly served as the deputy commander of the Armor Center at Fort Knox and was a fan of SIMNET. To this lunch General Sullivan carried with him a copy of the *Stars and Stripes* newspaper. Pointing to a headline, "Ghost Troops Battle at the 73 Easting," General Sullivan asked Reis if DARPA could put the Battle of 73 Easting in reverse simulation, as a training tool. Reis said he would see what he could do.

Reis brought the idea to Neale Cosby at the IDA SIMNET Center. "I told Vic it was a great idea," Colonel Cosby recalled in

2014. "I said, we can do it and we should do it." Reverse simulation of the Battle of 73 Easting, he thought, would be "the ultimate after-action report." There was much to learn from technology.

In a matter of days, a team from DARPA, led by Colonel Gary Bloedorn, flew to Iraq to interview soldiers who had fought in the battle. Bloedorn and the DARPA team heard varying accounts, read notes and radio transcripts, and listened to an audiotape made by a soldier in one of the command vehicles. The team traveled to the GPS gridline at 73 Easting, where they walked around the battlefield, recorded forensic evidence, and measured distances between U.S. firing positions and destroyed Iraqi vehicles. Then they returned to IDA to input data and reconstruct the battle down to fractions of seconds. The process took six months.

With a draft version complete, the reconstruction team traveled to Germany, where most of the battle's participants were stationed. The DARPA team showed the soldiers the SIMNET version of the battle, took notes, and made final adjustments for accuracy. Back at IDA the team worked for another six months, then met with the key leaders of the battle one last time for a final review. They proved that "capturing live combat" after the fact could be done, says Cosby. Now it was time to take the show to Congress.

On May 21, 1992, members of the Senate Armed Services Committee were shown the DARPA simulation of the Battle of 73 Easting. Retired general Paul Gorman led the opening remarks. But before playing the SIMNET simulation, Gorman pointed to the simulator and introduced the machine.

"This somewhat daunting graphic apparatus before you is an instrument of war," Gorman told the committee members, "a mechanism designed to enable humans to understand the complexity, the kinetics, the chaos of battle." Gorman reminded his audience what General Patton once said, "that it is men, not machines, who fight and win wars." But the world had changed, Gorman said, and now machines were there to help. In the past, war stories were the only record of battle. Computer simulation had now changed that.

"I am here to urge [you] that all must recognize that simulation is fundamental to readiness for war," Gorman said. With that, he played the twenty-three-minute simulation of the Battle of 73 Easting. Congress, Cosby recalled, was "wowed." The military services would begin moving toward computer simulation as a primary training tool for war.

DARPA's Assault Breaker concept had delivered results in the Gulf War, and at the Pentagon, renewed excitement was in the air. Ever since the Vietnam War, the Defense Department had struggled with a public perception of the military rooted in impotency and distrust. The Gulf War had changed that. The Pentagon was potent once again. The Gulf War was over fast, the death toll remarkably low: 390 Americans died, with 458 wounded in action. There were 510 casualties from all allied forces. President George H. W. Bush even triumphantly declared, "By God, we've licked the Vietnam Syndrome once and for all!"

But the optimism would not last long.

It was the early afternoon of October 3, 1993, in Mogadishu, Somalia, a lawless, famine-stricken city run by armed militias and warlords. What had begun as a peacekeeping mission ten months prior had devolved into a series of quick-action Special Forces operations. On this particular day, a joint special operations task force named Task Force Ranger, made up of elite U.S. military personnel including Army Rangers, Navy Seals, and Delta Force, embarked on a mission to capture two high-level Somali lieutenants working for the warlord and president-elect General Mohamed Farrah Aidid. A group of Aidid's lieutenants were holed up in a two-story building downtown, not far from the Olympic Hotel.

It was fifteen minutes into the mission and everything was going according to plan. Ground forces had arrived at the target location and were loading twenty-four captured Somali militants into convoy trucks when a series of deadly events began to unfold. A Black Hawk helicopter, call sign Super 61, was heading toward the target building with a plan in place to transport U.S. soldiers back to base, when suddenly a group of Somali militants scrambled onto a nearby rooftop, took aim at the helicopter, and fired a rocket-propelled grenade.

Norm Hooten, one of the Special Operations team leaders, watched in horror. The Black Hawk "took a direct hit toward the tail boom and it started a slow rotation" down, Hooten recalled. "It was a catastrophic impact." Super 61 began spinning out of control. It crashed in the street below, killing both pilots on impact. In a videotape recording of the crash released by the Defense Department in 2013, a voice can be heard shouting over the military communications system, "We got a Black Hawk going down! We got a Black Hawk going down!"

A fifteen-man combat search and rescue team and an MH-6 Little Bird helicopter raced to the crash site to assist. But hundreds of angry Somalis were gathering in the surrounding streets, creating barricades made of burning tires and garbage, inhibiting access. A firefight ensued, trapping the Americans and pitting them against a violent mob. The situation grew dramatically worse when a second Black Hawk, call sign Super 64, was shot down. Another mob of Somalis charged to the second crash site, where they killed everyone except one of the pilots, Michael Durrant. Ranger and Delta Force teams took to the streets in an attempt to provide search and rescue, and cover to their trapped fellow soldiers. A chaotic, deadly battle ensued, lasting all through the night and into the morning. By the time it was over, eighteen Americans, one Pakistani, and one Malaysian soldier were dead and eighty were injured. An unknown number of Somalis, estimated to be roughly three thousand, had been killed.

The 15-megaton Castle Bravo thermonuclear bomb, exploded in the Marshall Islands in 1954, was the largest nuclear weapon ever detonated by the United States. If unleashed on the eastern seaboard today it would kill roughly 20 million people. With this weapon, authorized to proceed in secret, came the certainty of the military-industrial complex and the birth of DARPA. (U.S. Department of Energy)

An elite group of weapons engineers rode out the Castle Bravo thermonuclear explosion from inside this bunker, code-named Station 70, just nineteen miles from ground zero. (The National Archives at Riverside)

In the 1950s, John von Neumann—mathematician, physicist, game theorist, and inventor—was the superstar defense scientist. No one could compete with his brain. (U.S. Department of Energy)

Rivalry spawns supremacy, and in the early 1950s, a second national nuclear weapons laboratory was created to foster competition with Los Alamos. Ernest O. Lawrence (left) and Edward Teller (center) cofounded the Lawrence Livermore National Laboratory. Herb York (right) served as first director. In 1958, York became scientific director of the brand new Advanced Research Project Agency (ARPA), later renamed DARPA. (Lawrence Livermore National Laboratory)

In his farewell address to the nation in January, 1961, President Eisenhower warned the American people about the "total influence" of the military-industrial complex. The warning was a decade too late. (Dwight D. Eisenhower Presidential Library)

Edward Teller and Herb York—shown here with Livermore colleague Luis Alvarez—envisioned a 10,000-megaton nuclear weapon designed to decimate and depopulate much of the Soviet Union. (Lawrence Livermore National Laboratory)

Harold Brown was twenty-four years old when he was put in charge of thermonuclear bomb work at Livermore. He followed Herb York to the Pentagon and oversaw ARPA weapons programs during the Vietnam War. In 1977, Harold Brown became the first scientist to be secretary of defense. (U.S. Department of Defense)

Physicist and presidential science advisor Marvin "Murph" Goldberger cofounded the Jason advisory group in 1959, paid for solely by ARPA until the end of the Vietnam War. The Jasons, still at work today, are considered the most influential and secretive defense scientists in America. Photographed here in his home, age 90 in 2013, Goldberger examines a photo of himself and President Johnson. (Author's collection)

Senator John F. Kennedy visiting Senator Lyndon B. Johnson at the LBJ ranch in Texas. Each man, as President, would personally authorize some of the most controversial ARPA weapons programs of the Vietnam War. (Lyndon B. Johnson Presidential Library, photo by Frank Muto)

In 1961 Kennedy sent Johnson to Vietnam to encourage South Vietnamese President Ngo Dinh Diem to sign off on ARPA's weapons lab in Saigon. In this photograph are (roughly front to back) Ngo Dinh Diem, Lady Bird Johnson, Madame Nhu, Lyndon Johnson, Nguyen Ngoc Tho, Jean Kennedy Smith, Stephen Smith, and Ngo Dinh Nhu, the head of the secret police. In 1963, Diem and Nhu were murdered in a White House–approved coup d'état. (Lyndon B. Johnson Presidential Library, photo by Republic of Vietnam)

President Diem's small-in-stature army had difficulty handling large, semi-automatic weapons carried by U.S. military advisors in Vietnam. ARPA's William Godel cut through red tape and sent 1,000 AR-15 rifles to Saigon. In 1966 the weapon was adapted for fully automatic fire and re-designated the M16 assault rifle. "One measure of the weapon's success is that it is still in use across the world," says DARPA. (NARA, photo by Dennis Kurpius)

The use of the chemical defoliant Agent Orange was an ARPA-devised scheme. "Your decision is required because this is a kind of chemical warfare," advisor Walt Rostow told President Kennedy, who signed off on the program in 1961. In 2012 Congress determined that between 2.1 million and 4.8 million Vietnamese were directly exposed to Agent Orange with the number of U.S. veterans remaining the subject of debate. (NARA, photo by Bryan K. Grigsby)

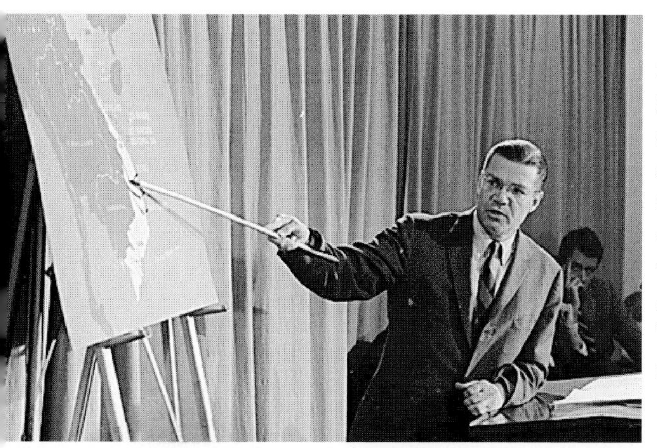

Secretary of Defense Robert S. McNamara explains the situation in Vietnam, during a Pentagon press conference in February 1965. Many of today's advanced technology weapons systems were developed by ARPA during the Vietnam War. (U.S. Department of Defense)

In 1965, the Jason scientists studied the use of tactical nuclear weapons in Vietnam to close off supply routes on the Ho Chi Minh Trail. (U.S. Army)

The Jason scientists were the brains behind McNamara's electronic fence, a system of advanced sensors designed to detect Viet Cong trail traffic. Initially ridiculed and later embraced, DARPA advanced the concept into Combat Zones That See. In this photo, an Air Delivered Seismic Intrusion Detector (ADSID) sensor is about to be dropped on the trail, near Khe Sanh. (U.S. Air Force)

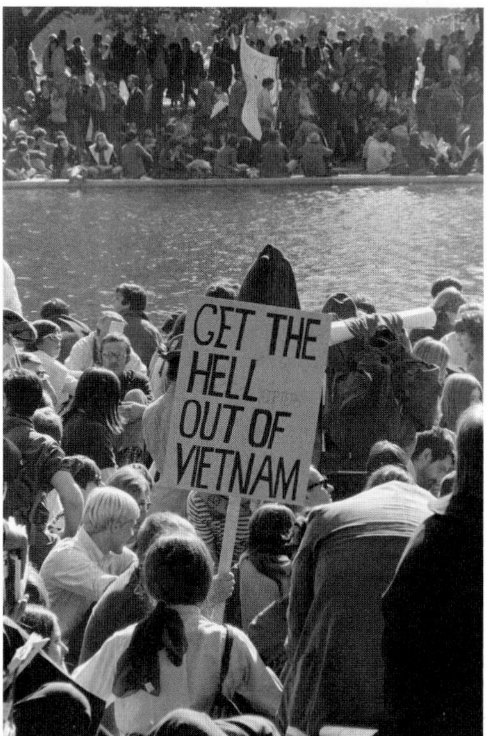

No amount of technology could stop Vietnam War protesters from gaining control of the war narrative. (Lyndon B. Johnson Presidential Library, photo by Frank Wolfe)

As the seventeenth secretary of defense Richard "Dick" B. Cheney oversaw the Gulf War in Iraq, which put decades of DARPA's advanced weapons technology on display. (Office of the Secretary of Defense)

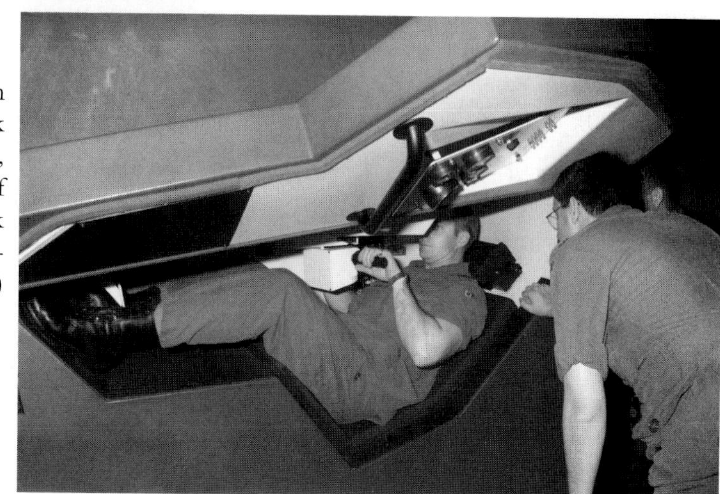

Students train in an M1 Abrams tank SIMNET simulator, the brainchild of DARPA's Jack Thorpe. (U.S. Department of Defense)

A staff sergeant armed with an M16A2 assault rifle maintains security over an F-117 stealth fighter, during refueling. (U.S. Department of Defense)

The superiority of U.S. weapons technology used in the Gulf War is made evident along Iraq's Highway 80, or "Highway of Death." (U.S. Department of Defense, Tech Sgt. Joe Coleman)

A U.S. Marine helicopter flies over a residential area in Mogadishu, Somalia, in 1992. The following year, the Battle of Mogadishu caused DARPA to rethink what future weapons systems would be needed for urban combat. (U.S. Department of Defense, Tech Sgt. Perry Heimer)

An early 1990s model of what the Pentagon thought an urban combat scenario might look like, seen here at the Military Operations in Urban Terrain (MOUT) training center. But combat zones like Mogadishu, Fallujah, and Kabul look nothing like this. (U.S. Department of Defense, Visual Information Center)

Retired Vice Admiral John M. Poindexter, known for his role in the Iran-Contra affair, served as director of DARPA's Information Awareness Office, starting in 2001. Allegedly shut down, many electronic surveillance programs were transferred to NSA. (NARA)

President George W. Bush and Secretary of Defense Donald Rumsfeld at the western face of the Pentagon, the day after the 9/11 terrorist attacks. (U.S. Department of Defense, photo by R. D. Ward)

U.S. and coalition flags fly outside Saddam Hussein's former Al Faw Palace, taken over by U.S. military and renamed Camp Victory, Iraq. Master Sergeant Craig Marsh lived here and oversaw the efforts of bomb disposal (EOD) technicians and DARPA robots. (U.S. Department of Defense, photo by Staff Sgt. Caleb Barrieau)

DARPA's Talon robot approaches a deadly improvised explosive device (IED) in Rajah, Iraq. (U.S. Army, photo by Specialist Jeffrey Sandstrum)

A micro air vehicle (MAV) prepares for its first combat mission in Iraq, in 2005. Many of DARPA's advanced MAV's are now small enough to fit in the palm of the hand. (U.S. Department of Defense, photo by Sgt. Doug Roles)

The seven-ounce Wasp drone, part of DARPA's Combat Zones That See, gathers real-time video and works in a swarm. (U.S. Department of Defense)

Vice President Cheney, his wife, and their daughter are greeted by General David Petraeus in Baghdad, in 2008. Petraeus wrote the first U.S. Army counterinsurgency manual since Vietnam and supported the DARPA-born Human Terrain System program which focused on winning "the hearts, minds, and acquiescence of the population." (U.S. Department of Defense, photo by Master Sgt. Jeffrey Allen)

The Predator drone inside a hangar at Creech Air Force Base, Nevada, in 2009. (Author's collection)

The charred alley in Chehel Gazi, Afghanistan, where Human Terrain Team member Paula Loyd was set on fire by an emissary of the Taliban. (USA Criminal Investigation Command)

DARPA Director Arati Prabhakar and Marine Corps Commandant General James F. Amos pose with DARPA's LS3 land robot, designed to carry heavy equipment over rugged terrain, in 2014. (U.S. Marine Corps, photo by Sgt. Mallory S. VanderSchans)

An armored truck with an assault rifle mounted on top keeps guard outside the Los Alamos National Laboratory where Dr. Garrett Kenyon and his team work on artificial intelligence for DARPA. (Author's collection)

When the IBM Roadrunner supercomputer was built for Los Alamos, in 2008, it was the fastest computer in the world, able to perform 1 million billion calculations per second. By 2013, advances in chip technology rendered it obsolete. In 2014, part of what remains of Roadrunner is used to power DARPA's artificial intelligence project. (Los Alamos National Laboratory)

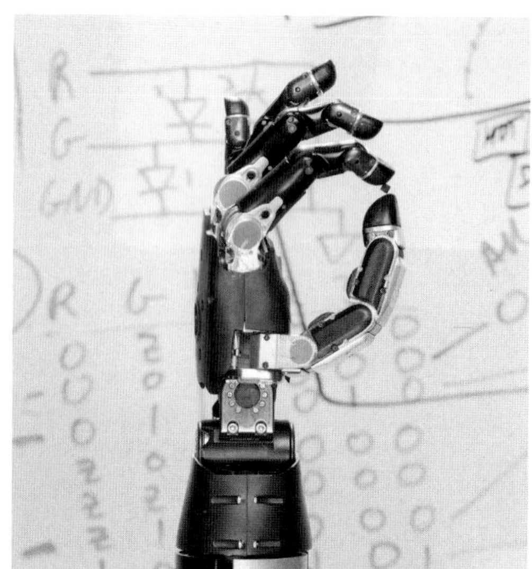

The DARPA Modular Prosthetic Limb. The work advances robotics but is it helping warfighters who lost limbs? (U.S. Department of Defense, courtesy of Johns Hopkins University Applied Physics Laboratory)

DARPA's Atlas robot is a high-mobility humanoid robot built by Boston Dynamics. Its "articulated sensor head" has stereo cameras and a laser range finder. (Defense Advanced Research Projects Agency)

Allen Macy Dulles and his sister, Joan Dulles Talley. A brain injury during the Korean War, in 1952, made it impossible for Dulles to record new memories. DARPA's brain prosthetics program alleges to help brain-wounded warriors like Dulles, but program details remain highly classified. (Author's collection)

The Modular Advanced Armed Robotic System, or MAARS robot kills human targets from almost two miles away. MAARS robots have motion detectors, acoustic sensors, siren and speaker systems, non-lethal laser dazzlers, less-than-lethal grenades, and encryption technology to make the robotic killer "extremely safe and tamper proof," says DARPA. (U.S. Army)

DARPA Headquarters in Arlington, Virginia, bears no identifying signs and maintains a "force protection environment," for security purposes. (Author's collection)

The Pentagon. (U.S. Department of Defense, photo by Senior Airman Perry Aston)

This was asymmetric warfare—a battle between two groups with radically different levels of military power. The superior military force, the United States, killed a far greater number of the opposition while its own losses were played out on television screens around the world. Videotaped images of mobs of Somalis dragging the semi-naked, bloodied bodies of the dead American pilots and soldiers through the streets were shocking.

It was a watershed moment and a turning point in modern U.S. military affairs. The might and morale of the United States military, made evident in the Gulf War, had been weakened. Every war planner, going back at least 2,500 years, knows better than to fight a battle in a crowded place. "The worst policy," wrote Sun Tzu, "is to attack cities." The battle of Mogadishu was not part of any plan. There was no rehearsal for what happened. U.S. forces were drawn into a hellish situation, and the result was more lives lost than in any other combat situation since Vietnam.

"The Americans were not supermen," commented Somali clan leader Colonel Aden. "In these dusty streets, where combat was reduced to rifle against rifle, they could die as easily as any Somali." Technologically advanced weaponry had been disabled by sticks, stones, AK-47s, and a few rocket-propelled grenades.

After the battle of Mogadishu, DARPA convened a senior working group (SWG) to analyze what had happened in Somalia and make recommendations for how the Pentagon could best prepare for future conflicts of a similar nature—situations called Military Operations Other Than War, or OOTW. The group, led by General Carl W. Stiner, former commander in chief of the U.S. Special Operations Command, focused on solutions that would require new technologies to be developed. The group involved itself in ten study sessions over two months and spent six months preparing a written report.

The opening lines read like a salvo. "The world is no longer bipolar," the Senior Working Group wrote. "The post–Cold War strategic environment is ill-defined, dynamic and unstable." During the Cold War, America knew who the enemy was. Not so anymore. Terrorist organizations, paramilitary groups, and militia were destined to emerge from multiple chaotic urban environments around the globe. Third World instability, ideological and religious extremism, and intentional terrorism and narco-terrorism meant that the whole world was the new battlefield. In future military operations other than war, irregular enemy forces would include a "diverse range of adversaries equipped with an ever increasing array of sophisticated weapons," including some that were atomic, chemical, and biological in design. The United States was not properly prepared to deal with these emerging new threats, the SWG warned. DARPA needed to refocus its attention on urban warfare. It needed to research and develop new weapons systems to deal with this threat, now growing across the Third World.

In one part of the report, the group listed dangerous insufficiencies that DARPA had to shore up at once: "Inadequate nuclear, BW, CW [biological weapon, chemical weapon] detection; inadequate underground bunker detection; limited secure, real-time command and control to lower-echelon units [i.e., getting the information to soldiers on the ground]; limited ISR [intelligence, surveillance, and reconnaissance] and dissemination; inadequate mine, booby trap and explosive detection capabilities; inadequate non-lethal capabilities [i.e., incapacitating agents]; inadequate modeling/simulation for training, rehearsal and operations; no voice recognition or language translation; inadequate ability to deal with sniper attacks." The SWG proposed that DARPA accelerate work in all these areas and also increase efforts in robotics and drones, human tagging and tracking, and nonlethal weapons systems for crowd control.

DARPA had its work cut out. The agency had been leading military research and development for decades against a different enemy, one with an army of tanks and heavy weaponry. The new focus was on urban warfare. What happened in Mogadishu was a cautionary tale. "Military operations that were of little consideration a decade ago are now of major concern," the study group warned.

The following year, DARPA asked RAND to study OOTW and write an unclassified report. The RAND report was called "Combat in Hell: A Consideration of Constrained Urban Warfare." It began with the prescient words: "Historical advice is consistent. Sun Tzu counseled that 'the worst policy is to attack cities.'" Accordingly, avoid urban warfare.

CHAPTER SEVENTEEN

Biological Weapons

On December 11, 1991, a mysterious forty-one-year-old Soviet scientist named Dr. Kanatjan Alibekov arrived in Washington, D.C., one of a thirteen-man Soviet delegation. The group was part of a trilateral mission that also involved scientists from the United States and Great Britain. The purpose of this visit was allegedly to allow each delegation to inspect the other countries' military facilities that had, decades earlier, been involved in biological weapons programs. But really there was a lot more than just that going on. Back in 1972, the Biological Weapons Convention Treaty had made germ weapons illegal, and all three countries had pledged to renounce biological warfare. But recently American intelligence officers had discovered that the Soviets had not given up bioweapons work and instead had created a far more nefarious and frightening program than any military scientist in the Western world had imagined. This information was first learned two years earlier, in October 1989, and the Americans and the British had been puzzling out what to do about it ever since. This trilateral mission was a piece of that puzzle.

In December 1991 the Soviets did not know that American and British intelligence officers were aware of their covert bioweapons program, which was called Biopreparat. Nor did the Soviets realize that American intelligence officers knew that the mysterious Dr. Kanatjan Alibekov was deputy director of Biopreparat, meaning he was second in command of a program that involved roughly forty thousand employees, working in forty facilities, twelve of which were used solely for offensive biological weapons work.

That the Soviet delegation was in the United States at all was a highly sensitive issue. Secretary of Defense Cheney did not want the details made public, and to ensure secrecy, his office issued a press blackout around the mission. The only people outside the Defense Department cleared on the Soviet scientists' whereabouts were individuals with the U.S. Army Medical Research Institute of Infectious Diseases (USAMRIID), who served as escorts.

The group traveled to Dugway Proving Grounds, in Utah, where deadly pathogens had once been tested in the open air, but whose Cold War–era buildings had since been abandoned. They traveled to Pine Bluffs Arsenal, in Arkansas, where the United States had once manufactured biological weapons on an industrial scale, but where there was now nothing left but weedy fields and rusting railroad tracks. They went to Fort Detrick, in Frederick, Maryland, the former locus of U.S. bioweapons research and development, where USAMRIID now had its headquarters.

Years later Dr. Alibekov would write a memoir, and in it he described the 1991 trip as one on which he was less interested in what he saw at the former weapons facilities than in the lifestyle of abundance that so many Americans seemed to enjoy. He regarded with wonderment "the well-paved highways, the well-stocked stores, and the luxurious homes where ordinary Americans lived." Democracy, he concluded, offered more to its citizens than communism ever did.

The trip to America in 1991 was Dr. Alibekov's first. He spoke not a word of English and had met just thirteen Westerners in his lifetime, all members of this same trilateral mission who had visited the Soviet Union earlier that same year. During that visit, Dr. Alibekov had acted as one of the tour guides. The Soviets were producing germ weapons, and it was Alibekov's job to make sure that the Western scientists were steered clear of any sights that might belie the Soviets' illegal weapons work.

Born in Kazakhstan in 1950, Alibekov had trained as an infectious disease physician, specializing in microbiology and epidemiology. At the age of twenty-four, he joined the military faculty at the Tomsk Medical Institute in Siberia and began working inside what he later described as "a succession of secret laboratories and installations in some of the most remote corners of the Soviet Union." With each job came financial privilege, which was unusual for a non-Russian. Kazakhs were generally considered second-class citizens during the Cold War. But Alibekov was a talented microbiologist and a hard worker, which served him well and paid off. By the 1990s, "with the combined salary of a senior bureaucrat and high-ranking military officer," he wrote, "I earned as much as a Soviet government minister."

As the tour of the American facilities was taking place, Russia was in a state of pandemonium. The Berlin Wall had come down two years earlier, but the red flag of the Soviet Union still flew over the Kremlin. The geopolitical landscape between the superpowers was in flux. "It wasn't so clear the [Soviet leaders] weren't going to re-form," remembers Dr. Craig Fields, DARPA's director at the time. "There was a lot of anxiety about the fact that they might re-form." The two nations had been moving toward normalized relations, but for the Pentagon this was a time of great instability. While the world rejoiced over the fall of the Berlin Wall, the Defense Department had been coping with a myriad of national security unknowns. Would a unified Germany join NATO? How to handle troop reductions throughout Europe? What about all the nuclear weapons the Soviets possessed? The Soviet Union had spent the past five decades building up its weapons of mass destruction, in a shoulder-to-shoulder arms race with the United States. Who, now, would control the Soviet arsenals of WMD? At any given moment the Russians had more than eleven thousand nuclear warheads aimed at carefully selected targets inside the United States, as well as an additional fifteen thousand nuclear warheads stored in facilities across the sprawling Russian countryside, including mobile systems fitted onto railway cars.

One person uniquely familiar with these kinds of questions, numbers, and threats was Lisa Bronson, the Pentagon official leading the delegation of Soviet scientists on their tour. Still in her thirties, Bronson was a lawyer and a disarmaments expert. As deputy director for multilateral negotiations with the Office of the Secretary of Defense, Bronson had helped conceive and design the visit by the Soviet team. She had also accompanied the U.S. and British scientists on their tour around Soviet facilities earlier in the year. She was one of the thirteen Westerners Dr. Alibekov had met before this trip. Now, with the facilities visited and the mission coming to a close, Lisa Bronson took the Russian scientists on a walking tour of the nation's capital.

It was during this part of the trip that a fortuitous exchange of words between Dr. Alibekov and Lisa Bronson occurred. Alibekov recalled the conversation in his memoir. "At various stops along the way, she had challenged us about the Soviet biological weapons program," he wrote. "Naturally, we denied we had one. But I admired her persistence."

Standing on Pennsylvania Avenue, just down the road from the White House, one of Alibekov's colleagues asked Bronson how much money an American scientist could earn in a year.

"That depends on your experience," she answered. "A government scientist can make between fifty thousand and seventy thousand dollars, but a scientist in the private sector could earn up to two-hundred thousand dollars a year," about $350,000 in 2015.

Alibekov was astonished. Throughout the trip he remained impressed by how much better everything was in America, from public infrastructure to personal living conditions. He thought of his own life in Moscow. How hard he worked and how little he had to show for it in comparison. And most of all how grim the future looked now that the wall was down. "At the time," he wrote, "a top-level Russian scientist could make about one hundred dollars a month." Emboldened, Alibekov decided to speak up. Through an interpreter he asked Bronson a question of his own.

"With my experience could I find a job here?" he asked.

Bronson gently told Dr. Alibekov that he would have to learn English first.

Through the translator, Alibekov thanked his Pentagon host. Then he made a joke. "Okay," he said, "if I ever come here, I'll ask for your help."

Lisa Bronson just smiled.

"Everyone started to laugh," Alibekov recalled, "including me."

Dr. Kanatjan Alibekov returned to Moscow with the Soviet delegation. Just a few days later, on December 25, 1991, President Mikhail Gorbachev resigned. On New Year's Eve, the red flag of the Soviet Union, with its iconic hammer and sickle beneath a gold star, was taken down from the flagpole at the Kremlin. The tricolored flag of the newly formed Russian Federation was raised in its place. The Soviet Union ceased to exist.

Two weeks later, Dr. Alibekov handed the director of Biopreparat, General Yury Kalinin, his resignation papers in Moscow. Then, using an intermediary, Alibekov reached out to Lisa Bronson to let her know that he wanted to defect to the United States. This was a military intelligence coup for the Pentagon. For two years now, all the intelligence on Biopreparat—including the revelation that it existed in the first place—had come from a single source, a former senior-level Soviet scientist named Vladimir Pasechnik, now in British custody. The Pentagon wanted its own high-level defector. Soon they would have Dr. Kanatjan Alibekov.

As for Vladimir Pasechnik, his defection had come out of the blue. In October 1989 Pasechnik had been sent to France on an official business trip, to purchase laboratory equipment. Instead, he called the British embassy from a phone booth and said he was a Soviet germ warfare scientist who wanted to defect to England. British Secret Intelligence Service agents picked him up in a car, flew him to England, and took him to a safe house in the countryside.

The handler assigned to Pasechnik was a senior biological warfare specialist on Britain's defense intelligence staff named Christopher Davis. Pasechnik stunned Davis with a legion of extraordinary facts. The fifty-one-year-old Pasechnik had worked under Dr. Alibekov in a Biopreparat facility in Leningrad called the Institute of Ultra-Pure Biological Preparations. As a senior scientist at Ultra-Pure, Pasechnik had made such significant contributions that he was given the honorary military title of general. At Biopreparat, scientists weaponized classic pathogens like anthrax, tularemia, and botulinum toxin, standard operating procedure in a bioweapons program. But at Ultra-Pure, scientists had been working to genetically modify pathogens so they were resistant to vaccines and antibiotics. Pasechnik told Davis that at Ultra-Pure, he had been assigned to work on a strategic antibiotic-resistant strain of the mother of all pathogens, bubonic plague.

The Soviets called their laboratory-engineered version of history's most prolific killer Super Plague. In the thirteenth century, the bubonic plague killed off roughly every third man, woman, and child in Europe; but it lost its potency in the twentieth century, when scientists discovered that the antibiotic streptomycin was effective against the infectious disease. When Christopher Davis learned that the Soviets were developing a genetically modified, antibiotic-resistant strain of plague, he interpreted it to mean one thing. "You choose plague because you're going to take out the other person's country," Davis said. "Kill all the people, then move in and take over the land. Full stop. That's what it is about."

For months, Christopher Davis and an MI6 colleague spent long hours debriefing Pasechnik. The information was then shared with American intelligence counterparts. In the first month alone, Vladimir Pasechnik provided the British government with more information about the Soviet biological weapons program than all the British and American intelligence agencies combined had been able to piece together without him over a period of more than twenty-five years. The United States' vast network of advanced sensor technology had proved useless in detecting biological weapons. Bioweapons can be engineered inside laboratories hidden in buildings or underground. Unlike work on missiles, which require launch tests from proving grounds that are easily observable from overhead satellites or aircraft, biological weapons work can continue for decades undetected. And at Biopreparat it did.

Despite hundreds of billions of dollars spent by U.S. military and intelligence agencies on high-tech reconnaissance and surveillance systems, on the ground, in the air, and in space, collecting SIGINT, MASINT, OSINT, GEOINT, and other forms of technology-based intelligence, a single human being had delivered so much that was unknown simply by opening his mouth. Pasechnik provided HUMINT, human intelligence.

"The fact that Vladimir [Pasechnik] defected was one of the key acts of the entire ending of the Soviet Union and the end of the Cold War," says Davis. "It was the greatest breakthrough we ever had." Once Davis briefed his U.S. counterparts on Pasechnik's information, things moved quickly. The United States sent the Nobel Prize–winning microbiologist Dr. Joshua Lederberg to England on a secret mission to interview Pasechnik. Lederberg came home unnerved. That the Soviets were working on Super Plague was shocking. But Lederberg also learned that scientists at Biopreparat had been working to weaponize smallpox, which was duplicitous. In the late 1970s the international health community, including doctors from the Soviet Union, had worked together on a worldwide effort to eradicate the killer virus. In 1980 the World Health Organization declared smallpox dead. That the Soviets would weaponize smallpox by the ton was particularly nefarious.

Lederberg confirmed for the Pentagon that Vladimir Pasechnik was credible, level-headed, and blessed with an impeccable memory. "He never, ever stretched things," says Christopher Davis. Using classified CIA satellite data, including photographs going back decades, the Pentagon located, then confirmed, the multiple biological weapons facilities revealed in Pasechnik's debriefings. Many of the key photographs were from ARPA satellites that had been sent aloft in the earliest days of the technology. With confirmation in place, it was now time to tell President George H. W. Bush about the Soviets' prodigious, illegal biological weapons program.

The wall had been down for only a few months, and from the perspective of the Pentagon, it was a precarious time as far as international security was concerned. There was a growing worry that President Mikhail Gorbachev was losing control of the Russian military. With this in mind, in the winter of 1990, President Bush decided it was best to keep the Soviets' biological weapons program a secret. To reveal it, Bush decided, would make Gorbachev appear weak. Gorbachev was being hailed internationally as a reformer. He needed credibility to keep moving his country out of a Cold War mentality and into the twentieth century. The world could not allow Russia to fall into chaos. The revelation of the Soviet bioweapons program could backfire. It needed to stay hidden, at least for now.

The single greatest unknown at this juncture was how much, if anything, did President Gorbachev actually know? Vladimir Pasechnik could not say with authority. The Pentagon needed a second source. Back in the fall of 1989 and the winter of 1990, no such second source existed. Pasechnik had been reticent at first but gradually became more comfortable with his British handlers. Then he started to name names, including that of Dr. Kanatjan Alibekov, deputy director of Biopreparat.

The Pentagon got to work setting in motion the trilateral mission—which is how Alibekov and twelve colleagues wound up at Fort Detrick in December 1991. After the U.S. trip, Alibekov had been back in Russia for just three weeks when he made up his mind to defect to the United States. Arrangements were made. In the dead of night, Alibekov left Russia with his wife and children, never to return.

By the time Gorbachev was set to leave office, U.S. intelligence had confirmed that he had in fact been aware of the Soviet bioweapons program. Gorbachev had received classified memos regarding operations, including how to deceive U.S. inspectors during trilateral mission facilities tours. The CIA also confirmed that Russia's new president, Boris Yeltsin, had been made aware of the program—and that he was allowing it to move forward. On January 20, 1992, British ambassador Rodric Braithwaite and Foreign Secretary Douglas Hurd met with President Yeltsin in Moscow. Since Pasechnik's defection, Ambassador Braithwaite had been trying, to no avail, to get the Russians to admit that they had a biological weapons program, which would be the first step toward its safe dissolution. This time, when the subject was brought up, Yeltsin stunned the British diplomats by acknowledging that he knew about Biopreparat.

"I know all about the Soviet biological weapons program," Yeltsin confessed. "It's still going ahead." He also said that the Russian scientists who ran the program were determined to continue their work. "They are fanatics, and they will not stop voluntarily," Yeltsin said. He vowed to put an end to it. "I'm going to close down the institutes," he promised, to "retire the director of the [Biopreparat] program."

"We were stunned," Braithwaite recalled in his memoir, "and we could do no more than thank him."

Boris Yeltsin had admitted what every other Soviet leader, including Gorbachev, had been lying about for twenty-three years. With the information now public, the U.S. Congress got involved. So did the American press. Countering biological weapons was poised to become a massive new industry, expanding and proliferating at a phenomenal rate. DARPA would lead the way.

In America, Dr. Alibekov changed his name to sound more American. He was Dr. Ken Alibek now. He moved his family into a home in the suburbs outside Washington, D.C. This was the Soviet scientist who, over decades, had weaponized the bacterial infection glanders, orchestrated test trials of Marburg hemorrhagic fever, overseen the creation of the Soviet Union's first tularemia bomb, and created a "battle strain" of anthrax, Strain 836, hailed as "the most virulent and vicious strain of anthrax known to man." He was working for the U.S. government now.

Each day Alibek drove along the well-paved highways, past the big homes and the well-stocked stores, to an office building in Virginia just twenty minutes outside the nation's capital, where he now worked. There, inside a secure room on the second floor, he answered questions asked of him by individuals from a wide variety of U.S. intelligence agencies, military agencies, and civilian organizations about Russia's biological weapons programs.

Alibek confirmed what Vladimir Pasechnik had told British intelligence about Soviet advances in biotechnology and the development of Super Plague. But as deputy director of Biopreparat, Alibek had had access to many more classified programs than Pasechnik did, including delivery systems for the germ bombs. This work, Alibek said, took place inside a top secret unit of Biopreparat called the Biological Group, located inside the Soviet General Staff

Operations Directorate. Here, weapons designers crafted specially designed missiles that would be used in a biological warfare attack against the United States. Weaponized pathogens are, for the most part, fragile microbes. They generally cannot withstand extreme temperature fluctuations, as happens in flight. The Soviets had solved this problem, Alibek said, by retrofitting long-range ICBM missiles with mini–space capsules, like the ones astronauts rode in. The missile was a MIRV, a multiple independently targetable reentry vehicle, meaning each ICBM was capable of carrying ten warheads over a range of six thousand miles. Its NATO reporting name was SS-18 Satan.

Alibek also provided chilling details about a Soviet bioweapons programs called Chimera, whereby genetic material from two or more different organisms was combined to produce more virulent germs. Alibek told his handlers they should be very worried about this program, and said he had direct knowledge of a trial developed in the late 1980s in which a chimera, or hybrid, strain was created by inserting Venezuelan equine encephalomyelitis genes into smallpox. One of the ultimate goals of Chimera, Alibek said, was to create a monster hybrid of smallpox and Ebola. Alibek warned his handlers that the Soviets had sold secrets about genetically modified bioweapons to Libya, Iran, Iraq, India, Cuba, and former Soviet bloc countries in eastern Europe. U.S. officials took notes and listened. Alibek's greatest frustration, he would later say, was that these officials did not seem to comprehend the potentially catastrophic consequences of the Soviet program.

"They did not care about our genetic work," Alibek lamented. "When it came to strategic questions," his interrogators told him that they were uninterested in what he had to say. "We are only interested in what you know," they said, "not what you think could happen." The Pentagon was happy to learn what he knew about the inner workings of Biopreparat. Alibek's information was useful, he was told, but his opinions were unwelcome. Soon, this too would change.

There had been a blind spot at the Pentagon and at DARPA since the earliest days of the Cold War, an aloof indifference to the opinions of biologists. Officials at the White House and the Defense Department were much more interested in what the hard scientists, like the Jason scientists, had to say. Back in 1968 Nobel laureate Joshua Lederberg pointed out this disadvantage in a science column he wrote regularly for the *Washington Post,* accusing the federal government of "blindness to the pace of biological advance and its accessibility to the most perilous genocidal experimentation." Lederberg was referring to biological weapons. Starting in 1945, with the advent of the atomic bomb, the Pentagon had largely relied on the advice and counsel of physicists and mathematicians as far as advanced weaponry was concerned, but rarely biologists.

If World War I had been the chemists' war and World War II the physicists' war, now, given the threats facing the Pentagon, would World War III be the biologists' war?

Briefed on Alibek's revelations about the Soviet bioweapons program, DARPA was quick to note this blind spot and to take action. "DoD had very little capability in biology" in the early 1990s, recalls Larry Lynn, DARPA's director from 1995 to 1998. Now DARPA recognized just how worrisome it was that biology, and the life sciences in general, could lead the next revolution in military affairs, and recognized, too, that the Department of Defense was behind the curve. The Pentagon needed its own core group of advisors, American scientists at the leading edge of biology. The Jason scientists were contacted.

Since leaving the Institute of Defense Analyses in 1973, the Jason scientists had had several homes. For the first eight years they received their defense contracts through the Stanford Research Institute in Menlo Park, California. SRI was a longtime ARPA contractor and an information technology pioneer, and had been one of the first four nodes on the ARPANET. Under the SRI in the 1970s, the

Jasons brought several computer scientists and electrical engineers into their ranks. And because they no longer served ARPA alone, their client list had expanded. Under the SRI banner, the Jasons conducted studies and wrote reports for the CIA, the Navy, NASA, the Department of Energy, the Defense Nuclear Agency, the National Science Foundation, and others.

In 1981 the Jason scientists moved their headquarters to the east coast once again, this time under the MITRE Corporation banner. There, Gordon MacDonald, himself a Jason scientist, served as MITRE's chief scientist. Business continued to grow, with the Jasons still conducting most of their work as summer studies.

In 1986, defense contractor General Dynamics gave the Jason scientists their own room, back in California again, on its sprawling 120-acre La Jolla campus, which they still used as of 2014. "It's a SCIF," Murph Goldberger explained in a 2014 interview, referring to a "sensitive compartmented information facility," meaning it was built to Defense Department security specifications and ringed by a barbed-wire perimeter. The room at General Dynamics was not exactly a college dormitory with a view of the ocean, but as Goldberger noted, "times have changed."

After the Berlin Wall came down and the bioweapons threat ratcheted up, Jason "was told it was wise to bring biologists into the ranks," said Goldberger. DARPA director Larry Lynn reached out personally to Joshua Lederberg. After decades of forewarning, Lederberg was finally brought on board as a defense scientist. He would now serve as chairman of DARPA's science advisors for biology. In 1994, DARPA director Larry Lynn and a team traveled to Moscow, laying plans for how to use technology to keep track of what was going on there. The details of this trip remain classified.

Biological weapons were the new national security concern, and in the fall of 1995, in an effort to have sanctions against his country relieved, Iraqi president Saddam Hussein disclosed to the

United Nations that Iraq had been producing biological weapons by the ton, including botulinum toxin, camelpox, and hemorrhagic conjunctivitis. Iraq admitted it had hundreds of scientists working in at least five separate facilities, a number of which were located underground, and which had survived destruction in the Gulf War. In 1996, the CIA provided President Clinton with reports on the biological weapons programs believed to be in existence inside North Korea, Iran, Iraq, Libya, and Syria—all still classified in 2015. In 1997, the Jasons were asked to conduct a summer study on biological weapons threats. The group had a new scientist in their ranks, the microbiologist Stephen M. Block, who, several years later, published some of the unclassified findings of this Jason summer study.

The most significant threat, noted Block, was the accelerated pace at which discoveries in molecular biology were being made. "Recent advances in life sciences have changed the nature and scope" of microbiology, he wrote, revealing "inevitably, a dark side." The Jason scientists warned just how dangerous the threat of genetically engineered pathogens had become. Modern bioscience has made "possible the creation of entirely new WMD, endowed with unprecedented power to destroy," Block wrote. "Was [this alarmist] hype, or largely warranted?" he asked. Block said the Jason scientists had concluded "the latter." In Block's opinion, "it seems likely that such weapons will eventually come to exist, simply because of the lamentable ease with which they may be constructed." They were cheap, easy to make, and, if you knew what you were looking for and could find out how to create them, freely available in the public domain.

The ability to genetically engineer pathogens had raised the threat level. For use as a weapon, the possibilities were limitless. "If you were to mix Ebola with the communicability of measles to create a pathogen that would continue to alter itself in such a way to evade treatment," wrote Block, the rate of Ebola's transmission and infectivity would skyrocket. These stealth viruses, which Alibek called chimeras, were even more menacing from a psychological perspective, Block said.

"The basic idea behind a stealth virus is to produce a tightly regulated, cryptic viral infection, using a vector that can enter and spread in human cells, remaining resident for lengthy periods without detectable harm," Block wrote, calling this a "silent viral load." One example that exists naturally is herpes simplex, or the common cold sore. The virus lies dormant until it is one day triggered by what is believed to be an environmental assault on the body, like sunburn or stress. Similarly, an unwitting population could be "slowly pre-infected with a stealth virus over an extended period, possibly years, and then synchronously triggered," Block wrote. This wicked concept had enormous potential in the realm of psychological warfare. As far as using a stealth virus as a weapon, the Jasons were dually concerned. Stealth viruses carried with them "a utility beyond that of traditional bioweapons," they concluded. "For example they could be disseminated and used to blackmail a population based on their activation."

If the notion of a stealth virus, or silent load, sounded improbable, Block cited a little-known controversy involving the anti-polio vaccination campaign of the late 1950s and early 1960s. According to Block, during this effort millions of Americans risked contracting the "cryptic human infection" of monkey virus, without ever being told. "These vaccines," writes Block, "were prepared using live African green monkey kidney cells, and batches of polio vaccine became contaminated by low levels of a monkey virus, Simian virus 40 (SV40), which eluded the quality control procedures of the day. As a result, large numbers of people—probably millions, in fact—were inadvertently exposed to SV40." Block says that two possible outcomes of this medical disaster remain debated. One side says the 98 million people vaccinated dodged a bullet. The other side believes there is evidence that the vaccine did harm. "A great deal of speculation occurs about whether [simian virus] may be responsible for some disease" that manifests much later in the vaccinated person's life, says Block, including cancer. The subject remains highly contentious, with vaccine makers and the National Institutes for Health engaged in acrimonious debate with scientists who have found the SV40 monkey virus in cancerous human tumors.

The 1997 Jason report on biological weapons remains classified. Shortly after it was completed, President Clinton issued two Presidential Decision Directives, PDD 62 and PDD 63, both of which addressed the biological weapons threat and both of which also remained classified as of 2015. Biological warfare defense was now a "very high DARPA priority." In 1996, DARPA opened a new office called the Unconventional Countermeasures Program. Congress quickly funded this "high-priority initiative" with $30 million for its first fiscal year. "DARPA is seeking partnerships with the research community and the biotechnology and pharmaceutical industries to develop innovative new treatment, prevention and diagnostic strategies for biological warfare threats," read one of the earliest program overview memos.

Initially, DARPA's primary focus was on protecting U.S. soldiers. An internal memo noted, "Troops, ports, airfields, supply depots, etc. are vulnerable to biological attacks," and yet, paradoxically, "most likely first use [of bioweapons] will be against population centers of ours or our allies." DARPA had a mission to develop "broad strategies to counter the threat." This effort explored four areas: sensing, protection, diagnosis, and countermeasures. But DARPA as an agency was dedicated to advanced research and development, and the first three areas, sensing, protection, and diagnosis, were "only marginally protective." DARPA wanted its scientists and researchers to strive for revolutionary goals, to focus on innovative countermeasures that did not yet exist. Larry Lynn told program managers that he wanted to create the "Star Wars of biology," a reference to President

Reagan's Strategic Defense Initiative. Lynn challenged DARPA scientists to push existing biotech boundaries and to come up with a vaccine, gene, or chemical that could allow the human body to "incapacitate or debilitate" a biological agent on its own, before the pathogen made its host sick. It was a brilliant, bold idea. But could it work? Was there time?

The 1994 international nonfiction best-seller *The Hot Zone,* by Richard Preston, is about the origins of, and incidents involving, the Ebola virus. Three years later, in 1997, Preston wrote a fictional account of a bioterrorism attack in New York City, titled *The Cobra Event.* Preston's genetically engineered biological weapon, a chimera virus called Cobra, is imaginary, but his information was based on real reporting. He had interviewed Christopher Davis, the Royal Navy surgeon who had been Vladimir Pasechnik's original handler, as well as Ken Alibek and many top scientists at USAMRIID.

President Clinton read *The Cobra Event* shortly after it was published and was alarmed. He asked Secretary of Defense William Cohen to read the book and have an intelligence analysis of the viability of a real-life Cobra event written up. Secretary of Health and Human Services Donna E. Shalala also read *The Cobra Event* and included a plot summary in a journal article she authored for the Centers for Disease Control and Prevention. The following year, in 1998, Richard Preston testified before Congress in Senate hearings on the question "Threats to America: Are We Prepared?"

"Biopreparat was like an egg," Preston said of the Soviet program. "The outside part was devoted to peaceful medical research. The hidden inner part, the yolk, was devoted to the creation and production of sophisticated bioweapons powders—smallpox, black plague, anthrax, tularemia, the Marburg virus, and certain brain viruses." In this public forum, Preston outlined Russia's capacity to launch a biological weapons attack on the United States. Using smallpox as an example, Preston said that as recently as a few years prior, Soviet-era ICBMs fitted with specially loaded MIRV warheads stood ready and able to launch. Those warheads, Preston said, carried "twenty tons of freeze-dried small-pox powder" and "probably . . . an equal number of Black Death [plague] warheads." Before the Berlin Wall came down, Preston summarized, if the Soviets had decided to launch a biological weapons attack against the United States, his research indicated that they "could have easily hit the one-hundred largest cities in the United States with devastating combined outbreaks of strategic smallpox and Black Death, an attack that could easily kill as many people as a major nuclear war." The Soviet Union no longer existed, but the warheads and their contents did. The congressional hearings supported the idea that biological warfare was an apocalyptic nightmare waiting to happen. Something radical had to be done. The bioweapons defense industry was like a sleeping giant, now awakened.

Ken Alibek had been in the United States for six years. He spoke English now, had friends, held lucrative defense contractor jobs, and was primed to enter the public domain. In February 1998 Alibek made his first television appearance on the ABC News program *Primetime Live.* In planning for World War III, Alibek said, the Russians had prepared "hundreds of tons" of bioweapons. Now, even with the wall down, Alibek said, the Russians "continue to do research to develop new biological agents." In March, Richard Preston profiled Dr. Alibek for the *New Yorker* magazine. Copies of the article were distributed to members of Congress through the *Congressional Record.*

Before the *Primetime Live* airing, Ken Alibek was not a public figure. He had been moving quietly in U.S. government, military, and intelligence circles, sharing information with individuals who held national security clearances similar to his own. Now, his opinions found a much wider audience. American citizens were interested in what he had to say and so were the Joint Chiefs of Staff. In May 1998 Alibek testified before a congressional committee hearing on terrorism and intelligence. He even had a private meeting at the Pentagon, in the E-Ring, where he briefed General Joseph W. Ralston, the vice chairman of the Joint Chiefs of Staff and the second-highest-ranking military officer in the United States. The narrative of the biological weapons threat was gaining traction in the mainstream press. In June 1998, President Clinton asked Congress to provide $294 million in funding for anti-bioterrorism programs. In October, Alibek was featured in the PBS *Frontline* documentary "Plague War."

In the six years since his defection, Ken Alibek had been a busy man professionally. For the first few years of his new life in America, he held various research and consulting positions at the National Institutes of Health and the CIA and with private defense contractors. Notably, he developed a relationship with Dr. Charles Bailey, former chief scientist at USAMRIID. "I helped to build Alibek's reputation with the military," said Bailey. "A lot of people were impressed with Alibek. I was impressed." When Bailey went to work for a defense contractor in Huntsville, Alabama, he brought Dr. Alibek along. Later, from 1996 to 1998, Alibek served as program manager at SRS Technologies, an information technology company based in California. In 1998 he and Bailey both worked as program managers for Battelle Memorial Institute, the defense contractor that handled ARPA's Vietnam-era Project Agile reports. In April 1999, Alibek became president of a defense contractor called Hadron Advanced Biosystems, Inc., located in Manassas, Virginia, whose mission was to "develop innovative solutions for the intelligence community...including intelligent weapons systems and biological weapons defense." Dr. Bailey served as vice president. Hadron became a go-to place for several former Soviet bioweapons engineers, microbiologists Alibek had formerly worked with at Biopreparat. Among them was Sergei Popov.

Popov was an expert in synthetic bioweapons and had been a member of the Biopreparat team that worked on the nefarious Chimera program in the Soviet Union, recombining genes to make stealth viruses. At Biopreparat, Popov had helped create a class of bioweapons with "new and unusual properties, difficult to recognize, difficult to treat," Popov told the PBS program *Nova* in 1998. "Essentially I arranged the research towards more virulent agents causing more death and more pathological symptoms." Like Alibek, Popov had defected to the United States after the Soviet Union ceased to exist.

At Hadron Advanced Biosystems, Alibek, Popov, and Bailey expressed their determination to find a cure-all against bioweapons, a broad-spectrum antidote that could shoot down dangerous pathogens in the body before they were able to infect a human host. This was similar to what DARPA director Larry Lynn was seeking when he asked his program managers to create a "Star Wars of biology" program. On *Nova,* Popov described what the doctors were working on as a countermeasure with the ability to "induce so-called 'unspecific immunity,' which would be efficient in protecting people against quite a big range of different diseases." Alibek called the concept an "immune booster." Other military research scientists called the idea impossible.

One noteworthy skeptic was Dr. Phillip K. Russell, the former commanding general of the Army Medical Research and Development Command. Dr. Russell told the *Wall Street Journal* that searching for a booster for the immune system was "complex and fraught with risk. Turn it on, and it does things that can be detrimental as well as protective." Dr. Russell also stated that Dr. Alibek was better at theorizing than at experimenting, and that the former Soviet bioweapons engineer was "as much an enigma as a scientist as he is as an individual."

Alibek stayed focused on his research goals. In 1999 he approached DARPA. Here was an agency that was willing to take risks. And with a recent infusion of money from Congress, there were many new contracts to be had in biological warfare defense. As the chief scientist at defense contractor Hadron, Dr. Ken Alibek was in a prime position to receive DARPA contracts.

In the fall of 1999, Hadron Advanced Biosystems was awarded its first one-year DARPA contract, for $3.3 million, roughly $4.6 million in 2015. Alibek issued a press statement reading, "We hope this [DARPA] program is just the beginning of new, innovative research, funded by government agencies." Alibek told colleagues that one day he hoped to build a drug manufacturing plant in the former Soviet republic of Ukraine. He also told colleagues that if terrorists got their hands on biological weapons, all of America would be at risk.

In October 1999, DARPA invited Dr. Alibek to testify before the House Committee on Armed Services' Subcommittee on Research and Development and Subcommittee on Procurement. In his opening statement, Alibek told members of Congress in no uncertain terms what they should be afraid of. "What we need to expect," Alibek said, is biological weapons in the hands of "some terrorist organization."

Which is exactly what may or may not have happened two years later, in October 2001.

CHAPTER EIGHTEEN

Transforming Humans for War

Retired four-star general Paul F. Gorman recalls first learning about the "weakling of the battlefield" as a young soldier in the 1950s. This was before Gorman fought in Vietnam, before he served as special assistant to the Joint Chiefs of Staff, before the Department of Defense detailed him to the CIA, and before he completed his uniformed service and became commander in chief of the U.S. Southern Command.

"Soldiers get tired and soldiers get fearful," said Gorman, age eighty-nine in 2014, in an interview for this book. "Frequently, soldiers just don't want to fight. Attention must always be paid to the soldier himself." Since its inception in 1958, DARPA's focus has been on the research and development of vast weapons systems of the future. Starting in 1990, and owing to individuals like General Gorman, a new focus was put on soldiers, airmen, and sailors. On transforming humans for war.

General Gorman learned about the weakling of the battlefield while reading S. L. A. Marshall, the U.S. Army combat historian during World War II. After interviewing soldiers who participated in the Normandy beach landings, Marshall concluded, "On the field of battle man is not only a thinking animal but a beast of burden." It was fatigue that was responsible for an overwhelming number of casualties, Marshall learned.

"I didn't know my strength was gone until I hit the beach," Sergeant Bruce Hensley told Marshall. "I was carrying part of a machine gun. Normally I could run with it... but I found I couldn't even walk with it.... So I crawled across the sand dragging it with me. I felt ashamed of my own weakness, but looking around I saw the others crawling and dragging the weights they normally carried."

And Staff Sergeant Thomas B. Turner told Marshall, "Under fire we learned what we had never been told—that fear and fatigue are about the same in their effect on an advance," such as storming a beach.

Reading these soldiers' accounts of exhaustion from the sheer weight of what they carried into battle planted an idea in Paul Gorman's brain. Decades later, in the 1970s, Gorman was at the Los Alamos National Laboratory, in New Mexico, "working on a sensitive program," when he got an idea about how to strengthen the weakling of the battlefield. It could be done, he thought, with a strength-amplifying mechanical suit.

"Los Alamos was developing a suit for people who had to be encapsulated because they were working in a radioactive environment," Gorman recalls. The suits were lead-lined, heavy, and cumbersome. "Much of the science focused on how to lighten the load." But Gorman noticed something else as well. "The [people] inside the suits struggled with sensory deprivation," he says, "and when deprived of sensory inputs, a person cannot function at capacity for very long." Soldiers need strength and endurance, which led to Gorman's pioneering idea for a battle suit of the future: the "quintessential man-machine interface [for] the soldier who fights on foot."

General Gorman retired from the Army in 1985 and began working for DARPA. In 1990 he wrote a paper describing an "integrated powered exoskeleton" that could transform the weakling of the battlefield into a veritable super-soldier. Gorman's SuperTroop concept would make the soldier stronger and give him enhanced command, control, communication, and intelligence capabilities. This was the origin of the now famous DARPA exoskeleton.

The exoskeleton Gorman proposed offered protection against chemical, biological, electromagnetic, and ballistic threats, including direct fire from a .50 caliber bullet. It "incorporated audio, visual and haptic [touch] sensors," Gorman explains, including thermal imaging for the eyes, sound suppression for the ears, and fiber optics from head to fingertips. Its interior would be climate controlled, and each soldier would have his own physiological specifications embedded on a chip within his dog tags. "When a soldier donned his ST [SuperTroop] battledress," Gorman wrote, "he would insert one dog-tag into a slot under the chest armor, thereby loading his personal program into the battle suit's computer," giving the twenty-first-century soldier an extraordinary ability to hear, see, move, shoot, and communicate. "The exoskeleton would require a very powerful computer," Gorman surmised. Since the technology did not yet exist, he proposed that the SuperTroop concept be fielded first through SIMNET simulators. A program called the Soldier System Model and Simulation was born, and work on the DARPA exoskeleton began.

DARPA had spent the previous three decades focusing on advancing weapons platforms. Now the agency would research and develop technologies for the dismounted soldier. The biological weapons threat caused DARPA to bring biologists into its ranks, and with the life sciences at the fore, DARPA began to look inside the human body, toward a scientific capability that could transform soldiers from the inside out.

Throughout the 1990s, the exponential progress of three technologies made this possible: biotechnology, information technology, and nanotechnology. In 1999 DARPA created the Defense Sciences Office (DSO) and made Michael Goldblatt its director. With twenty-eight program managers under his control, Goldblatt would be overseeing the single largest number of program managers at DARPA, an agency that in 1999 had 140 program managers in total.

Michael Goldblatt came to DARPA with a radical vision. He believed that through advanced technology, in twenty or fifty years' time, human beings could be the "first species to control evolution." In an interview for this book in 2014, Goldblatt described the climate at DARPA when he arrived. "Biology was an area where the Defense Department was underserved. War was shifting. The pattern of warfare was shifting. So was the thinking." The turn of the century "was a radical time to be at DARPA," Goldblatt says, and in this time of momentous change he saw great opportunity. "Suddenly, there were zoologists in the office." As director of DSO at DARPA, Goldblatt believed that defense sciences could demonstrate that "the next frontier was inside of our own selves." In this way, at DARPA, Goldblatt became a pioneer in military-based transhumanism—the notion that man can and will alter the human condition fundamentally by augmenting humans with machines and other means.

When Goldblatt arrived at DARPA in 1999, the Biological Warfare Defense Program was two and a half years old. "The threat was growing far faster than the solutions were coming in. It was a hard problem," Goldblatt recalls. "[President] Clinton gave lots of money to the countermeasures program for unconventional pathogens," he says. "There was lots of money for biology programs at DARPA." Goldblatt saw the creation of the super-soldier as imperative to twenty-first-century warfare. "Soldiers having no physical, physiological, or cognitive limitation will be key to survival and operational dominance in the future," Goldblatt told his program managers just a few weeks after arriving at DARPA.

How did Michael Goldblatt, a biologist and venture capitalist from the Midwest, end up running what would be one of the most consequential defense sciences programs of the early twenty-first century?

"In the mid-1990s I had not heard of DARPA," Goldblatt insists. But as chief science officer and vice president of research, development, and nutrition at McDonald's, the world's largest fast food restaurant chain, Goldblatt had his finger on the pulse of food-related national health scares. When, in 1993, four children died and 623 people fell seriously ill after eating *E. coli*–infected hamburgers sold at Jack in the Box restaurants, Goldblatt became hyper-aware. All of a sudden, a previously unknown bacterium, O157:H7, "was on everybody's radar," says Goldblatt. Every person in the fast food business "was on pathogen alert."

Goldblatt, the venture capitalist, got an idea. "In an effort to identify ways to enhance food safety and eliminate unwanted pathogens, a guy I was working with, Alvin Chow, and I came up with a technology for self-sterilizing packages—packages that sterilized products in the field." McDonald's decided not to use the technology that Goldblatt and Chow had developed, so the two men sought out a different buyer. "We thought this technology would be useful to the government," Goldblatt says. "We did some research and found this group called DARPA. I called them. No response. I wrote to them. No response. I called again. I said, 'This is Michael Goldblatt from McDonald's. I'd like to speak with Larry Lynn,'" the director of DARPA. "After a short while, he called me back. He thought I was with McDonnell Aircraft. I said, 'No, McDonald's hamburgers.' There was riotous laughter," Goldblatt recalls. "I told Larry about the self-sterilizing packages. How they could be used in field hospitals or on the battlefield. Larry was blown away. He said, 'We want you to come to DARPA.' And I did."

At DARPA, Goldblatt realized that almost anything that could be imagined could at least be tried. In the Defense Sciences Office, programs were initiated to develop technologies that would make soldiers, also called warfighters, stronger, smarter, more capable, and would give them more endurance than other humans. One program, called Persistence in Combat, addressed three areas that slowed soldiers down on the battlefield: pain, wounds, and excessive bleeding.

Goldblatt hired a biotechnology firm to develop a pain vaccine. "It works with the body's inflammatory response that is responsible for pain," Goldblatt explained in 2014. The way the vaccine would work is that, if a soldier got shot, he would experience "ten to thirty seconds of agony then no pain for thirty days. The vaccine would reduce the pain triggered by inflammation and swelling," allowing the warfighter to keep fighting so long as bleeding could be stopped. To develop new ways to try to stop bleeding, Goldblatt initiated another program that involved injecting millions of microscopic magnets into a person, which could later be brought together into a single area to stop bleeding with the wave of a wand. The scientist in charge of that program, Dr. Harry T. Whelan, worked on several "rapid healing" programs under the banner "DARPA Soldier Self Care."

Another idea regarding ways to allow wounded soldiers to survive blood loss and avoid going into shock involved figuring out a way to get a human to go into a kind of hibernation, or suspended animation, until help arrived. Achieving this goal would give a soldier precious hours, or even days, to survive while awaiting evacuation or triage. Bears hibernate. Why can't man? DARPA DSO scientists asked these and other questions, including, could a chemical compound like hydrogen sulfide produce a hibernation-like state in a man?

Sleep was another field of intense research at DSO. In the Continually Assisted Performance program, scientists worked on ways to create a "24/7 soldier," one who required little or no sleep for up to seven days. If this could be achieved, the enemy's need for sleep would put them at an extreme disadvantage. Goldblatt's program managers hired marine biologists studying certain sea animals to look for clues. Whales and dolphins don't sleep; as mammals, they would drown if they did. Unlike humans, they are somehow able to control the lobes of their left and right brains so that while one lobe sleeps, the opposite lobe stays awake, allowing the animal to swim. While some DARPA scientists ruminated over the question of how humans might one day control the lobes of their own brains, other scientists experimented with drugs like Modafinil, a powerful medication used to counter sleep apnea and narcolepsy, to keep warfighters awake.

To address strength and endurance issues, Goldblatt initiated a program called the Mechanically Dominant Soldier. What if soldiers could have ten times the muscle endurance of enemy soldiers? What if they could leap seven feet and be able to cool down their own body temperature? What if the military benchmark of eighty pull-ups a day could be raised to three hundred pull-ups a day? "We want every war fighter to look like Lance Armstrong as far as metabolic profile," program manager Joe Bielitzki told *Washington Post* reporter Joel Garreau a decade before Armstrong resigned from athletics in disgrace.

Under the DSO banner, in a program called the Brain-Machine Interface, DARPA scientists studied how brain implants could enhance cognitive ability. The program's first goal was to create "a wireless brain modem for a freely moving rat," said DARPA's Dr. Eric Eisenstadt in 1999. The scientists would implant a chip in the rat's brain to see if they could remotely control the animal's movements. "The objective of this effort," Eisenstadt explained, "is to use remote teleoperation via direct interconnections with the brain." DARPA's bigger vision for its Brain-Machine Interface program was to allow future "soldiers [to] communicate by thought alone."

Dr. Eisenstadt asked his program managers to "picture a time when humans see in the UV [ultraviolet] and IR [infrared] portions of the electromagnetic spectrum, or hear speech on the noisy flight deck of an aircraft carrier." What might sound like science fiction elsewhere in the world at DARPA was future science. "Imagine a time when the human brain has its own wireless modem so that instead of acting on thoughts, warfighters have thoughts that act," Eisenstadt suggested. Fifteen years later, the Brain-Machine Interface program would astound. But turn-of-the-millennium critics cried foul, and a spotlight was turned on DARPA's super-soldier pursuits. Critics said that the quest to enhance human performance on the battlefield would lead scientists down a morally dangerous path. Michael Goldblatt disagreed.

"How is an exoskeleton or a brain implant different from a pacemaker or a cochlear implant or a prosthetic?" Goldblatt asked in a 2014 interview. For Goldblatt, the scientific exploration into transhumanism is personal. His daughter Gina was born with cerebral palsy, a group of permanent physical disorders related to movement that get worse over time, never better. Goldblatt believes that the physically impaired or weak have every right to compete with their fellows, and if science allows them a way and a means to do so, that science should be pursued. "When we learned Gina had cerebral palsy," said Goldblatt, "I called the smartest person I knew. He said to me, 'It's permanent. Now accept that.'" Goldblatt could still recall the long, dark silence that followed that statement until finally the smart person on the other end of the phone said to him, "Now ask yourself, what are you going to do about it?"

For Goldblatt, the answer was clear. He would provide his daughter with every opportunity to compete with other children, through performance enhancements like a motorized wheelchair and the best computers available, with everything in her bedroom remotely controlled. This vision carried over to DARPA, where, as director of DSO, Goldblatt would oversee performance enhancements for the warfighter on a national scale, spending over $100 million on programs to reengineer the twenty-first-century soldier fighting on foot.

Asked about that morally dangerous path, Goldblatt rephrases his question, "How is having a cochlear implant that helps the deaf hear any different than having a chip in your brain that could help control your thoughts?" When questioned about unintended consequences, like controlling humans for nefarious ends, Goldblatt insists, "There are unintended consequences for everything."

It was June 2001 and the new president, George W. Bush, had been in office for six months. The biological weapons threat continued to interest the public and was regularly featured in the news. And war games, including the computer-based SIMNET, had become an integral part of national security strategizing. But in some arenas, old school role-playing prevailed. In the third week of June, a group of fifteen former senior officials and two journalists assembled at Andrews Air Force Base in Washington, D.C., to carry out a script-based, asymmetrical attack simulation called *Dark Winter.* In the fictional game scenario, the nation has been pummeled into chaos after terrorists attack Oklahoma with a biological weapon containing smallpox. The *Dark Winter* exercise involved three National Security Council meetings taking place over a period of two weeks. In the war game, the National Security Council members were role-played by former officials. The onetime U.S. senator and chairman of the Senate Armed Services Committee, Sam Nunn, played *Dark Winter*'s fictional president; the former special counselor to the president and White House communications director, David Gergen, played the national security advisor; a former vice chief of staff of the U.S. Army, General John. H. Tilelli, played the chairman of the Joint Chiefs of Staff; the former director of the CIA, James Woolsey, played *Dark Winter*'s fictional CIA, director; and the sitting governor of Oklahoma, Frank Keating, played the fictional governor of Oklahoma. *Dark Winter*'s war game plot revolved around how the players would respond to a hypothetical biological weapons attack.

First, the game players were "briefed" on background events.

"Last month Russian authorities, with support from the FBI, arrested Yusuuf Abdul Aziiz, a known operative in Al-Qaida and a close personal friend and suspected senior lieutenant of Usama bin Laden," read the *Dark Winter* script. "Yusuuf was caught in a sting operation that had been developing during the last year. He was attempting to acquire 50 kilograms of plutonium and was also attempting to arrange the purchase of several biological pathogens that had been weaponized by the Soviet Union."

The war game scenario also involved Iraq. *Dark Winter* game players were told that two days earlier, "Iraqi forces in the South of Iraq moved into offensive positions along the Kuwaiti border," just as they had done in real life in 1990, which set the Gulf War in motion. Also on background, the war gamers learned about domestic conditions: "US Economy is in good shape. Polls show a slim majority of Americans oppose a major deployment of US troops to the Persian Gulf. Most Americans agree that Saddam's Iraqi regime represents a real threat to stability in the region and to American interests." It is worth noting that in real life, the first two fictional statement were based in fact, but the third one, that most Americans saw Saddam's Iraq as a threat, was not a fact. What was factual was that the man who had been secretary of defense during the Gulf War, Dick Cheney, was now the vice president of the United States, and he saw Saddam's Iraq as a threat. As for *Dark Winter,* the game began when the fictional governor of Oklahoma informed the National Security Council that his state has been attacked with a smallpox weapon.

Over the course of the fourteen days, for the game players, the scenario went from bad to worse to calamitous. Entire states shut down, chaos reigned, massive traffic jams ensued, civil liberties were suspended, many banks and post offices closed. As vaccines ran out, "angry citizens denounce[d] the government's failure to stop the smallpox epidemic." Civilians started shooting policemen. The National Guard started shooting civilians. Finally, a fictional "prominent Iraqi defector claim[ed] that Iraq arranged the bioweapons attack on the US through intermediaries," most likely Yusuuf Abdul Aziiz, the fictional deputy of the real Osama bin Laden.

In the *Dark Winter* war game, 3 million Americans died of smallpox. As a result, a fictional CNN-Gallup poll revealed that 48 percent of Americans wanted the president to consider using nuclear weapons in response. The game ended there.

One month later, on July 23, 2001, former chairman of the Senate Armed Services Committee Sam Nunn—the man who played *Dark Winter's* fictional president—told Congress during a House hearing on combating biological terrorism that the real emergency revealed in the war game was just how unprepared America was to handle an actual biological weapons attack.

"I was honored to play the part of the President in the exercise *Dark Winter,*" Nunn told Congress. "You often don't know what you don't know until you've been tested," he said. "And it's a lucky thing for the United States that, as the emergency broadcast network used to say, 'this is just a test, this is not a real emergency.' But Mr. Chairman, our lack of preparation is a real emergency."

No one said, "But *Dark Winter* was only a game."

Lines were being blurred. Games were influencing reality. Man was merging with machine. What else would the technological advances of the twenty-first century bring?

In August 2001, scientists from Los Alamos and the Lawrence Livermore National Laboratory—renamed in honor of its founder, Ernest O. Lawrence—traveled to the West Desert Test Center at Dugway Proving Ground in Utah. There, inside the Special Programs Division, the scientists tested a new sensor system designed to detect killer pathogens such as anthrax and botulinum toxin. The name of the program was the Biological Aerosol Sentry and Information Systems, or BASIS. It was hailed as a plan for "guarding the air we breathe." In truth, all BASIS could do was "detect to treat." Unlike chemical weapons, the presence of which could now be identified before release through an advanced technology called acoustic detection, biological weapons could be detected only after the fact. Even worse, the sensor systems were notorious for giving false alarms; the filter system was flawed. In open literature, Livermore acknowledged that false alarms were a serious concern but did not admit that their own problem was widespread. "Any technology that reports a terrorist incident where none exists may induce the very panic and social disruption it is intended to thwart. Therefore, the rate of false-positive alarms must be zero or very nearly so."

By the summer of 2001, Vice President Cheney was becoming increasingly concerned about a possible biological weapons attack directed at the White House. Plans were put in place to install Livermore's BASIS system throughout the White House and its grounds.

In the summer of 2001, DARPA's biological weapons defense initiative was one of the fastest-growing programs in the defense sciences world. A decade earlier, before the defection of the Soviet scientists, the threat was not even known to exist. Now the industry was a several-hundred-million-dollar-a-year field.

Programs were largely speculative: as of yet, in a conundrum that ran parallel to ARPA's first quandary, ballistic missile defense, there was no way to defend against a biological weapons attack. Only if there were a terrorist attack involving the release of a deadly pathogen on American soil could biological weapons defense truly be put to the test. Defensive programs and countermeasure programs would then skyrocket. Which is exactly what happened next.

PART IV

THE WAR ON TERROR

CHAPTER NINETEEN

Terror Strikes

Early on the morning of September 11, 2001, twenty-four-year-old David A. Bray was in Atlanta, at the U.S. Centers for Disease Control (CDC), for a briefing with the Laboratory Response Network for Bioterrorism. Bray was the information technology chief for the Bioterrorism Preparedness and Response Program at CDC, a program established by President Clinton under his U.S. policy on counterterrorism. It was Bray's job to make sure people got good information when and as they needed it. There was so much information out there, filtering out the important information was key. A man cannot drink from a fire hose. The meeting on September 11 was supposed to start at 9:00 a.m.

"When I signed up for work in bioterrorism I thought to myself, what kind of world requires my job?" asks Bray. That spring, he says, "we had received a memo that said, 'Be on alert for Al Qaeda activity June through August 2001.' It specifically ended in August."

It was September now, and Bray and his team were getting ready for the Bioterrorism Preparedness and Response team briefing when an airplane hit the North Tower of the World Trade Center.

"We got the news. Details were sketchy." At 9:03, he recalls, "when the second airplane hit, we definitely knew it was a terrorism event."

Many of the CDC employees were dispatched elsewhere. "A large group started piling computers into cars and were sent to an undisclosed off-site bunker," says Bray, explaining, "We were concerned that a second event would involve bioterrorism."

David Bray has always been a remarkably focused person. His area of expertise is informatics, the science of how information is gathered, stored, and retrieved. The son of a minister and a teacher, Bray started winning national science prizes in middle school. By age fifteen, he had his first job with the federal government, with the Department of Energy at its Continuous Electron Beam Accelerator Facility in Newport News, Virginia.

"I was trying to understand the universe, and the lab was looking for new energy sources," Bray says of his youth, when he had to get a special permit to work for the Department of Energy so as to comply with federal laws regarding child labor. By the time Bray was sixteen, he had been written up in the *Washington Post* for inventing a prizewinning computer program that predicted how best to clean up an oil spill. At age seventeen Bray was working for the Department of Defense. Before he had turned twenty-one, he had added jobs with the National Institutes of Health and the Department of Agriculture to his résumé. In between jobs he attended college, studying science, biology, and journalism. One summer he worked in South Africa as a health reporter for the *Cape Argus News.* What interested Bray most was information. How people get information and what they do with the information they have.

As a reporter covering the AIDS crisis in South Africa, Bray observed how informed people were still willing to ignore dangers right in front of them. In 1997 more than one out of six people in South Africa had the AIDS virus, and the epidemic was spreading out of control. Bray went around the countryside talking to South African students about the risks they faced, and how easily they could protect themselves with prophylactics. "They knew that they should wear protection," Bray says, "but I asked them if they would wear protection, and they said they would not." This was hardly shocking. Bray said many Americans had the same attitude: "It's not going to happen to me." He began thinking about how to get people to follow the best course of action, certainly as far as public health goes, based on the information they have. At the Centers for Disease Control, he found a place where he could focus on this idea.

The terrorist attacks on the morning of September 11 created what Bray calls a "hyper-turbulent environment." In this kind of fear-fueled setting, "knowledge is the most strategically significant resource of an organization," says Bray. Not more knowledge but better knowledge. Good, clear, factual information. Data about what is going on. Immediately after 9/11, says Bray, "we began reaching out to fifty states. We worked from the idea that the second event would be a biological event. We wanted to have information channels [open] with all fifty states" in the event that a bioterrorism attack were to occur.

DARPA had been sponsoring a surveillance program called Bio-ALIRT, for Bio-Event Advanced Leading Indicator Recognition Technology, an information-based technology program designed to enable computers to quickly recognize a bioweapons attack. To get a computer to "recognize" a bioweapons attack from the data was an extraordinary enterprise, and the program wasn't capable enough by 9/11.

Originally designed to protect troops on foreign soil, the program had recently expanded with plans for a national surveillance program of U.S. civilians, using an individual's medical records. The ramifications for collecting medical information on Americans for purposes of national security, but without their knowledge or consent, were profound. The Bio-ALIRT program fell under an emerging new industry called "biosurveillance," a contentious concept that has largely avoided public scrutiny. DARPA's military partner in this effort was the Walter Reed Army Institute of Research. Its civilian partners were the Johns Hopkins Applied Physics Laboratory, the University of Pittsburgh and Carnegie Mellon University, and the Stanford University Medical Informatics group. DARPA's defense contractor partners were General Dynamics Advanced Information Systems and the IBM Corporation.

The science behind Bio-ALIRT was intended to determine whether or not "automated detection algorithms" could identify an outbreak in either a bioweapons attack or a naturally occurring epidemic, like bird flu. Never mind the people—the doctors, nurses, and clinicians—reporting from the field. The idea behind Bio-ALIRT was to take human "bias" out of the equation and allow computers to do the job faster. As part of Bio-ALIRT, supercomputers would scan vast databases of medical records, in real time, as doctors entered data. Simultaneously, and also as part of Bio-ALIRT, supercomputers would scan sales at pharmacies of both prescription and nonprescription drugs, in real time. A privately held company called Surveillance Data, Inc., was hired to provide "de-identified" outpatient data, meaning that Surveillance Data, Inc., would "scrub" the medical information of personal details, such as names, social security numbers, and home addresses. It is unclear how much medical history was considered personal and how much the Bio-ALIRT supercomputers needed to differentiate between chronic medical conditions and new symptoms.

There were many flaws in the system, privacy issues among them, but one flaw rendered the program all but worthless. Bio-ALIRT's automated detection algorithms—the software that told the supercomputers what to look for—were based on data from the World Health Organization's International Classification of Diseases, ninth revision, known as ICD-9. But the biological weapons that were the most deadly—the chimera viruses and the recombinant pathogens like the ones the Soviet defectors Ken Alibek, Vladimir Pasechnik, Sergei Popov, and others had been working on at Biopreparat—were neither listed in nor identifiable by ICD-9. If Bio-ALIRT programs had been further along than in their earliest stages, the CDC could potentially have benefited from the system. But on 9/11, the biosurveillance industry was still in its infancy, and the Laboratory Response Network for Bioterrorism, which Bray led as information chief, had to rely on humans in all fifty states for receiving information. Bray and his team had an overwhelming amount of work cut out for themselves in this hyper-turbulent environment. Bray welcomed the challenge.

"It was a very long day," recalls Bray, who was personally doing the work that one day a computer might do.

On the morning of September 11, 2001, when the first airplane hit the North Tower of the World Trade Center, at 8:46 a.m., Vice President Dick Cheney was sitting in his office in the West Wing of the White House. He immediately focused his attention on the television screen. "It was a clear day, there were no weather problems, and then we saw the second airplane hit," Cheney recalled in his memoir. "At that moment, you knew this was a deliberate act. This was a terrorist act."

Vice President Cheney called President Bush, who was in Sarasota, Florida, visiting an elementary school. Vice President Cheney was on the phone with a presidential aide in Florida when his door burst open and a Secret Service agent rushed in. "He grabbed me and propelled me out of my office, and into the underground shelter in the White House," Cheney told CNN's John King. Later that same night, the Secret Service transferred the vice president to a more secure underground location outside the capital. En route from the White House in a helicopter, Cheney asked to view the damage to the Pentagon, which had been struck by a third plane at 9:37 a.m. "As we lifted off and headed up the Potomac, you could look out and see the Pentagon, see that black hole where it'd been hit," Cheney recalled. For the first time in the Pentagon's history, the very symbol of American military power stood broken and exposed with a huge gash in one of its five sides.

Cheney was helicoptered to an "undisclosed location," which was Site R, the underground bunker facility inside the Raven Rock Mountain Complex seventy-five miles from the White House, near Camp David. The location was disclosed in 2004 by journalist James Bamford. This was the Cold War–era underground command center that had caused President Eisenhower so much grief back in 1956, during the heated post–Castle Bravo debate over civil defense. Site R was originally designed to be the place where the president would be taken in the event of a nuclear attack. Eisenhower had struggled with the concept throughout his presidency, mindful that it was designed to provide safety for the president and his close advisors during a time when the very population the president was sworn to protect would be most vulnerable, exposed, and unaware.

At Raven Rock, Vice President Cheney began laying plans for war.

Also on the morning of September 11, 2001, shortly before 9:40 a.m., Secretary of Defense Donald Rumsfeld was sitting in his office on the third floor of the Pentagon listening to a prescheduled briefing by the CIA. Rumsfeld took notes on a small, round wooden table once used by General William Tecumseh Sherman, famous for his scorched earth and total war policies, and for saying, "War is hell." Earlier that same morning, terrorists had hijacked four airplanes and had, by now, flown two of them into the North and South towers of the World Trade Center in New York. Outside the door of the office of the secretary of defense, a Pentagon police officer named Aubrey Davis was standing guard.

"There was an incredibly loud 'boom,'" Davis later told British journalist Andrew Cockburn. Terrorists had just crashed an American Airlines commercial jet into the Pentagon. Secretary Rumsfeld emerged from his office and asked Davis what was going on. Davis, relaying information that was coming over his portable radio, told the secretary of defense that he was getting reports that an airplane had hit the Pentagon. Rumsfeld listened, then hurried down the corridor. Davis followed after him. The smell of smoke filled the air. People were running down the hallways, yelling and screaming. "They're bombing the building, they're bombing the building!" someone hollered. After several minutes of walking, Rumsfeld, Davis, and others who had joined the group arrived at what looked like a wall of fire.

"There were flames, and bits of metal all around," Davis recalled. A woman was lying on the ground right in front of him, her legs horribly burned. "The Secretary picked up one of the pieces of metal," Davis remembered. "I was telling him that he shouldn't be interfering with a crime scene when he looked at the inscription on it and [it read], 'American Airlines.'" Amid the chaos and smoke, there were shouts and cries for help. Someone passed by with an injured person laid out on a gurney. Secretary Rumsfeld helped push the gurney outside.

By 10:00 a.m. Rumsfeld was back inside the Pentagon. After calling the president from his office in the E-Ring, he was moved to a secure location elsewhere in the building, likely underground. From there, Rumsfeld spoke with Vice President Cheney, who was still in the bunker beneath the White House. At 12:05 p.m. Rumsfeld received a call from CIA director George Tenet, who reported that the National Security Agency had just intercepted a call between one of Osama bin Laden's deputies and a person in the former Soviet Republic of Georgia discussing the "good news," a clear reference to the terrorist strikes. Osama bin Laden and Al Qaeda were responsible for the attacks, the CIA director told the secretary of defense.

A little after 2:00 p.m. Rumsfeld gathered a core group of military advisors and Pentagon staff and began discussing what steps he wanted taken next. The people in the room included General Richard Myers, acting chairman of the Joint Chiefs of Staff; Stephen Cambone, Rumsfeld's undersecretary for intelligence; Victoria Clarke, a Pentagon spokeswoman; and a Pentagon lawyer. Cambone and Clarke took notes with pen and paper. During the meeting, Rumsfeld discussed the possibility of going after Saddam Hussein and Iraq as a response to that morning's terrorist attack. The notes of the undersecretary for intelligence, later reviewed by the 9/11 Commission, revealed that Rumsfeld asked for "Best info fast...judge whether good enough [to] hit S.H. [Saddam Hussein] @ same time—not only UBL [Usama bin Laden]." Rumsfeld asked the lawyer in the room to discuss with Deputy Secretary of Defense Paul Wolfowitz "connection with UBL [Usama bin Laden]" and Iraq.

Two days later, on September 13, Vice President Dick Cheney, Secretary of Defense Donald Rumsfeld, Secretary of State Colin Powell, and national security advisor Condoleezza Rice gathered for dinner at Holly Lodge, Camp David, which is located just a few miles from the Site R underground command center. The topic discussed, according to matching accounts in three of the four advisors' memoirs, was how America would respond to the 9/11 attacks.

"We all knew the outcome would be a declaration of war against the Taliban," Rice wrote. "But the discussion was useful in teasing out the questions the President would need to address."

"We were embarking on a fundamentally new policy," Cheney wrote in his memoir. "We were not simply going to go after individual cells of terrorists responsible for 9/11. We were going to bring down their networks and go after the organizations, nations, and people who lent them support."

"I argued that our strategy should be to put them on the defensive," wrote Rumsfeld. "The emphasis on a global campaign was important, I believed." Preemption was the new way forward. Thwarting the enemy before he made his next move.

On September 16, CIA director George Tenet sent out a memo to CIA staff. In the "Subject" line he wrote, "We're at war." Tenet told his CIA staff that in order to successfully "wage a worldwide war against al-Qa'ida and other terrorist organizations... [t]here must be absolute and full sharing of information, ideas, and capabilities." For George Tenet, information was the way to win this war.

At the CDC in Atlanta, David Bray and his colleagues continued to work around the clock, keeping channels open between the CDC and health professionals in all fifty states. Each day that passed without receiving health-related information that might suggest a bioterrorism event was under way meant another day of relief. "On October first we were told to stand down," Bray recalls. On October 3, he flew to CIA headquarters in Langley, Virginia. There, inside the George H. W. Bush Center for Intelligence, Bray gave the Interagency Intelligence Committee on Terrorism a briefing about what the CDC's Laboratory Response Network would do in the event of a bioterrorism attack. It was a seminal moment for Bray, only twenty-four years old and with considerable responsibility, and there was something he learned at CIA headquarters that still amazed him fourteen years later.

"The agency didn't know we existed," says Bray. He was the chief technology officer for the CDC team that would handle a biological weapons event were it to happen, and yet, according to Bray, no one in the audience at CIA headquarters seemed to know anything about it. For Bray, it was a revelatory moment.

"We were created by public law, Presidential Decision Directive Thirty-nine," Bray explains. "But they [the CIA] did not have that information." If knowledge is the most strategically significant resource of an organization, as David Bray believes and as George Tenet stated in his "We're at war" memo, the U.S. bioterrorism defense community had a very long way to go. For Bray, bridging the gap between having good information and effectively disseminating good information would become a professional crusade. He would continue this work over the next decade as an information specialist for DARPA in Afghanistan, for James Clapper in the Office of the Director of National Intelligence in Washington, D.C., and as the chief information officer for the Federal Communications Commission, starting in 2013. The lessons learned in the hyper-turbulent environment would shape his career.

The day after David Bray briefed an auditorium full of intelligence officials at CIA headquarters in Langley, he traveled back to the CDC's Atlanta offices, where he learned about a serious new development. Bray was told that a sixty-three-year-old Florida man had been hospitalized in Boca Raton with inhalation anthrax.

"You're joking," Bray remembers saying. The man was Bob Stevens, and he was a photo editor with American Media, Inc., the publisher of the *National Enquirer.* Twenty-four hours later, Bob Stevens was dead.

Things very quickly went from bad to worse. The FBI was now involved. On October 12, an NBC employee in New York City tested positive for anthrax. On October 15, Senate majority leader Tom Daschle told reporters that anthrax had been found in his Senate office. The Hart Senate Office Building was evacuated and put under quarantine. Hundreds of people lined up for anthrax tests. The Capitol itself was swept clear of vehicles and nonessential visitors. A bunker mentality took hold. "A war of nerves is being fought in Washington," a senior White House official told the *New York Times,* "and I fear we're not doing as well as we might be."

Over the next few days, more individuals tested positive for anthrax poisoning after letters containing the substance were mailed to ABC, CBS, and the U.S. State Department. People were beginning to die. When the 1,271,030-square-foot Hart Building needed to be decontaminated, DARPA was asked to provide science advisors to help with the enormous undertaking. A team of DARPA scientists reviewed decontamination technologies and delivered "quick turn-around testing on three separate candidates to determine efficacy." The test that proved most effective happened to be the "chlorine dioxide approach." This approach was based on technology that DARPA's Defense Sciences Office director, Michael Goldblatt, together with scientist Alvin Chow, had created for self-sterilizing packages in the wake of the *E. coli* Jack in the Box scandal. "We'd created it in a solid-state form to be triggered by light or humidity," Goldblatt explains. "My interpretation was a human scale; [DARPA's] solution was a huge scale." For this, says Goldblatt, he feels "a little bit of pride."

Three days after Senator Daschle told reporters that anthrax had been found in his office, Vice President Cheney paid a visit to ground zero, his first visit to the World Trade Center site since the 9/11 attacks. It was a little after 1:00 p.m. on October 18, 2001, when Cheney boarded *Air Force Two* and headed to New York City. He had been airborne for just a short time when his chief of staff, Lewis "Scooter" Libby, received a telephone call.

"There had been an initial positive test result indicating a botulinum toxin attack on the White House," Cheney revealed in his memoir. "If the result was confirmed, it could mean the president and I, members of the White House staff, and probably scores of others who had simply been in the vicinity had been exposed to one of the most lethal substances known to man." Botulinum toxin was a deadly neurotoxin for which there was no reliable antidote or cure. It kills by attacking the central nervous system and causing death by paralysis.

The positive hits had come from the BASIS sensor system that had been installed throughout the White House complex shortly after the *Dark Winter* bioterrorism attack war game. Livermore and Los Alamos had promoted the BASIS system as being able to deliver "a virtually zero rate of false-positive detection." Cheney also knew that "a single gram of botulinum toxin, evenly dispersed and inhaled, can kill a million people." He needed to call the president but decided to have Scooter Libby get a second set of test results first.

In the interim, the vice president stuck to his schedule. He met with Mayor Rudy Giuliani and Governor George Pataki for a briefing on New York City affairs. He toured ground zero. He shook hands with recovery workers who were sorting through rubble at the crash site. When he returned to his hotel room at the Waldorf Astoria later that afternoon, he discovered Libby waiting for him there, with very bad news. "He told me there had been two positive hits for botulinum toxin on one of the White House sensors," wrote Cheney. More tests were being run and results would be available at noon the following day. It was time to call the president.

Cheney was scheduled to deliver the keynote address at the annual Alfred E. Smith Memorial Foundation dinner that evening in the Waldorf Astoria ballroom. Wearing white tie and tails, he sat down in front of a secure video screen in his hotel room and called President Bush, who was attending a summit in Shanghai. Accompanying the president were Colin Powell and Condoleezza Rice. All three had been in the White House complex; all three could have been exposed to botulinum toxin.

"Mr. President," Vice President Cheney said, "the White House biological detectors have registered the presence of botulinum toxin, and there is no reliable antidote. We and many others may well have been exposed," Cheney recalled telling the president.

President Bush turned to Condoleezza Rice, who was standing beside him in Shanghai. In her memoir, Rice recalls hearing the president say, "Go call Hadley and find out what the hell is going on." Stephen Hadley was the president's deputy national security advisor. Hadley told Rice that lab mice were now being tested.

"Let's put it this way," said Hadley, who could also have been exposed. "If the mice are feet down tomorrow, we are fine. If they're feet up, we're toast."

In New York City, Vice President Cheney headed downstairs. During his speech, he talked about the bravery, generosity, and grace shown to him by average Americans digging through the rubble at ground zero that day. "I promised to deliver justice to the people responsible," Cheney said. He talked about the dilemma that America would now face with this new enemy, the terrorist. "We are dealing here with evil people who dwell in the shadows, planning unimaginable violence and destruction," he said. The banquet hall at the Waldorf Astoria erupted into resounding applause.

The following day, the results of the BASIS sensor system were returned. The $50 million system had delivered a false positive. There had been no biological weapons attack. No terror strike on the White House. If knowledge is the most strategically significant resource in a hyper-turbulent environment, scientists at Lawrence Livermore and Los Alamos national laboratories had failed. Still, in his 2003 State of the Union address, President Bush announced he was "deploying the nation's first early warning network of sensors to detect biological attack." BASIS sensors would now be set up in more than thirty cities around the country, at an initial cost of roughly $30 million, with another $1 million per city, per year, estimated in maintenance costs. Between 2003 and 2008, newspapers reported more than fifty false alarms from BASIS sensors in public spaces. The full details of BASIS, including its locations, operational costs, and precise number of false positives, as well as emergency response efforts, if any, to those false positives, remain classified.

But in Shanghai, in October 2001, Condoleezza Rice happily received the good news.

"Feet down, not up," she told President Bush. "The President smiled," she wrote in her memoirs. "I'm sure the Chinese thought it was some kind of coded message."

The president, vice president, secretary of state, national security advisor, and others had dodged a bullet. A photo editor, two postal workers, a female hospital employee, and a ninety-four-year-old woman from Connecticut were dead from anthrax. As of 2014, the mystery of who killed them has yet to be definitively solved.

At the end of October, ABC News reported that the anthrax mailed to Senator Daschle's office could be tied to the Iraqi bioweapons program through an additive called bentonite. The White House denied the link. A few nights later, ABC News reported that the ringleader of the 9/11 hijackers, Mohammed Atta, "had met at least once with a senior Iraqi intelligence agent in Prague." The report kicked off a firestorm of related news articles, including some that confirmed the story of the Iraq link, some that discredited the story, and some that blamed the CIA for engaging in a disinformation campaign.

Congress asked DARPA director Anthony Tether to brief the House Armed Services Committee on efforts currently being undertaken by DARPA with regard to its Biological Warfare Defense Program. Tony Tether had been DARPA director for only three months when the airplanes hit the buildings, but he had decades of experience in the Department of Defense and the CIA. Tether had a Ph.D. in electrical engineering from Stanford University, and a long career at the Pentagon and in the intelligence world. Since 1978 he had been working in both intelligence and defense, serving as the director of the national intelligence office in the Office of the Secretary of Defense from 1978 to 1982, and from 1982 to 1986 as the director of DARPA's Strategic Technology Office, the agency's liaison to the CIA. The specifics of his job remain classified, but as an indication of his significance, at the end of his tenure in 1986, Director of Central Intelligence Bill Casey honored him with the National Intelligence Medal, while his superior at the Pentagon, Secretary of Defense Caspar Weinberger, presented him with the Department of Defense Civilian Meritorious Service Medal.

In information submitted to Congress, Tether categorized biological weapons defense according to what DARPA considered to be the five stages of a biological weapons attack, in chronological order. "Prior to a BW attack" involved the development of vaccines. "During an attack" focused on cutting-edge sensor and biosurveillance technologies. "In the minutes and hours after an attack" included developing immediate ways to protect people. "In the hours and days after an attack" involved more efficient ways to get information out to first responders and better management of medical systems. "In the days and perhaps years after an attack" focused on decontamination technology, Tether said.

In February 2002, just four months after the first U.S. murder by anthrax, Congress approved a $358 million budget for biological warfare defense for the next year, nearly three times what it had been the year before the 9/11 terror attacks. That same month, George Mason University announced it would be building a Center for Biodefense "to address issues related to biological terrorism and the proliferation of biological weapons." A press release stated, "Kenneth Alibek, former first deputy chief of the civilian branch of the Soviet Union's Offensive Biological Weapons Program, and Charles Bailey, former commander for Research at the U.S. Army Medical Research Institute of Infectious Diseases," would serve as executive administrators of the center. "Alibek was now in charge of finding solutions to problems he helped create," says Michael Goldblatt, who oversaw some of Alibek's work for DARPA.

In May, DARPA awarded Alibek's company an additional $2 million to create "prototype biodefense products," the silver bullet DARPA was still looking for. Alibek spoke to reporters about the exciting prospects that lay ahead. The goal was to create a product that could "enhance the body's innate immune response against a wide variety of biological weapons threats," Alibek said. "Our research continues to yield promising results, and we are pleased that DARPA has awarded us additional funding to develop advanced protection against biological threat agents." Ken Alibek also used the opportunity to talk about future business prospects for his new corporate ventures. "At the appropriate time, our Company intends to explore potential opportunities to license its developing technology to, or seek a joint venture with, a partner to complete the necessary clinical trials, regulatory approvals, and the development, manufacturing, and marketing of any future products that might arise from this work." Some months later, another company run by Alibek began selling pills on the Internet with labels that read "Dr. Ken Alibek's Immune System Support Formula." The pills claimed to help the body's innate immune system defend against a wide variety of harmful pathogens. They could be purchased for $60 a bottle at a website called DrAlibek.com.

In government, it is a generally accepted rule that someone has to take the blame when government fails. For DARPA, whose job it was to safeguard the nation from technical surprise, there was no clear mission failure on 9/11, at least not in the public eye. The weapons used by the terrorists were fixed-blade utility knives, invented during the Great Depression. The flint knife, prehistory's utility blade, is roughly 1.4 million years old. Al Qaeda used American technology against America, hijacking four fully fueled aircraft and successfully piloting three of them, as missiles, to their targets. It is believed that Al Qaeda spent less than $500,000 planning and executing the attacks.

The public's perception, generally, was that the intelligence community was to blame for 9/11, a surprise attack that rivaled Pearl Harbor in its death toll and future consequence. Most fingers were pointed at the CIA and the FBI. Because the National Security Agency maintained a lower public profile at the time, it was not held accountable to the same degree. History has made clear, however, that errors by the NSA were indelible. On September 10, 2001, it intercepted from terrorists, already being monitored by the NSA, two messages in Arabic.

"The match is about to begin," read one message.

"Tomorrow is zero hour," read the other message.

The sentences were not translated until September 12. "In fact these phrases [might] have not been translated with such a quick turnaround had the horrific events not happened," in-house DARPA literature notes. DARPA is responsible for much of the technology behind advanced information collection as well as real-time translation capabilities. In the wake of 9/11, DARPA rapidly began to advance these technologies, and others related to them, so its partner, NSA, could do its job better.

Despite all the advanced technology at the disposal of the U.S. government, the national security establishment did not see the September 11, 2001, terrorist attack coming. Nor was its arsenal of advanced technology able to stop the attack once it began. As a consequence, the American military establishment would begin a hyper-militarization not seen since the explosion of the 15-megaton Castle Bravo hydrogen bomb on Bikini Atoll in 1954.

CHAPTER TWENTY

Total Information Awareness

The nuclear physicist John Poindexter is rarely noted for his prowess in nuclear physics. Instead he is almost always referred to as the retired Navy admiral and former national security advisor to President Ronald Reagan during the Iran-Contra affair who was convicted on five felony counts of lying to Congress, destroying official documents, and obstructing congressional investigations.

The day after the terrorist attacks of 9/11, Poindexter was pulling his car out of the quiet suburban subdivision where he lived outside Washington, D.C., when he was struck with an idea for DARPA. He had worked for the agency before, as a defense contractor in the late 1990s. By then Poindexter's Iran-Contra notoriety had died down, and he was able to return to public service. A U.S. court of appeals had reversed all five of Poindexter's felony convictions on the grounds that his testimony had been given under a grant of immunity.

In the decade after the scandal, Poindexter put his focus into computer technology. Because he had retained his full Navy pension after Iran-Contra, he did not have to look for a job. Fascinated by computers, Poindexter began teaching himself computer programming languages, and soon he could write code. In 1995, through a defense contractor called Syntek, Poindexter began working on a DARPA project called Genoa. The goal of Genoa was to develop a complex computer system—an intelligent machine—designed to reach across multiple classified government computer databases in order to predict the next man-made cataclysmic event, such as a terrorist attack. Poindexter, a seafaring man, especially liked Genoa's name. A genoa is a boat's jib, or foresail, typically raised on a sailboat to increase speed.

Poindexter's boss on the project, the person in charge of all "next-generation" information-processing ideas at DARPA in the late 1990s, was a man named Brian Sharkey. After a little more than a year working on the project, Syntek's contract ended. Poindexter and Sharkey had gotten along well during phase one of Genoa and kept each other's contact information. The way Poindexter tells the story, on the morning after the 9/11 terrorist attacks, he was struck with the idea that the time had come to revitalize the Genoa program. He pulled his car to the side of the road and began scrolling through contacts on his cell phone until he found Brian Sharkey's number.

"That's funny," Poindexter recalls Sharkey saying to him. "I was just thinking about calling you."

Both men agreed that it was time to accelerate the Genoa program. Sharkey had left DARPA to serve as senior vice president and chief technology officer for the California-based defense contracting giant Science Applications International Corporation, or SAIC. With so many surveillance-related defense contracts on its roster, SAIC was often jokingly referred to as NSA West. Another one of SAIC's prime clients was DARPA. Brian Sharkey knew the current DARPA director, Tony Tether, quite well.

"We need to talk to Tony," Poindexter told Sharkey.

In Washington, Tony Tether was well regarded as a top innovator. Someone who saw the future and made it happen. When he was serving as director of DARPA's Strategic Technology Office, back in the 1980s, he advocated maximizing technology for surveillance capabilities. Now, two decades later, these kinds of technologies had advanced exponentially. In this post-9/11 environment, Tether's enthusiasm for, and experience in, surveillance collection would prove invaluable in his role as DARPA director.

Brian Sharkey and Tony Tether knew each other from SAIC. In the 1990s, after leaving government service for defense contracting, Tether had served as vice president of SAIC in its advanced technology sector. Now Sharkey was a senior vice president at SAIC. During the September 12 phone call between Sharkey and Poindexter, the men agreed that Sharkey would set up a meeting with Tether to discuss Genoa.

Since 1995, DARPA had spent roughly $42 million advancing the Genoa concept under the Information Systems Office. The program was part of a concept DARPA now called Total Information Awareness (TIA). But the existing Genoa program was nowhere near having the "intelligence" necessary to recognize another 9/11-style plot. Poindexter and Sharkey aimed to change that.

The following month, on October 15, 2001, Sharkey and Tether met at a seafood restaurant in Arlington, Virginia, Gaffney's Oyster and Ale House, to discuss Total Information Awareness. Tether embraced the idea, so much so that he asked Brain Sharkey to leave his job at SAIC and return to DARPA to lead the new effort. But Sharkey did not want to leave his job at SAIC. The corporation was one of the largest employee-owned companies in America, and Sharkey had accumulated considerable stock options. If he were to return to government service, he would have to let go of profit participation. John Poindexter was the man who should serve as the director of the Total Information Awareness program, Sharkey said. SAIC could act as DARPA's prime contractor.

A few days later, Sharkey and Poindexter went sailing on Poindexter's yacht, *Bluebird,* to discuss next steps. Poindexter later recalled feeling excited. He had big ideas. He believed he knew exactly how extensive this program had to be to succeed. Poindexter knew what the subtitle of the program should be. In his pitch to Tether, his opening slide would read "A Manhattan Project on Countering Terrorism." Artificially intelligent computers were the twenty-first century's atomic bomb.

Tether had Poindexter come to his office at DARPA and present the slide show. Poindexter's background was in submarines, and there was an analogy here, he told Tether. Submarines emit sound signals as they move through the sea. The 9/11 hijackers had emitted electronic signals as they moved through the United States. But even if the NSA had been listening, its system of systems was not intelligent enough to handle the load in real time. The hijackers had rented apartments, bought airplane tickets, purchased box cutters, received emails and wire transfers. All of this could have been looked at as it was happening, Poindexter said. Terrorists give out signals. Genoa could find them. It would take enormous sums of time and treasure, but it was worth it. The 9/11 attacks were but the opening salvo, the White House had said. The time was right because the climate was right. People were terrified.

Tony Tether agreed. If John Poindexter was willing to run the Information Awareness Office, DARPA would fund it. In January 2002 the Information Awareness Office was given the green light to proceed, with a colossal initial start-up budget of $145 million and another $183.3 million earmarked for the following year. John Poindexter was now officially DARPA's Total Information Awareness czar.

"In our view, information technology is a weapon," says Bob Popp, the former deputy director of the Information Awareness Office, John Poindexter's number two. Popp is a computer scientist with a Ph.D. in electrical engineering, a prolific author and patent holder. He rides a motorcycle and is an active participant in and lifetime member of HOG, or Harley Owners Group. His areas of expertise include anti-submarine warfare and ISR (intelligence, surveillance, and reconnaissance). When he was a younger man, Popp welded Trident nuclear submarines for General Dynamics.

Before 9/11, "information technology was a huge unexploited weapon for analysts," Popp says. "They were using it in a very limited capacity. There were a lot of bad guys out there. No shortage of data. Analysts were inundated with problems and inundated with data. The basic hypothesis of TIA was to create a system where analysts could be effective. Where they were no longer overwhelmed."

It was Bob Popp's job as John Poindexter's deputy to oversee the setting up of multiple programs under the TIA umbrella. The Evidence Extraction and Link Discovery program (EELD) was a big office with a large support staff. Its function was to suction up as much electronic information about people as possible—not just terror suspects but the general American public. The electronic information to be gathered was to include individual people's phone records, computer searches, credit card receipts, parking receipts, books checked out of the library, films rented, and more, from every military and civilian database in the United States, with the hope of determining who were the terrorists lurking among ordinary Americans. The primary job of the EELD office was to create a computer system so "intelligent" it would be able to review megadata on 285 million people a day, in real time, and identify individuals who might be plotting the next terror event.

In 2002, DARPA senior program manager Ted Senator explained how EELD would work. The plan, Senator said, was to develop "techniques that allow us to find relevant information—about links between people, organizations, places, and things—from the masses of available data, putting it together by connecting these bits of information into patterns that can be evaluated and analyzed, and learning what patterns discriminate between legitimate and suspicious behavior." It was not an easy task. Using the needle-in-the-haystack metaphor, Senator explains just how hard it was. "Our task is akin to finding dangerous groups of needles hidden in stacks of needle pieces. This is much harder," he points out, "than simply finding needles in a haystack: we have to search through many stacks, not just one; we do not have a contrast between shiny, hard needles and dull, fragile hay; we have many ways of putting the pieces together into individual needles and the needles into groups of needles; and we cannot tell if a needle or group is dangerous until it is at least partially assembled." So, he says, "in principle at least, we must track all the needle pieces all of the time and consider all possible combinations."

Because terrorists do not generally act as lone wolves, a second program would be key to TIA's success, namely, the Scalable Social Network Analysis. The SSNA would monitor telephone calls, conference calls, and ATM withdrawals, but it also sought to develop a far more invasive surveillance technology, one that could "capture human activities in surveillance environments." The Activity Recognition and Monitoring program, or ARM, was modeled after England's CCTV camera. Surveillance cameras would be set up across the nation, and through the ARM program, they would capture images of people as they went about their daily lives, then save these images to massive data storage banks for computers to examine. Using state-of-the-art facial recognition software, ARM would seek to identify who was behaving outside the computer's preprogrammed threshold for "ordinary." The parameters for "ordinary" remain classified.

Facial recognition software expert Jonathan Phillips was brought on board to advance an existing DARPA program called Human Identification at a Distance. Computer systems armed with algorithms for the faces of up to a million known terrorists could scan newly acquired surveillance video, captured through the ARM program, with the goal of locating a terrorist among the crowd.

TIA was a many-tentacled program. The problem of language barriers had also long been a thorn in the military's side. DARPA needed to develop computer-based translation programs in what it called "the war languages," Arabic, Pashto, Urdu, Dari, and other Middle Eastern and South Asian dialects. Charles Wayne was brought on board to run two programs, TIDES and EARS, to develop computer programs that could convert foreign languages to English-language text. There would be a war games effort inside TIA, too, called War Gaming the Asymmetric Environment, and led by Larry Willis. In this office, terrorism experts would create fictional terror networks, made up of individual characters, like avatars, who would begin plotting fake terror attacks. The point was to see if TIA's myriad of surveillance programs, working in concert, could identify the avatar-terrorists as they plotted and planned. To further this effort, a group inside the group was formed, called the Red Team, headed by former DARPA director Stephen Lukasik. Red teaming is a role-playing exercise in which a problem is examined from an adversary's or enemy's perspective.

Finally there was Genoa II, the centerpiece of the program, the software that would run the system of information systems. Its director, Thomas P. Armour, described Genoa II as a "collaboration between two collaborations." One group of collaborators were the intelligence analysts, whose goal was "sensemaking," Armour said. These collaborators had the tricky job of collaborating among themselves, across multiple organizations, including the CIA, NSA, DIA, and others. It was the job of the sensemakers to construct models or blueprints of how terrorists might act. This group would then collaborate with "policymakers and operators at the most senior level," who would evaluate the intelligence analysts' work and develop options for a U.S. response to any given situation. Genoa II, Armour told his team, "is all about creating the technology to make these collaborations possible, efficient, and effective."

To Armour, there was hardware, meaning the machinery, software, meaning the computer programs, and wetware, meaning the human brain. Armour saw the wetware as the weakest link. The challenge was that intelligence agencies historically preferred to keep high-target terrorist information to themselves. "The 'wetware' whose limitations I mentioned is the human cognitive systems," Armour told defense contractors who were bidding on the job. "Its limitations and biases are well documented, and they pervade the entire system, from perception through cognition, learning, memory, and decision," Armour told his team. In this system of systems, which was based on collaborative efforts between humans and their machines, Armour believed that the humans represented the point where the system was most vulnerable. "These systems," said Armour, referring to human brains, "are the product of evolution, optimized by evolution for a world which no longer exists; it is not surprising then that, however capable our cognitive apparatus is, it too often fails when challenged by tasks completely alien to its biological roots."

Unlike so many of the new technologists working on TIA, Tom Armour was a Cold Warrior. He was also a former spy. After flying combat missions during Vietnam as a U.S. Air Force navigator on the AC-119K gunship, he began a long career with the CIA, starting in 1975. Armour was an expert on Soviet nuclear weapons systems, missile technology, and strategic command and control. At the CIA, under the Directorate of Intelligence, he served as chief of computing and methodological support, bringing the agency into the twenty-first century with computers for intelligence analysis.

But when the Berlin Wall came down, Armour saw new threats cropping up everywhere. "People then were talking giddily about a 'peace dividend,'" he told a group of DARPA technologists at a conference in 2002, but reminded the audience that his former boss at the CIA, James Woolsey, knew better. "Woolsey pointedly said that while the 'big bad bear' was gone, the woods were still filled with lots of poisonous snakes," Armour said. The terrorists had since emerged as the new snakes, "what we now call the asymmetric threat." Armour believed that the job of the twenty-first-century intelligence analyst was to find the snakes, using computers.

Humans were frail. As technical collectors, they could be manipulated either by assets trying to give them bad information or by their own biases and mental blocks. This weakness "has long been called 'deception and denial' in intelligence circles," Armour said. Genoa II's predecessor, Genoa, was about making the machines smarter. Each machine had been overseen by what was called a "Lone Ranger," a single intelligence analyst. With Genoa II, Armour wanted to get "smarter results." He wanted "cognitive amplification." Smarter machines and smarter humans.

Armour created what he called "bumper sticker phrases" that captured Genoa II's automation goals, phrases that read like words George Orwell could have written in the dystopian novel *Nineteen Eighty-Four* because they sounded like doublethink. "Read everything without reading everything," Armour told Genoa II analysts. "There is too much that must be read to actually read." Armour also said that TIA analysts would need to "begin the trip to computers as servants, to partners, to mentors," meaning that analysts needed first to view their computers as assistants and eventually view them as advisors. Ultimately, Genoa II's computers would know more than a human could know.

As John von Neumann had predicted on his deathbed in "The Computer and the Brain," the "artificial automaton" would one day be able to *think*. TIA was a system of information systems that could read everything without reading everything. It was a system of systems that could observe and then connect everything the human eye could not see.

On January 14, 2002, the Information Awareness Office opened its doors, temporarily, on the fourth floor of the DARPA office building at 3710 North Fairfax Drive in Arlington, while John Poindexter worked to secure an independent facility where TIA analysts could settle permanently. One of the first people Poindexter would visit was Secretary of Defense Donald Rumsfeld. Over lunch in Rumsfeld's office in the Pentagon, the two men discussed TIA. It was agreed that DARPA would build the system, then help its customers get the system up and running. The customers were the CIA, FBI, and NSA, but also the service agencies. Tether felt that the best place to house the new Total Information Awareness system was at Fort Belvoir, Virginia, a division of the Army's Intelligence and Security Command, INSCOM.

Tony Tether set up a meeting with INSCOM's commanding officer, Lieutenant General Keith Alexander. At Fort Belvoir, Alexander ran his operations out of a facility known as the Information Dominance Center, with an unusual interior design that deviated significantly from traditional military decor. The Information Dominance Center had been designed by Academy Award–winning Hollywood set designer Bran Ferren to simulate the bridge of the Starship *Enterprise,* from the *Star Trek* television and film series. There were ovoid-shaped chairs, computer stations inside highly polished chrome panels, even doors that slid open with a whooshing sound. Alexander would sit in the leather captain's chair, positioned in the center of the command post, where he could face the Information Dominance Center's twenty-four-foot television monitor. General Alexander loved the science-fiction genre. INSCOM staff even wondered if the general fancied himself a real-life Captain Kirk.

An arrangement was made between DARPA and INSCOM whereby General Alexander gave John Poindexter and his team an area to work out of inside the Information Dominance Center. "The initial TIA experiment was done at INSCOM, worldwide command," says Bob Popp. "The plan was to have attachments, or nodes, across the world. Multiple agencies would work on multiple problems." Poindexter began inviting other agencies to work alongside TIA as collaborators. One by one they joined, including the CIA, NSA, and FBI.

Poindexter believed that another attack was already well along in its planning phase. It could happen at any time. Many other senior officials were motivated by the same fear.

"We felt as if we were really battling terrorism," says Popp. "The network grew. We set up another node in Germany." The future of TIA seemed bright. Then suddenly, as Bob Popp recalls, "we had our own battle, with Congress."

In August 2002, John Poindexter unveiled TIA at the DARPATech conference in Anaheim, California. This technology conference marked the beginning of the program's public end. In November 2002, a *New York Times* headline read "Pentagon Plans a Computer System That Would Peek at Personal Data of Americans." Reporter John Markoff wrote that the Department of Defense had initiated a massive computer-based domestic surveillance program, "a vast electronic dragnet, searching for personal information as part of the hunt for terrorists around the globe—including the United States... without a search warrant." Markoff named DARPA as the agency in charge, and reported that the computer system was called Total Information Awareness. The logo of the Information Awareness Office became the focus of much ire. It featured the Eye of Providence icon—the same as the one on the back of the dollar bill—casting a searchlight over a globe. DARPA's Latin motto, *Scientia Est Potentia,* or "Knowledge Is Power," fueled its own comparisons to George Orwell's *Nineteen Eighty-Four.*

Several days later, columnist William Safire wrote about TIA, focusing on the fact that John Poindexter, of the Iran-Contra affair scandal, was its director. The Pentagon had given a "disgraced admiral... a $200 million budget to create computer dossiers on 300 million Americans," Safire wrote, listing the myriad of electronic transactions a person makes in any day, week, or year: "Every purchase you make with a credit card, every magazine subscription you buy and medical prescription you fill, every Web site you visit and e-mail you send or receive." If DARPA got its way, the TIA program would be able to monitor them all. "This is not some far-out Orwellian scenario," Safire wrote. "It is what will happen to your personal freedom in the next few weeks if John Poindexter gets the unprecedented power he seeks."

When Safire's column ran, TIA's existence had been a matter of public knowledge for seven months but no one had paid much attention to it. In the thirty days after Safire's column appeared, there were 285 stories about TIA, the majority of which were overwhelmingly negative. Many of the articles focused on the $200 million figure cited by Safire. In a press conference on November 20, Undersecretary of Defense for Acquisition, Logistics and Technology Edward "Pete" Aldridge stated that the budget for the TIA system was $10 million through the 2003 fiscal year. This was highly inaccurate. According to records from the Defense Technical Information Center comptroller's office, the actual budget for the Information Awareness Office through fiscal year 2003 was $586.4 million. The true numbers had been concealed inside other DARPA Research, Development, Test and Evaluation budgeting. Although the numbers controversy wouldn't be revealed for months, the privacy concerns took center stage.

Americans wanted answers. Lawmakers sent a list of questions for DARPA. John Poindexter was sent to Capitol Hill, where he was expected to clarify details about TIA to roughly fifty members of Congress and their staff. Bob Popp went too. "Me, Poindexter, Tony [Tether], and our Hill liaison went to the Hill to brief the House and Senate," Popp recalled in 2014. Their meeting with the House Permanent Select Committee on Intelligence "went well," Popp says. "Questions, answers, fine." Then they moved on to the Senate Permanent Select Committee on Intelligence.

At the Senate, Poindexter began his testimony with a background of his own personal history, starting with his early education at a military academy. After roughly fifteen minutes, a Senate staffer shouted out, "Hey, when are you going to start talking about the reason you're here?"

"Poindexter said, 'If you'll just give me a chance—'" Popp recalls.

At which point, Poindexter was interrupted by another staffer.

"What's all this invasion of privacy!" someone else yelled.

Popp says, "John Poindexter was polite, but stern."

"Get to the data mining!" the staffer yelled, which infuriated Poindexter.

The staffer shouted, "We want answers now!"

Which is when John Poindexter lost his composure. "Will you sit down!" he shouted back, far too loudly. Then, "I'm not going to let you drive the agenda!"

Poindexter gave the rest of his presentation, but word of what had happened was already making its way back to the Pentagon. It was the beginning of the end of TIA. Secretary of Defense Donald Rumsfeld was brought into the loop. What was DARPA to do? Rumsfeld issued an order. John Poindexter was not to speak to anyone. No interviews with anyone from Congress. No interviews with the press.

Poindexter's second fall from grace happened quickly. With him went the program, at least as far as the public was told. A multitude of newspaper articles generated a further wave of public outcry, including over the fact that the Pentagon had allocated a quarter of a billion dollars for TIA through 2005. Poindexter was portrayed as a villain and DARPA was cast as a surveillance machine.

A reporter asked Secretary Rumsfeld about TIA. "I don't know much about it," Rumsfeld answered. Poindexter "explained to me what he was doing at DARPA," he said, "but it was a casual conversation. I haven't been briefed on it; I'm not knowledgeable about it. Anyone who is concerned ought not be." When asked about Poindexter the man, Rumsfeld said he didn't "remember him much." Rumsfeld told the reporter that, as was often the case with the American public, there was far too much "hype and alarm." Of the surveillance program Rumsfeld said, "Anyone with any concern ought to be able to sleep well tonight." TIA was a research program, he clarified, not an intelligence-gathering operation.

In the wake of the scandal, the Total Information Awareness program was briefly renamed the Terrorism Information Awareness program, but the public controversy did not die down. Secretary of Defense Donald Rumsfeld made it clear that John Poindexter would resign or be fired. Ultimately, Poindexter offered his resignation to Tony Tether and told reporters he was leaving DARPA and looking forward to spending more time sailing on the Chesapeake Bay. Secretary Rumsfeld then went back to making plans to invade Iraq.

Months later, in the fall of 2003, Congress eliminated funding for the Total Information Awareness program, saying it was "concerned about the activities of the Information Awareness Office." The House and Senate jointly directed "that the Office be terminated immediately."

But "the [TIA] programs did not end," Bob Popp explained in 2014. Instead, many of the clandestine electronic surveillance programs were classified and transferred to NSA, DHS, CIA, and the military services. Program names were changed. Certain members of Congress were cleared to know about some of them, but not all of them. Major elements of DARPA's Evidence Extraction and Link Discovery (EELD) and Genoa II programs, including the physical nodes that already existed at INSCOM and in Germany, were folded into a classified NSA system called PRISM—a massive covert electronic surveillance and data-mining program that would create an international uproar in 2013 after NSA whistleblower Edward Snowden leaked thousands of pages of classified documents to the press.

Some DARPA programs with public faces were transferred to the Department of Homeland Security, including the Computer Assisted Passenger Prescreening System (CAPPS), Activity Recognition and Monitoring (ARM), and Human Identification at a Distance (HumanID). These programs, managed by the Office of Biometric Identity Management and the TSA, oversaw identity recognition software systems at airports and borders, and in public transportation systems and other public spaces.

For use abroad, other TIA programs were transferred to the Army for its Biometrically Enabled Intelligence programs, meant ultimately to collect biometrics on foreign individuals using eye scans, fingerprint scans, and facial scans. And the CIA initiated a program called Anonymous Entity Resolution, based on TIA's Scalable Social Network Analysis (SSNA), examining links between individuals through electronic systems like ATM withdrawals and hotel reservations.

For use in future war zones, DARPA recycled some of the most invasive TIA surveillance and data-mining technologies into a program designed for video collection, pattern analysis, and targeting acquisition for use in military operations in urban terrain. This program was called Combat Zones That See.

Any future invasion strategy needed a "new strategic context," according to Secretary Rumsfeld. Future wars would be fought according to DARPA's system of systems concept—advanced weapons platforms linked by a network of advanced computer systems. In 2003 this could not exactly be sold to the American people as "Assault Breaker Warfare," which would require a paragraph of explanation and sounded dull. Rumsfeld had been thinking about articulating a new strategic context for the Department of Defense ever since he took office, and shortly after the 9/11 attacks he tasked the job of choosing a name to retired vice admiral Arthur Cebrowski, director of the Office of Force Transformation.

The Office of Force Transformation was an in-house Pentagon think tank personally created by Rumsfeld in the wake of 9/11. The mandate of this new office was "to challenge the status quo with new concepts for American defense to ensure an overwhelming and continuing competitive advantage." The name that the Office of Force Transformation came up with for this new way of waging war was "network-centric warfare." It was a phrase DARPA had been using for years, based on its Assault Breaker concept back in 1974. Soon the whole world would start hearing about network-centric warfare. When Secretary Rumsfeld presented the Pentagon's "Transformation Planning Guidance" to the president in the winter of 2003, he summed up the way forward as "drawing upon unparalleled Command, Control, Communications, Computers, Intelligence, Surveillance, and Reconnaissance (C4ISR) capabilities." So much had changed since the days of command and control.

Arthur Cebrowski was a decorated Navy pilot who had flown 154 combat missions during the Vietnam War. He had also served in Operation Desert Storm, commanding a carrier air wing, a helicopter carrier, and an aircraft carrier. He retired from the Navy in August 2001. Regarding this naming issue, in internal documents sent to Rumsfeld in 2003 Cebrowski simplified why the concept of network-centric warfare would work. It offered a "New Theory of War based on information age principles and phenomena," Cebrowski wrote. And network-centric warfare offered a "new relationship between operations abroad and homeland security," meaning the lines between homeland security and fighting foreign wars would become intentionally blurred. Finally, Cebrowski wrote, network-centric warfare would provide a "new concept/sense of security in the American citizen." Cebrowski was an avowed American patriot, and he believed that everyone else should be too. Network-centric warfare "had great moral seductiveness," Cebrowski said.

With the doctrine of network-centric warfare in place, on March 19, 2003, the United States and its allies launched Operation Iraqi

Freedom and invaded Iraq. After the U.S. military completed its so-called "major combat operations" in just twenty-one days of "shock and awe," Cebrowski told PBS how pleased he was. "The speed of that advance was absolutely unheard of," he said. He attributed this "very high-speed warfare" to "network-centric warfare." He espoused the idea that a war that relied on advanced technology was a morally superior war. America did not have to resort to "wholesale slaughter" anymore, Cebrowski said. We did not have to "kill a very large number of them," meaning Iraqis, or "maim an even larger number," because advanced technology now allowed the Defense Department to target specific individuals. This, said Cebrowski, was a good and moral thing.

"There's a temptation to say that to develop that sense in the minds of an enemy that they are in fact defeated, you have to kill a very large number of them, maim an even larger number, destroy a lot of infrastructure and key elements of their civilization, and then they will feel defeated. I think that's wrong," Cebrowski said. "I think we are confronted now with a new problem, in a way the kind of problem we always wanted to have, where you can achieve your initial military ends without the wholesale slaughter. Because, remember," he said, "this always cuts two ways. You have a moral obligation not just to limit your own casualties and casualties of nonparticipants but also those of the enemy itself. So we're moving in the more moral direction, which is appropriate.... We need to come to grips with this reality."

History would reveal that Arthur Cebrowski spoke too soon. All the technology in the world could not win the war against terrorists in Iraq or Afghanistan. Local populations did not see network-centric warfare and targeted killing by drones, in their neighborhoods, as morally superior. And a new wave of terrorist organizations would emerge, form, and terrorize.

CHAPTER TWENTY-ONE

IED War

On May 26, 2003, Private First Class Jeremiah D. Smith, a twenty-five-year-old soldier from Missouri, was driving in an Army vehicle outside Baghdad when the convoy he was traveling in came upon a canvas bag lying in the road. It was Memorial Day, which meant that back in the United States this was a day to remember the millions of American soldiers who died while serving in the armed forces. Private Smith had been a proud member of the U.S. Army for a little over a year.

Three and a half weeks earlier, on May 1, 2003, President George W. Bush had stood on the deck of the USS *Abraham Lincoln* and announced that major combat operations in Iraq were over. "In the battle of Iraq, the United States and our allies have prevailed," he declared. The invasion, which began on March 21, had been swift. Baghdad fell on April 9. Standing on the deck of the aircraft carrier in a dark suit and a red tie (he'd more memorably arrived on board wearing a flight suit), the president exuded confidence. A banner behind him, designed by the White House art department, read "Mission Accomplished." At one point during his speech, the president gave the thumbs-up.

Now it was Memorial Day, and Private Smith was heading into dangerous territory. His convoy was escorting heavy equipment out of Baghdad, traveling west. Smith was a gunner and was sitting on the passenger side of the Humvee. As the vehicle approached the canvas bag lying in the road, not far from the Baghdad International Airport, the driver had no way of knowing it contained an improvised explosive device, or IED, and he simply drove over it. As the vehicle passed over the bag, the device exploded, killing Private Smith. In his death, Smith became the first American to be killed by an IED in the Iraq war.

The blast could be heard for miles. Twenty-two-year-old Specialist Jeremy Ridgley was one of the first people to come upon the inferno. "I was a gunner in the Eighteenth Military Police Brigade," recalled Ridgley in a 2014 interview. "We were driving about five hundred yards behind, in a totally separate convoy. The explosion was extremely loud. We'd been informed that people were dropping things off overpasses, so every time we went under one, we sped up and came out in a different lane. Someone threw something at our vehicle, then I heard the explosion. I swung my gun around. It all happened so fast." The explosion Ridgley heard was the IED detonating as Private Smith's vehicle drove over it.

Ahead of him, Ridgley saw the burning Humvee in the road. Two bloodied soldiers emerged from the thick black smoke and staggered toward his vehicle, dazed. "One of the guys was trying to push something up his arm," recalls Ridgley, "like he was trying to fix his sleeve. When he got closer I saw it was skin. Skin was just falling off of his arm." A second bloodied soldier followed behind. "He asked me if he had something on his face," Ridgley recalls. "Most of his face was missing. It was horrible. He was horribly, horribly burned."

Ridgley's team leader, Sergeant Phillip Whitehouse, ran toward the burning vehicle. Whitehouse discovered Private First Class Jeremiah Smith unconscious, trapped inside. "He pulled Smith out. That's when the vehicle started to cook off," Ridgley remembers. "All the ammo inside started to catch on fire. There were massive explosions going off all around. I caught some shrapnel. A little burn near my sleeve. I was sitting on the gun platform thinking, I need to call in a report."

Ridgley called for a Medevac and remembers looking around. "There were these Iraqi kids playing soccer in a field," Ridgley recalls, "and I told the Medevac the helicopter could land there. Everything seemed like slow motion." Ridgley had never seen mortally wounded people before, and he was having trouble focusing. "The Medevac arrived and the soldiers were loaded onboard. From the time I called it in until the time the helicopter took off was about twenty minutes," recalls Ridgley. "But it sure seemed like it lasted all day," he says. "Time stood still." Later, Jeremy Ridgley learned that Private First Class Jeremiah Smith had died.

On May 28, the Department of Defense identified Private Smith as having been killed in Iraq while supporting Operation Iraqi Freedom. The Pentagon attributed Smith's death to "unexploded ordnance," as if what had killed him had been old or forgotten munitions left lying in the road. Two weeks later, in an article in the *New York Times* titled "After the War," a Defense Department official conceded that the unexploded ordnance that killed Smith might have been left there deliberately.

An IED is made up of five components: the explosive, a container, a fuse, a switch, and a power source, usually a battery. It does not require any kind of advanced technology. With certain skills, an IED is relatively easy to make. The primary component of the IED is the explosive material, and after the invasion, Iraq was overflowing with explosives.

"There's more ammunition in Iraq than any place I've ever

been in my life, and it's not securable," General John Abizaid, commander of the U.S. Central Command (CENTCOM), told the Senate Appropriations Committee in September 2003. "I wish I could tell you we had it all under control, but we don't."

The month after Private Smith was killed by an IED, the casualty toll from IED attacks began to climb. In June there were twenty-two incidents. By August the number of soldiers killed by IEDs in Iraq was greater than the number of fatalities by direct fire, including from guns and rocket-propelled grenades. By late 2003, monthly IED fatalities were double that of deaths by other weapons. In a press conference, General Abizaid stated that American troops were now fighting "a classical guerrilla-style campaign" in Iraq. This kind of language had not been used by the Defense Department since the Vietnam War.

"A new phenomenon [was] at work on the battlefield," says retired Australian brigadier general Andrew Smith, who also has a Ph.D. in political studies. "IEDs caught coalition forces off guard. 'Surprise' is not a word you want to hear on the battlefield." Smith was one of the first NATO officers to lead a counter-IED working group for Combined Joint Task Force 7, in Baghdad. Later, in 2009, Brigadier General Smith oversaw the work of 350 NATO officials at CENTCOM, all dealing with countering IEDs. "The sheer volume of unsecured weapons in Iraq was staggering," Smith says, "a whole lot of explosives left over from Saddam." In 2003, there were an estimated 1 million tons of unsecured explosives secreted around the country in civilian hands. These were former stockpiles once controlled by Saddam Hussein's security forces, individuals who quickly abandoned their guard posts after the invasion. A videotape shot by a U.S. Army helicopter crew in 2003 shows the kind of explosive material that was up for grabs across Iraq. In the footage, an old aircraft hangar is visible, stripped of its roof and its siding. From the overhead perspective, row after row of unguarded bombs can be seen. One of the men in the helicopter says, "It looks like there's hundreds of warheads or bombs" in there.

The IEDs kept getting more destructive. Three months after Private First Class Jeremiah Smith was killed, a truck bomb was driven into the United Nations headquarters in Baghdad, killing twenty-two people, including the UN special envoy to Iraq, Sergio Vieira de Mello. The Pentagon added a new IED classification to the growing roster. This was called the VBIED, or vehicle-borne improvised explosive device, soon to be joined by the PBIED, a person-borne improvised explosive device, or suicide bomber. When Al Qaeda in Iraq claimed responsibility for the IEDs, the resounding psychological effects were profound. Before the invasion, there had been no Al Qaeda in Iraq.

DARPA's long-term goals were now subordinated to this immediate need inundating the Pentagon. Initial counter-IED efforts involved Counter Radio-Controlled Electronic Warfare (CREW) systems, or jamming devices, that were installed on the dashboards of Army vehicles and cost roughly $80,000 each. The triggering mechanism on most IEDs consisted of simple wireless electronics, including components found in cell phones, cordless telephones, wireless doorbells, and key fobs. Early jammers were designed to interrupt the radio signals insurgents relied on to detonate their IEDs. First dozens, then hundreds of classified jamming systems made their way to coalition forces in Iraq, with code names like Jukebox, Warlock, Chameleon, and Duke. At the same time, DARPA worked on a next generation of jammers, developing technology that could one day locate IEDs by sensing chemical vapors from the relative safety of a fast-moving vehicle. The program, called Recognize IED and Report, or RIEDAR, would work from a distance of up to two miles away. The ideal device would be able to search 2,700 square meters per second, could be small and portable, and able to alert within one second of detection. But these were future plans, and the Pentagon needed ways to counter the IED threat now. By February 2004, IED attacks had escalated to one hundred per week. The five hundred jammers already in Iraq were doing only a little good. In June, General Abizaid sent a memo to Secretary Rumsfeld and Chairman of the Joint Chiefs of Staff Richard Meyers, sounding an alarm. The Pentagon needed what Abizaid called a "Manhattan-like project" to address the IED problem.

In Washington, Congress put DARPA in the hot seat when, in the spring of 2004, in a research study report for Congress, the concept of network-centric warfare was taken to task. Congress asked whether the Department of Defense had "given adequate attention to possible unintended outcomes resulting from over-reliance on high technology," with the clear suggestion being that it had not. The unintended consequence that had Congress most concerned was the IED, presently killing so many American soldiers in Iraq. In its report, Congress wondered if, while the Pentagon had been pursuing "networked communications technology," the terrorists were gaining the upper hand by using "asymmetric countermeasures." Congress listed five other areas of concern: "(1) suicide bombings; (2) hostile forces intermingling with civilians used as shields; (3) irregular fighters and close-range snipers that swarm to attack, and then disperse quickly; (4) use of bombs to spread 'dirty' radioactive material; or (5) chemical or biological weapons."

To the press, Arthur Cebrowski claimed that he had been misunderstood. The so-called godfather of network-centric warfare complained that Congress was misinterpreting his words. "Warfare is all about human behavior," said Cebrowski, which contradicted hundreds of pages of documents and memos he had sent to Secretary Rumsfeld. "It's a common error to think that transformation has a technology focus. It's one of many elements," Cebrowski said. Even the Defense Department's own Defense Acquisition

University, a training and certification establishment for military personnel and defense contractors, was confused by the paradox and sent a reporter from its magazine *Defense AT&L* to Cebrowski's office to clarify. How could the father of network-centric warfare be talking about human behavior, the reporter asked. "Network-centric warfare is first of all about human behavior, as opposed to information technology," Cebrowski said. "Recall that while 'a network' is a noun, 'to network' is a verb, and what we are focusing on is human behavior in the networked environment."

It seemed as if Cebrowski was stretching to make sense, or at least resorting to semantics to avoid embarrassing the secretary of defense. Nowhere in Secretary Rumsfeld's thirty-nine-page monograph for the president, a summation of Cebrowski's vision titled "Transformation Planning Guidance," was human behavior mentioned or even alluded to. While Cebrowski did television interviews addressing congressional concerns, the Office of Force Transformation added four new slides to its "Transforming Defense" PowerPoint presentation. One of the two new slides now addressed "Social Intelligence as a key to winning the peace," and the other addressed "Social Domain Cultural Awareness" as a way to give warfighters a "cognitive advantage."

On *PBS NewsHour,* Cebrowski defended network-centric warfare and again reminded the audience that the United States had, he believed, achieved operational dominance in Iraq, completing major combat operations in just twenty-one days. "That speed of advance was absolutely unheard of," Cebrowski said. But now, "we're reminded that warfare is more than combat, and combat's more than shooting." It was about "how do people behave?" To win the war in Iraq, Cebrowski said, the military needed to recognize that "warfare is all about human behavior." And that was what network-centric warfare was about: "the behavior of humans in the networked environment... how do people behave when they become networked?"

If Cebrowski could not convincingly speak of human behavior, he found a partner in someone who could. Retired major general Robert H. Scales was a highly decorated Vietnam War veteran and recipient of the Silver Star. As the country sought a solution to the nightmare unfolding in Iraq, Scales proposed what he called a "culture-centric" solution. "War is a thinking man's game," Scales wrote in *Proceedings* magazine, the monthly magazine of the United States Naval Institute. "Wars are won as much by creating alliances, leveraging nonmilitary advantages, reading intentions, building trust, converting opinions, and managing perceptions—all tasks that demand an exceptional ability to understand people, their culture, and their motivation." As if reaching back in time to the roundtable discussions held by JFK's Special Group and Robert McNamara's Pentagon, Scales was talking about motivation and morale.

In 2004, amid the ever-growing IED crisis, Scales proposed to Cebrowski that the Pentagon needed a social science program to get inside how the enemy thought. The United States needed to know what made the enemy tick. Cebrowski agreed. "Knowledge of one's enemy and his culture and society may be more important than knowledge of his order of battle," Cebrowski wrote in *Military Review,* a bi-monthly Army journal. The Office of Force Transformation now publicly endorsed "social intelligence" as a new warfighting concept, the idea that in-depth knowledge of local customs in Iraq and elsewhere would allow the Pentagon to better determine who was friend and who was foe in a given war theater. "Combat troops are becoming intelligence operatives to support stabilization and counterinsurgency operations in Iraq," Cebrowski's office told *Defense News* in April 2004. It was hearts and minds all over again, reemerging in Iraq.

With chaos unfolding across Iraq, all the agencies and military services attached to the Pentagon were scrambling to find solutions. At DARPA, the former deputy director of the Total Information

Awareness program, Bob Popp, got an idea. "I was the deputy director of an office that no longer existed," said Popp in a 2014 interview. The Information Awareness Office had been shut down, and Poindexter's Total Information Awareness program was no more, at least as far as the public was concerned. "Some of the TIA programs had been canceled, some were transitioned to the intelligence community," says Popp with an insider's knowledge available to few, most notably because, he says, "the transitioning aspects were part of my job." Popp was now serving as special assistant to DARPA director Tony Tether. "Tony and I met once a month," recalls Popp. "He said, 'Put together another program,' and I did."

Working with DARPA's Strategic Technology Office, Popp examined data on what he felt was the most important element of TIA, namely, "information on the bad guys." After thinking through a number of ideas, Popp focused on one. "I started thinking, why do certain areas harbor bad guys?" He sought counsel within his community of Defense Department experts, including strategists, economists, engineers, and field commanders. Popp was surprised by the variety of answers he received, and how incongruous the opinions were. "They were not all right and they were not all wrong," Popp recalls. But as far as harboring bad guys was concerned, Popp wanted to know who was harboring them, and why. He wanted to know what social scientists thought of the growing insurgencies in Iraq and Afghanistan. "I looked around DARPA and realized there was not a single social scientist to be found," Popp says, so he began talking to "old-timers" about his idea of bringing social scientists on board. "Most of them were cautious. They said, 'Oh, I don't know. You should listen to the commanders in Afghanistan and Iraq.'" Then someone suggested to Bob Popp that he talk to an anthropologist named Montgomery McFate.

When Bob Popp first spoke with McFate in 2004, she was thirty-eight years old and worked as a fellow at the Office of Naval Research. Before that, McFate worked for RAND, where she wrote an analysis of totalitarianism in North Korean society. A profile in the *San Francisco Examiner* describes her as "a punk rock wild child of dyed-in-the-wool hippies... close-cropped hair and a voice buttery... a double-doc Ivy Leaguer with a penchant for big hats and American Spirit cigarettes and a nose that still bears the tiny dent of a piercing 25 years closed." If her personal background seemed to separate her from the conservative organizations she worked for, her ideas made her part of the defense establishment.

McFate says that in addition to being approached by DARPA's Bob Popp for help in social science work, she also received a call from a science advisor to the Joint Chiefs of Staff, Hriar S. Cabayan, who was calling from the war theater. "We're having a really hard time out here," McFate remembers Cabayan saying. "We have no idea how this society works.... Could you help us?"

In 2004 the insurgency in Iraq was growing at an alarming rate. Criticism of the Pentagon was reaching new heights, most notably as stories of dubious WMD intelligence gained traction in Congress and around the world. For the Department of Defense, it was a tall order to locate anthropologists willing to work for the Pentagon. Academic studies showed that politically, the vast majority were left-leaning, with twenty registered Democrats to every one registered Republican. Not only was McFate rare for an anthropologist, but also she was enthusiastic about the war effort. Like many Americans, she had been propelled into action by 9/11. In 2004, Montgomery McFate decided to make it her "evangelical mission" to get the Pentagon to understand the culture it was dealing with in Iraq and Afghanistan.

In November 2004, DARPA co-sponsored a conference on counterinsurgency, or COIN, with the Office of Naval Research. For the first time since the Vietnam War, DARPA sought the advice of behavioral scientists to try to put an end to what General Abizaid called a "guerrilla-style" war. The DARPA conference, called the Adversary Cultural Knowledge and National Security

Conference, was organized by Montgomery McFate and took place at the Sheraton Hotel in Crystal City, Virginia. The key speaker was retired major general Robert Scales. From the podium, the decorated Vietnam War veteran told his audience what he believed was the key element in the current conflict: winning hearts and minds. Scales was famous for his role in the battle of Dong Ap Bia, known as the Battle of Hamburger Hill because the casualty rate was so high, roughly 70 percent, that it made the soldiers who were there think of it as a meat grinder.

An entire generation of Vietnam War officers like himself had retired or were in the process of retiring, Scales told his audience. He and his colleagues were men who had engaged in battle before the age of "network-centric warfare." Vietnam-era officers had been replaced by technology enthusiasts, Scales said, many of whom "went so far as to claim that technology would remove the fog of war entirely from the battlefield." These were the same individuals who said that one day soon, ground forces would be unnecessary. That the Air Force, the Navy, and perhaps a future space force would be fighting wars from above, seated in command centers far away from the battlefield. Scales said it was time to reject this idea. Guerrilla warfare was back, he warned. Just like in Vietnam. Technology did not win against insurgents, Scales said. People did.

"The nature of war is changing," Scales wrote that same fall in *Proceedings* magazine. "Fanatics and fundamentalists in the Middle East have adapted and adopted a method of war that seeks to offset U.S. technical superiority with a countervailing method that uses guile, subterfuge and terror mixed with patience and a willingness to die." Scales warned that this new kind of warfare would allow the weaker force, the insurgents in Afghanistan and Iraq, to take on the stronger force, the United States, and win. Since the Israeli War of Independence, Scales wrote, "Islamic armies are 0 and 7 when fighting Western style and 5 and 0 when fighting unconventionally against Israel, the United States, and the Soviet Union."

The Pentagon moved forward with DARPA's idea to bring anthropologists into the Iraq war, and McFate garnered exclusive permission to interview Marines coming home from Iraq. In July 2005 she authored a paper in *Joint Force Quarterly,* a magazine funded by the Department of Defense, titled "The Military Utility of Understanding Adversary Culture." In it she stated clearly her opinion about what had gone wrong in Iraq. "When the U.S. cut off the hydra's Ba'thist head, power reverted to its most basic and stable form—the tribe," wrote McFate. "Once the Sunni Ba'thists lost their prestigious jobs, were humiliated in the conflict, and got frozen out through de-Ba'thification, the tribal network became the backbone of the insurgency." As an anthropologist, McFate believed that "the tribal insurgency is a direct result of our misunderstanding the Iraqi culture."

Soldiers in the field had information, McFate said, but it was the wrong information. "Soldiers and Marines were unable to establish one-to-one relationships with Iraqis, which are key to both intelligence collection and winning hearts and minds." McFate issued a stern warning to her Pentagon colleagues: "Failure to understand culture would endanger troops and civilians at a tactical level. Although it may not seem like a priority when bullets are flying, cultural ignorance can kill."

McFate was hired to perform a data analysis of eighty-eight tribes and sub-tribes from a particular province in Iraq, and the behavioral science program she was proposing began to have legs. At DARPA, Bob Popp was enthusiastic. "It was not a panacea," he says, "but we needed nation rebuilding. The social science community had tremendous insights into [the] serious problems going on [there], and a sector of DoD was ready to make serious investments into social sciences," he says of DARPA's efforts.

Arthur Cebrowski died of cancer the following year. The Office of Force Transformation did not last long without him and within a year after his death closed down, but the social intelligence programs forged ahead. Montgomery McFate found a new advocate in General David Petraeus, commander of the Multi-National Security Transition Command, Iraq, who shared her vision about the importance of winning hearts and minds. Petraeus began talking about "stability operations" and using the phrase "culture-centric warfare" when talking to the press. He said that understanding people was likely to become more important in future battles than "shock and awe and network-centric warfare."

The DARPA program originally conceived broadly by Bob Popp to bring social scientists and anthropologists into the war effort was fielded to the U.S. Army. Montgomery McFate became the lead social scientist in charge of this new program, now called the Human Terrain System. But what did that mean? The program's stated mission was to "counter the threat of the improvised explosive device," which seemed strangely at odds with a hearts and minds campaign. Historically, the battle for hearts and minds focused on people who were not yet committed to the enemy's ideology. The Army's mission statement made the Human Terrain System sound as if its social scientists were going to be persuading terrorists not to strap on the suicide vest or bury the roadside bomb after all. The first year's budget was $31 million, and by 2014, the Pentagon would spend half a billion dollars on the program. Unlike in ARPA's Motivation and Morale program during the Vietnam War, the social scientists who were part of the Human Terrain System program during the war on terror would deploy into the war zone for tours of six to nine months, embedded with combat brigades and dressed in full battle gear. Many would carry guns. So many elements of the program were incongruous, it was easy to wonder what the intent actually was.

"I do not want to get anybody killed," McFate told the *New Yorker.* "I see there could be misuse. But I just can't stand to sit back and watch these mistakes happen over and over as people get killed, and do nothing." Major General Robert Scales, the keynote speaker at the DARPA counterinsurgency conference organized by McFate, wrote papers and testified before Congress in support of this new hearts and minds effort in Iraq and Afghanistan. In the *Armed Forces Journal* Scales wrote, "Understanding and empathy will be important weapons of war." Then he made a bold declaration. "World War I was a chemists' war," Scales said. "World War II was a physicists' war," and the war on terror was "the social scientists' war."

The program quickly gathered momentum. The Human Terrain System was a countermeasure against IEDs, and counterinsurgency was back in U.S. Army nomenclature. In December 2006 the Army released its first counterinsurgency manual in more than twenty years, *Counterinsurgency, Field Manual*, No. 3-24. Lieutenant General David Petraeus oversaw the manual's publication. Montgomery McFate wrote one of the chapters. "What is Counterinsurgency?" the manual asks its readers. "If you have not studied counterinsurgency theory, here it is in a nutshell: Counterinsurgency is a competition with the insurgent for the right to win the hearts, minds, and acquiescence of the population." As it had done in Vietnam, the COIN manual stressed nation-building and cultural understanding as key tactics in winning a guerrilla war.

It was as if the Vietnam War had produced amnesia instead of experience. On its official website, the U.S. Army erroneously identified the new Human Terrain System program as being "the first time that social science research, analysis, and advising has been done systematically, on a large scale, and at the operational level" in a war.

CHAPTER TWENTY-TWO

Combat Zones That See

For the Pentagon, trying to fight a war in an urban center was like fighting blind. From the chaotic marketplace to the maze of streets, there was no way of knowing who the enemy was. DARPA believed that superior technology could give soldiers not just sight but omnipotence. Their new effort was to create "Combat Zones That See."

In the second year of the Iraq war, DARPA launched its Urban Operations Program, the largest and most expensive of the twenty-first century, as of 2014. "No technological challenges are more immediate, or more important for the future, than those posed by urban warfare," DARPA's deputy director, Dr. Robert Leheny, told a group of defense contractors, scientists, and engineers in 2005. "What we are seeing today [in Iraq] is the future of warfare." While the short-term priority remained the IED, the long-term solution required a larger vision. It was less about locating the bombs than about finding the bomb makers, Tony Tether told Congress in 2005. With Vietnam came the birth of the electronic fence, with a goal of sensing and hearing what was happening on the Ho Chi Minh Trail. With Iraq came the birth of the electronic battle space, with eyes and ears everywhere—on the ground, in the air, behind doorways and walls. DARPA needed to bolster its research and development programs to produce wide-scale surveillance technology for urban combat zones—total surveillance of an area wherever and whenever it was needed. This was the plan for Combat Zones That See.

"We need a network, or web, of sensors to better map a city and the activities in it, including inside buildings, to sort adversaries and their equipment from civilians and their equipment, including in crowds, and to spot snipers, suicide bombers, or IEDs," Tether told the Senate Armed Services Committee. "We need to watch a great variety of things, activities, and people over a wide area and have great resolution available when we need it." Through information technology the United States could gain the upper hand against the terrorists in Iraq and places like it. "And this is not just a matter of more and better sensors," he explained, "but just as important, the systems needed to make actionable intelligence out of all the data." Director Tether requested half a billion dollars to fund the first phase of development.

The timing was right. Congress had eliminated funding for DARPA's Total Information Awareness programs in the fall of 2003, citing privacy concerns. But Iraq was a "foreign battle space." Civil liberties were not at issue in a war zone. "Closely related to this [network of sensors] are tagging, tracking, and locating (TT&L) systems that help us watch and track a particular person or object of interest," said Tether. "These systems will also help us detect the clandestine production or possession of weapons of mass destruction in overseas urban areas."

DARPA partnered with the National Geospatial-Intelligence Agency (NGA), a dual combat support and intelligence agency that had been drawing and analyzing military maps since 1939. With the invention of the satellite, NGA became the lead agency responsible for collecting "geospatial intelligence," or GEOINT, interpreting that intelligence, and distributing its findings to other agencies. The NGA remains one of the lesser-known intelligence agencies. The majority of its operations are born classified.

In Iraq, DARPA and the NGA worked together to create high-resolution three-dimensional maps of most major cities and suspected terrorist hideouts. The mapping efforts became part of a system of systems, folded into a DARPA program called Heterogeneous Urban Reconnaissance, Surveillance and Target Acquisition, or HURT. Entire foreign civilian populations and their living spaces would be surveyed, observed, and scrutinized by the U.S. military and American allies so that individual people—insurgents—could be targeted, then captured or killed. In urban warfare situations, DARPA knew, terrorists tried to blend in among heterogeneous crowds, much as the Vietcong had done with trees on the trail. DARPA'S HURT program was technology designed to deprive terrorists of people cover.

To implement the terrain-based elements of the HURT program, hundreds, perhaps thousands, of defense contractors were dispatched to Iraq, capturing digital imagery along at least five thousand miles of streets using techniques similar to those used for Google Maps. Many details of the program remain classified, including which cities were targeted and in what order, but from Tether's own testimony Congress learned that thousands of tiny surveillance cameras and other microsensing devices had been discreetly mounted on infrastructure, designed to work like England's CCTV system. Tether described these surveillance cameras to Congress as "a network of nonintrusive microsensors." Unclassified documents from the NGA described these sensors as including low-resolution video sensors placed close to the ground to monitor foot traffic; medium-resolution video sensors placed high on telephone poles to watch motor vehicle and pedestrian streams, and high-resolution video sensors placed at an opportune height to capture "skeletal features and anthropometric [body measurement] cues." The resulting three-dimensional maps laid the groundwork for the first of many Combat Zones That See. DARPA program managers joked that their goal was "to track everything that moves."

One of the drones in the HURT program was the Wasp, a tiny unmanned aerial vehicle with a fourteen-inch wingspan and weighing only 430 grams, or less than a pound. Providing real-time overhead surveillance to soldiers on the ground, a fleet of Wasps took to the airspace over Iraqi cities and supply routes. The Wasp was one of the smartest drones in the drone fleet in 2005. Powered by batteries, it flew low and carried an exceptional payload of technology packed inside, including a color video camera, altimeter, GPS, and autopilot. The Wasps worked together in the system of systems, bird-sized drones flying in pairs and in threes.

"The [HURT] system can get reconnaissance imagery that high-altitude systems can not," says Dr. Michael A. Pagels, a HURT program manager who oversaw field operations in Iraq. "It can see around and sometimes into buildings." Because of the Wasp's micro size, some could enter into buildings undetected, through open windows and doorways, then fly around inside. The drones' capabilities were tailored for specific urban combat needs. If two of the Wasps were taking surveillance photos of the same area, their advanced software was able to merge the best of both images in a "paintbrush-like effect," updating the images captured in near real time, then sending them to small computers carried by soldiers on the ground. At a soldier's behest, the HURT system could pause, rewind, and play back the Wasp's surveillance video. This was a key feature if a soldier was hunting a terror cell planting an IED and needed to know what an area looked like three minutes, or three hours, before. The HURT system even had several self-governing features. It knew when one of its drones was low on fuel and could coordinate refueling times to ensure that surveillance was maintained by other drones in the system. The Wasp was also designed to recognize when it was running low on battery power. It could transmit its status to an operator. "HURT is designed to be agnostic," Pagels says, meaning that if one part of the system goes down, the other parts of the system quickly adapt to compensate for the loss. Mindful of what DARPA called the "chaotic fog of war and the mind-numbing complexity of the urban environment," the system's creators aimed to achieve "Persistent Area Dominance." HURT was part of that domination. With HURT, humans and machines would work together to maintain situational awareness in dangerous urban environments.

Giant unmanned blimps were also involved in surveillance, in DARPA's Tactical Aerostat program, also called the "unblinking eye." Originally designed for U.S. border patrol surveillance, these forty-five-foot-long airships were tethered to mobile launching platforms by reinforced fiber-optic cable. The moored balloons were then raised to heights of between one thousand and three thousand feet. They were designed to be compact and portable, able to go up and down before insurgents could shoot them out of the sky. Fiber optics allowed for secure communication between the classified surveillance systems carried inside the blimps and the operators on the ground. The blimps were helpful for keeping watch over increasingly dangerous roads, like Main Supply Route Tampa, a fifteen-mile stretch of road out of Baghdad, and Route Irish, the deadly road to the Baghdad International Airport.

Unclassified DARPA literature reveals that sometimes the system of systems worked. Other times, elements failed. Sandstorms made visibility difficult, and when that happened, terrorists could sneak in and plant their IEDs under cover of weather. When the sandstorm cleared, it was often impossible to distinguish wind-blown trash from newly planted bombs. Several of the blimps and drones also either were shot down or crashed on their own.

But DARPA's defense contractors and scientists back home

persevered. The system of systems being built by DARPA was long term, and had ambitious, well-funded goals. The ultimate objective for Combat Zones That See was to be able to track millions of people and cars as they moved through urban centers, not just in Iraq but in other urban areas that potentially posed a threat. Cars would be tracked by their license plates. Human faces would be tracked through facial recognition software. The supercomputers at the heart of the system would process all this information, using "intelligent computer algorithms [to] determine what is normal and what is not," just as the Total Information Awareness office proposed. Combat Zones That See was similar to TIA's needle-in-a-haystack hunt. It was bigger, bolder, and far more invasive. But would it work?

In Combat Zones That See, DARPA's goal was for artificially intelligent computers to process what it called "forensic information." Computers could provide answers to questions like "Where did that vehicle come from? How did it get here?" In this manner, the computers could discover "links between places, subjects and times of activities." Then, with predictive modeling capabilities in place, the artificially intelligent computers would eventually be able to "alert operators to potential force protection risks and hostile situations." In other words, the computers would be able to detect non-normal situations, and to notify the humans in the system of systems as to which hostile individuals *might* be planning an IED or other terrorist attack.

In the winter of 2005, the *Washington Post* reported that an IED attack occurred inside Iraq every forty-eight minutes. The primary countermeasure was still the electronic jamming device, designed to thwart IED activation by remote control. But these jammers were doing only a little good. In Iraq, coalition forces were up against an electromagnetic environment that was totally unpredictable and impossible to control. Iraq had an estimated 27 million people using unregulated cell phones, cordless phones, walkie-talkies, and satellite phones, and DARPA jammers were failing to keep up. Jammers were even getting jammed: Al Qaeda bomb makers developed a rudimentary radio-controlled jamming signal decoder that the Americans called the "spider." The U.S. military appeared to be losing control. Despite DARPA's lofty goals of Persistent Area Dominance through battle space surveillance, in reality the Combat Zones That See concept was collecting lots of information but providing little dominance.

DARPA had dozens of potential solutions in various stages of development. The Stealthy Insect Sensor Project, at Los Alamos National Laboratories, was now ready to deploy. As part of the animal sentinel program, going back to 1999, scientists had been making great progress training honeybees to locate bombs. Bees have sensing capabilities that outperform the dog's nose by a trillion parts per second. Using Pavlovian techniques, scientists cooled down groups of bees in a refrigerator, then strapped them into tiny boxes using masking tape, leaving their heads, and most of their antennae, poking out the top. Using a sugar water reward system, the scientists trained the bees to use their tongues to "sniff out" explosives, resulting in a reaction the scientists call a "purr." After training, when the scientists exposed the bees to a six-second burst of explosives, some had learned to "purr."

DARPA officials traveled to Los Alamos to observe the tests, filming the event for later review. The bees, transported in little boxes, were tested with various explosives, including TNT and C4. As a proof-of-concept test, a van configured like a vehicle-borne improvised explosive device, or VBIED, was packed with explosives. Remarkably, the bees were able to sniff out the explosive material inside, their tiny tongues "purring" when they came in proximity. The DARPA team was excited by the science and the prospects. But when the Army learned that DARPA planned to send bees to Iraq as a countermeasure to the IED threat, they rejected the idea. The reality of depending on insect performance in a war zone was implausible, the Army said, so the Los Alamos bees never traveled to Iraq.

On the urban battlefield the casualty rate continued to escalate. An even more deadly IED emerged, called the explosively formed penetrator, or EFP. Crafted from a cylindrical firing tube and packed with explosives, the unique EFP had a front end that was sealed by a concave liner, usually a copper disk. When the EFP fired, the intense heat of the blast turned the copper disk into an armor-piercing molten slug, propelling itself forward on a straight path at 2,000 meters per second, more than double the speed of a .50 caliber bullet. The EFP was designed with an infrared trigger, which meant it was largely jammer proof. As for other IEDs, terrorists had created new measures to defeat U.S. jamming countermeasures. They were now engineering IEDs to be "victim activated," triggered by a human foot or vehicle tire. By 2006, roughly two thousand jammers had been installed on the dashboards of coalition force vehicles in Iraq. None of these could defeat the dreaded "victim activated" pressure plate.

DARPA enhanced its body armor efforts through a program called Hardwire HD Armor. Scientists and engineers developed an entirely new class of body armor made of a hybrid metallic-composite material that weighed less than steel armor but could defend better against armor-piercing rounds. The manufacturing company Hardwire LLC specialized in building blast-resistant bunkers before it started designing bulletproof vests. But the IEDs kept coming, increasing in lethality and terror. Armor protects the chest but leaves limbs, sexual organs, and the brain exposed. All across Iraq, from Mosul to Najaf, IEDs continued to rip apart soldiers' bodies, tearing away their limbs, shredding their penises and testicles, gravely injuring their brains. The improvised explosive device—a low-technology bomb constructed for as little as $25—was now responsible for 63 percent of all coalition force deaths.

By 2006, the Pentagon had spent more than $1 billion on "defeat-the-IED" technology. Deputy Secretary of Defense Paul Wolfowitz recommended the creation of a permanent program, and on February 14, 2006, the Joint Improvised Explosive Device Defeat Organization (JIEDDO) was established to deal with the ever-increasing IED threat. With a first-year budget of $3.6 billion, JIEDDO was described as its own mini–Manhattan Project. Hundreds more electronic warfare specialists were sent to the war theater in Iraq. To the explosive ordnance disposal technicians, called EOD techs, working to defuse bombs in the war theater, there was something that DARPA was working on that could not get there fast enough: its force of next-generation robots.

Master Chief Petty Officer Craig Marsh was a Master Explosive Ordnance Disposal (EOD) technician, assigned to the first ever Combined Joint Counter-IED Task Force, otherwise known as CJTF Troy. EOD techs are part of the Special Operations community and frequently operate alongside Navy Seals, Green Berets, and other Special Warfare units on classified missions. In 2006, Marsh deployed to Iraq to help establish CJTF Troy as the Operations (J3) senior noncommissioned officer. Marsh was trained to respond to and dispose of bombs planted underwater and aboveground, including nuclear, chemical, and biological weapons. When he was a younger sailor, he served on the classified Mark 6 Marine Mammal System program, swimming with highly trained bottlenose dolphins to detect and mark the location of underwater intruders and explosives.

In Iraq, the daily work of EOD techs was among the most crucial, most deadly, and most nerve-racking of jobs. IEDs were ubiquitous. Defusing these homemade bombs, and collecting intelligence about the bombs and the bomb makers, made for an extraordinarily stressful workload. In Hollywood, the efforts of EOD technicians would be made famous by the Academy Award–winning film *The Hurt Locker.* In Iraq, the work was overwhelming, and many of the younger technicians were largely unprepared for what they were up against. "We were dealing with thousands and thousands of IEDs," Craig Marsh recalls. "Ninety-five percent of the guys had never seen an IED before."

At forty-two years old, Marsh had nearly twenty years of experience in the EOD community defusing bombs. In Baghdad, it was his job to oversee the work of eighty EOD teams spread across Iraq, each composed of two or three technicians, and he was to coordinate the fragmentary orders (FRAGOs) from the Multi-National Corps-Iraq three-star generals across the entire Joint Task Force Troy.

At Task Force Troy, Marsh lived on the fourth floor of the Al Faw Palace, or Water Place, formerly inhabited by Saddam Hussein and his entourage. The palace had roughly sixty-two rooms and twenty-nine bathrooms. It was loaded with garish gold chandeliers and expensive marble tile. The Al Faw was surrounded by artificial ponds filled with large, hungry carp, notorious for attacking and devouring ducks that landed on its shimmering surface. The Americans set up a headquarters here and renamed the place Camp Victory, Iraq. Combined Joint Task Force Troy lived inside.

Over time, Camp Victory would grow larger and come to be encircled in twenty-seven miles of concrete wall, making it the largest of a total of 505 bases operated by the United States in Iraq. Even Saddam Hussein and his cousin Ali Hassan al Majeed, known as "Chemical Ali," lived at Camp Victory during the war. The two men were imprisoned in a top secret building on an island in the center of one of the ponds. Accessible only by a drawbridge, the prison was code-named Building 114. In the mornings, Marsh would pass by the island on his morning jog.

Task Force Troy was the first operational counter-IED task force in U.S. military history, and the unit was only a few months old when Marsh arrived. "In 2006, everyone was still running around with their hair on fire," he recalls. "We were still trying to determine who the good guys were and who the bad guys were." There were thousands of bombs to defuse. Too many to count. "All eighty teams would be out in the field, working eighteen, twenty hours a day. Some guys would clear ten locations, then come back, then get sent back to the same hole" after another IED had been planted in it. "There were snipers to deal with. The cost was tremendous," Marsh says. Death was commonplace. "It was painful and frustrating. Within the first couple of months, one of the sailors I was working with was blown up and killed."

Another part of Craig Marsh's job was to coordinate the work between the teams that were trying to locate bomb makers and the lab technicians examining evidence. At every location, before and after an IED blast, there was forensic evidence to collect, a potential means of identifying and capturing members of local terrorist cells. Task Force Troy worked in concert with a forensic counter-IED team called the Combined Explosive Exploitation Cell, or "sexy" (CEXC) for short. CEXC had an electronics shop and laboratory at Camp Victory where technicians worked around the clock examining evidence. This was home to some of the most technologically advanced forensic equipment in the world, including high-powered microscopes, reflective ultraviolet imaging system fingerprint scopes, and x-ray photographing machines.

Task Force Troy had access to some sensor technology, but it did not do much good in the field. "Sensors are great for identifying anomalies at the bottom of the ocean," says Marsh. "Technology can be very good for gathering intelligence. But when it comes to assessing technology, nothing comes close to an experienced human. The 'ah-hah' moments almost always came from a guy in the lab at CEXC."

Human intelligence, HUMINT, offered Task Force Troy some of the best leads in trying to identify who might be building and planting the IEDs. Task Force Troy teams would go out in the field and talk to locals, taking paper-and-pen notes. "We'd follow up on these leads," relates Marsh, only to discover "we were now dealing with death squads." For Iraqis, working with Americans carried a high price. "These guys would kill entire families just for talking to us. It was brutal. We'd find vans stuffed with bodies. Villagers who talked to us would wind up dead, blindfolded, left by the side of the road." Corpses went unidentified and lay rotting in the streets because extended family members were afraid to claim the bodies, fearing reprisal. As the violence swelled, trust disappeared.

The psychological toll grew heavy. Marsh remembers being back at Camp Victory one night, longing for some kind of a break, when he and a colleague were watching a training video illustrating how a DARPA robot could allow first sighting of visible wires and other components of a partially buried IED. Marsh recalls what he saw. "The robot's working the road. Then the robot blows up. The dust clears. Along comes another robot and it starts working on a second IED in the road." EOD teams had used DARPA robots before, "but there were not enough of them to go around," says Marsh. "The few robots [we had] were taking a beating due to IED blasts. DARPA was the momentum behind pushing the much-needed volume of robots into the hands of those of us who really needed them." When Marsh learned more robots were coming to Task Force Troy, "that was a 'thank God' moment," he recalls.

The workhorse of all the counter-IED robots was DARPA's Talon robot, first developed for DARPA by Foster-Miller, Inc., in 1993. The robot was originally conceived as a counter-mine robot, designed to work in shallow ocean waters, called the surf zone. In the aftermath of the Bosnian war, Talon robots were used to remove unexploded munitions. On 9/11, Talon robots were used on-site at the World Trade Center, searching through the rubble for survivors. And Talon robots were the first robots used in the war on terror. They accompanied Special Forces during action against the Taliban and Al Qaeda on a classified mission in Afghanistan in

2002. "Talon robots have been in continuous active military duty ever since," DARPA literature reports.

Now, a fleet of combat-ready, man-portable Talon robots was finally ready for battle in Iraq. It was 2006. This generation of Talon was small and squat, weighing just one hundred pounds. It had a robotic arm and was mounted on a four-wheeled platform that rolled along on two tank treads. The robot was operated from a portable control unit through a two-way radio or a fiber-optic link.

The EOD techs gave the Talons high praise—and human names.

"Sorry for the late report on Gordon the robot," reads one EOD operator report. "While I was in direct control of Gordon, 8 deep buried IED's were disposed of, 7 houses were cleared of possible HBIEDs [house-borne improvised explosive devices], 13 Unexploded Ordinances (UXO) found in houses that were to be placed as IEDs, 18 landmines. Approximately 300 lbs of HME [homemade explosive] was disposed of."

Several days after that report, Gordon the robot was launched out the back of an EOD truck and was searching an intersection for a deeply buried IED when a bomb detonated approximately ten feet from where Gordon was working. "Still functioning, he continued to search the area," the EOD tech reported. "On the opposite side of the road, another IED was detonated and had turned him upside down. Everything was still working until a fire fight started. Gordon took 7 rounds to the underside and was done for the day." The EOD technician took Gordon back to the robot shop for repair. He was fixed, returned to the team, and sent back out into the field.

Not long after, Gordon was searching a gate near a house, looking for possible booby traps, when an IED detonated right next to where he was working. "Gordon was mangled beyond repair. Now his replacement, 'Flash,' is here to finish his job," wrote the tech. The beauty of robots, says Craig Marsh, is simple to understand. "Some leaders say you can't take the man out of the mine field. But the bottom line is, robots save lives. EOD technicians will choose to work smarter instead of harder when at all possible." The Talon robots cost between $60,000 and $180,000 per unit, depending on what sensor technology the robot is fitted with.

The longer-term goal of Task Force Troy was to turn the bomb detection and defusing technology over to the Iraqis themselves. "We were trying to establish a partnership with the Iraqi Ministry of Police, but we got a lot of pushback," Marsh recalls. "We'd say, here's how DNA works. Here's how fingerprinting works. And they'd look at us like we were talking about magic." In Marsh's experience, the way the Iraqi police force worked in 2006 was based on a man's word. "They'd ask someone, a suspect, 'Did you build this IED?' And if he said 'no,' that worked for them. Proof to them was an eyewitness. Judges would ask, 'Are there any eyewitnesses to back this up?' If the answer was no, and [the suspect] said he didn't do it, he would be let go. The system was based on deceptions. On a lot of untruths."

Task Force Troy worked with CEXC to build what it called "targeting packages," files of evidence that could be used by Iraqi police before a judge. "It made things complicated and frustrating. Trying to assist the Iraqi judicial system—we were not supposed to say 'train'—and to prosecute the war."

There was a major turning point in cooperative science on February 22, 2006. Early that morning, sixty-five miles north of Baghdad, in the city of Samarra, a massive IED blast tore apart the Golden Dome of the Askariya Shrine, one of Shia Islam's holiest shrines. "This is like 9/11 in the United States," declared Abdel Abdul Mahdi, one of Iraq's two vice presidents, a Shiite Muslim.

When Craig Marsh learned about the bombing, he walked across the Al Faw Palace compound to update his commander, Colonel Kevin Lutz, on the other side of Camp Victory. The two men discussed next steps. "There was so much evidence to collect at the Golden Dome," says Marsh. "We wanted to get eyes on the incident site and at least do our best to preserve the evidence for collection without damaging an already sensitive relationship with Iraqi leadership. CEXC guys were well equipped to handle that." The Iraqi government in Baghdad was not. But now they saw how they could "benefit from the science," says Marsh. For the first time since Task Force Troy had been set up, the government of Baghdad, which was led by Shiite Muslims, agreed to allow CEXC to investigate something that had nothing to do with coalition force deaths. A team of Task Force Troy CEXC technicians descended on the rubble of the Golden Mosque.

In working with forensic science to identify the terrorists who blew up the Golden Dome, Iraqi leaders in Baghdad warmed to science in general, says Marsh. Then advances in science took a bizarre and tragic turn. Marsh learned that Iraqi security forces were relying on a device to detect bombs that had no science behind it at all. Word was the device, called the ADE 651, "was a totally bogus piece of equipment," he says. It was a small handheld black box with a swiveling antenna attached to the top. The Iraqi Ministry of the Interior's General Directorate for Combating Explosives had purchased more than 1,500 of the devices from a private company in England called ATSC.

Craig Marsh took the problem to senior officers, who invited top Iraqi officials to Task Force Troy for a technology demonstration. "We had the Iraqis come to the laboratory and we had DoD guys demonstrate" that it did not work, Marsh recounts. The ADE 651 "did not detect explosives of any kind. We took it apart. We had it x-rayed. It had no electronic components inside." There was also no power source. The Iraqis insisted the device worked on "nuclear magnetic resonance, or NMR." Despite overwhelming evidence coming from the CEXC lab at Task Force Troy that the device had no scientific value whatsoever, Iraqi officials stood behind the ADE 651 bomb detector, which cost $60,000 per device. Soon, almost every Iraqi guard at every major checkpoint across the country was using the worthless device in place of any kind of physical inspection. It was dangerous and frustrating. "Insurgents were able to get dump truck bombs past checkpoints" into Baghdad, Marsh says. "Coalition checkpoints did not use this device because we had actual explosive detection systems at our disposal." The ADE 651 "was nothing more than a magic wand."

"Whether it's magic or scientific, what I care about is it detects bombs," Major General Jehad al-Jabiri, head of the General Directorate for Combating Explosives, told the *New York Times*. "I know more about this issue than the Americans do. In fact, I know more about bombs than anyone in the world."

Years later, the maker of the phony device, ATSC president Jim McCormick, was arrested in England and convicted for fraud after a whistleblower revealed that McCormick knew he was selling bogus equipment. In 2011, Major General al-Jabiri was arrested for taking millions of dollars in bribes from McCormick. As of 2014 he had not been tried, and the bogus devices were still being used in Iraq.

The same month that terrorists in Iraq blew up Shia Islam's revered shrine, attacks against coalition forces numbered more than two an hour, or fifty a day. By 2007 that figure had doubled to one hundred attacks a day, or three thousand a month. An estimated $15 billion had been spent by that point on counter-IED efforts—on jammers, robots, surveillance systems, and more. The situation was only getting worse. DARPA's Combat Zones That See program was having little effect on the war effort, despite a classified number of dollars being spent on a program that collected video images of Iraqi citizens walking around cities and driving in cars and housed them in classified data storage facilities for access at a later date. America was rapidly losing control of the war, and in response, in January 2007, an additional thirty thousand troops were deployed to Iraq in what would become known as "the surge."

To support the tens of thousands of new soldiers heading into battle, Tony Tether appeared before the House Armed Services Committee to discuss several new technology programs DARPA was sending into the war zone. The Boomerang was DARPA's response to sniper threats, Tether said. It was an acoustic sensor system made up of seven small microphones that attached to a military vehicle, listened for shooter information, and notified soldiers precisely where the fire was coming from, all in less than a second. The Boomerang system was able to detect shock waves from a sniper's incoming bullets, as well as the muzzle blast, then relay that information to soldiers. For example, when a shot was detected, Boomerang might call out, "Shot. Two o'clock. 400 meters." Tether told Congress that DARPA had fielded sixty Boomerang units to the Army, Marine Corps, and Special Forces, and was now working on a more advanced Boomerang-based technology called CROSSHAIRS (Counter Rocket-Propelled Grenade and Shooter System with Highly Accurate Immediate Responses).

CROSSHAIRS was a vehicle-mounted system that fused radar and signal-processing technologies to quickly detect much larger projectiles coming at coalition vehicles, including rocket-propelled grenades, antitank guided missiles, and even direct mortar fire. A sensor system inside the CROSSHAIRS would be able to identify where the shot came from and relay that information to all other vehicles in a convoy. The terrorists would be able to get one shot off, then Boomerang and CROSSHAIRS would allow coalition shooters to respond by targeting and killing the enemy shooter—in under one second.

To help snipers with accuracy, immediacy, and portability, DARPA was also fielding the smallest, lightest-weight sniper rifle in the history of warfare, the DARPA XM-3.

Tether also told Congress about DARPA's new Radar Scope, a tiny, 1.5-pound handheld unit that allowed U.S. forces to "sense" through nonmetallic walls, including concrete, and determine if a human was hiding inside a building or behind a wall. In the winter of 2007, DARPA fielded fifty Radar Scopes to the Army, Marines, and Special Forces for evaluation in the war theater. Tether hinted at bigger plans for this same technology, including ways to sense human activity underground, up to fifty feet deep.

Broad intelligence, surveillance, and reconnaissance efforts fused with massive data collection and data-mining operations would continue to be DARPA's priority in urban area operations, Tether told Congress. "By 2025, nearly 60 percent of the world's population will live in urban areas," Tether said, "so we should assume that U.S. forces will continue to be deployed to urban areas for combat and post-conflict stabilization." Tether listed numerous unclassified programs, each with a suitable acronym. DARPA's WATCH-IT (Wide Area All Terrain Change Indication Technologies) program analyzed data collected from foliage-penetrating radar. DARPA's LADAR (Laser Detection and Ranging) program sensors obtained "exquisitely detailed, 3-D imagery through foliage to identify targets in response to these cues." DARPA's ASSIST (Advanced Soldier Sensor Information System and Technology) program allowed soldiers to collect details about specific Iraqi neighborhoods and then upload that information into a database for other soldiers to use.

DARPA's HURT (Heterogeneous Urban Reconnaissance, Surveillance and Target Acquisition) program was flying more than fifty drones in support of coalition infantry brigades. HURT was able to reconnoiter over hundreds of miles of roadways, support convoys, and EOD tech teams. HURT provided persistent perimeter surveillance at forward operating bases and was playing a role in stopping an ever-increasing number of suicide bombers who were targeting U.S. military bases. In 2007 the HURT program would discreetly change its name to HART (Heterogeneous Airborne Reconnaissance Team) after unnamed sources suggested that the acronym was in poor taste.

To merge its growing number of surveillance and data-collection technologies, DARPA engineered a multimedia reporting system called TIGR (Tactical Ground Reporting) to be used by soldiers on the ground in Iraq. Congress was told that TIGR's web-based multimedia platform "allows small units, like patrols, to easily collect and quickly share 'cop-on-the-beat' information about operations, neighborhoods, people and civil affairs." It was like a three-dimensional Wikipedia for soldiers in combat zones. U.S. soldiers told *MIT Technology Review* that TIGR allowed them to "see locations of key buildings, like mosques," and to access data on "past attacks, geo-tagged photos of houses... and photos of suspected insurgents and neighborhood leaders." In testimony the following year, the Armed Services Committee was told that TIGR was "so successful in Operation Iraqi Freedom, it was [being] requested by brigades going to Afghanistan." Which, in the fall of 2008, was where tens of thousands of additional coalition forces would soon be headed.

After five years of relative stability in Afghanistan, the country was again spiraling into violence and chaos. Critics cried foul, declaring that the Bush administration had lost control of an insurgency force it had already defeated and pacified in 2002. That in diverting the great majority of American military resources, as well as intelligence and reconstruction resources, from Afghanistan into Iraq, the White House and the Pentagon had created a dual insurgency nightmare. Afghanistan and Iraq were being called quagmires in the press. These wars were unwinnable, critics said. This was Vietnam all over again. And, as had been the case for fifty years, DARPA was heading straight into the war zone.

CHAPTER TWENTY-THREE

Human Terrain

At 9:20 p.m. on the night of June 13, 2008, two truck bombs, or vehicle-borne IEDs (VBIEDs), pulled up to the gates of the Sarposa prison in Kandahar, Afghanistan, and exploded in massive fireballs, knocking down large sections of the mud brick walls. Taliban militants on motorcycles quickly swarmed into the area in a coordinated attack, firing rocket-propelled grenades and assault rifles at prison guards, killing fifteen of them. It was a scene of carnage and mayhem. By the time coalition forces arrived, roughly an hour later, not one of the 1,200 incarcerated prisoners remained. In the morning, Ahmed Wali Karzai, brother of President Hamid Karzai and the head of the provincial council in Kandahar, declared that "all" of the Sarposa prisoners had escaped, including as many as four hundred hard-core Taliban.

The prison break was dangerous for the citizens of Kandahar and embarrassing for NATO-led coalition forces, officially called the International Security Assistance Force. The Taliban issued a press release claiming responsibility and stating that the freed prisoners were happy to be back living in their Kandahar homes.

Coalition force soldiers conducted door-to-door searches looking for Taliban escapees, but there was almost no way to determine who had been in the prison. Fifteen prison guards were dead, and those still alive were not cooperating.

As a result of the security failure, the Pentagon redoubled efforts regarding its biometrics program in Afghanistan. Thousands of Handheld Interagency Identity Detection Equipment (HIIDE) units were shipped to coalition forces with instructions on how to collect eye scans, fingerprints, facial images, and DNA swabs from every Afghan male between the ages of fifteen and sixty-four that coalition soldiers and Afghan security forces came into contact with. The wars in Iraq and Afghanistan had given birth to a new form of U.S. intelligence exploitation called bio-intelligence, or BIOINT. This concept found its genesis in DARPA's Information Awareness Office. The mission of BIOINT, bulleted out in a DARPA program memo from 2002, was to "produce a proto-type system to [gather] biometric signatures of humans." The biometrics system had been fielded to the Army, with the first hardware units appearing in Fallujah, Iraq, in December 2004.

The U.S. commander in Iraq, General David Petraeus, was an advocate of collecting biometrics in counterinsurgency operations. "This data is virtually irrefutable and generally is very helpful in identifying who was responsible for a particular device [i.e., an IED] in a particular attack, enabling subsequent targeting," Petraeus said. "Based on our experience in Iraq, I pushed this hard here in Afghanistan, too, and the Afghan authorities have recognized the value and embraced the systems." Over the next three years, coalition forces would collect biometrics on more than 1.5 million Afghan men, roughly one out of every six males in the country. In Iraq the figure was even higher—reportedly 2.2 million male Iraqis, or one in four, had biometric scans performed on them.

The month after the Sarposa prison break, in July 2008, Democratic presidential candidate Senator Barack Obama took his first official trip to the region, spending two days in Iraq and two days in Afghanistan. Senator Obama called the situation in Afghanistan "precarious and urgent," and said that if elected president, he would make Afghanistan the new "central front in the war against terrorism." Two days later the chairman of the Joint Chiefs of Staff, Admiral Mike Mullen, appeared on *PBS NewsHour* to discuss the growing violence in Afghanistan and the need for a ten-thousand- to twenty-thousand-troop surge there.

Summer became fall, and now it was November 2008. It had been four years since DARPA had sponsored its first social science and counterinsurgency conference since the Vietnam War, the Adversary Cultural Knowledge and National Security Conference organized by Montgomery McFate. The results of the conference had borne fruit in what was now the Army's Human Terrain System program, and at least twenty-six teams of social scientists and anthropologists had been sent to Iraq and Afghanistan. On November 4, one of those Human Terrain Teams was a three-person unit stationed at Combat Outpost Hutal, Afghanistan, fifty miles west of Kandahar. On this day back home, Americans were voting for a new president, and here in the war theater, anthropologist Paula Loyd, security contractor Don Ayala, and former combat Marine Clint Cooper were heading out on regular patrol.

The area around Kandahar was particularly dangerous and hostile to coalition forces. Kandahar had long been the spiritual center of the Taliban, and now, after the prison break five months earlier, an unusual number of hard-core Taliban were living among the people, making the situation even more precarious. On patrol that November morning, Paula Loyd, Don Ayala, and Clint Cooper were accompanied by three local interpreters and one platoon of U.S. Army infantry soldiers with C Company, 2-2 Infantry Battalion. Paula Loyd was a dedicated anthropologist, a Wellesley College graduate, thirty-six years old and engaged to be married. Petite and striking, with long blond hair hanging out the back of her combat helmet, Loyd had served in the U.S. Army for four years after college, including a post as a vehicle mechanic in the DMZ in South Korea. She was hardworking, curious, and respected by her peers; one former colleague said, "An indefinable spirit defined her." Nearing the central market in the village of Chehel Gazi, the Human Terrain Team spread out. Paula Loyd stopped in a dirt alleyway and started handing out candy and pens to local children walking to school. The alleyway was about twenty-five feet wide and lined on either side by tall mud brick walls. Running down the center of the alleyway was a shallow creek, its sloping banks lined with tall leafy trees. As adults passed by, through an interpreter Loyd asked questions about the local price of cooking fuel, a key indicator as to whether or not the Taliban had hijacked supply lines. As Loyd interviewed people, she took notes in her notebook, information that was to be uploaded into a military database at the end of each day.

A young bearded man walked up to Loyd, shooing the local children away. The man carried a container, like a jug. Loyd asked her interpreter to translate.

"What's in your jug?" Loyd asked the man.

He told her it was fuel. Gasoline for his water pump at home.

"How much does petrol cost in Maiwand?" Loyd asked.

He told her it was very expensive. She asked about his job. He said he worked for a school.

"Would you like some candy?" she asked.

"I don't like candy," the man said. His name was Abdul Salam. He wore blue sweatpants, a long-sleeved shirt, and a blue-striped vest. Abdul Salam asked Loyd's interpreter if she smoked. The conversation continued for a while, then tapered off. Then Abdul Salam wandered away. After a while he came back. The interpreter noticed he was playing with a plastic lighter, turning it over in one hand. In the other hand he held the jug of fuel.

In a flash, Abdul Salam raised the jug and poured gasoline over

Paula Loyd. He struck the lighter and set her on fire. Some witnesses described hearing a *whoosh* sound. Others described seeing Paula Loyd being consumed by an inferno of flames. The heat was so intense and powerful that no one near her could immediately help without catching fire as well. Loyd's interpreter later recalled seeing her burning as his mind raced for a way to put the fire out. She called out his name. Nearby, a twenty-six-year-old platoon leader named Matthew Pathak shouted out that soldiers should get her into the creek. He filled his helmet with water and threw it on Loyd. People tossed dirt and sand on her, trying to get the fire out. Finally, soldiers dragged her across the alleyway and into the creek. The flames were not out. Loyd had third-degree burns on 60 percent of her body. She was still conscious.

"I'm cold," she said. "I'm cold." It was one of the last things she said.

When Abdul Salam set Paula Loyd on fire, people started screaming. Human Terrain Team member Don Ayala was standing roughly 150 feet down the alleyway. He drew his pistol and raced toward the commotion. As Ayala ran toward Loyd, Abdul Salam was running away from the crime scene, toward Ayala. Soldiers pursuing Salam screamed, "Stop that man! Shoot him!" Ayala tackled Salam and, with the help of two soldiers, put him in flex cuffs.

Don Ayala was not a social scientist or an anthropologist; he was a security contractor, or bodyguard. Ayala had previously guarded Afghan president Hamid Karzai and Iraqi prime minister Nouri al-Maliki. His job was to keep Paula Loyd from getting killed. Witnesses watched him work to immobilize Abdul Salam, who resisted detention, while soldiers and interpreters about 150 feet away tried to help the critically injured Loyd, whose clothes had melted into her skin and who was in terrible pain. Specialist Justin Skotnicki, one of the U.S. Army infantry soldiers who had witnessed the attack, went over to Ayala and told him what had happened to Paula Loyd, that Abdul Salam had thrown gasoline on her and set her on fire. Ayala called out for an interpreter.

"Don had the interpreter inform [Abdul Salam] that Don thought the man was the devil," Skotnicki later recalled. Then Don Ayala pulled his 9mm pistol from his belt, pressed it against Abdul Salam's temple, and shot him in the head, killing him.

Paula Loyd was transported to Brooke Army Medical Center in San Antonio, Texas. She was in the burn unit there for two months until she died of her injuries on January 7, 2009. The Taliban claimed credit for her death.

Earlier that spring, in May, Don Ayala was tried for murder in a Louisiana courtroom. He pled guilty to manslaughter. U.S. District Senior Judge Claude Hilton showed leniency and gave Ayala probation and a $12,500 fine instead of jail time. "The acts that were done in front of this defendant would provide provocation for anyone" who was present, Judge Hilton said. "This occurred in a hostile area, maybe not in the middle of a battlefield, but certainly in the middle of a war."

The entire situation was grotesque. An anthropologist handing out candy to children was set on fire by an emissary of the Taliban and died a horrible death. The security contractor hired to protect the anthropologist was unable to do so and instead took justice into his own hands. But none of this was exactly as it seemed. Why was Ayala on the Human Terrain Team in the first place? He had no qualifications in anthropology or social science. Why weren't the U.S. Army infantry soldiers considered capable of protecting her? According to Montgomery McFate, all Human Terrain Team members "advise brigades on economic development, political systems, tribal structures, etc.; provide training to brigades as requested; and conduct research on topics of interest to the brigade staff," but Ayala was not qualified in any of those areas, except for the "etc." part.

Court documents revealed that Don Ayala was paid $425 a day, each day he worked in Afghanistan, and that in Iraq he had been paid $800 a day, which meant he earned more in two days than any of the soldiers in C Company made in a month. What service could Don Ayala perform that the C Company soldiers were unable to do? Over the next five years the Human Terrain System would cost taxpayers $600 million. What actual purpose did it serve? The answer would ultimately lead back to DARPA.

But first there was subterfuge and misinformation, starting with the wide gap between how McFate and other social scientists presented the program to the public—knowingly or not—and how the program was actually positioned in the Defense Department hierarchy.

To the public, the Human Terrain System was sold as a culture-centric program, a hearts and minds campaign. But in U.S. Army literature, the Human Terrain System was in place "to help mitigate IEDs," and the program was funded by the Joint Improvised Explosive Device Defeat Organization (JIEDDO), with members like Paula Loyd working alongside EOD technicians, DARPA jammers, and Talon robots. In press releases, the Army was oblique. "Combat commanders [do] not have a good understanding of the cultural and social implications of military operations in urban environments," said one. Anthropologists and social scientists were going into the battle zone "to provide social science support to military commanders." The important word was "support." It would take until this book for a fuller picture to emerge of what was being supported.

The Human Terrain System program was controversial from the start. The American Anthropological Association, which was founded in 1902, and whose credo for anthropologists was "first do no harm," denounced the program as "a disaster waiting to unfold." Its executive board condemned the Human Terrain System as "a problematic application of anthropological expertise, most specifically on ethical grounds," and in a letter to Congress called the program "dangerous and reckless" and "a waste of the taxpayers' money." In an article for *Anthropology Today,* Roberto González, associate professor of anthropology at San Jose State University, called the program "mercenary anthropology." Catherine Lutz, chair of the anthropology department at Brown University, charged that the Defense Department was promoting a dangerous and false idea "that anthropologists' 'help' will create a more humane approach on the part of the U.S. military towards the Iraqi people." Lutz believed the notion of helping people to be "a very seductive idea," but she encouraged anthropologists to step back and ask, "Help what? Help whom, to do what?"

Hugh Gusterson, professor of anthropology at George Mason University, accused the Army of trying to convince anthropologists that "Americans have a mission to spread democracy" and that "Americans have only the well-being of other people in mind." Gusterson saw that as manipulative and believed that once a person convinced himself or herself of that, "you start to think of it [war] as some kind of cultural miscommunication. And you start to ask naive, misshapen questions [like],'If we only understood their culture, how could we make them like us? Why do they hate us so much?'" Gusterson believed the answer was simple. "They hate us because we are occupying their country, not because they don't understand our hand signals and because occasionally we mistreat their women," Gusterson said. "So if you ask the wrong questions you get the wrong answers and more people on both sides will die."

"I think the idea that there can be a kinder, gentler counterinsurgency war is a myth," said González. "I think it's a hope that many people have. It's a kind of dream that they [anthropologists] can somehow do things differently. I do think it's a myth, though, and I think we have lots of historical evidence to back that up."

With the debate escalating, the Pentagon cultivated two succinct narratives regarding the Human Terrain System, as exemplified in educational courses taught at the U.S. Army School of Advanced Military Studies at Fort Leavenworth, Kansas, the U.S.

Army War College in Carlisle, Pennsylvania, and the U.S. Naval War College in Newport, Rhode Island. One narrative was that Human Terrain Teams helped make way for "the moral prosecution of warfare." That time and again, the teams enabled soldiers to narrowly avert disaster. That putting anthropologists on the battlefield made soldiers better able to engage in so-called "honorable warfare." The experiences of Major Philip Carlson and his unit in the wrongful arrest of an Iraqi village elder, as taught by the Army, illustrate this point of view.

"My very first time out in an HTT [Human Terrain Team] in Iraq, we had a company airmobile to the countryside because of the IED threat on the road," said Carlson. The Human Terrain Team was attached to a patrol fire squadron in the Second Armored Cavalry Regiment and was carrying out "random interviews and know and search operations." Carlson was having problems with his local interpreters, whom he described as "young, gung-ho Shi'ites who were motivated to capture terrorists." In one particular house, Major Carlson recalled, coalition forces discovered an older man in possession of a rifle scope and a closetful of books. The interpreters insisted that the books were "jihadist in nature and the [rifle] scope was for a sophisticated sniper rifle," said Carlson. The man, Mr. Alawi, was arrested and "paraded through the village back to the patrol base." There, a Human Terrain Team's cultural expert, Dr. Ammar, questioned Alawi further and decided he was not a radical but a "kindly old school teacher." His books, said Carlson, were textbooks from a school. The scope was from an air rifle that he used to shoot birds.

According to Major Carlson, if the Human Terrain Team had not been present, the coalition forces would not have understood how important it was to restore Alawi's honor. They simply would have released him and let him return to his house on his own. This would have been a grave mistake, said Dr. Ammar, who instructed the soldiers on the specifics of honor restoration. In the

Army-sanctioned story, Major Carlson did not elaborate on what the specifics of honor restoration entail, nor did he explain what happened to the gung-ho Shi'ite interpreters who presented their U.S. Army employers with false information. According to Carlson, "the news [of the honor restoration] spread like wildfire." Instead of having created a foe in Mr. Alawi, they had created a friend. The son of the village elder showed Major Carlson where an IED was buried and where eighty mortar tubes were hidden. "That is the power of understanding and operating appropriately within a culture," said Major Carlson.

A second Pentagon narrative, conveyed by the Navy, held that work done by the Human Terrain Teams sometimes seemed futile but had positive outcomes later on. This narrative is exemplified by the writings of Human Terrain Team advisor Norman Nigh. In "An Operator's Guide to Human Terrain Teams," written for the U.S. Naval War College's Center on Irregular Warfare and Armed Groups, Nigh asks, when considering counterinsurgency doctrine and COIN application, "Can doctrine be applied despite an unwilling population?" To answer the question, he tells the story of an Afghan village elder called Haji Malma.

Norman Nigh was a member of a Human Terrain Team attached to a group of coalition forces from Canada, assigned to the village of Nakhonay, Afghanistan, located about ten miles southwest of Kandahar, in the Taliban heartland, not far from where Paula Loyd was set on fire. Most of the soldiers on Nigh's combat patrol despised Haji Malma, "a stoic village elder, known Taliban judge, and suspected architect of countless Canadian deaths." For several years, NATO forces had been trying to build a case against Haji Malma and other Taliban leaders like him, but could not. Malma reveled in the fact that there was nothing the coalition forces could do to him, Nigh says. "Like most sophisticated Taliban leaders in Afghanistan," Nigh explains, "Malma was taking advantage of [America's] COIN war. On the surface, he appeared to be a benign village elder, interested only in the well-being of the people of Nakhonay," when in fact he was a "key Pakistani-educated Al-Qaida supporter who controlled one of the most dangerous and strategically important areas in Kandahar."

Haji Malma regularly sought development funds from aid organizations and NATO troops, and regularly received financial support. The same went for the rest of the duplicitous elders running Nakhonay village affairs. The Human Terrain Team found that the situation was infuriating soldiers, who were "unable to realize justice for the friends they've lost." This, says Nigh, was dangerous for the broader effort in Afghanistan, since "these heightened emotions often blur an operator's ability to understand the population and wage an effective COIN war."

The Human Terrain Team suggested that coalition forces, in this case Task Force Kandahar, "pull back and take a long-horizon perspective." Nigh and his colleagues determined that Afghanistan was "a country that lacks a rule of law," ranking 176 out of 178 on the State Department's Corruption Perception Index. "Corruption and kickbacks of public procurement act as a necessary evil to mitigate risk, leverage against liabilities, and promote cooperation." The Human Terrain Team also conducted a comprehensive ethnographic study on the topic of corruption, interviewing the majority of villagers and asking them what they thought. "Virtually the entire village agreed that the Western term 'bribery' was nothing more than *tarrun,* an Afghan word for contract or agreement," Nigh explained.

Right around this same time, Task Force Kandahar was preparing for what was called a "clearing operation" in the area—the removal of Taliban leaders and the installation of more coalition-friendly men. But in the opinion of the Human Terrain Team, "many previous clearing operations had resulted in little to no change." They suggested a different strategy, something Nigh referred to as the "oil spot plan...to divide and conquer the population." The oil spot COIN strategy worked analogously to the way cheesecloth works, writes Nigh, with each drop of oil representing a stability initiative, or a municipal service, or an offer of agricultural development assistance. "Drops of oil, one at a time and over time, eventually cover the entire cloth," according to Nigh, "each oil spot [representing] a visible manifestation of the desired end state for the entire war." The oil spot concept was a strategy endorsed by Dr. Karl Slaikeu, the psychologist and conflict resolution specialist who replaced Paula Loyd. The oil spot strategy was put into effect in Nakhonay, and in his Naval War College narrative Nigh writes, "The strategy appears to be working." The international press did not agree. In an October 2010 issue of *Military World Magazine,* published in England, Nakhonay would be described as "a town now infamous as a killing zone."

The mainstream press largely disparaged the program as the deaths of Human Terrain Team members made headline news. Michael Bhatia, an anthropologist with degrees from Brown University and Oxford University, and who was working on a Ph.D. dissertation on the mujahedeen of Afghanistan, was killed in May 2008 while traveling through Khost, Afghanistan. His unit was en route to help negotiate a peace process between two warring tribes when his vehicle drove over an IED buried in the road. Witnesses say the explosion was loud, horrific, and all-consuming. Bhatia and two Army soldiers were instantly killed. As an Associated Press article about his death put it, "Michael Bhatia was on the frontlines of a Pentagon experiment." The following month, in Iraq, Human Terrain Team member Nicole Suveges, a political scientist from Johns Hopkins University, was also killed by an IED, planted by terrorists inside a district council building in Sadr City. Killed alongside Suveges were eleven other people, military and civilian, including U.S. soldiers, Iraqi government officials, and U.S. Embassy personnel. Her team was trying to identify ways that ordinary Iraqi citizens could learn how to assist a transitioning government achieve their political aims, according to the Pentagon.

The Human Terrain System continued to grow. In 2010 it was reported that team members earned $200,000 a year. Ever vilified by the press, Human Terrain Team members were likened to de facto intelligence agents because the judgments they provided to coalition forces about who was friend and who was foe often amounted to who would live and who would die. Comparisons were made to the CIA's Vietnam-era Phoenix and CORDS programs, whereby the CIA enlisted local Vietnamese leaders to help choose targets for assassination. The truth about the Human Terrain System was hidden in plain sight. It was, truly, about human terrain. In the same way that cartographers map terrain, the U.S. Army was mapping people. The program supported DARPA's technology-driven concept of creating Combat Zones That See.

Each day, after going out on patrol, Human Terrain System members fed information into a mega-database, called Map-HT, or Mapping Human Terrain. Map-HT uses a suite of computer tools to record data gathered by Army intelligence officers, Human Terrain Team members, and coalition forces, including HUMINT and BIOINT. All the information is uploaded into a massive database. Some of the information is sent to the Human Terrain System Reach-Back Research Center at Fort Leavenworth. The more sensitive information "is stored in a classified facility at the National Ground Intelligence Center, outside Charlottesville, Virginia," says former Army lieutenant colonel Troy Techau, who served as director of the Biometrics Program of U.S. Central Command J2X in post-invasion Iraq.

When retired vice admiral Arthur Cebrowski told *PBS NewsHour* that network-centric warfare was about "the behavior of humans in the networked environment," he was speaking factually. To fight the war on terror, the Pentagon would collect, synthesize, and analyze information on as many humans as possible, and maintain that information in classified and unclassified networked databases.

"People use human networks to organize the control of resources and geography," explains Tristan Reed, an analyst with the private intelligence firm Stratfor Intelligence. "No person alone can control anything of significance. Presidents, drug lords, and CEOs rely on people to execute their strategies and are constrained by the capabilities and interests of the people who work for them."

Afghanistan was a nation controlled by warlords. Iraq was a nation controlled by religious militia groups. The Pentagon needed to understand who was controlling what, and how. Mapping the terrain of individual humans was a means of connecting the networks' data points. In 2012, coalition forces withdrew from Iraq, and with them the Human Terrain Teams. In Afghanistan, thirty-one teams continued to map the human terrain. Army intelligence took over parts of the program from JIEDDO and retooled it for "Phase Zero pre-conflict," or the phase before the next war.

"Whether it's counterinsurgency, or whether it's Phase Zero pre-conflict, there are critical questions to ask before you decide on a course of action or if you decide to take any action," says U.S. Army colonel Sharon Hamilton, who directs the program. "If we raise the level of understanding [among the U.S. military], we establish a context baseline of beliefs, values, dreams and aspirations, needs, requirements, security—if we can do all that in Phase Zero, we might not be talking about being somewhere else for 10 years." As of 2014, there are MAP-HT teams operating all over the globe, from Africa to Mexico.

In Iraq and Afghanistan, by 2011 the Army had intrusively mapped the human terrain of at least 3.7 million foreigners, many of whom were enemy combatants in war zones. Apart from the effectiveness of any of that work—and as of 2015 the Islamic State controlled much of Iraq, while Afghanistan was spiraling into further chaos—there exists an important question for Americans to consider. In the summer of 2013, whistleblower Edward Snowden released classified information that showed the National Security

Agency had a clandestine data-mining surveillance program in place, called PRISM, which allowed the NSA to collect information on millions of American citizens. Both of these programs had origins in DARPA's Total Information Awareness program. In the wake of the Snowden leak, the NSA admitted, after first denying, that it does collect information on millions of Americans but stated that none of the information is synthesized or analyzed without a warrant. But the data are all stored in classified NSA facilities, available for NSA reach-back. Is the NSA mapping the human terrain in America in this same way?

Several data-mining surveillance programs described in the fiscal year 2015 budget estimate for the Defense Advanced Research Projects Agency raise privacy concerns. For its biomedical technology program, an element of "bio-warfare defense," DARPA requested from Congress $112 million to develop a technology "to allow medical practitioners the capability to visualize and comprehend the complex relationships across patient data in the electronic medical records system." Specifically, the technologies being developed ostensibly would allow practitioners "to assimilate and analyze large amounts of data and provide tools to make better-informed decisions for patient care." It is not clear under what authority patient data would be shared with the federal government, and DARPA declined to answer questions for this book.

The Nexus 7 program, whose 2015 budget was classified, monitors social media networks. Specifically, Nexus 7 "applies forecasting, data extraction and analysis methodologies to develop tools, techniques and frameworks for [examining] social networks." The classified program was used operationally in Afghanistan by a unit called DARPA Forward Cell and won the Defense Department Joint Meritorious Unit Award. From 2007 to 2011, dozens of DARPA personnel traveled "far behind enemy lines...to ensure the latest research and technological advances inform their efforts," according to DARPA literature associated with the award. The unit emplaced High-Altitude LIDAR Operations Experiment (HALOE) sensors into the battle space as well as Vehicle and Dismount Exploitation Radar (VADER) pods. How Nexus 7 is used in the United States is classified, and DARPA declined to answer general questions.

For the Deep Exploration and Filtering of Text (DEFT) program, DARPA requested from Congress $28 million to develop computer algorithms to allow machines to scour a vast array of text-based messages from "free-text or semi-structured reports, messages, documents or databases," so as to pull "actionable intelligence" of ambiguously worded messages. "A key DEFT emphasis is to determine the implied and hidden meaning in text through probabilistic inference, anomaly detection and disfluency analysis." The only way to determine if a person's message or part of a message was anomalous or irregular would be to have a much larger database of that user's messages to compare it to. How DEFT is used in the United States is classified, and DARPA declined to answer general questions. These are just three out of nearly three hundred DARPA programs that were in development for fiscal year 2015, with a requested budget of $2.91 billion, not counting classified budgets.

It is impossible for American citizens to know about and to comprehend more than a fraction of the advanced science and technology programs that DARPA is developing for the government. And at the same time, it is becoming more possible for the federal government to monitor what American citizens are doing and saying, where they are going, what they are buying, who they are communicating with, what they are reading, what they are writing, and how healthy they are.

All this raises an important question. Is the world transforming into a war zone and America into a police state, and is it DARPA that is making them so?

PART V

FUTURE WAR

CHAPTER TWENTY-FOUR

Drone Wars

In May 2013, President Barack Obama gave a long-anticipated speech at the National Defense University, at Fort McNair in Washington, D.C., in which he said it was time to bring the war on terror to a close. "This war, like all wars, must end," he said, and quoted the 1795 warning by James Madison, who stated, "No nation could preserve its freedom in the midst of continual warfare." It was President Obama's first war speech of his second term.

In the context of the history of the modern American war machine—the advanced science and technology of which is spearheaded by DARPA—there was significance in the president's words and symmetry in the locale. It was here at Fort McNair that, fifty-five years earlier, twenty-two defense scientists gathered to produce ARPA Study No. 1, the first of thousands of secret and unclassified DARPA studies outlining which weapons would best serve the United States in coming wars.

"America is at a crossroads," President Obama said. "We must define the nature and scope of this struggle"—meaning the war on terror—"or else it will define us." Much of the rest of the president's speech focused on the use of armed drones. He mentioned drone strikes on fourteen separate occasions in his roughly fifteen-minute talk. The summary point reported across news outlets was that President Obama was curtailing the use of drones.

He was doing no such thing, nor, really, did the president say he was. He merely said, "I've insisted on strong oversight of all lethal action," meaning that White House and CIA lawyers would continue to be in the loop before individual terrorists were targeted for assassination by unmanned systems, including American citizens living overseas. As commander in chief, the president had twice endorsed significant Department of Defense reports, "Unmanned Systems Integrated Roadmap FY 2011–2036" and "Unmanned Systems Integrated Roadmap FY 2013–2038," which called for the amplification, not the curtailment, of the Pentagon's pursuit of robotic warfare. These two reports, roughly three hundred pages in total, made clear that Pentagon drones were positioned to lead the way forward over the next twenty-five years of war.

DARPA's vast weapon systems of the future will involve an entire army of drones. They will include unmanned aerial vehicles (UAV), unmanned ground systems (UGS), unmanned surface vehicles (USV), unmanned maritime systems (UMS), and unmanned aircraft systems (UAS), weapons that reach from the depths of the ocean into outer space. At present and in the future, the Pentagon's drones will fly, swim, crawl, walk, run, and swarm as they conduct missions around the globe. Some of these drones will be cyborgs, or what DARPA calls "biohybrids," which are part animal and part machine. And the technology, which has been building for decades, is closer than the average citizen might think.

In the very heart of Washington, D.C., across the street from the White House, sits a public park called Lafayette Square, so named to honor the Revolutionary War hero the Marquis de Lafayette.

The park has a storied history. It briefly housed a graveyard and for a while a racetrack. Slaves were sold here. During the War of 1812, the seven-acre park served as a soldiers' encampment. In the modern era it has become home to war protests. It was here, during an antiwar rally in the fall of 2007, that Bernard Crane, a prominent Washington, D.C., attorney, saw one of the strangest things he had ever seen in his life.

"My daughter had asked me to take her to the demonstration, so I did," Crane explains. "I certainly wouldn't have been there on my own. I was half-paying attention to what was going on onstage and half-looking around when I saw three incredibly large dragonflies overhead," says Crane. "They moved in unison, as if they were in lockstep. My first thought was, 'Are those dragonflies mechanical? Or are they alive?' "

Nearby, someone shouted, "Oh my God, look at those!" Many people looked up. Vanessa Alarcon, a college student from New York, recalled her reaction. "I'm like, 'What the hell is that?' They looked kind of like dragonflies or little helicopters." But she felt certain about one thing. "Those are not insects," Alarcon said.

Likewise, Bernard Crane surmised that the creatures were not hatched of this world. "All three moved together," says Crane. "They would move to the left together, then they would move to the right together." It was bizarre. "I had just returned from a two-week vacation at a lake house in Maine," Crane says. "I'd spent a lot of time lying on my back watching dragonflies. I'd become familiar with how they move. How they hover. How they generally fly alone. Dragonflies are not like carpenter ants. They don't do the same thing as the next dragonfly over, certainly not at the same time."

At the protest in Lafayette Square, Bernard Crane scrutinized the flying objects. Around him, protesters led by the antiwar activist Cindy Sheehan waved signs that read "End the War!" Onstage, the Libyan-born surgeon and president of the Muslim American

Society, Dr. Esam Omeish, railed against the U.S. government and insisted that President Bush be impeached. "We must prosecute those who are responsible!" Omeish shouted. "Let us cleanse our State Department, our Congress, and our Pentagon of those who have driven us into this colossal mistake!"

The war in Iraq was at a boiling point in 2007. Despite the recent U.S. troop surge there, violence, mayhem, and death had reached astonishing new levels. One month earlier, in a single day of carnage, terrorists detonated multiple truck bombs in public places, killing 500 people and wounding 1,500 others—the worst coordinated attacks of the war by a factor of three. From the podium in Lafayette Square, Omeish blamed this kind of horror—the "blood of the Middle East people"—on the Bush administration. "Impeach Bush today!" he shouted again and again.

Dr. Esam Omeish was a controversial figure. He served on the board of directors of the Dar Al-Hijrah Islamic Center, the Virginia mosque where two of the 9/11 hijackers prayed before the terrorist attacks. Omeish reportedly played a role in hiring the mosque's imam during that dark time, a radical cleric named Anwar Al-Awlaki. By 2007, Al-Awlaki, a U.S. citizen, had fled to Yemen, where he was revealed to be a member of the Al Qaeda leadership. From Yemen, Al-Awlaki encouraged Muslims around the world to commit terrorist attacks against the United States. (Some would, including Major Nidal Hasan, who killed thirteen people and injured at least thirty more in a mass shooting at Fort Hood in Texas in 2009.) Al-Awlaki also served as imam at the Dar Al-Hijrah mosque, from January 2001 to April 2002. Not for another four years would Anwar Al-Awlaki become the first U.S. citizen officially assassinated by the U.S. government, in a drone strike on a desert highway in Yemen. Dr. Esam Omeish had been an associate of Anwar Al-Awlaki, through Dar Al-Hijrah, but association is not a crime. Were the dragonflies in Lafayette Park insect-inspired drones sent to spy on the doctor and the antiwar crowd? Or were they just unusually large dragonflies?

The month after the Lafayette Square rally, the *Washington Post* reported a handful of similar sightings of insect-shaped spy drones flying overhead at political events in Washington and New York. "Some suspect the insect-like drones are high-tech surveillance tools," wrote *Post* reporter Rick Weiss. "Others think they are, well, dragonflies—an ancient order of insects that even biologists concede look about as robotic as a living creature can look." No federal agency would admit to having deployed insect-sized spy drones. "But a number of U.S. government and private entities acknowledge they are trying," wrote Weiss.

By the time of the 2007 antiwar protest, DARPA had been actively developing insect-inspired drones, called micro air vehicles (MAVs), for at least fourteen years. The first DARPA micro air vehicles feasibility study was conducted in 1993, by the RAND Corporation. "Insect-size flying and crawling systems could help give the United States a significant military advantage in the coming years," the RAND authors wrote. Shortly thereafter, DARPA began soliciting scientists and awarding grants under its Tactical Technology Office.

DARPA's original insect-drone prototype, called Black Widow, was built by AeroVironment, a defense contractor in Simi Valley, California. The six-inch mini-drone weighed 40 grams and had wings fashioned from plastic model airplane propellers, cut and sanded for better lift. For years, scientists with AeroVironment struggled to get Black Widow to fly with a payload, and by March 1999, with help from MIT's Lincoln Laboratory, DARPA finally had its first-generation micro air vehicle able to fly reconnaissance missions. Powered by two lithium batteries, this 56-gram variant of Black Widow carried a black-and-white micro video camera, had excellent maneuverability, and could even hover, or loiter, for up to twenty-two minutes before returning to its base. Black Widow "cannot be heard above ambient noise at 100 feet," reported scientists in the field, "and unless you're specifically looking for [it] you can't see it." Even birds were fooled. "It looks more like a bird than an airplane," the scientists wrote. "We have seen sparrows and seagulls flocking around the MAV several times."

DARPA was enthusiastic; remember, this was March 1999. "The Black Widow MAV program has been quite successful in proving that a 6-inch aircraft is not only feasible, but that it can perform useful missions that were previously deemed impossible," read an after-action report. Then came the more important idea. A RAND analyst named Benjamin Lambeth concluded that mini-drones like the Black Widow had enormous potential, not just in intelligence, surveillance, and reconnaissance, but ultimately as a means of assassination. Mini-drones disguised as insects, Lambeth wrote, could one day be outfitted with "micro-explosive bombs... able to kill moving targets with just grams of explosive."

DARPA expanded its micro air vehicle program to include at least three research efforts, or "thrusts," each of which relies on the animal kingdom for inspiration and ideas. The results of these programs are called biosystems, biomimetics, and biohybrids. Biosystems involves the use of living, breathing insects or animals trained for military use. During the Vietnam War, German shepherds were trained to track Vietcong fighters tagged with chemicals. During the Iraq war, scientists at Los Alamos National Laboratory in New Mexico trained bees to locate buried IEDs. These are two examples of biosystemic programs.

Biomimetics research is a field closely related to bionics. In DARPA's biomimetics programs, scientists build mechanical systems to imitate creatures from the natural world. DARPA designed biomimetic drones, like the Black Widow MAV, including ones that appear to be hummingbirds, bats, beetles, and flies. If DARPA has dragonfly drones, they would fall under the rubric of biomimetics. Biomimetic drones have been used by the intelligence community since at least 1972, when the CIA built a prototype dragonfly drone it called "insectothopter." A miniature engine powered the drone's wings to move up and down. Insectothopter ran on a thimbleful of gas.

Biohybrids tread on entirely new ground. DARPA's micro air vehicle programs are built on decades of aviation technology, aerospace engineering, computer science, and nanotechnology, which is the science of making things small. Then at the turn of the twenty-first century, a new field called nanobiology, or nanobiotechnology, came into being. Once relegated to the pages of science fiction, this burgeoning new discipline allows scientists to "couple" biological systems with machines. In 1999 DARPA awarded grants for biohybrid programs. The stated goal was to create cyborgs—part living creatures, part machines.

DARPA's biohybrid programs remain shrouded in mystery. Biohybrid military applications are largely classified, but a few prototype programs have been unveiled. As nanobiotechnology advanced in the early years of the twenty-first century, tiny machines could realistically be wired into animals' brains, bodies, and wings. Starting in 2002, DARPA began periodically releasing incremental information into the public domain.

That year, news of an early prototype emerged from a DARPA-funded laboratory at the State University of New York's Downstate Medical Center in Brooklyn, led by researcher Sanjiv Talwar. Scientists implanted electrodes in the medial forebrain bundle of a rat's brain, a region that senses reward. Wires the size of a human hair connected the electrodes to a microprocessor sewn onto the rat's back, like a backpack. From a laptop 500 meters—a third of a mile—away, Talwar and his team of scientists sent electronic pulses to the rat's medial forebrain. After using Pavlovian techniques to train the rat to respond to stimuli, DARPA scientists were able to control the rat, steering it left, right, and forward through a maze via brain stimulation.

Animal rights activists cried foul. "The animal is no longer functioning as an animal," lamented Gary Francione, an animal welfare expert at Rutgers University School of Law. But for the majority of Americans, lab rats are synonymous with scientific experimentation. The idea being it's okay to experiment on rats, to control their brains, in the spirit of progress. The rat was not generally perceived as a cyborg per se. It was just a lab rat hooked up to a machine.

Over the next five years, DARPA's biohybrid programs advanced at an astonishing pace. Microprocessor technology was doubling in capacity every eighteen months. By June 29, 2007, when Apple rereleased its first-generation iPhone, Americans could now carry in their pockets more technology than NASA had when it sent astronauts to the moon.

One of the first insect cyborgs was unveiled in 2009. Inside a DARPA-funded laboratory at the University of California, Berkeley, Professor Michel Maharbiz and his colleagues coupled a green June beetle with a machine. The scientists implanted electrodes into the brain and wings of a 2-centimeter-long beetle and sewed a radio receiver onto its back. By remotely delivering electrical pulses to the beetle's brain, they were able to start and stop the beating of the beetle's wings, thereby steering and controlling the insect in flight.

In 2014, DARPA scientists working at North Carolina State University again broke new ground, this time with the *Manduca sexta* moth, or goliath worm, an insect with a metamorphic life cycle that lasts forty days. During the late pupa stage, DARPA scientist Dr. Alper Bozkurt and his team surgically inserted an electrode in the dorsal thorax of the moth, between its neck and abdomen. "The tissue develops around the implanted electrodes and secures their attachment to the insect's body over the course of a few days," explains team member Alexander Verderber. "The electrodes emerge as a part of the insect's body in the final adult stage as a moth." By "taking advantage of the rebuilding of the insect's entire tissue system during metamorphic development," says Verderber, the scientists were able to create a steerable cyborg, part insect, part machine. "One use of the biohybrid would be for use in applications such as search and rescue operations," Bozkurt says. DARPA scientists working on such cyborg programs invariably describe the programs as designed to help society. Certainly, subjects like free will, ethics, and the consequences of manufacturing cyborgs are worthy of and ripe for discussion. Another question: What are DARPA's plans for augmenting humans with machines?

By 2014, DARPA had handed over many of its micro air vehicle programs to the military services. An unclassified in-house 2013 U.S. Air Force Research Laboratory animated video revealed the burgeoning new role that biosystemic, biomimetic, and biohybrid micro air vehicles would play in future weapons systems. The video begins with hundreds of mini-drones, shaped like living creatures, being dropped from a much larger drone. The MAVs rain down onto an urban center below. At ground level, a man parks a van in front of a cement-block safe house. Across the street, a pigeon sits on an electrical wire.

"The small size of MAVs allows them to be hidden in plain sight," says the video's narrator. A close-up of the "pigeon" reveals that the bird is a surveillance drone, its head a high-resolution video camera. "Once in place," the narrator explains, "an MAV can enter a low-power, extended surveillance mode for missions lasting days or weeks. This may require the MAV to harvest energy from environmental sources such as sunlight or wind, or from manmade sources such as power lines and vibrating machinery."

The pigeon drone transmits information to an Air Force technician sitting at a desk in an information operations center at a remote location. Using biometrics, the technician confirms that the man driving the van is a terror suspect.

The man exits the van and walks down an alleyway. The pigeon takes flight, now joined by a beetle-shaped drone. The pigeon falls away and the beetle MAV follows the suspect through a maze of alleyways. "MAVs will use micro-sensors and microprocessor technology to navigate and track targets through complicated terrain such as urban areas," says the narrator. As the terror suspect enters an apartment building, the beetle drone follows along. "Small in size, agile flight will enable MAVs to covertly enter locations inaccessible by traditional means of aerial surveillance," the narrator says, but "MAVs will use new forms of navigation, such as a vision-based technique called 'optic flow.' This remains robust when traditional techniques such as GPS are unavailable." The drone can navigate and see on its own.

In the video, once inside the building, the beetle drone hovers near an apartment, loitering above the doorway, out of sight. When the door opens, a man steps out into the hallway and looks around before exiting the apartment. He closes the door behind him, but not before the beetle drone is able to slip surreptitiously inside. Now, a swarm of additional flying insect drones join in the mission. "Multiple MAVs, each equipped with small sensors, will work together to survey a large area," the narrator explains. "While some MAVs may be used purely for visual reconnaissance, others may be used for targeting or tagging of sensitive locations." Inside the apartment, a terrorist with a high-powered sniper rifle is seen setting up a kill shot. As the enemy sniper prepares to fire his weapon out an open window, one of the beetle-sized micro air vehicles flies toward him and hovers near the back of his head.

"Individual MAVs may perform direct attack missions," says the narrator, "can be equipped with incapacitating chemicals, combustible payloads, or even explosives for precision targeting capabilities." As the beetle hovers near the sniper's head, its payload explodes. The sniper falls over, dead. The animated video ends.

In addition to missions that involve targeted kills, DARPA's vast weapon systems of the future will involve an army of drones on intelligence, surveillance, and reconnaissance (ISR) missions. The MAVs are but one element. DARPA has scores of programs for biologically inspired robotic systems that fly. While micro air vehicles will fly slow and low, DARPA's hypersonic stealth drones will fly high and fast. The armed Falcon HTV-2, launched from a rocket, will travel at Mach 20 (13,000 miles per hour), or twenty-two times faster than a commercial jet. According to DARPA documents, "at HTV-2 speeds, flight time between New York City and Los Angeles would be less than 12 minutes." The Mach 20 drone will be able to strike any target, anywhere in the world, in less than an hour. As the Defense Department grows increasingly reliant on satellite technology, DARPA must provide the Pentagon with "quick, affordable and routine access to space," says DARPA. The XS-1 experimental space drone, announced in the fall of 2013, is DARPA's seminal hypersonic low-earth-orbit drone, designed to be able to fly faster on consecutive around-the-world missions than any other drone in U.S. history. Specifics about the weapons systems on board the XS-1 are classified.

The oceans are vast, and DARPA's plans for unmanned underwater vehicles (UUVs) are equally immense. One program is Hydra, an undersea system that includes a fleet of baby submersibles combined with a mother ship. The baby UUVs are being designed to deploy from the mother ship into shallow coastal waters and harbors, and then return. Integrated into this underwater system will also be airborne drones, with encapsulated UAVs able to eject from the Hydra mother ship, surface, launch, become airborne, and fly reconnaissance or combat missions. In this way, Hydra will serve as a submarine, a transport aircraft, and a communications center in one. In another undersea DARPA program, called Upward Falling Payloads, unmanned sensor systems are placed on the deep-ocean floor, where they lie undetected for years at a time, gathering intelligence. "These deep-sea nodes could be remotely activated when needed and recalled to the surface," according to DARPA; hence "they fall upward."

Ground robotic systems are advancing with equal pace. There is Atlas, a high-mobility humanoid robot, strong and coordinated enough to navigate rough outdoor terrain, climb stairs, and manipulate environments with its hands. Atlas's head, made up of sensors, includes stereo cameras and a laser range finder. Similarly anthropomorphic is the six-foot-two Valkyrie robot, built by NASA for the DARPA robotics challenge. It opens windows and wears clothes. NASA hopes to send Valkyrie to Mars as a humanoid avatar and one day assemble structures there.

Accompanying the humanoid robots are Unmanned Ground System robots, many of which resemble animals. The AlphaDog robot, which is about the size of a small rhinoceros, is able to traverse rugged terrain with the ease of a four-legged animal while carrying 400 pounds of military equipment. It can recognize its squad leader's commands and right itself after falling over. The MIT cheetah robot, presently the fastest legged robot in history, can run twenty-eight miles per hour and jump over obstacles in its path. Cheetah runs on a quiet electric motor, giving it stealth like a cat. Other land-based robots roll over terrain on continuous track treads. There is the Talon SWORD (Special Weapons Observation Reconnaissance Detection System) robot, one of the fastest in the fleet, and a next-generation incarnation of the bomb disposal robots fielded to EOD technicians in Iraq. The Talon SWORD carries an M249 Squad Automatic Weapon and a 6mm rocket launcher, each of which can be remotely controlled from half a mile away. Its more powerful cousin, the MAARS (Modular Advanced Armed

Robotic System), is designed to conduct reconnaissance and surveillance missions, and then to kill human targets from almost two miles away. In addition to firing machine guns and grenade launchers from their robotic arms, the MAARS robots are equipped with motion detectors, acoustic sensors, siren and speaker systems, nonlethal laser dazzlers, less-than-lethal grenades, and encryption technology to make the robotic killer "extremely safe and tamper proof," according to unclassified DARPA documents.

DARPA's LANdroids (Local Area Network droids) program is one of the smallest of the tread-borne robotic ground systems. LANdroids are "small, inexpensive, smart robotic radio network relay nodes" that work in a fleet, or swarm, says DARPA. These hand-size robots are dropped by dismounted soldiers as they deploy into urban combat zones, capable of leveraging their stealth and mobility "to coordinate and move autonomously" on their own. If one of the LANdroids is destroyed in battle, the others rearrange themselves accordingly. The LANdroids program aims to develop "intelligent autonomous radio drones," a concept that is critical to understanding where the Pentagon's army of robots is headed over the next twenty-five years.

"The program seeks to demonstrate the capabilities of self-configuration, self-optimization, self-healing, tethering, and power management," according to DARPA. In this sense, DARPA's LANdroids program is a prototype for future robotic systems that aim toward autonomy, or self-governance. Autonomy lies at the heart of the Pentagon's newest revolution in military affairs. To be clear about what "autonomy" is, the concept is spelled out by the Pentagon, using a drone as an example: "When an aircraft is under remote control, it is not autonomous. And when it is autonomous, it is not under remote control." It governs itself.

Vice Chairman of the Joint Chiefs of Staff James A. Winnefeld made this explicit in the Pentagon's drone warfare report: "The autonomous systems are self-directed toward a goal in that they do not require outside control, but rather are governed by laws and strategies that direct their behavior." The nontechnical term for an autonomous drone is a hunter-killer robot, a robotic system "intelligent" enough to be shown a photograph of a person and told to return when the target has been killed.

This is science, not science fiction. It is also Pentagon policy. Department of Defense Directive 3000.09, "Autonomy in Weapon Systems," released in 2012, mandates that "autonomous and semi-autonomous weapon systems shall be designed." And like all advanced scientific endeavors, the technology must evolve, from vision to reality. It is DARPA's job to lead the way. "DoD envisions unmanned systems seamlessly operating with manned systems while gradually reducing the degree of human control and decision making . . . with an ultimate goal of full autonomy."

According to the Defense Department's 2011 "Unmanned Systems Integrated Roadmap," the progression from semiautonomy to full autonomy over the next twenty-five years would be a fourfold process. To begin with, unmanned systems would be "human operated," or entirely controlled by man, as they are today. The second step involves "human delegated" systems, with drones learning how to "perform many functions independently of human control." The third level involves "human supervised" systems, in which the machines perform tasks independently after being given "top-level permissions or directions by a human." Finally, the robotic systems would become "fully autonomous," whereby "the system receives goals from humans and translates them into tasks to be performed without human interaction." A note accompanies the level-four goal: "A human could still enter the loop in an emergency or change the goals, although in practice there may be significant time delays before human intervention occurs." Time is everything. It still takes only 1,600 seconds for a nuclear weapon to travel halfway around the earth.

The world has reached an epoch-defining moment the magnitude of which has not been seen since the decision to engineer the thermonuclear bomb. If we give machines autonomy, the potential for unintended consequences is unparalleled. Some civilian-sector robotics experts say the technology for self-governing machines is simply not there, and won't be for decades. That autonomous machines require true artificial intelligence, and AI capabilities are not yet anywhere near the threshold of self-governance. But at least one very powerful individual at the Pentagon disagrees. "Dramatic progress in supporting technologies suggests that unprecedented, perhaps unimagined degrees of autonomy can be introduced into current and future military systems," Ashton B. Carter, then undersecretary of defense, wrote in 2010 in a letter tasking defense scientists to study the technology. "This could presage dramatic changes in military capability and force composition comparable to the introduction of 'Net-Centricity.'" In February 2015, Ashton Carter took office as President Obama's secretary of defense.

So what is the status of artificial intelligence? Are hunter-killer robots right around the bend? In order to discern DARPA's AI capabilities, I traveled to the Los Alamos National Laboratory in New Mexico. It was here, starting in 1943, that U.S. defense scientists engineered the world's first atomic bomb. And it is here, in the spring of 2014, that DARPA scientists were working to create an artificial brain.

CHAPTER TWENTY-FIVE

Brain Wars

The Los Alamos National Laboratory sits at the top of a mountain range in the high desert of northern New Mexico. It is a long, steep drive to get there from the capital city of Santa Fe, through the Tesuque Indian Reservation, over the Rio Grande, and into the Santa Fe National Forest. I am headed to the laboratory of Dr. Garrett T. Kenyon, whose program falls under the rubric of synthetic cognition, an attempt to build an artificial brain. Roboticists define artificial brains as man-made machines designed to be as intelligent, self-aware, and creative as humans. No such machine yet exists, but DARPA scientists like Dr. Kenyon believe that, given the rapid advances in DARPA technologies, one day soon they will. There are two technologies that play key roles in advancing artificial intelligence, and they are computing, which involves machines, and neuroscience, which involves the human brain.

During the recent wars in Iraq and Afghanistan, of the 2.5 million Americans who served, more than 300,000 returned home with brain injuries. DARPA calls these individuals brain-wounded warriors. One of the most severe forms of brain injury sustained by brain-wounded warriors is traumatic brain injury, or TBI, which occurs when an object, such as a bullet or piece of mortar or shrapnel from an IED, pierces the skull and enters the brain tissue. To address TBI, as well as other brain injuries sustained in modern warfare, DARPA has publicly stated that it has a multitude of science and technology programs in place. The agency's long-term goals in brain science research, it says, revolve around trying to restore the minds and memories of brain-wounded warriors. Through the Office of the Secretary of Defense (OSD), I submitted multiple written requests to interview one or more brain-wounded warriors who are currently participating in DARPA's brain research programs. OSD and DARPA repeatedly declined.

Traumatic brain injury is as old as war. U.S. soldiers have sustained traumatic brain injuries in each and every one of America's wars since the Revolution. When I learned that Allen Macy Dulles, the brain-wounded warrior from the Korean War, was, at age eighty-four, living just down the road from the Los Alamos National Laboratory, I arranged to visit him—before heading to Dr. Kenyon's laboratory and its artificial brain.

Allen Macy Dulles, the only son of the former CIA director Allen Welsh Dulles, lives off the old Santa Fe Trail, down a small side road, inside a large brown adobe brick home. When I visit him in the spring of 2014, he has been living with a severe form of traumatic brain injury for almost sixty-two years. Allen Macy Dulles stopped being able to record new memories back in November 1952, when he was twenty-two years old. He was the young soldier I wrote about earlier in this book, the Marine Corps officer who went out on patrol on the western front in Korea, near a hilltop called Outpost Bunker Hill, and got hit by enemy mortar fire. He has been alive all this time and has been well taken care of by his older sister and guardian, Joan Dulles Talley.

When I arrive, he looks like any elderly gentleman might look, sitting in a chair in his kitchen, waiting for his lunch. There are flowers on the table and there is artwork on the walls. Physically Allen Macy Dulles is healthy, with a big smile and a neatly combed mustache. "He looks just like our father," Joan Dulles Talley says. I come in and sit down across from him, take out my digital tape recorder, and begin our interview. Allen speaks clearly and eloquently. Remarkably, he can discuss the Egyptian pharaohs and the ancient Greeks with the ease of the classics scholar he once was, because he studied and learned these subjects before his brain was injured. His neural network allows him to access this information, as memory, and yet he cannot recall what he had for dinner last night or for breakfast this morning. When I leave, he will have no memory of my having been here, his sister Joan explains.

Joan Talley, a Jungian analyst by training, age ninety in 2014, is tall, gentle, fiercely knowledgeable, and has Katharine Hepburn's voice. Her first husband worked as a spy during World War II and later served as the U.S. ambassador to Iran. After their divorce, Joan Talley moved to Switzerland, where she trained as a psychotherapist specializing in the psychology of the unconscious, and regularly visited her brother Allen at the mental institution where he lived for a while, on Lake Geneva. After their father died, Joan Talley brought her brother back to America and has been his guardian ever since.

The injury in Korea left Allen Macy Dulles mostly deaf in his left ear. To compensate for this deficiency he uses a machine, a 1990s-era listening aid that includes a handheld transmitter, and a microphone attached to the transmitter by long wires. In his left ear he wears an earpiece. To speak with him, I pick up the microphone and talk into it. To Allen, this is high technology and does not make much sense. It did not exist in the world he is capable of remembering, the world before November 1952.

"What are your plans for the day?" I ask.

"Nothing in particular," he says, "although I do like going to secondhand stores."

"What do you buy?"

"Anything that happens to do with books or scientific devices," Allen says. He delivers a short lecture on scientific devices. But he is talking about science from before 1952.

"Will you remember this conversation in an hour?" I ask.

"Probably not," he says. "As you know, my [short-term] memory is practically nonexistent."

I ask Allen to share a memory with me from before his brain injury, something from high school.

"I remember a good class on constitutional interpretation," he says.

"Why did you decide to join the Marines?" I ask.

"Well, you see," he says with conviction, "I was seventeen years old, I had the opportunity to enlist. The war in Europe had ended. I knew there were going to be more wars. There is no shortage of wars."

Allen discusses war. Greek warfare. The wars in Europe. The war with Nazi Germany. The war in Korea against the Chinese. He can talk about all the wars leading up to 1952, and then his knowledge of war, and of the science and technology that have resulted from wars, abruptly ends for him. He has lived through every event and invention discussed in this book—the Castle Bravo bomb, the ICBM, the ARPANET, the Internet, the Vietnam War, the Gulf War, GPS, stealth technology, robots and computers, 9/11, the wars in Iraq and Afghanistan—but he has no memory or knowledge of any of it having happened. Allen Macy Dulles is a living anachronism. He belongs to a world that no longer exists. For him, time stands still. It stopped in 1952, before science and technology transformed and shaped the modern world in which we live.

Carl Sagan once stated, "It is suicidal to create a society dependent on science and technology in which hardly anybody knows anything about the science and technology." But I imagine if Carl

Sagan had met Allen Macy Dulles, he would have given the man a pass. As for the rest of us, Sagan's message applies.

DARPA leads the nation in advancing science and technology. DARPA makes the future happen. Starting in 2013, DARPA teamed up with the White House on the BRAIN (Brain Research through Advancing Innovative Neurotechnologies) initiative and declared this decade to be the decade of the brain. The White House calls the BRAIN initiative "a bold new research effort to revolutionize our understanding of the human mind and uncover new ways to treat, prevent, and cure brain disorders like Alzheimer's, schizophrenia, autism, epilepsy and traumatic brain injury." These are important goals. But DARPA's stated goal is advancing weapons technology, not curing mental illness. What is DARPA's primary goal in researching the brain?

To help brain-wounded warriors, DARPA has several programs of note. In Restoring Active Memory (RAM), scientists have developed and are testing implantable wireless "neuroprosthetics" as a possible means of overcoming amnesia. As part of the RAM program, soldiers allow the tiny machines, or chips, to be implanted in their brain. The Reorganization and Plasticity to Accelerate Injury Recovery (REPAIR) program seeks to understand how the brain makes computations and organizes them. This too requires the surgical implantation of a brain chip, as does the Restorative Encoding Memory Integration Neural Device (REMIND). Despite multiple appeals through the Office of the Secretary of Defense, DARPA declined to grant me an interview with any of these brain-wounded warriors. DARPA would also not answer specific questions about RAM, REPAIR, or REMIND.

According to the Pentagon, "mental disorders are the leading cause of hospital bed days and the second leading cause of medical encounters for active duty servicemembers." To address this problem, DARPA has developed brain implants for the treatment of war-related mental, or neuropsychological, illnesses. The Systems-Based Neurotechnology for Emerging Therapies (SUBNETS) program seeks to treat post-traumatic stress disorder (PTSD) by surgically implanting multiple electrodes in various regions of the brain as well as a microchip between the brain and skull of the brain-wounded warfighter. The chips wirelessly transmit data back to an information operations center, which has the capacity to send electrical impulses remotely to different regions of the warfighter's brain to relieve symptoms like anxiety and delayed reaction time—a kind of twenty-first-century electroshock therapy on the go. In technical terms, DARPA states that its goals are a way to "incorporate near real-time recording, analysis and stimulation in next-generation devices inspired by current Deep Brain Stimulation (DBS)." The Office of the Secretary of Defense and DARPA declined to grant access to any SUBNETS test subjects or to answer specific questions about the program.

If the past teaches us about the present, it is clear that DARPA's stated goals regarding its brain programs are not DARPA's only goals. DARPA is not primarily in the business of helping soldiers heal; that is the job of the U.S. Department of Veterans Affairs. DARPA's job is to "create and prevent strategic surprise." DARPA prepares vast weapons systems of the future. So what are the classified brain programs really for? What is the reason behind the reason?

DARPA's limb prosthetics program might offer a number of clues. In 2005, with IEDs dominating the war news, DARPA initiated a program called Revolutionizing Prosthetics. Over the next two years the program was split in two parts. DEKA Research and Development Corporation, in New Hampshire, was given a DARPA contract to make a robotic prosthetic arm. Johns Hopkins University's Applied Physics Laboratory was given a DARPA contract to create a "thought-controlled" robotic arm. These were highly ambitious goals.

Of Johns Hopkins's amazing progress, *MIT Technology Review* reported in 2007, "They have demonstrated for the first time that neural activity recorded from a monkey's brain can control fingers on a robotic hand, making it play several notes on a piano." But this was not entirely accurate, according to Jonathan Kuniholm, a former engineer officer with the First Battalion, Twenty-third Marines. Kuniholm lost his right arm to an IED buried along the Euphrates River in Haditha, Iraq. The homemade bomb was disguised as a discarded olive oil can. After recuperating, Kuniholm signed on with DARPA and Revolutionizing Prosthetics. "The Intrinsic hand was physically capable of all the individual movements necessary to play the piano," Kuniholm wrote in *IEEE Spectrum,* the trade magazine for the world's largest professional association for the advancement of technology, "but it could not be controlled by a person in real time. There was no muscle twitch or electrical signal being decoded by signal-processing algorithms in real time. The hand was preprogrammed, like a player piano." In some regards, Revolutionizing Prosthetics did more for DARPA's image than it did for warfighters who had lost limbs in war.

Major news organizations wrote stories about the DEKA arm, hailing it as revolutionary, spectacular, and astounding. In 2009, Dean Kamen, DEKA's founder, recalled on *60 Minutes* what it was like when DARPA officials came to him proposing to build a robotic arm. "They said, 'We want these kids to have something put back on them that will essentially allow one of these kids to pick up a raisin or a grape off the table, know the difference without looking at it.'" Kamen welcomed the challenge, and he and his team of forty engineers spent a year working on the problem; DARPA spent $100 million.

But when the cameras go off, the arms usually go back to the DARPA laboratories, where they generally sit on shelves. "Most of us strap back on our Captain Hook arms," said one participant, who lost an arm in Iraq and who has appeared on national television modeling the DEKA arm but asked not to be identified by name. This individual has become frustrated with DARPA, whose motives he sees as something other than getting better prosthetics to war veterans, though he does not claim to know what DARPA's ulterior motives might be. The DEKA arm, which costs up to $650,000 to engineer, has yet to find a partner to mass-produce its system. In November 2014 the FDA approved marketing the device, which reportedly can respond to multiple simultaneous commands from a wearer's brain. In a press statement, DARPA said it was happy "to repay some of the debt we owe to our Service members," but acknowledges there is no timeline on when the DEKA arm will become available to amputees. America's wounded warriors continue to wear what amputees have worn since World War I, the so-called Captain Hook arm, which is officially called the Dorrance hook, invented by D. W. Dorrance in 1912.

It is likely that DARPA's primary goal in advancing prosthetics is to give robots, not men, better arms and hands. Robotics expert Noel Sharkey, who serves as a United Nations advisor and chairman of the International Committee for Robot Arms Control, explains: "You hear DARPA talk about a robot they are designing, being able to turn a valve inside a Fukushima-type power plant. Yes, that is an example of robots keeping humans safe. But that robotic hand will also soon be able to turn a valve onboard, say, a ship." A ship that a robot has been sent to take over in a military operation.

The technologies DARPA is pursuing in its brain and prosthetics programs have dual use in DARPA's efforts to engineer hunter-killer robots. Coupled with the quest for artificial intelligence, all this might explain why DARPA is so focused on looking inside people's brains.

High on the top of a forested plateau in the Jemez Mountains, the Los Alamos National Laboratory is a storied place with a rich and complex history of nuclear weapons research. The Los Alamos National Laboratory is also one of the largest producers of defense science in the nation, with a mission statement that reads, "Delivering science and technology to protect our nation and promote world stability." Although the list of DARPA contracts here at Los Alamos is not public knowledge, it is voluminous. Most of the contracts are classified. These are not the programs that DARPA's public affairs officers are quick to promote in the press. The classified programs are not like the ones people read about in mainstream magazines and newspapers, about bullets that bend, prosthetics that can pick up a grape, cars that can drive themselves, technology you can swallow, and robots that can fall down and get back up again. Here, in the classified laboratories at Los Alamos National Laboratory, and in other classified national laboratories and research facilities like this one, is where some of DARPA's highest-risk, highest-payoff programs evolve. The consequential weapons systems of the future are born black, as in classified, and, like the hydrogen bomb, McNamara's electronic fence, Assault Breaker, and stealth technology, are unveiled to the public only after they have created a revolution in military affairs.

Within the thirty-six-square-mile Los Alamos campus, there are 1,280 buildings, eleven of which are nuclear facilities. Even the cooks who work in some of the kitchens have top secret Q clearances. There are sixty-three miles of gas lines inside the laboratory campus, thirty-four miles of electrical lines, and a power plant. There are roughly ten thousand employees and contract workers at the lab, and according to the historian at the Los Alamos Historical Society, roughly half of them have Ph.D.s. One scientist who has a DARPA contract and is at liberty to discuss some of his work on the artificial brain is Dr. Garrett T. Kenyon.

Outside Dr. Kenyon's office at Los Alamos there is an armored truck with a machine gun mounted on top. It is parked in the red zone, by the front entrance. Inside the building, Dr. Kenyon and his team work on artificial intelligence, man's quest to create a sentient machine. Dr. Kenyon is part of the synthetic cognition group at Los Alamos National Laboratory. He and his team are simulating the primate visual system, using a supercomputer to power the operation. Specifically, the team is trying to create a precise computer model of the human eye, including all of its neural networks, to understand the relationship between visual cognition and the brain. This is not necessarily an impossible task, but it does require one of the fastest computers in the world to model such a complex neural network as that of the human eye. Neuroscientists currently believe that there are 100 billion neurons inside a human brain and that every sensory message the brain receives involves an exponential number of neural connections between these networks.

To do their work, Dr. Kenyon and his team use a part of the IBM Roadrunner supercomputer, or what is left of it. When Roadrunner was built in 2008 it was the fastest computer in the world, able to perform 1 million billion calculations per second, setting the world's record for petaflops per second data-processing speeds. That is a far cry from the World War II–era ENIAC computer at the University of Pennsylvania's Moore School, which completed five thousand operations per second. But science builds. Visions become reality. Thus the ENIAC inspired John von Neumann to build MANIAC, which inspired Daniel Slotnick to build the ILLIAC IV, which led to the IBM Roadrunner. In 2014, the world's fastest supercomputer, located at China's National University of Defense Technology and called Tianhe-2, could reportedly perform some 30 quadrillion calculations per second, or 33.86 petaflops.

As for the IBM Roadrunner supercomputer, between its unveiling in 2008 and my visit in 2014, it has become obsolete. The machine cost $100 million to build but has since become too power-inefficient to continue to run. The machine cannot be recycled, though, because it holds many of the nation's nuclear secrets. Computers never entirely lose the information they record. Because of this, and since the Los Alamos National Laboratory requires a bigger, faster, more efficient computer, Roadrunner is being destroyed.

Some of what is left of it is being used by Dr. Kenyon's team in their quest for artificial intelligence. The banks of computers they use fit into a room about the size of a basketball court.

Dr. Kenyon takes me to look at the supercomputer. It is located inside the brick and glass building that houses his laboratory, beyond the armored truck, down a long corridor and behind a single locked door. Dr. Kenyon and I peer in through a small window at the Roadrunner supercomputer. The lights are low. The banks of processors are alight with tiny red and white blinking lights. There are racks of machines in rows. There are bundles of cables on the floor. Kenyon points inside. "It's a giant abacus," he says. "The real power is in the human brain." Kenyon taps his forehead. "So small, so infinite."

We walk through another part of the building. While we wait for an elevator, Dr. Kenyon unfolds a dinner-size napkin and holds it up in the air in front of his forehead. "This is about the size of your brain, spread out," he says. "The part that matters. The cerebral cortex." The 100 billion neurons there are also known as the brain's gray matter. "And the human brain does things beyond anyone's comprehension. Evolution created the smartest machine in this world."

Dr. Kenyon explains the concept behind the DARPA-funded project he is working on, in layman's terms. "Today, my twelve-year-old daughter reprogrammed my smart phone so it has facial recognition software," he says. "But seventy to eighty percent of the time it doesn't recognize me." He holds up his phone to his face. "The smart phone can't always see it's me. I can see it's me. There's the double chin, like it or not. So why can't my phone recognize me all the time? Why can't it perform a function that my dog can, the minute I walk in the door? For all the things the smart phone can do, it can't do the simplest things that biological systems can. Recognize someone all the time."

Kenyon notes that if a person's teenaged child recognized him only 70 to 80 percent of the time, there would be something seriously wrong with the child's brain. "Sentient beings recognize through sight," he explains. "My phone, on the other hand, is just comparing a set of stored features with a set of features extracted from the input coming from its camera. It's not 'seeing' anything. My phone is not resolving the pixels into a rich scene, with all the interrelationships implicit therein. My phone is just finding a few key points and constructing a high-dimensional feature vector that it can compare to a stored feature vector."

At present, true recognition—as in *cognition,* or acquiring knowledge and understanding through thought, experience, and the senses—is done only by sentient beings. "We think that by working hard to understand how biological systems solve this problem, how the primate visual system recognizes things, we can understand something fundamental about how brains solve the problems they do, like recognition. Until then, computers are blind," Kenyon says. "They can't see."

Which raises at least one technical problem regarding artificial intelligence and autonomous hunter-killer drones. "I think robot assassins are a very bad idea for a number of reasons," Garrett Kenyon asserts. "Moral and political issues aside, the technical hurdles to overcome cannot be understated," he says. "It's misleading to think just because my smart phone can 'identify' me seventy percent of the time that it has thirty percent to go." We are talking about orders of magnitude. "The chances that my daughter might not recognize me, or misidentify me from a short distance, or because I am wearing a hat," he says, "are about one in 0.0001. And we still do not understand how neural systems work."

Dr. Kenyon is excited by his research. He is convinced that neuroscientists of today are like alchemists of the Middle Ages trying to understand chemistry. That all the exciting discoveries lie ahead. "Think of how much chemists in the Dark Ages did not understand about chemistry compared to what we know now. We neuroscientists are trapped in a bubble of ignorance. We still don't have a clue about what's going on in the human brain. We have theories; we just don't know for sure. We can't build an electrical circuit, digital or analogue or other, that mimics the biological system. We can't emulate the behavior. One day in the future, we think we can."

Dr. Kenyon says that one of the most powerful facts about DARPA as an organization is that it includes theoretical scientists and engineers in its ranks. The quest for artificial intelligence, he says, is similar to getting humans to Mars. Once you have confidence you can do it, "then getting to Mars is an engineering problem," he says. In his laboratory, metaphorically, "we just don't know where Mars is yet." But Dr. Kenyon and his team are determined. "I don't think it's that far away," he says of artificial intelligence. "The question is, who will be the Columbus here?"

Columbus was an explorer looking for a new land. DARPA is looking for ways to use science to fight future wars.

Interviews with DARPA scientists of today give a sense that in the twenty-first century, programs that once existed in the realm of science fiction are rapidly becoming the science of the here and now. If Dr. Garrett Kenyon's Los Alamos laboratory represents the future of the mind, the laboratory of Dr. Susan V. Bryant and Dr. David M. Gardiner at the University of California, Irvine, represents the future of the human body. Dr. Bryant and Dr. Gardiner are a husband-and-wife team of regeneration biologists. Dr. Bryant also served as the dean of the School of Biological Sciences and the vice chancellor for research at U.C. Irvine. Dr. Gardiner is a professor of developmental and cell biology and maintains the laboratory where he does research as a regenerative engineer.

This laboratory looks like many university science labs. It is filled with high-powered microscopes, dissection equipment, and graduate students wearing goggles and gloves. The work Dr. Gardiner and Dr. Bryant do here is the result of a four-year contract with DARPA and an extended five-year contract with the Army. Their work involves limb regeneration. Gardiner and Bryant believe that one day soon, humans will also be able to regenerate their own body parts.

Dr. David Gardiner, who is in his sixties, examines a set of lab trays on the countertop. Crawling around inside the trays are multi-limbed aquatic salamanders called axolotls. The creatures look both prehistoric and futuristic, with large, bug-like eyes. Some are pink; others are unpigmented, a naturally occurring mutation that makes them look transparent; you can see the bones and blood vessels inside. This species of salamander, a urodele amphibian, is able to regenerate lost body parts as an adult.

"Regeneration is really coming alive now," Dr. Gardiner says. "Sue and I have been studying the science for years. DARPA was the first time anyone ever asked us to regenerate anything. They did this with the mouse digit," he says, referring to the tip of a mouse finger, which they and another team of scientists had been able to get to grow back, thereby setting a scientific milestone. "DARPA said, 'Great. Can you scale it up?' As in pigs. As in humans. They asked, 'Is this possible?' We said yes. They asked, 'Do you know how to do it?' We said no. They said, 'Well, then, we'll fund you.'" Gardiner believes that therein lies the genius of DARPA. "DARPA funds questions," he says.

Dr. Gardiner searches through the trays of salamanders and locates the one he is looking for. This axolotl has an extra limb coming out the right side of its body. A second right front limb. "If we look at this extra limb on the salamander, we understand we [humans] have all the info to make an arm."

To explain the concept of limb regeneration, Dr. Gardiner first provides a brief summary of mutagenesis, the process by which an organism's genetic information is changed, resulting in a mutation. "Mutations occur in nature, as the result of exposure to a mutagen," he says. "Natural mutations can be beneficial or harmful to an organism, and this drives evolution. Mutations can also be performed as experiments, in laboratories. DNA can be modified artificially, by chemical and biological agents, resulting in mutations." One consequential example of harmful mutagenesis that we discuss occurred as a result of ARPA's Project Agile defoliation campaign. People who were exposed to Agent Orange during the Vietnam War suffer a higher rate of children born with mutations. This includes Vietnamese people who were sprayed with the herbicides and also a vigorously debated number of American servicemen who were involved in the spraying.

"Mutations tell us about signals," Gardiner explains. "Cells talk to each other using signals. Every cell has an identity. All cells have information. There are no dumb cells. Cells talk to each other to stimulate growth. They talk to each other to make new patterns." Pointing to the see-through axolotl with the extra limb, Gardiner says, "People look at this salamander and say, 'Salamanders are special. We [humans] will never regenerate like a salamander.'" Dr. Gardiner and Dr. Bryant do not agree. "We say, 'Oh, really? How do you know?' The most compelling evidence is you have an arm."

There is no regeneration gene, says Gardiner. It happens at a cellular level. "People regenerate. Look how we started *ab initio.* As a single cell. Once upon a time, each one of us was a one-cell embryo that divided. Every human being on this planet regenerated his or her own cells, in the womb."

Dr. Bryant uses differentiation to simplify things. "The difference between salamanders and humans," she says, "is that when salamanders' limbs are amputated, they grow new ones. When humans' limbs are amputated, they produce scar tissue. We humans respond to injury by making scar tissue. Why?" she asks.

"At the heart of limb regeneration is evolution," Dr. Gardiner adds. What his wife is pointing out, he says, is that "at the heart of genetics is diversity."

"Some people make mega-scars," says Dr. Bryant. "The scars

can be bigger than the wound. If you cut the scar tissue off, it grows back. There is the same evidence at the other end of the scarring spectrum. Some people produce scars that can go away."

Dr. Gardiner suggests looking at cancer research as an analogy. "Cancer equals our bodies interacting with the environment," he says. "Cancer shows us we have remarkable regenerative ability. The pathways that drive cancer are the same pathways that cause regeneration. In the early days, no one had any idea about cancer. There was one cancer. Then along came the idea of 'cancer-causing' carcinogens. Well, we have found salamanders are very resistant to cancer. Inject a carcinogen into a salamander and it regulates the growth and turns it into an extra limb."

"Where is this leading?" I ask.

"We are driving our biology toward immortality," Dr. Gardiner says. "Or at least toward the fountain of youth."

In April 2014, scientists in the United States and Mexico announced they had successfully grown a complex organ, a human uterus, from tissue cells, in a lab. And in England, that same month, at a North London hospital, scientists announced they had grown noses, ears, blood vessels, and windpipes in a laboratory as they attempt to make body parts using stem cells. Scientists at Maastricht University, in Holland, have produced laboratory-grown beef burgers, grown in vitro from cattle stem cells, which food tasters say taste "close to meat."

"Can science go too far?" I ask Dr. Gardiner and Dr. Bryant.

"The same biotechnology will allow scientists to clone humans," says Dr. Gardiner.

"Do you think the Defense Department will begin human cloning research?" I ask.

"Ultimately, it needs to be a policy decision," Gardiner says.

In 2005 the United Nations voted to adopt the Declaration on Human Cloning, prohibiting "all forms of human cloning inasmuch as they are incompatible with human dignity and the protection of human life." But in the United States there is currently no federal policy banning the practice. The Human Cloning Prohibition Act of 2007 (H.R. 2560) did not pass. So the Defense Department could be cloning now. And while neither Dr. Bryant nor Dr. Gardiner has the answer to that question, we agree that what is possible in science is almost always tried by scientists.

"These are discussions that need to be had," Dr. Gardiner says.

In the twenty-first-century world of science, almost anything can be done. But should it be done? Who decides? How do we know what is wise and what is unwise?

"An informed public is necessary," Dr. Bryant says. "The public must stay informed."

But for the public to stay informed, the public has to be informed. Dr. Bryant and Dr. Gardiner's program was never classified. They worked for DARPA for four years, then both parties amiably moved on. What DARPA is doing with the limb regeneration science, DARPA gets to decide. If DARPA is working on a cloning program, that program is classified, and the public will be informed only in the future, if at all.

If human cloning is possible, and therefore inevitable, should American scientists be the first to achieve this milestone, with Pentagon funding and military application in mind? If artificial intelligence is possible, is it therefore inevitable?

Another way to ask, from a DARPA frame of mind: Were Russia or China or South Korea or India or Iran to present the world with the first human clone, or the first artificially intelligent machine, would that be considered a *Sputnik*-like surprise?

DARPA has always sought the technological and military edge, leaving observers to debate the line between militarily useful scientific progress and pushing science too far. What is right and what is wrong?

"Look at Stephen Hawking," says Dr. Bryant.

Hawking, a theoretical physicist and cosmologist, is considered one of the smartest people on the planet. In 1963 he contracted motor neuron disease and was given two years to live. He is still alive in 2015. Although Hawking is paralyzed, he has had a remarkably full life in the more than fifty years since, working, writing books, and communicating through a speech-generating device. Hawking is a proponent of cloning. "The fuss about cloning is rather silly," he says. "I can't see any essential distinction between cloning and producing brothers and sisters in the time-honored way." But Hawking believes that the quest for artificial intelligence is a dangerous idea. That it could be man's "worst mistake in history," and perhaps his last. In 2014 Hawking and a group of colleagues warned against the risks posed by artificially intelligent machines. "One can imagine such technology outsmarting financial markets, out-inventing human researchers, out-manipulating human leaders, and developing weapons we cannot even understand. Whereas the short-term impact of AI depends on who controls it, the long-term impact depends on whether it can be controlled at all."

Stephen Hawking is far from alone in his warnings against artificial intelligence. The physicist and artificial intelligence expert Steve Omohundro believes that "these [autonomous] systems are likely to behave in anti-social and harmful ways unless they are very carefully designed." In Geneva in 2013, the United Nations held its first-ever convention on lethal autonomous weapons systems, or hunter-killer drones. Over four days, the 117-member coalition debated whether or not these kinds of robotic systems should be internationally outlawed. Testifying in front of the United Nations, Noel Sharkey, a world-renowned expert on robotics and artificial intelligence, said, "Weapons systems should not be allowed to autonomously select their own human targets and engage them with lethal force." To coincide with the UN convention, Human Rights Watch and the Harvard Law School International Human Rights Clinic released a report called "Losing Humanity: The Case Against Killer Robots."

"Fully autonomous weapons threaten to violate the foundational rights to life," the authors wrote, because robotic killing machines "undermine the underlying principles of human dignity." Stephen Goose, Arms Division director at Human Rights Watch, said, "Giving machines the power to decide who lives and dies on the battlefield would take technology too far."

In an interview for this book, Noel Sharkey relayed a list of potential robot errors he believes are far too serious to ignore, including "human-machine interaction failures, software coding errors, malfunctions, communication degradation, enemy cyber-attacks," and more. "I believe there is a line that must not be crossed," Sharkey says. "Robots should not be given the authority to kill humans."

Can the push to create hunter-killer robots be stopped? Steve Omohundro believes that "an autonomous weapons arms race is already taking place," because "military and economic pressures are driving the rapid development of autonomous systems." Stephen Hawking, Noel Sharkey, and Steve Omohundro are three among a growing population who believe that humanity is standing on a precipice. DARPA's goal is to create and prevent strategic surprise. But what if the ultimate endgame is humanity's loss? What if, in trying to stave off foreign military competitors, DARPA creates an unexpected competitor that becomes its own worst enemy? A mechanical rival born of powerful science with intelligence that quickly becomes superior to our own. An opponent that cannot be stopped, like a runaway train. What if the twenty-first century becomes the last time in history when humans have no real competition but other humans?

In a world ruled by science and technology, it is not necessarily the fittest but rather the smartest that survive. DARPA program managers like to say that DARPA science is "science fact, not science fiction." What happens when these two concepts fuse?

CHAPTER TWENTY-SIX

The Pentagon's Brain

In April 2014 I interviewed Charles H. Townes, the Nobel Prize–winning inventor of the laser. When we spoke, Professor Townes was just about to turn ninety-nine years old. Lucid and articulate, Townes was still keeping office hours at the University of California, Berkeley, still writing papers, and still granting reporters' requests. I felt delighted to be interviewing him.

Two things we discussed remain indelible. Charles Townes told me that once, long ago, he was sharing his idea for the laser with John von Neumann and that von Neumann told him his idea wouldn't work.

"What did you think about that?" I asked Townes.

"If you're going to do anything new," he said, "you have to disregard criticism. Most people are against new ideas. They think, 'If I didn't think of it, it won't work.' Inevitably, people doubt you. You persevere anyway. That's what you do." And that was exactly what Charles Townes did. The laser is considered one of the most significant scientific inventions of the modern world.

The second profound thing Charles Townes said to me, and I

mentioned it earlier in this book, was that he was personally inspired to invent the laser after reading the science-fiction novel *The Garin Death Ray,* written by Alexei Tolstoi in 1926. It is remarkable to think how powerful a force science fiction can be. That fantastic, seemingly impossible ideas can inspire people like Charles Townes to invent things that totally transform the real world.

This notion that science fiction can profoundly impact reality remains especially interesting to me because in researching and reporting this book, I learned that during the war on terror, the Pentagon began seeking ideas from science-fiction writers, most notably a civilian organization called the SIGMA group. Its founder, Dr. Arlan Andrews, says that the core idea behind forming the group was to save the world from terrorism, and to this end the SIGMA group started offering "futurism consulting" to the Pentagon and the White House. The group's motto is "Science Fiction in the National Interest."

Those responsible for safeguarding the nation "need to think of crazy ideas," says Dr. Andrews, and the SIGMA group helps the Pentagon in this effort, he says. "Many of us [in SIGMA] have earned Ph.D.'s in high tech fields, and some presently hold Federal and defense industry positions." Andrews worked as a White House science officer under President George H. W. Bush, and before that at the nation's nuclear weapons production facility, Sandia National Laboratories, in New Mexico. Of SIGMA members he says, "Each [of us] is an accomplished science fiction author who has postulated new technologies, new problems and new societies, explaining the possible science and speculating about the effects on the human race."

One of the SIGMA group members is Lieutenant Colonel Peter Garretson, a transformation strategist at the Pentagon. In the spring of 2014 Garretson arranged for me to come to the Pentagon with two colleagues, Chris Carter and Gale Anne Hurd. Chris Carter created *The X-Files,* one of the most popular science-fiction television dramas of all time. The *X-Files* character the Cigarette Smoking Man is a quintessential villain who lives at the center of government conspiracies. Gale Anne Hurd co-wrote *The Terminator,* a science-fiction classic about a cyborg assassin sent back across time to save the world from a malevolent artificially intelligent machine called Skynet. In *The Terminator,* Skynet becomes smarter than the defense scientists who created it and initiates a nuclear war to achieve machine supremacy and rid the earth of humankind.

Carter and Hurd have joined me on a reporting trip to the Pentagon not to offer any kind of futurism consulting but to listen, discuss, and observe. It's a warm spring day in 2014 when we arrive at the Pentagon. The five-sided, five-floored, 6.5-million-square-foot structure looms like a colossus. We pass through security and check in. Security protocols require that we are escorted everywhere we go, including the bathroom. We head into the Pentagon courtyard for lunch, with its lawn, tall trees, and wooden picnic tables. Garretson's colleague Lieutenant Colonel Julian Chesnutt, with the Defense Intelligence Agency, Defense Clandestine Service, tells us a story about the building at the center of the Pentagon courtyard, which is now a food court but used to be a hot dog stand. Chesnutt explains that during the height of the Cold War, when satellite technology first came into being, Soviet analysts monitoring the Pentagon became convinced that the building was the entrance to an underground facility, like a nuclear missile silo. The analysts could find no other explanation as to why thousands of people entered and exited this tiny building, all day, every day. Apparently the Soviets never figured it out, and the hot dog stand remained a target throughout the Cold War—along with the rest of the Pentagon. It's a great anecdote and makes one wonder what really is underneath the Pentagon, which is rumored to have multiple stories belowground.

During lunch, seated at a long picnic table, we engage in a thought-provoking conversation with a group of Pentagon "future thinkers" about science fact and science fiction. These defense intellectuals, many of whom have Ph.D.s, come from various military services and range in age from their late twenties to early sixties. Some spent time in the war theater in Iraq, others in Afghanistan. The enthusiasm among these futurologists is palpable, their ideas are provocative, and their commitment to national security is unambiguous. These are among the brains at the Pentagon that make the future happen.

After lunch we are taken to the E-Ring, home to the Joint Chiefs of Staff and the secretary of defense. The maze-like corridors buzz with fluorescent lighting as we pass through scores of security doors and travel up and down multiple flights of stairs. Finally, we arrive in the hallway outside the office of the secretary of defense. Hanging on the corridor walls are large life-sized oil portraits of the nation's former defense secretaries. I see the five past secretaries of defense portrayed in this book. Neil McElroy asked Congress to approve the creation of DARPA, which he promised would steward America's vast weapons systems of the future, and it has. Robert McNamara believed that intellect and systems analysis could win wars, and peopled the upper echelons of the Pentagon with whiz kids to accomplish this goal. Harold Brown, hydrogen bomb weapons engineer, became the first physicist secretary of defense and gave America its offset strategy—the ability of commanders to fight wars from a continent's distance away. Dick Cheney demonstrated to the world that overwhelming force could accomplish certain goals. Donald Rumsfeld introduced the world to network-centric warfare.

As we walk the corridors looking at artwork and photographs of weapons systems adorning the Pentagon's walls, our group expands, as does the conversation about science fact and science fiction. One officer says he has a poster of the Cigarette Smoking Man hanging on his office wall. Another says that for an office social event, his defense group made baseball caps with *Skynet* written across the front. Science fiction is a powerful force. Because of the fictional work of Carter and Hurd, many sound-minded people take seriously at least two significant science-fiction concepts: that (as in *The Terminator*) artificially intelligent machines could potentially outsmart their human creators and start a nuclear war, and that (as in *The X-Files*) there are forces inside the government that keep certain truths secret. As a reporter, I have learned that these concepts also exist in the real world. Artificially intelligent hunter-killer robots present unparalleled potential dangers, and the U.S. government keeps dark secrets in the name of national security. I've also found that some of the most powerful Pentagon secrets and strategies are hidden in plain sight.

The day after the Pentagon reporting trip, I went to see Michael Goldblatt, the man who pioneered many of DARPA's super-soldier programs. Goldblatt, a scientist and venture capitalist, ran DARPA's Defense Sciences Office from 1999 until 2004, and oversaw program efforts to create warfighters who are a mentally and physically superior breed. Goldblatt asked me to come to his home for our interview, and as a car took me from my hotel room in Pentagon City out to where Goldblatt lives in the suburbs, the trip took on the feel of an *X-Files* episode. Traveling through the woodsy environs of McLean, Virginia, down Dolley Madison Boulevard (Dolley's husband, James Madison, called war the dreaded enemy of liberty), we passed by the entrance to CIA headquarters, Langley, and turned in to a nearby residential neighborhood.

Inside his home, Michael Goldblatt and I discussed transhumanism, DARPA's efforts to augment, or increase, the performance of warfighters with machines, pharmaceuticals, and other means. Under Goldblatt's tenure, unclassified programs included Persistence in Combat, Mechanically Dominant Soldier, and Continually Assisted Performance. These programs focused on augmenting the physical body of warfighters, but today I am most interested in the DARPA programs that focus on augmenting the human brain. Not just the brains of brain-wounded warriors but those of healthy soldiers as well. DARPA calls this area of research Augmented Cognition, or AugCog. The concept of AugCog sits at the scientific frontier of human-machine interface, or what the Pentagon calls Human-Robot Interaction (HRI). In DARPA's robo-rat and *Manduca sexta* moth programs, scientists created animal-machine biohybrids that are steerable by remote control. Through Augmented Cognition programs, DARPA is creating human-machine biohybrids, or what we might call cyborgs.

DARPA has been researching brain-computer interfaces (BCI) since the 1970s, but it took twenty-first-century advances in nanobiotechnology for BCI to really break new ground. DARPA's AugCog efforts gained momentum during Goldblatt's tenure. By 2004, DARPA's stated goal was to develop "orders of magnitude increases in available, net-thinking power resulting from linked human-machine dyads." In 2007, in a solicitation for new programs, DARPA stated, "Human brain activity must be integrated with technology." Several unclassified programs came about as a result, including Cognitive Technology Threat Warning System (CT2WS) and Neurotechnology for Intelligence Analysts (NIA). Both programs use "non-invasive technology" to accelerate human capacity to detect targets. The CT2WS program was designed for soldiers looking for targets on the battlefield and for intelligence operatives conducting surveillance operations in hostile environments. The NIA was designed for imagery analysts looking for targets in satellite photographs. The program participants wear a "wirelesss EEG [electroencephalography] acquisition cap," also called a headset, which jolts their brains with electrical pulses to increase cognitive functioning. DARPA scientists have found that by using this "non-invasive, brain-computer interface," they are able to accelerate human cognition exponentially, to make soldiers and spies think faster and more accurately. The problem, according to DARPA program managers, is that "these devices are often cumbersome to apply and unappealing to the user, given the wetness or residue that remains on the user's scalp and hair following removal of the headset." A brain implant would be far more effective.

After Goldblatt left the agency, in scientific journals DARPA researchers identified a series of "groundbreaking advances" in "Man/Machine Systems." In 2014 DARPA program managers stated that "the future of brain-computer interface technologies" depended on merging all the technologies of DARPA's brain programs, the noninvasive and the invasive ones, specifically citing RAM, REPAIR, REMIND, and SUBNETS. Was DARPA conducting what were, in essence, intelligence, surveillance, and reconnaissance missions inside the human brain? Was this the long-sought information that would provide DARPA scientists with the key to artificial intelligence? "With respect to the President's BRAIN initiative," write DARPA program managers, "novel BCI [brain-computer interface] technologies are needed that not only extend what information can be extracted from the brain, but also who is able to conduct and participate in those studies."

For decades scientists have been trying to create artificially intelligent machines, without success. AI scientists keep hitting the same wall. To date, computers can only obey commands, following rules set forth by software algorithms. I wondered if the transhumanism programs that Michael Goldblatt pioneered at DARPA would allow the agency to tear down this wall. Were DARPA's brain-computer interface programs the missing link?

Goldblatt chuckled. He'd left DARPA a decade ago, he said. He could discuss only unclassified programs. But he pointed me in a revelatory direction. This came up when we were discussing the Jason scientists and a report they published in 2008. In this report, titled "Human Performance," in a section called "Brain Computer Interface," the Jasons addressed noninvasive interfaces including DARPA's CT2WS and NIA programs. Using "electromagnetic signals to detect the combined activity of many millions of neurons and synapses" (in other words, the EEG cap) was effective in augmenting cognition, the Jasons noted, but the information gleaned was "noisy and degraded." The more invasive programs would produce far more specific results, they observed, particularly programs in which "a micro-electrode array [is] implanted into the cortex with connections to a 'feedthrough' pedestal on the skull." The Jason scientists wrote that these chip-in-the-brain programs would indeed substantially improve "the desired outcome," which could allow "predictable, high quality brain-control to become a reality."

So there it was, hidden in plain sight. If DARPA could master "high quality brain-control," the possibilities for man-machine systems and brain-computer interface would open wide. The wall would come down. The applications in hunter-killer drone warfare would potentially be unbridled. The brain chip was the missing link.

But even the Jasons felt it was important to issue, along with this idea, a stern warning. "An adversary might use invasive interfaces in military applications," they wrote. "An extreme example would be remote guidance or control of a human being." And for this reason, the Jason scientists cautioned the Pentagon *not* to pursue this area, at least not without a serious ethics debate. "The brain machine interface excites the imagination in its potential (good and evil) application to modify human performance," but it also raises questions regarding "potential for abuses in carrying out such research," the Jasons wrote. In summary, the Jason scientists said that creating human cyborgs able to be brain-controlled was not something they would recommend.

This warning echoed an earlier Jason warning, back during the Vietnam War, when Secretary of Defense Robert McNamara asked the Jasons to consider using nuclear weapons against the Ho Chi Minh Trail. The Jasons studied the issue and concluded it was *not* something they could recommend. Using nuclear weapons in Vietnam would encourage the Vietcong to acquire nuclear weapons from their Soviet and Chinese benefactors and to use them, the

Jasons warned. This would in turn encourage terrorists in the future to use nuclear weapons.

In their 2008 study on augmented cognition and human performance, the Jason scientists also said they believed that the concept of brain control would ultimately fail because too many people in the military would have an ethical problem with it. "Such ethical considerations will appropriately limit the types of activities and applications in human performance modification that will be considered in the U.S. military," they wrote.

But in our discussion of the Jason scientists' impact on DARPA, Goldblatt shook his head, indicating I was wrong.

"The Jason scientists are hardly relevant anymore," Goldblatt said. During his time at DARPA, and as of 2014, the "scientific advisory group with the most influence on DARPA," he said, "is the DSB," the Defense Science Board. The DSB has offices inside the Pentagon. And where the DSB finds problems, it is DARPA's job to find solutions, Goldblatt explained. The DSB had recently studied man-machine systems, and it saw an entirely different set of problems related to human-robot interactions.

In 2012, in between the two Pentagon roadmaps on drone warfare, "Unmanned Systems Integrated Roadmap FY 2011–2036" and "Unmanned Systems Integrated Roadmap FY 2013–2038," the DSB delivered to the secretary of defense a 125-page report titled "The Role of Autonomy in DoD Systems." The report unambiguously calls for the Pentagon to rapidly accelerate its development of artificially intelligent weapons systems. "The Task Force has concluded that, while currently fielded unmanned systems are making positive contributions across DoD operations, autonomy technology is being underutilized as a result of material obstacles within the Department that are inhibiting the broad acceptance of autonomy," wrote DSB chairman Paul Kaminski in a letter accompanying the report.

The primary obstacle, said the DSB, was trust—much as the

Jason scientists had predicted in their report. Many individuals in the military mistrusted the idea that coupling man and machine in an effort to create autonomous weapons systems was a good idea. The DSB found that resistance came from all echelons of the command structure, from field commanders to drone operators. "For commanders and operators in particular, these challenges can collectively be characterized as a lack of trust that the autonomous functions of a given system will operate as intended in all situations," wrote the DSB. The overall problem was getting "commanders to trust that autonomous systems will not behave in a manner other than what is intended on the battlefield."

Maybe the commanders had watched too many *X-Files* episodes or seen any of the *Terminator* films one too many times. Or maybe they read Department of Defense Directive 3000.09, which discusses "the probability and consequences of failure in autonomous and semi-automatic weapons systems that could lead to unintended engagements." Or maybe commanders and operators want to remain men (and women), not become cyborg man-machines. But unlike the Jason scientists, the Defense Science Board advised the Pentagon to *accelerate* its efforts to change this attitude—to persuade commanders, operators, and warfighters to accept, and to trust, human-robot interaction.

"An area of HRI [human-robot interaction] that has received significant attention is *robot ethics,*" wrote the DSB. This effort, which involved internal debates on robot ethics, was supposed to foster trust between military personnel and robotic systems, the DSB noted. Instead it backfired. "While theoretically interesting, this debate on functional morality has had unfortunate consequences. It increased distrust in unmanned systems because it implies that robots will not act with bounded rationality." The DSB advised that this attitude of distrust needed to change.

Perhaps it's no surprise that DARPA has a program on how to manipulate trust. During the war on terror, the agency began working with the CIA's own DARPA-like division, the Intelligence Advanced Research Projects Agency, or IARPA, on what it calls Narrative Networks (N2), to "develop techniques to quantify the effect of narrative on human cognition." One scientist leading this effort, Dr. Paul Zak, insists that what DARPA and the CIA are doing with trust is a good thing. "We would all benefit if the government focused more on trusting people," Zak told me in the fall of 2014, when I visited his laboratory at Claremont Graduate University in California. When I asked Zak if the DARPA research he was involved in was more likely being used to manipulate trust, Zak said he had no reason to believe that was correct.

Paul Zak is a leader in the field of neuroeconomics and morality, a field that studies the neurochemical roots of making economic decisions based on trust. Zak has a Ph.D. in economics and postdoctoral training, in neuroimaging, from Harvard. In 2004 he made what he describes as a groundbreaking and life-changing discovery. "I discovered the brain's moral molecule," Zak says, "the chemical in the brain, called oxytocin, that allows man to make moral decisions [and that] morality is tied to trust." In no time, says Zak, "all kinds of people from DARPA were asking me, 'How do we get some of this?' " Zak also fielded interest from the CIA. For DARPA's Narrative Networks program, Zak has been developing a method to measure how people's brains and bodies respond when oxytocin, i.e., "The brain's moral molecule," is released naturally.

Researchers at the University of Bonn, not affiliated with DARPA, have taken a different approach with their studies of oxytocin. In December 2014, these researchers published a study on how the chemical can be used to "erase fear." Lead researcher Monika Eckstein told *Scientific American* that her goal in the study was to administer oxytocin into the noses of sixty-two men, in hopes that their fear would dissipate. "And for the most part it did," she said. A time might not be too far off when we live in a world in which fear can be erased.

★ ★ ★

Why is the Defense Science Board so focused on pushing robotic warfare on the Pentagon? Why force military personnel to learn to "trust" robots and to rely on autonomous robots in future warfare? Why is the erasure of fear a federal investment? The answer to it all, to every question in this book, lies at the heart of the military-industrial complex.

Unlike the Jason scientists, the majority of whom were part-time defense scientists and full-time university professors, the majority of DSB members are defense contractors. DSB chairman Paul Kaminski, who also served on President Obama's Intelligence Advisory Board from 2009 to 2013, is a director of General Dynamics, chairman of the board of the RAND Corporation, chairman of the board of HRL (the former Hughes Research Labs), chairman of the board of Exostar, chairman and CEO of Technovation, Inc., trustee and advisor to the Johns Hopkins Applied Physics Lab, and trustee and advisor to MIT's Lincoln Laboratory—all companies and corporations that build robotic weapons systems for DARPA and for the Pentagon. Kaminski, who also serves as a paid consultant to the Office of the Secretary of Defense, is but one example. Kaminski's fellow DSB members, a total of roughly fifty persons, serve on the boards of defense contracting giants including Raytheon, Boeing, General Dynamics, Northrop Grumman, Bechtel, Aerospace Corporation, Texas Instruments, IBM, Lawrence Livermore National Laboratory, Sandia National Laboratories, and others.

One might look at DARPA's history and say that part of its role—even its entire role—is to maintain a U.S. advantage in military technology, in perpetuity. Former DARPA director Eberhardt Rechtin clearly stated this conundrum of advanced technology warfare when he told Congress, back in 1970, that it was necessary to accept the "chicken-and-egg problem" that DARPA will always face. That the agency must forever conduct "pre-requirement research," because by the time a technological need arises on the battlefield, it becomes apparent, too late, that the research should already have been done. DARPA's contractors are vital parts of a system that allows the Pentagon to stay ahead of its needs, and to steer revolutions in military affairs. To dominate in future battles, never to be caught off guard.

One might also look at DARPA's history, and its future, and say that it's possible at some point that the technology may itself outstrip DARPA as it is unleashed into the world. This is a grave concern of many esteemed scientists and engineers.

A question to ask might be, how close to the line can we get and still control what we create?

Another question might be, how much of the race for this technological upper hand is now based in the reality that corporations are very much invested in keeping DARPA's "chicken-and-egg" conundrum alive?

This is what President Eisenhower warned Americans to fear when he spoke of the perils of the military-industrial complex in his farewell speech in January 1961. "We have been compelled to create a permanent armaments industry of vast proportions," the president said.

In the years since, the armaments industry has only grown bigger by the decade. If DARPA is the Pentagon's brain, defense contractors are its beating heart. President Eisenhower said that the only way Americans could keep defense contractors in check was through knowledge. "Only an alert and knowledgeable citizenry can compel the proper meshing of the huge industrial and military machinery of defense with our peaceful methods and goals, so that security and liberty may prosper together."

Anything less, and civilians cede control of their own destiny.

The programs written about in this book are all unclassified. DARPA's highest-risk, highest-payoff programs remain secret until they are unveiled on the battlefield. Given how far along DARPA is in its quest for hunter-killer robots, and for a way to couple man with machine, perhaps the most urgent question of all might be whether civilians already have.

Can military technology be stopped? Should it be? DARPA's original autonomous robot designs were developed as part of DARPA's Smart Weapons Program decades ago, in 1983. The program was called "Killer Robots" and its motto offered prescient words: "The battlefield is no place for human beings."

This book begins with scientists testing a weapon that at least some of them believed was an "evil thing." In creating the hydrogen bomb, scientists engineered a weapon against which there is no defense. With regard to the thousands of hydrogen bombs in existence today, the mighty U.S. military relies on wishful optimism—hope that the civilization-destroyer is never unleashed.

This book ends with scientists inside the Pentagon working to create autonomous weapons systems, and with scientists outside the Pentagon working to spread the idea that these weapons systems are inherently evil things, that artificially intelligent hunter-killer robots can and will outsmart their human creators, and against which there will be no defense.

There is a perilous distinction to call attention to: when the hydrogen bomb was being engineered, the military-industrial complex—led by defense contractors, academics, and industrialists—was just beginning to exert considerable control over the Pentagon. Today that control is omnipotent.

Another difference between the creation of the hydrogen bomb in the early 1950s and the accelerating development of hunter-killer robots today is that the decision to engineer the hydrogen bomb was made in secret and the decision to accelerate hunter-killer robots, while not widely known, is not secret. In that sense, destiny is being decided right now.

ACKNOWLEDGMENTS

The Pentagon's Brain begins in 1954 with defense scientists who worked on the hydrogen bomb and ends in 2015 with defense scientists who work on robots, cyborgs, and biohybrids. In researching a book about extreme science, one very human nonscientific story stands out. Richard "Rip" Jacobs shared it with me during an interview. Jacobs was a member of the VO-67 Navy squadron whose job it was to lay down military sensors on the Ho Chi Minh Trail during the Vietnam War. I write about the experiences of Jacobs and his fellow airmen from Crew Seven earlier in this book; they were shot down over enemy territory on February 27, 1968. Two were killed, the rest of them—somewhat miraculously—survived.

Forty-two years later, in 2010, sixty-six-year-old Rip Jacobs had just finished playing golf and was walking back to his car, parked in the Lake Hefner Golf Club parking lot in Oklahoma City, Oklahoma, when he spotted a bumper sticker on a nearby car. In an instant, billions of neurons fired in his brain as memory flooded back. The bumper sticker contained the logo of the Jolly Green Giants, the helicopter search and rescue squadrons from the Vietnam War.

Rip Jacobs stared at the image. As his neurons sparked he remembered being tangled up in a tree in the jungle canopy over the Ho Chi Minh Trail, forty-two years earlier. After parachuting out of a crashing aircraft, Jacobs had landed in the trees with his parachute's lanyards wrapped around him in a way that made it impossible for him to wriggle free. Everything hurt. He was covered in blood. Immobile, and with his senses heightened, he remembered hearing the dreaded sounds of small arms fire on the ground as Vietcong searched for him. In his memory, Rip Jacobs recalled the internal panic he felt decades before over whether or not he'd set off his locator button. If he had, there was a chance that a Jolly Green helicopter might be able to locate and rescue him. If he hadn't, surely he'd die. And then he remembered hearing the whap-whap-whap of the Jolly Green helicopter blades and knowing that his fellow Americans were coming to rescue him. Forty-two years had passed, but as Rip Jacobs stood there in the golf club parking lot, he could almost see the little seat come out of the helicopter, see the two arms that reached out for him back on February 27, 1968. Then the memory was gone.

"I found a pen and paper and I left a note on the windshield of the car," Rip Jacobs recalls. "In the note I said something like, 'if you know anything about the Jolly Green Giants in Vietnam, please call me.' I signed my name."

That night the phone rang.

The person on the telephone line introduced himself as Chief Master Sergeant Clarence Robert Boles Jr. "He said he was eighty-six years old," Jacobs remembers. "He said I'd left a note on his car."

Rip Jacobs asked Clarence Boles if he knew anything about the Jolly Greens in Vietnam. Boles said, "I was with one of the Jolly Greens working out of Nakhon Phanom, Thailand." Then Boles said something astounding. "In fact," Bole said, "I recognize your name. I was the guy that rescued you out of that tree."

How could that be?

Clarence Boles drove over to Rip Jacobs's house. The local television news channel came too. The reporters filmed a segment on the amazing, chance reunion of the two former Vietnam veterans, after forty-two years. Back during the Vietnam War, when Rip Jacobs was in the rescue helicopter, after Boles had cut his parachute lanyards with his knife, Jacobs never said a word. He was in shock. But Clarence Boles kept a list of the names of every person his Jolly Green team rescued that day and all the other days. And for decades, Boles had been telling the story of the person he'd rescued from the tree. Boles never imagined he'd meet the man he rescued again and he didn't particularly feel the need to search him out. It was a story from the past, a moment in a war. The incident in the golf club parking lot was an astonishing coincidence that brought the two men together again. And to think that they were living in nearby towns in Oklahoma, just a few dozen miles away from each other.

How could that be? It's hard to explain some things. Not every answer is found in science. Some of the most mysterious and powerful puzzles are simply about being human.

Researching and reporting this book required the assistance of many individuals who generously shared their wisdom and experiences with me. I wish to thank all the scientists, engineers, government officials, defense contractors, academics, soldiers, sailors, and warfighters who spoke to me on the record and all those who spoke on background and asked not to be named. I thank Joan Dulles Talley, Murph Goldberger, and Michael Goldblatt for allowing me to interview them in their homes. Thank you Garrett Kenyon, Paul Zak, Sue Bryant, and David Gardiner for inviting me into their laboratories. I thank Peter Garretson for arranging for Gale Anne Hurd, Chris Carter, Dori Carter, and me to come to the Pentagon. Thanks to David A. Bray for inviting the four of us to join his group for Chinese food. Thank you Fred Hareland for taking me to China Lake, Damon Northrop for showing me around SpaceX, and Robert Lowell for the visit to JPL. Thank you Dr. Steve Bein for your generosity with the introductions. I thank Finn Aaserud for compiling the Jason scientists' oral histories in the

1980s; this book benefited greatly as a result. And thank you Richard Van Atta for taking the time to speak with me and for stewarding so much of the historical record on DARPA over the past several decades.

At the National Archives and Records Administration, College Park, MD, I would like to thank Richard Peuser, David Fort, and Eric Van Slander. At the National Archives at Riverside, thank you Matthew Law and Aaron Prah. Thank you Aaron Graves, Major Eric D. Badger, and Sue Gough in the Office of the Secretary of Defense; Thomas D. Kunkle and Kevin Neil Roark, Los Alamos National Laboratory; Karen Laney, National Nuclear Security Administration; Byron Ristvet, Defense Threat Reduction Agency; Christopher Banks, LBJ Library; Eric J. Butterbaugh, DARPA Public Affairs; Robert Hoback, U.S. Secret Service; Chris Grey, USA Criminal Investigation Command (CID), Quantico, VA; Pamela Patterson, Lawrence Berkeley National Laboratory.

I am most grateful to the team. Thank you John Parsley, Jim Hornfischer, Steve Younger, Tiffany Ward, Nicole Dewey, Liz Garriga, Malin von Euler-Hogan, Morgan Moroney, Heather Fain, Michael Noon, Amanda Heller, and Allison Warner. Thank you Alice and Tom Soininen, Kathleen and Geoffrey Silver, Rio and Frank Morse, Marion Wroldsen, Keith Rogers, and John Zagata. And my fellow writers from group: Kirston Mann, Sabrina Weill, Michelle Fiordaliso, Nicole Lucas Haimes, and Annette Murphy.

The only thing that makes me happier than finishing a book is the daily joy I get from Kevin, Finley, and Jett. You guys are my best friends.

NOTES

Abbreviations Used in Notes

ARCHIVES

CIA	Central Intelligence Agency Library, digital collection
DSOH	U.S. Department of State, Office of the Historian, digital collection
Geisel	Geisel Library, University of California, San Diego, CA
JFK	John F. Kennedy Presidential Library and Museum, Boston, MA
LANL	Los Alamos National Laboratory Research Library, Los Alamos, NM
LOC	Library of Congress, Washington, DC
NACP	National Archives and Records Administration at College Park, MD
NAR	National Archives and Records Administration at Riverside, CA
UCSB	American Presidency Project, University of California, Santa Barbara, CA
VO67A	VO-67 Association, Navy Observation Squadron Sixty-Seven, digital collection

GOVERNMENT AGENCIES & AFFILIATES

ARPA	Advanced Research Projects Agency
DARPA	Defense Advanced Research Projects Agency
DNA	Defense Nuclear Agency
GAO	General Accounting Office
IDA	Institute for Defense Analyses

Prologue

5 DARPA as an agency: Inspector general's report, "Defense Advanced Research Projects Agency Ethics Program Met Federal Government Standards," January 24, 2013; "Breakthrough Technologies for National Security," DARPA 2015.

7 "We are faced": DARPA press release,"President's Budget Request for DARPA Aims to Fund Promising Ideas, Help Regain Prior Levels," March 5, 2014.

8 eighty-seven nations: Interview with Noel Sharkey, August 2013.

Chapter One *The Evil Thing*

11 "an evil thing": "Minority report," General Advisory Committee, U.S. Atomic Energy Commission, October 30, 1949, LANL.

11 facing an unknown fate: Eyewitness information is from interviews with Alfred O'Donnell, 2009–2013; interviews with Jim Freedman, 2009–2011. See also O'Keefe, *Nuclear Hostages;* Ogle, *Daily Diary, 1954,* LANL; DNA, *Castle Series 1954,* LANL.

12 miniaturized: Principles of the hydrogen bomb were demonstrated two years earlier with Ivy Mike, which was the size of a small factory and weighed eighty-two tons.

12 buried under ten feet of sand: Holmes and Narver photographs, W-102–5, RG 326, Atomic Energy Commission, NAR.

12 scientists running this secret operation: Ogle, *Daily Diary, 1954,* 95-99, LANL.

13 "In the bunker": Quotes are from O'Keefe, 166, 173–175.

14 Out at sea: Quotes are from interview with Jim Freedman; See also *Castle Series 1954*, 123.

15 largest-ever nuclear fireball: Memorandum to Dr. John von Neumann from Lt. Col. N. M. Lulejian, February 23, 1955, LANL; In time, the Soviets' Tsar Bomba would be larger.

15 weather station: Hansen, *Swords of Armageddon,* IV-285.
16 No one had any idea: Joint Task Force Seven, *Operation Castle,* 46–61.
16 wind direction: "The Effects of Castle Detonations Upon the Weather," Task Force Weather Central, Special Report, October 1954, 3–7, LANL; Hansen, *Swords of Armageddon,* IV-289–290.
17 "The explosion": Quotes are from O'Keefe, *Nuclear Hostages*, 178.
18 scientist in charge: John C. Clark, "We Were Trapped by Radioactive Fallout," *Saturday Evening Post,* July 20, 1957.
19 mystical apparition: Lapp, 28.
19 unprecedented destruction: *Castle Series 1954*, 182–185. It would take Atomic Energy Commission historians thirty-four years to acknowledge that technical success was a veil and "just behind it were the frightening problems—some that threatened human existence itself."
19 news blackout: Memorandum from Brigadier General K. E. Fields to Alvin Graves, March 4, 1954, LANL.
20 "very inconsequential": Dwight D. Eisenhower, "The President's News Conference," March 10, 1954, UCSB.
20 "routine atomic test": Memorandum from Brigadier General K. E. Fields, director of Military Application, USAEC to CJTF 7, March 15, 1954, LANL; Hansen, *Swords of Armageddon,* IV-298.
21 fallout pattern: RG 326 Atomic Energy Commission, "Distance From GZ, Statute Miles, Off-site dose rate contours in r/hr at H+1 hour," Document 410526, figures 148–150, NAR.
21 roentgens: Hewlett and Holl, 182.
22 "exterminating civilian populations": Memorandum, General Advisory Committee, October 25, 1949, LANL. Secrecy elements are discussed in York, *Advisors,* 51.
23 fierce competition: "Race for the Superbomb," *American Experience,* PBS, January 1999.
23 "We must know more": Quotes are from York, *Advisors,* 60-65.
23 "taking profit out of war": Ernest Lawrence, transcript, Bohemian Club Speech, February 8, 1951, York Papers, Geisel.
24 "horse laughs": York, *Advisors,* 134.
25 Castle series: Ogle, *Daily Diary, 1954,* LANL. A total of 22.5 megatons would be detonated.
26 "weapons obsolete": Minutes, Forty-first Meeting of the General Advisory Committee (GAC), U.S. Atomic Energy Commission, July 12–15, 1954, 12–24, LANL; Fehner and Gosling, 116.
27 only surviving record: Ibid.
27 "quantitative advantage": York, *Making Weapons,* 77.

Chapter Two *War Games and Computing Machines*

28 U.S. Air Force brawn: Abella, photographs, (unpaginated).

28 game pieces scattered: Leonard, 339.

29 "credibility": York, *Making Weapons,* 89.

29 remarkable child prodigy: S. Bochner, *John Von Neumann, 1903–1957, National Academy of Sciences,* 442–450.

29 "unsolved problem": P. R. Halmos, "The Legend of John Von Neumann," *Mathematical Association of America,* Vol. 80, No. 4, April 1973, 386.

29 "He was pleasant": York, *Making Weapons,* 89.

30 "I think": Kaplan, *Wizards of Armageddon,* 63.

30 "all-out atomic war": Whitman, 52.

30 maximum kill rate: "Citation to Accompany the Award of the Medal of Merit to Dr. John von Neumann," October 1946, Von Neumann Papers, LOC.

31 "a mentally superhuman race": Dyson, *Turing's Cathedral,* 45.

32 Prisoner's Dilemma: Poundstone, 8-9, 103-106.

33 something unexpected: Abella, 55–56; Poundstone, 121-123.

33 "How can you persuade": McCullough, 758.

35 Goldstine explained: Information on Goldstine comes from Jon Edwards, "A History of Early Computing at Princeton," *Princeton Alumni Weekly,* August 27, 2012.

35 von Neumann declared: Dyson, *Turing's Cathedral,* 73.

36 "Our universe": George Dyson, "'An Artificially Created Universe': The Electronic Computer Project at IAS," Institute for Advanced Study, Princeton (Spring 2012), 8-9.

36 secured funding: Maynard, "Daybreak of the Digital Age," *Princeton Alumni Weekly,* April 4, 2012.

37 he erred: Jon Edwards, "A History of Early Computing at Princeton," *Princeton Alumni Weekly,* August 27, 2012, 4.

38 Wohlstetter's famous theory: Wohlstetter, "The Delicate Balance of Terror," 1-12.

40 Debris: Descriptions of shock wave and blast effects are described in Garrison, 23-29.

40 Georg Rickhey: Information on Rickhey comes from Bundesarchiv Ludwigsburg and RG 330 JIOA Foreign Scientist Case Files, NACP. See also Jacobsen, *Operation Paperclip,* 252.

40 a hospital, chapel, barbershop: Interview with Dr. Leonard Kreisler, March 2012. Kreisler was the post doctor at Raven Rock.

41 "land of the blind": Keeney, 19.

41 the senators had questions: For testimony from the hearings, see U.S. Senate Committee, *Hearings Before the Subcommittee on Civil Defense of the Committee on Armed Services,* 119–21.

44 speck of plutonium: Dyson, *Turing's Cathedral,* podcast.

44 "Johnny was": York, *Making Weapons,* 96-97.

45 He theorizes: John von Neumann, "The Computer and the Brain," 60, 74.

Chapter Three *Vast Weapons Systems of the Future*

46 "successful satellite": Details of this incident are from Brzezinski, 164-165.

47 "portrays a United States": Cited in "Missile and Satellite Hearings." *CQ Almanac 1958,* 14th ed., 11-669-11-671. Washington, DC: Congressional Quarterly, 1959. The actual title was "Deterrence & Survival in the Nuclear Age," York Papers, Geisel.

47 national hysteria: *DARPA: 50 Years of Bridging the Gap,* 20.

47 presidential research committee: Gaither had to withdraw because of illness in September 1957.

48 "The issue": For this account, see York, *Making Weapons,* 98.

50 Russians were not preparing: Interview with Hervey Stockman, August 2009; Jacobsen, *Area 51,* 86–89.

50 in error: Allen Dulles, "Memorandum from the Director of Central Intelligence to the Executive Secretary of the National Security Council," December 24, 1957, CIA. According to Dulles, the CIA's information was "far more detailed than that contained in the Gaither report itself."

51 "Soap operas sell": Hafner and Lyon, 14.

51 He proposed: McElroy wanted to create the agency without authorization from Congress. He first ran the idea by his general counsel, who informed him that he did not have the authority to create such an agency. As per the National Security Act of 1947, McElroy would have to notify the chairman of the Armed Services Committee and present him with a proposal.

51 "vast weapons systems": House Subcommittee on Department of Defense Appropriations, *The Ballistic Missile Program, Hearings,* 85th Cong., 1st sess., November 20–21, 1957, 7.

51 "the new dimension": Quotes and information in this section are from *The Advanced Research Projects Agency, 1958–1974,* Richard J. Barber Associates, December 1975 (hereafter Barber), II-1-22, located in York Papers, Geisel.

52 their service's domain: *Aviation Week,* February 3, 1958.

54 State of the Union: Dwight D. Eisenhower, "Annual Message to the Congress on the State of the Union," January 9, 1958, UCSB.

54 unpublished history: Barber, II-10–25.
55 grandfather made caskets: General Biographical History, Notes, Series 1: biographical materials, York Papers, Geisel.
55 "From the earliest times": York, *Making Weapons,* 7.
56 "I made my way with difficulty": General Biographical History, Notes, Series 1: biographical materials, York Papers, Geisel.
56 von Braun's 113 German colleagues: Jacobsen, *Operation Paperclip,* 16–17, 88, 95–96.
57 "not acceptable": Barber, II-25.
57 good for national security: Kistiakowsky, 198.
58 York explained: York, *Making Weapons,* 117.
58 "Traitorous!": Herken, *Brotherhood of the Bomb,* 318.
58 "I formally proposed": Dwight D. Eisenhower, Letter to Nikita Khrushchev, Chairman, Council of Ministers, U.S.S.R., on the Discontinuance of Nuclear Weapons Tests, May 16, 1959, UCSB.
58 "If we stop testing": "Lawrence in the Cold War, Ernest Lawrence and the Cyclotron," American Institute of Physics, History Center Exhibit, digital collection.
59 about to get to work: Barber, IV-27. Vela started small, officially in ARPA's second year. The scientific limitations in nuclear detection were not entirely clear at the 1958 Geneva Conference of Experts. It was after Project Argus that scientists first determined how difficult it was to detect nuclear explosions in space.
59 Vela Sierra monitored: Information about Vela follow-on programs can be found in Van Atta et al, *DARPA Technical Accomplishments*, Volume 3, II-2, III-4; Barber, IV-28–30.

Chapter Four *Emergency Plans*

60 York's desk: Details from this section are from Herb York, Diaries Series, appointment books, date books, and wall calendars, York Papers, Geisel.
60 Keeney made public: Keeney, 22–33.
64 on account of a theory: Barber, II-27.
64 the "Christofilos effect": Advanced Research Projects Division, *Identification of Certain Current Defense Problems and Possible Means of Solution,* IDA-ARPA Study No. 1, August 1958 (hereafter IDA-ARPA Study No. 1); interview with Charles Townes, March 2014.
64 Project Floral: DNA, *Operation Argus 1958,* 3, 53.
65 code name, Project 137: IDA-ARPA Study No. 1; Wheeler oral history interview, 61–63.
65 "defense problems": Finkbeiner, 29.

65 "its own special clearance": Quotes are from interviews with Marvin "Murph" Goldberger, June–August, 2013. See also Goldberger oral history interview.
66 "ingenuity, practicality and motivation": Finkbeiner, 28.
66 Astrodome-like shield: Barber, VI-II. For quotes from York, see *Making Weapons,* 129–30.
67 unusual backstory: Melissinos, *Nicholas C. Christofilos: His Contributions to Physics,* 1–15.
69 "responsible people": IDA-ARPA Study No. 1, 19.
69 "The group has": IDA-ARPA Study No. 1, 19.
70 Brazilian Anomaly: *Operation Argus 1958*, 19.
70 so many moving parts: Ibid., 22-26.
71 missile trajectory: Ibid., 48; list of shipboard tests and remarks, 56.
71 "Doctor Livingstone, I presume?": Ibid., 34.
72 watched fireworks: Childs, 525.
72 "The President has asked": Ibid., 521.
73 detection facilities: *DARPA: 50 Years of Bridging the Gap,* 58.
73 Wissmer examined Lawrence: Childs, 526.
73 had Harold Brown participate: Supplement 5 to "Extended Chronology of Significant Events Leading Up to Disarmament," Joint Secretariat, Joint Chiefs of Staff, April 21, 1961, (unpaginated), York Papers, Geisel.
74 "I could never": Childs, 527.
74 Christofilos effect did occur: *Argus 1958,* 65–68; Interview with Doug Beason, June 2014; "Report to the Commission to Assess the Threat to the United States from Electromagnetic Pulse (EMP) Attack," 161.
75 The telegram marked: Edward Teller, telegram to General Starbird, "Thoughts in Connection to the Test Moratorium," August 29, 1958, LANL.

Chapter Five *Sixteen Hundred Seconds Until Doomsday*

76 "Our job": Interview with Gene McManus, October 2013.
77 "coldest thirteen miles": Berry, "The Coldest 13 Miles on Wheels," *Popular Mechanics,* February 1968.
79 twenty-four-hour operational mode: Richard Witkin, "U.S. Radar Scans Communist Areas: Missile Warning System at Thule Is Put in Operation on a 24-Hour Basis," *New York Times,* October 2, 1960.
79 sitting in the NORAD War Room: John G. Hubbell, "'You Are Under Attack!' The Strange Incident of October 5," *Reader's Digest*, April 1961.
79 coming in from the BMEWS J-Site: Interview with Gene McManus, who arrived at J-Site three months later. The story was legendary at

BMEWS. The technicians involved were McManus's colleagues. A NORAD spokesman described the conversation for the *Reader's Digest* magazine six months after the crisis.

81 the story broke: "Moon Stirs Scare of Missile Attack," Associated Press, December 7, 1961.

82 closer to $900 million: This information comes from ODR&E Report, "Assessment of Ballistic Missile Defense Program" PPD 61–33, 1961 (fifty-four pages, unpaginated), York Papers, Geisel.

82 Twenty-six minutes and forty seconds: Ibid.

83 "The nuclear-armed ICBM": Ibid.

83 "high confidence": Ibid., Appendix 1.

83 "I started Jason": Quotes are from interview with Murph Goldberger, June 2013. He passed away the following year, in November 2014.

84 had been entwined: Brueckner oral history interview, 4; Lukasik oral history interview, 27.

85 a little business": Brueckner oral history interview, 7.

85 most significant inventions: Interview with Charles Townes, March 2014.

85 IDA served: Interview with Richard Van Atta, May 2014; Barber, I-8.

86 most respected colleagues: Interview with Murph Goldberger, July 2013.

86 "tremendously bright squad": Kistiakowsky, 200–202.

86 contribute significantly: Interview with Murph Goldberger, June 2014. See also Finkbeiner.

86 official entity: Draft, DoD Directive, Subjects: Department of Defense Advanced Research Projects Agency, No. 5129.33, December 30, 1959, York Papers, Geisel.

87 Mildred Goldberger said: Interview with Murph Goldberger, June, 2014; see also Goldberger oral history interview.

88 "confuse satellite detection": Drell oral history interview, 14.

89 "imaginative thinking": Barber, V-24.

89 PENAIDS proof tests: Van Atta et al, *DARPA Technical Accomplishments,* Volume 2, IV-4–5; Hansen, *Swords of Armageddon,* Volume 7, 491.

89 "Pen X": Ruina oral history interview.

89 deceptive MIRVs: H. F. York, "Multiple Warhead Missiles," *Scientific American* 229, no. 5 (1973): 71.

90 Ruina and Townes reached an agreement: Ruina oral history interview.

90 "instantaneous kill": Barber, IX-31.

90 "whether you can use a particle beam": Finkbeiner, 53.

91 Project Seesaw: Barber, IV-23, IX-32; for Christofilos, see York, *Making Weapons,* 129–30.

91 "Seesaw was a sensitive": Barber, IX-31. See also Jason Division, IDA, *Project Seesaw (U)*.
91 "Directed energy": Interview with General Paul F. Gorman (retired), October 2014.

Chapter Six *Psychological Operations*

92 Thor Agena A: Ruffner, *Corona: America's First Satellite Program*, 16.
93 "the best specimens": Space and Missile Systems Organization, Air Force Systems Command, "Biomedical Space Specimens, Fact Sheet," June 3, 1959, Appendix C.
93 "We don't want to humanize": Bill Willks, "Satellite Carrying Mice Fails," *Washington Post,* June 4, 1959.
93 "dramatic rescue effort": Ruffner, *Corona: America's First Satellite Program*, 16.
94 classified spying mission: Ibid., x.
94 TIROS: Barber, III-15.
95 22,952 images: Conway, 29.
95 photographs of a storm front: John W. Finney, "U.S. Will Share Tiros I Pictures," *New York Times,* April 5, 1960.
96 "no information": Email correspondence with Mike Hanson, September 17, 2013.
96 story of intrigue: Files are from RG 330, Office of the Secretary of Defense, ARPA, Project Agile, NACP; RG 330, Records of Robert S. McNamara, 1961–1968, Defense Programs and Operations, NACP.
96 forged a brilliant record: Barber, V-37.
96 a limp: Interview with Kay Godel, September 2013. The limp was not always obvious.
97 "since Napoleon": Spector, 111.
97 "The Vietnamese refused": Ibid., 112.
99 "We hated to dig": Quotes throughout this discussion are from Abboud oral history interview, 15–16; see also Bernard C. Nalty, *Stalemate: U.S. Marines from Bunker Hill to the Hook,* 4.
99 Chinese land mines: Abboud oral history interview, 15.
100 both men came from privilege: All quotes in this section are from interviews and email correspondence with Joan Dulles Talley, March 2014–May 2015.
103 shadowy figure: Correspondence between Allen W. Dulles and Dr. Harold G. Wolff, New York Hospital, CIA; "Biographical Note," Harold Wolff, M.D. (1898–1962), Papers, Cornell University Archives, digital collection.
104 spin out of control: Memorandum, Gordon Gray to Allen Dulles, October 29, 1951, CIA.

104 Godel convened: As per National Security Council directives NSC 10/2, NSC 10/5, NSC 59/1, Papers of Gordon Gray, Harry S. Truman Library and Museum, digital collection.

104 "mind-annihilating methods": See "Forced Confessions," Memorandum for the Record, National Security Council Staff, May 8, 1953, and "Brainwashing During the Korean War," Psychological Strategy Board (PSB) Central Files Series, PSB 702.5 (no date), Dwight D. Eisenhower Library, digital collection.

105 "brainwashing": This account is drawn from Marks, 133.

106 "insectivization of human beings": Edward Hunter, "Brain-Washing Tactics Force Chinese into Ranks of Communist Party," *Miami News,* September 1950.

106 Congress invited Hunter: U.S. House of Representatives, Committee on Un-American Activities, "Communist Psychological Warfare (Brainwashing)," March 13, 1958.

106 Joost A. M. Meerloo: Tim Weiner, "Remembering Brainwashing," *New York Times,* July 6, 2008.

107 Schwable recanted: "Marines Award Schwable the Legion of Merit," *New York Times,* July 8, 1954.

108 mental breakdowns: Officers such as Frank Olson, a biological weapons expert who committed suicide, or was killed, when he suffered a breakdown after being covertly dosed with LSD by his CIA bosses.

109 Society for the Investigation of Human Ecology: Marks, chap. 9.

109 even more powerful position: Official Register of the United States Civil Service Commission, 1955, 108.

109 Godel was praised: Document 96, Foreign Relations, 1961–1963, Volume I, Vietnam, DSOH.

109 "collecting, evaluating and disseminating intelligence": Document 210, Foreign Relations, 1961–1963, Volume I, Vietnam, DSOH; IAC-D-104/4 23, April 1957, CIA.

110 Godel would say: Barber, V-36.

110 "bold summation": Ibid., V-37.

111 outlined his observations: W. H. Godel, director, Policy and Planning Division, ARPA, Memo for assistant secretary of defense, Subject: Vietnam, September 15, 1960, RG 330, Project Agile, NACP.

112 "applying scientific talent": Barber, V-39.

112 "anti-guerrilla forces at night": Spector, 111–114.

112 ARPA-financed fighters: In May 1960 three U.S. Army Special Forces Teams of ten men each arrived in Vietnam to work with President Diem. With them were thirteen U.S. Army intelligence specialists and three

psychological warfare specialists. They trained Vietnamese soldiers for roughly two months; Spector, 353.

112 "Godel continued": Barber, V-2, V-4.

112 departure of Herb York: For quotes, see York, *Making Weapons,* 194, 203.

Chapter Seven *Techniques and Gadgets*

117 pushed the muzzles: Karnow, 10.

118 Kennedy spent more time: Barber, V-39.

118 "Viet-nam counter-insurgency plan": "Summary Record of a Meeting, the White House," Washington, D.C., January 28, 1961, DSOH.

119 "to deter all wars": "Special Message to Congress on Urgent National Needs," May 25, 1961, National Security Files, JFK.

120 "techniques and 'gadgets'": Document 27, Foreign Relations, 1961–1963, Volume I, Vietnam, DSOH.

120 develop new weapons: Document 96, Foreign Relations, 1961–1963, Volume I, Vietnam, DSOH.

120 garner support: Document 59, Foreign Relations, 1961–1963, Volume I, Vietnam, DSOH.

121 Johnson asked Diem: Document 56, Foreign Relations, 1961–1963, Volume I, Vietnam, DSOH.

121 gave Godel authority: Barber, V-35.

122 Each building had: ARPA Field Unit, Vietnam, Monthly Report, CDTC, photographs (n.d.), RG 330, Project Agile, NACP.

122 entourage of military advisors: Ibid., photograph (n.d.).

122 laborers toiled away: Ibid., photographs (n.d.).

123 giving briefings: Viet-Nam Working Group Files, Lot 66, D 193, Minutes of Task Force Meetings, National Security Files, JFK.

123 canine program: "The Use of a Marking Agent for Identification by Dogs," March 11, 1966, RG 330, Project Agile, NACP; see also ARPA Field Unit, ARPA Order 262-67, July 7, 1961.

124 Godel called it: Document 96, Foreign Relations, 1961–1963, Volume I, Vietnam, DSOH.

125 AR-15 prototypes: Barber, V-44.

125 "would have caused death": Ezell, 187.

125 "development of the M-16": Barber, V-44.

127 "maximum effectiveness": Document 96, Foreign Relations, 1961–1963, Volume I, Vietnam, DSOH.

127 "subject to political-psychological restrictions": Letter from Brigadier General Edward G. Lansdale, assist. SECDEF to Dir/Defense Research &

Engineering, subject: Combat Development Test Center, Vietnam, May 16, 1961. National Security Files, JFK.

127 first batch: Buckingham, *Operation Ranch Hand,* 11, 208n.

127 first mission to spray herbicides: Brown, *Vegetational Spray Tests in South Vietnam,* 17, 23, 45.

128 more ambitious follow-up plan: Ibid., 68.

128 roughly half of South Vietnam: Buckingham, *Operation Ranch Hand,* 15.

129 "The first advice": Bradlee, 22.

129 General Maxwell Taylor: As Army chief of staff, Taylor believed the Eisenhower doctrine of massive retaliation put too much emphasis on nuclear weapons and not enough emphasis on the Army. Under Eisenhower, the Army was reduced by 500,000 men, while the Air Force gained 30,000. See also McMaster, *Dereliction,* 8-17.

129 According to a memo: Historical Division Joint Secretariat, Joint Chiefs of Staff, *The History of the Joint Chiefs of Staff: The Joint Chiefs of Staff and the War in Vietnam, 1960–1968,* ix, 74.

130 Godel took General Taylor: Document 169, Foreign Relations, 1961–1963, Volume I, Vietnam, DSOH.

130 Taylor-Rostow mission: Telegram from the President's Military Representative (Taylor) to the Department of State, Saigon, October 25, 1961, DSOH.

130 General Taylor described: Quotes are from "Vietnam Report on Taylor-Rostow Mission to South Vietnam," November 3, 1961, RDT&E Annex, National Security Files, JFK.

131 Radio Hanoi: "PsyWar Efforts and Compensation Machinery in Support of Herbicide Operations," Subject: Chemical Defoliation and Crop Destruction in South Viet-Nam, Washington, April 18, 1963, National Security Files, JFK.

131 "Joint Chiefs of Staff": Buckingham, *Operation Ranch Hand,* 16; McMaster, *Dereliction,* 114.

131 "Weed Killer": Memorandum from Rostow to President, November 21, 1961, National Security Files, JFK.

132 Kennedy approved: National Security Action Memorandum 115, Subject: Defoliant Operations in Viet-nam, November 30, 1961, National Security Files, JFK.

132 2012 congressional report: Martin, "Vietnamese Victims of Agent Orange and U.S.-Vietnam Relations," 2, 15.

132 "He was advised": RG 330, Project Agile ARPA Field Unit, Vietnam, Memorandum for record, "Meeting with Mr. William Godel,"

December 4 and December 12, 1961, NACP; Brown, *Anticrop Warfare Research, Task-01*, 135.

Chapter Eight *RAND and COIN*

133 lunchtime matches: Jardini, chap. 2. Jardini's book is available only on Amazon Kindle, hence no page numbers.

133 Project Sierra: Weiner, 4-9.

134 Tanham's observations: Elliott, 27. Mai Elliott's book is the definitive work on RAND during the Vietnam War era. She worked on ARPA programs, in Saigon, during the war.

134 Tanham's 1961 report: Elliott, 17–18; George K. Tanham, "Trip Report: Vietnam, January 1963," RAND Corporation, March 22, 1963.

135 Rand was needed: Deitchman, *Best-Laid Schemes*, 25.

135 generally looked down: Interview with Murph Goldberger, June 2013.

136 "weapons systems philosophy": George H. Clement, "Weapons Systems Philosophy," RAND Corporation, 1956.

136 first two RAND analysts: J. Donnell and G. Hickey, Memo RM-3208-ARPA, August 1962, ARPA Combat Development & Test Center, Vietnam, Monthly Report (n.d.), RG 330, Project Agile, NACP.

137 "Signs of conflict": Hickey, *Window*, 19, 90–91.

137 change of plans: Ahern, *CIA and Rural Pacification in South Vietnam (U)*, 114; Hickey, *Window*, 91.

138 effective means of pacification: Memorandum from the director of the CIA to Secretary of Defense McNamara on the Strategic Hamlet Program, July 13, 1962, CIA.

138 "monitor": Ehlschlaeger, "Understanding Megacities with the Reconnaissance, Surveillance, and Intelligence Paradigm," xii.

139 Cu Chu villagers: Hickey, *Window*, 93.

140 "I said, in essence": Ibid., 99.

141 Hickey recalled paraphrasing: Ibid., 99.

142 ARPA officials complained: Deitchman, *Best-Laid Schemes*, 342.

143 "more patient approach": Elliott, 33.

143 "ground to a pulp": Ibid., 38.

143 Tanham showed great optimism: Tanham, *War Without Guns*, 25-29.

144 "Given a little luck": Elliott, 31.

Chapter Nine *Command and Control*

146 command and control: "Special Message to Congress on the Defense Budget," March 28, 1961, JFK speeches, JFK.

146 Brown recruited J. C. R. Licklider: Ruina oral history interview.

146 world's authorities: Hafner and Lyon, 28.

147 Semi-Automatic Ground Environment: Interview with Jay Forrester, October 2013.

147 "Man-Computer Symbiosis:" J. C. R. Licklider, "Man-Computer Symbiosis," *IRE Transactions on Human Factors in Electronics,* volume HFE-1, March 1960, 4–11.

148 "in not too many years": Ibid., 4-5.

148 The agency inherited: Barber, V-4.

149 "Guess how many nuclear missiles": Interview with Paul Kozemchak, April 2014.

150 "The Soviets fired three": Peter Kuran, *Nukes in Space: The Rainbow Bombs,* DVD (2000).

150 could easily have misidentified: Interview with Gene McManus, October 2014.

150 "could have led to war": Kuran, *Nukes in Space.*

150 detonated... over Zhezqazghan: EIS [Electric Infrastructure Security] Council, "Report: USSR Nuclear EMP Upper Atmosphere Kazakhstan Test," 184, 1.

151 Licklider wrote: "Memorandum For: Members and Affiliates of the Intergalactic Computer Network, From: J. C. R. Licklider," April 23, 1963; discussed in Barber, V-50–53.

151 related to surveillance programs: Barber, VI-53.

151 used in conflict zones: Smithsonian Institution Archives, "Toward a Technology of Human Behavior for Defense Use (1962)," Record Unit 179, York Papers, Geisel.

151 "build a bridge": Cited in Barber, V-54.

152 "Computer assisted teaching": Ibid.

152 legally required: U.S. General Accounting Office, *Activities of the Research and Development Center: Thailand,* 13.

153 "Thailand was the laboratory": Woods oral history interview.

153 "The U.S. would need": ARPA, *Project Agile: Remote Area Research and Engineering, Semiannual Report, 1 July–31 December 1963,* 2.

153 miscataloged: Interview with archivist Eric Van Slander at National Archives, College Park, February 2014.

153 "policy not to release": Email correspondence with Charles E. Arp, Battelle Enterprise content manager, January 21, 2014.

154 "theoretical and experimental": Brundage, "Military Research and Development Center, Quarterly Report," October 1, 1963–December 31, 1963.

154 "Anthropometric Survey": Information is drawn from Robert White, "Anthropometric Survey of the Royal Thai Armed Forces."

155 They proposed that studies: Joseph Hanlon, "Project Cambridge Plans Changed After Protests," *Computer World,* October 22, 1969.

155 "barely scratched the surface": Salemink, 222.

155 "important tools": J. C. R. Licklider, *New Scientist,* February 25, 1971, 423.

155 monitored, analyzed, and modeled: *The Utilization of ARPA-Supported Research for International Security Planning,* 6, 13–15, 33–42.

156 Someone threw a grenade: U.S. Department of State Central Files, cable, POL 25, S Viet, May 9, 1963, DSOH.

157 "Flames were coming": Halberstam, *Making of a Quagmire,* 128.

158 "What have the Buddhist": Madame Nhu's response is viewable on YouTube. https://www.youtube.com/watch?v=d_PWM9gWR5E.

158 "I can scarcely believe": Cited in Mark Moyar, *Triumph Forsaken: The Vietnam War, 1954–1965* (Cambridge: Cambridge University Press, 2006).

Chapter Ten *Motivation and Morale*

160 with a team of ARPA officials: See Hickey, "The Military Advisor and His Foreign Counterpart."

160 "En route": Quotes are from Hickey, *Window,* 111.

161 "villagers were sick": Ibid., 124.

162 a massive explosion: Donlon, *Outpost of Freedom,* 139; Hickey, *Window,* 127.

162 Outside his bunkroom: The account of the ambush is drawn from Hickey, *Window,* 130; Hickey, "Military Advisor," iii.

163 "The July 1964": Hickey, *Window,* 147.

164 Collbohm and Pauker: Deitchman oral history interview, 71–72; Elliott, 48–49.

164 Deitchman: Trained as an engineer, Deitchman had been working at IDA when he was asked to take a two-year leave to work at the Pentagon, reporting directly to Harold Brown.

164 "Who are the Vietcong?": Information is from interviews with Joseph Zasloff, August–October 2014; Zasloff died in December 2014. Seel also Zasloff, *The Role of North Vietnam in the Southern Insurgency;* Donnell, Pauker, and Zasloff, *Viet Cong Motivation and Morale in 1964: A Preliminary Report;* Elliott, *RAND in Southeast Asia: A History of the Vietnam War Era,* Chapter Two.

165 "The original intent": Deitchman, *Best-Laid Schemes,* 235.

165 deal with the CIA: Ahern, *CIA and Rural Pacification in South Vietnam,* 23.

166 inhabited by ghosts: Tela Zasloff, *Saigon Dreaming,* 164.

167 Most farmers: Elliott, 59.

168 What motivated Vietcong fighters: Interview with Joseph Zasloff, October 2014.

168 Pauker forwarded: Pauker, "Treatment of POWs, Defectors, and Suspects in South Vietnam," 13.

169 "The motivation": Press, "Estimating from Misclassified Data," iii, 26.

170 identified by the Pentagon: McMaster, *Dereliction*, 143.

171 briefed General William Westmoreland: Interview with Joseph Zasloff, October 2014.

171 The insurgency: Quotes in this paragraph and the next are from Donnell, Pauker, and Zasloff, *Viet Cong Motivation and Morale in 1964: A Preliminary Report*.

172 other RAND officers: Interview with Joseph Zasloff, October 2014.

172 "I am looking for": Elliott, 88.

173 elite defense intellectuals: Louis Menand, "Fat Man: Herman Kahn and the Nuclear Age," *New Yorker,* June 27, 2005.

174 article attacking Gouré's work: Harrison E. Salisbury, "Soviet Shelters: A Myth or Fact?" *New York Times,* December 24, 1961.

174 "I get red": Interview with Joseph Zasloff, October 2014.

175 Brink Bachelor Officers Quarters: Karnow, 408–409.

175 "By and large": Gouré, "Southeast Asia Trip Report, Part I: The Impact of Air Power in South Vietnam."

175 "Gouré gave the Pentagon": Interview with Joseph Zasloff, October 2014.

176 "break the backbone": Elliott, 90; Gouré, *JCS Briefing on Viet Cong Motivation and Morale,* 7.

177 "Dan Ellsberg": Hickey, *Window,* 179.

178 reports for ARPA: Gouré, "Some Findings of the Vietcong Motivation and Morale Study: June–December 1965," 3.

178 copy of Gouré's findings: Malcolm Gladwell, "Viewpoint: Could One Man Have Shortened the Vietnam War?" *BBC News Magazine,* July 8, 2013.

178 Frelinghuysen said: Quotes are from Deitchman, *Best-Laid Schemes,* 235–39.

179 Fulbright wrote: Jardini (unpaginated).

179 62,000 pages: Phillips, *User's Guide to the Rand Interviews in Vietnam*, iii.

180 indicted Godel: Walter B. Douglas, "Accused Former Aides Cite Witnesses in Asia," *Washington Post,* January 9, 1965.

180 Godel was convicted: Peter S. Diggins, "Godel, Wylie Get 5 Years for Funds Conspiracy," *Washington Post,* June 19, 1965.

180 prison terms: "5-Year Term for Godel Is Upheld," *Washington Post,* May 21, 1966.

180 correctional institution in Allenwood: Interview with Kay Godel, September 2013.

180 personal financial benefit: "Embezzler Godel Sued to Repay Double," *Washington Post,* November 5, 1966.

Chapter Eleven *The Jasons Enter Vietnam*

181 secret, top secret, or secret restricted data: Interview with Murph Goldberger, June 2014.

181 closely intertwined: By example, William Nierenberg earned a Ph.D. under I. I. Rabi at Columbia. Edward Teller and Enrico Fermi were both on the faculty at the University of Chicago when Fermi took on Murph Goldberger and one other theoretical physicist as Ph.D. students. See also Finkbeiner.

182 "The high goals set": MacDonald, "Jason—The Early Years," informal presentation at the meeting of the Jason Advisory Board held at DARPA, Arlington, VA, December 12, 1986, York Papers, Geisel; MacDonald oral history interview.

182 Gell-Mann: Interview with Murph Goldberger, June 2013; Ruina oral history interview.

183 unsuccessfully tried: Johnson, 229.

183 "Jasons became intrigued": Interview with Murph Goldberger, June 2013; Johnson, 256.

183 "the Vietnam problem": William Nierenberg, "DCPG: The Genesis of a Concept," *Journal of Defense Research,* ser. B, Tactical Warfare (Fall 1969); declassified unpublished manuscript, November 18, 1971, York Papers, Geisel.

184 never been declassified: Harris, *Acoustical Techniques/Designs Investigated During the Southeast Asia Conflict: 1966–1972,* 3.

185 Powell said: "Colin L. Powell: By the Book," *New York Times Book Review,* July 1, 2012, 8.

186 "One very positive thing": MacDonald oral history interview, 3.

188 "He made a point": Fleming, 5.

188 "miserable": MacDonald oral history interview, 13.

188 venerable Dr. Walter Munk: Von Storch and Hasselman, 226.

189 "And with Adlai Stevenson": Quotes are from MacDonald oral history interview, 6, 10, 11.

190 *The World Tomorrow:* MacDonald oral history interview, 28.

190 elected chairman: *Weather and Climate Modification Problems and Prospects,* vol. 2, *Research and Development,* National Research Council, January 1, 1966.

190 "a deliberate and thoughtful review": Cited in Munk et al, "Gordon James Fraser MacDonald, July 30, 1929–May 14, 2002," 230.

191 "I became increasingly convinced": Ibid., 231.

191 "searching, almost desperately": MacDonald, "Jason and DCPG—Ten Lessons," 6.

191 Project EMOTE: Quotes are from Mutch et al., *Operation Pink Rose;* Chandler and Bentley, *Forest Fire as a Military Weapon, Final Report.*

192 "appreciable destruction": J. M. Breit, "Neutralization of Viet Cong Safe Havens," 13.

193 inferno: Mutch et al., *Operation Pink Rose,* iii, 116; Joseph Trevithick "Firestorm: Forest Fires as a Weapon in Vietnam," *Armchair General Magazine,* June 13, 2012.

193 forest flammability: Mutch et al., *Operation Pink Rose,* 103–112.

194 top secret report: Hanyok, *Spartans in Darkness,* 94–95. By war's end, the NSA estimated "as many as one million soldiers and political cadre" had traveled the trail during the Vietnam War.

194 sent the Jason scientists: Deitchman, "An Insider's Account: Seymour Deitchman," *Nautilus Institute for Security and Sustainability,* February 25, 2003. Deitchman's email interview conducted with Peter Hayes is available online at nautilus.org.

194 "anastomosed structure": Nierenberg, "DCPG—The Genesis of a Concept," declassified unpublished manuscript, November 18, 1971, York Papers, Geisel.

194 obstructing movement along the trail: Lewis oral history interview.

194 studies the Jasons performed: Interview with Murph Goldberger; see also Federation of American Scientists, list of Jason studies, digital archive.

195 "We did our studies": Interview with Murph Goldberger, June 2014, quoting/paraphrasing Jason Division, IDA, *Air-Supported Anti-Infiltration Barrier,* ii, as well as his interviews with Finkbeiner and Aaserud.

195 "think about using nuclear weapons": Deitchman, "An Insider's Account: Seymour Deitchman," *Nautilus Institute for Security and Sustainability,* February 25, 2003.

196 "the numbers": Jason Division, IDA, *Tactical Nuclear Weapons in Southeast Asia,* 27.

Chapter Twelve *The Electronic Fence*

197 "I stepped on": Interviews and email correspondence with Richard "Rip" Jacobs, June–August 2013. Information is from interviews with VO-67 crew members and the VO-67 Association digital archive and website.

198 Nine men KIA: VO-67 Crew 2 Memorial Pictures, VO-67 Crew 2 Summary-KIA, VO67A. Personnel in this incident: Denis Anderson, Delbert A. Olson, Richard Mancini, Arthur C. Buck, Michael Roberts, Gale Siow, Phillip Stevens, Donald Thoresen, Kenneth Widon.

198 Crew Five was lost: VO-67 Crew 5 Memorial Pictures, VO-67 Crew 5 Summary-KIA, VO-67A. Personnel in this incident: Glenn Miller Hayden, Chester Coons, Frank Dawson, Paul Donato, Clayborn Ashby, James Kravitz, James Martin, Curtis Thurman, James Wonn.

198 acoubuoys: For a technical discussion, see Office of the Secretary, Joint Staff, MACV, Military History Branch. *Command History, United States Military Assistance Command Vietnam: 1967.* Volume 3, 1105–1106; for a narrative discussion, see Rego 11–17, with photographs.

199 "how it happens": Interview with Tom Wells, June 2013.

200 "We couldn't control": Interview with Barney Walsh, June 2013.

202 Captain Milius: Milius was first listed MIA, but his status was later changed to PKIA (Presumed Killed in Action); the USS *Milius* is named in his honor.

203 McNamara...looked: Ruina oral history interview, 28; *Pentagon Papers* (Gravel), vol. 4, chap. 1, sec. 3, subsection 1.C. The idea had first been proposed by Harvard Law School professor Roger Fisher.

203 "Secretary McNamara asked me": Sullivan oral history interview, 53; Rego, 1.

204 high-technology sensors: Sensors are small, self-powered machines designed to measure physical qualities by mimicking biological senses including sight, hearing, smell, and touch. ARPA became an early pioneer in modern sensor technology when, in 1958, before NASA was created, it was put in charge of all U.S. space programs. The first American satellite, *Explorer I,* carried a sensor into space, a tiny Geiger counter that confirmed the presence of the Van Allen radiation belts.

204 classified sensor programs: MacDonald, "Jason and DCPG—Ten Lessons," 10, York Papers, Geisel.

204 listen for Vietcong: Gatlin, *Project CHECO Southeast Asia Report,* 32; Mahnken, 112.

205 the campus grounds: Interview with Goldberger; Fitch oral history interview. In defense of the Jasons' role in creating the barrier, Goldberger said the intention was to "kill fewer people" than the Air Force was killing with its two-thousand-pound bombs.

205 SADEYE cluster bombs: The bombs are discussed in Jason Division, IDA, *Air-Supported Anti-Infiltration Barrier,* 3–4.

206 held a seminar: Richard Garwin oral history interview.

206 "aspirin-size" mini-bombs: Jason Division, IDA, *Air-Supported Anti-Infiltration Barrier,* 30.

206 "20 million Gravel mines": Ibid., 5.

206 "It is difficult to assess": Ibid., 6, 9, and 13.

206 roughly one billion: In September 1966, the official figure the Jasons gave McNamara was $860 million. By the time the fence was operational, costs had reached $1.8 billion.

207 McNamara was impressed: Interview with Murph Goldberger, June 2013.

207 "The occasion": MacDonald, "Jason and the DCPG-Ten Lessons," 10.

208 belittled by most of the generals: All quotes from Office of the Secretary, Joint Staff, MACV, Military History Branch, *Command History, United States Military Assistance Command Vietnam: 1967,* Volume 3, 1072–1075.

208 with or without the support: Ibid., 1073.

209 General Starbird: Details are from Foster, "Alfred Dodd Starbird, 1912–1983," 317–321; interview with Edward Starbird, the general's son.

209 Joint Task Force 728: Office of the Secretary, Joint Staff, MACV, Military History Branch. *Command History, United States Military Assistance Command Vietnam: 1967.* Volume 3, 1072-1075.

210 "highest national priority": Document 233, Foreign Relations of the United States, 1964–1968, Volume IV, Vietnam, 1966, DSOH.

211 "We are on the threshold": Cited in Vernon Pizer, "Coming—The Electronic Battlefield," *Corpus Christi Caller-Times,* February 14, 1971.

211 "system of systems": MacDonald, "Jason and the DCPG—Ten Lessons," 8.

212 electronic battlefield concept: Half a century later, the results of the electronic fence are ubiquitous—not just on the battlefield but across America, in the civil sector. The legacy of the electronic fence is everywhere: home, phone, computer, car, airport, doctor's office, shopping mall.

212 "From its outset": Gatlin, *Project CHECO Southeast Asia Report,* 38.

Chapter Thirteen *The End of Vietnam*

213 received a tip: Quotes are from Finney, "Anonymous Call Set Off Rumors of Nuclear Arms for Vietnam," *New York Times,* February 12 and 13, 1968.

215 "It was a scary place": MacDonald, "Jason and the DCPG—Ten Lessons," 8–12.

215 "I had probably": Garwin oral history interview.

216 also allegedly stolen: James N. Hill, "The Committee on Ethics: Past, Present, and Future," 11–19. In *Handbook on Ethical Issues in Anthropology,*

edited by Joan Cassell and Sue-Ellen Jacobs, a special publication of the American Anthropological Association number 23, available online at aaanet.org.

216 "staggering 32K of memory": Maynard, 257n.

216 journalists also revealed: *Princeton Alumni Weekly,* September 25, 1959, 12.

217 students chained...shut: Maynard, 193; "Vote of Princeton Faculty Could Lead to End of University Ties to IDA," *Harvard Crimson,* March 7, 1968.

218 rare declassified copy: Quotes are from ARPA, *Overseas Defense Research: A Brief Survey of Non-Lethal Weapons (U)* (page numbers are illegible).

221 nonlethal weapons: Steve Metz, "Non-Lethal Weapons: A Progress Report," *Joint Force Quarterly* (Spring–Summer 2001): 18–22; Ando Arike, "The Soft-Kill Solution: New Frontiers in Pain Compliance," *Harper's,* March 2010.

221 famously gave birth to: LAPD, "History of S.W.A.T.," Los Angeles Police Foundation, digital archive.

222 came under fire: Barber, VIII-63–VIII-67; Van Atta, Richard H., Sidney Reed, and Seymour Deitchman, *DARPA Technical Accomplishments,* Volume 1. 18-1–18-11; Hord, 4–8.

222 developed his first thoughts: Hord, 245, 327.

222 a billion instructions per second: "A Description of the ILLIAC IV," Interim Report, IBM Advanced Computing Systems, May 1, 1967. The machine never actually achieved a billion operations per second, but it was at the time the largest assemblage of computer hardware ever amassed in a single machine.

222 designed to cut down: New to the mix was the concept of building a large-scale SIMD (single instruction, multiple data) machine. This would change the way data were stored in the computer's memory and how data flowed through the machine. *University of Illinois Alumni Magazine* 1 (2012): 30–35.

222 "ballistic missile defense": Roland and Shiman, 12; Hord, 9.

222 still-classified ARPA program: Author's FOIA requests were rejected by the departments of Commerce, Energy, and Defense.

223 "all the computational requirements": Cited in Muraoka, Yoichi. "Illiac IV." *Encyclopedia of Parallel Computing,* Springer US, 2011, 914–917.

223 Defense Department contract: Barber, VIII-63.

223 headline in the *Daily Illini:* Patrick D. Kennedy, "Reactions Against the Vietnam War and Military-Related Targets on Campus: The University of Illinois as a Case Study, 1965–1972," Illinois Historical Journal 84, 109.

224 "The horrors ILLIAC IV": All quotes are from the *Daily Illini,* January 6, 1970.

224 "If I could have gotten": Barber, VIII-63.
224 firebombed the campus armory: Kennedy, "Reactions Against the Vietnam War," Illinois Historical Journal 84, 110.
225 guarantee the safety: O'Neill, 31; Barber, VIII-62. According to ARPA, it was the agency that pulled ILLIAC IV, not the university.
226 classified program to track submarines: "US Looks for Bigger Warlike Computers," *New Scientist,* April 21, 1977, 140. By 1977, the ILLIAC IV was outdated. DARPA sought to build a new machine, one that could produce 10 billion instructions per second (BIPS).
226 Acoustic sensors: "U.S. Looks for Bigger, Warlike Computers." *New Scientist,* April 21, 1977, 140.
226 "practical outcomes": Roland and Shiman, 29.
227 "the epitome": Barber, IX-2.
227 "It wouldn't surprise me": Ibid., IX-19.
227 "The staff just didn't know": Ibid., VIII-79.
228 "chicken-and-egg problem": Ibid., VIII-74–77.
230 "the devil": Finkbeiner, 102.
230 "I'll talk about China": Interview with Murph Goldberger; Finkbeiner, 104.
231 "Jason made a terrible mistake": Joel Shurkin, "The Secret War over Bombing," *Philadelphia Inquirer,* February 4, 1973.
231 No Jason scientist: Interview with Charles Schwartz; file on "Jason controversy," York Papers, Geisel.
231 "This is Dick Garwin": Finkbeiner, 104.
231 "perfect occasion": Bruno Vitale, "The War Physicists," 3, 12.
232 European scientists: "Jason: survey by E. H. S. Burhop and replies, 1973," Samuel A. Goudsmit Papers, 1921–1979, Niels Bohr Library and Archives, digital archive.
232 "tried for war crimes": Ibid.
232 "We should": Interview with Murph Goldberger, June 2013.
232 "intellectual forefront": Lukasik oral history interview, 27, 32–33.
232 "an agreeable move": Interview with Murph Goldberger, June 2013.

Chapter Fourteen *Rise of the Machines*

238 in keeping with the Mansfield Act: Barber, IX-23. Staff supervision would remain under the control of DDR&E.
238 three former ARPA directors: Barber, VIII-43, VIII-50.
239 "high-risk projects": Barber, IX-7
240 "It was most difficult": Barber, IX-37. Lukasik would become a senior vice president of RAND for national security programs.
240 altered the opinions: *Commanders Digest,* September 20, 1973, 2.

241 radar cross-section: Interviews with Edward Lovick, 2009–2015; Jacobsen, *Area 51,* 97.

241 acoustically undetectable: Reed et al., *DARPA Technical Accomplishments.* Volume 1. 16-1–16-4.

241 "high-stealth aircraft": *DARPA: 50 Years of Bridging the Gap,* 152.

242 asked the CIA: Interviews with Ed Lovick, 2009–2015. After Heilmeier was briefed by Lockheed, the Skunk Works division was given a $1 contract by DARPA to "study" stealth, which essentially amounted to Lockheed handing over reports already done for CIA. I write about this in *Area 51,* having interviewed a number of program participants. The subject is discussed in *DARPA: 50 Years of Bridging the Gap* but because Project Oxcart had not been declassified by CIA when the monograph was written, most of the narrative refers to the SR-71.

242 "We designed flat, faceted panels": Interviews with Ed Lovick, 2009; Jacobsen, *Area 51,* 340.

243 Two significant ideas: RG 330, ARPA, Memo from George H. Lawrence to Deputy Director of Procurement, Defense Supply Service, Contract DAHC15-70-C-0144, NACP.

244 Doubling is a powerful concept: Garreau, 49.

245 "In a few years": J. C. R. Licklider and Robert W. Taylor, "The Computer as a Communication Device," *Science and Technology* (April 1968), 22.

245 text messages: K. Fisch, S. McLeod, and B. Brenman, "Did You Know, 3.0," *Research and Design* (2008): 2.

246 "Is it going to be": Taylor oral history interview.

247 "the most successful project": DARPA, *A History of the Arpanet: The First Decade,* I-2–5.

247 "to identify and characterize": Kaplan, *Daydream Believers,* 11. For a detailed discussion of Assault Breaker, see Van Atta et al., *Transformation and Transition,* Volume 1, Chapter Four.

247 Wohlstetter concluded: See Paolucci, "Summary Report of the Long Range Research and Development Planning Program."

247 "a circular error probable": Cited in Watts, "Precision Strike: An Evolution," 3, footnote 6.

248 best example was the bombing: Lavalle, 7.

248 "It appears": Kaplan, *Daydream Believers,* 13.

248 love of model airplanes: Van Atta et al., *Transformation and Transition,* Volume 1, 40.

248 Praerie and Calere: Ibid., 40–41.

249 forward-looking infrared: Interview with John Gargus, September 2011.

249 "more complicated" drone: Cited in Barber, VIII-53.

249 Nite Panther and Nite Gazelle: Gyrodyne Helicopter Historical Foundation, "Nite Panther: U.S. Navy's QH-50 Drone Anti-Submarine Helicopter (DASH) System," (n.d.).

250 TRANSIT: Reed et al., *DARPA Technical Accomplishments,* Volume 1, 3-1–9.

251 planning countermeasures: Watts, "Precision Strike: An Evolution," 12.

251 a master game theorist: Jardini (unpaginated). Andrew Marshall served eight consecutive U.S. presidents, thirteen secretaries of defense, and fourteen DARPA directors. After forty-two years of military forecasting, Marshall retired in January 2015 at the age of ninety-two. He was the longest-serving director inside the Office of Secretary of Defense in Pentagon history.

252 Soviets felt so threatened: Watts, "Precision Strike: An Evolution," 5, 7, 11–13.

252 "military-technical revolution": Marshal N. V. Ogarkov, "The Defense of Socialism: Experience of History and the Present Day," *Red Star,* May 9, 1984, trans. Foreign Broadcast Information Service, Daily Report, May 9, 1984.

252 "technology leadership": Interview with Richard Van Atta, May 2014.

253 being pursued, in the black: Barber, VIII-36, IX-7, IX-32–40; Reed et al., *DARPA Technical Accomplishments,* Volume 1, S-1–9.

253 got a radical idea: Interviews and email correspondence with Jack Thorpe, May 2014–March 2015. The idea, says Thorpe, developed over time while he was working at the Air Force Office of Scientific Research in Washington D.C.

253 hydraulic motion system: Michael L. Cyrus, "Motion Systems Role in Flight Simulators for Flying Training," Williams Air Force Base, AZ, August 1978.

253 "The other flyer's aircraft": Quotes are from interview with Jack Thorpe, May–October 2014; See also Thorpe, "Trends in Modeling, Simulation, & Gaming."

254 "a place where": Interview with Jack Thorpe, clarifying his original paper.

255 reviewed by senior Pentagon staff: Cosby, *Simnet: An Insider's Perspective,* 3.

256 TCP/IP: Roland and Shiman, 117.

257 C2U: Thorpe clarifies that C2U was a term that originated with DARPA's Command Post of the Future program.

257 "allowed to fail": *DARPA: 50 Years of Bridging the Gap,* 68.

257 "networked war-fighting system was impossible": Interview with Neale Cosby, March 2014.

257 "William Gibson didn't": Fred Hapgood,"Simnet," *Wired Magazine,* Vol. 5, no. 4, April 1997; Deborah Solomon, "Back From the Future Questions for William Gibson," *New York Times Magazine,* August 19, 2007.

258 Project Reynard: Interview with Justin Elliott; Justin Elliott and Mark Mazzetti, "World of Spycraft: NSA and CIA Spied in Online Games," *New York Times,* December 9, 2013.

Chapter Fifteen *Star Wars and Tank Wars*

259 He had just flown in: Teller, 531.

259 Poindexter suggested: Broad, 164.

260 lead agency: *DARPA: 50 Years of Bridging the Gap,* 67. The program would not be called SDI until later. DARPA's research and development efforts focused on directed energy systems and were later continued by the Strategic Defense Initiative Organization.

261 "But is it a bomb?": Robert Scheer, "X-Ray Weapon," *Los Angeles Times,* June 4, 1986.

261 a laser is: Interview with Charles Townes, March 2014; Townes, 4–6; Beason, 15.

261 had been inspired to create the laser: Interview with Charles Townes; Townes, 6. Charles Townes died in January 2015.

262 "array of small reflectors": Quotes are from interview with Charles Townes; Townes, 3.

263 "like an imaginary story": Hey, 95–96.

264 *Fiscal Times:* Merrill Goozner, "$100b and Counting: Missiles That Work... Sometimes," *The Fiscal Times,* March 24, 2012; Mark Thompson, "Why Obama Will Continue Star Wars," *Time Magazine,* November 16, 2008.

264 "capture the sense of tankness": Interviews with Jack Thorpe, May–October, 2014.

267 "The high rankers": Quotes are from interviews with Neale Cosby, May–October 2014.

268 DARPA and the Army spent: Cosby, 4.

268 The Internal Look war games: Interview with General Paul Gorman (retired), October 2014.

269 "We played Internal Look": Schwartzkopf, 10.

Chapter Sixteen *Gulf War and Operations Other Than War*

270 what struck him: Atkinson, *Crusade,* 25.

270 stealth fighter aircraft: For a comprehensive story of the DARPA stealth program, see Van Atta et al., *Transformation and Transition,* Volume 2, I-1–9.

271 "give them the full load": Atkinson, *Crusade,* 31.

271 "Two thoughts": Crickmore, 63.

271 "sophisticated video game": Ibid. Feest also discusses how war is like playing a video game in Richard Benke, "Right on Target," AP, January 14, 1996.

272 "video game was over": Crickmore, 63.

272 tactical advantage: Defense Department New Briefing, January 17, 1991, C-SPAN.org; Robert F. Dorr, 312. Numbers vary slightly, according to different sources.

273 Iraqi Scuds: Major General Jay Garner, "Army Stands by Patriot's Persian Gulf Performance," *Defense News* 7, no. 26 (1-4): 3; Atkinson, *Crusade,* 182; "Intelligence Successes and Failures in Operations Desert Shield/ Storm," Report of the Oversight and Investigations Subcommittee, Committee on Armed Services, U.S. House of Representatives, August 1993.

274 surrendering to a machine: Ted Shelsby, "Iraqi soldiers surrender to AAI's drones." *Baltimore Sun,* March 2, 1991.

274 JSTARS: U.S. Air Force, Fact Sheet, E-8C, Joint Stars (2005).

274 600,000 lines of code: Mahnken, 130.

274 "real-time tactical view": JOINT STARS, Transitions to the Air Force, Selected Technology Transition, 68.

275 ten thousand more missions: According to a Defense Department timeline of the Gulf War, www.defense.gov.

275 mind-numbing statistics: *USA Today World,* 1991 Gulf War chronology, September 3, 1996.

276 terrible weather: McMaster, "Battle of 73 Easting," 10–11.

276 wrote the first handbook: Wolfe, 3.

276 "We had thermal imagery": Interview with Douglas Macgregor, April 2014.

276 Eagle Troop: Interview with General Paul Gorman (retired) October 2014. The controversy continues over how long this battle actually lasted.

277 "slaughter for slaughter's sake": Powell, 505. All quotes in this section are from Powell's book.

277 "a great idea": Interview with Neal Cosby, May 2014.

278 Bloedorn and the DARPA team: Thorpe, "Trends in Modeling, Simulation, & Gaming," 12.

278 "capturing": Interview with Neal Cosby, May 2014.

278 "an instrument of war": This account is from Gorman and McMaster, "The Future of the Armed Services: Training for the 21st Century," Statement before Senate Armed Services Committee, May 21, 1992.

279 Task Force Ranger: Stewart, *The United States Army in Somalia, 1992–1994,* 10–11.

280 "a direct hit": Norm Hooten, interview with Lara Logan, CBS News, *60 Minutes,* October 6, 2013.

281 written report: Quotes are from *Report of the Senior Working Group on Military Operations Other Than War (OOTW).* Around this time, DARPA's name was briefly changed back to ARPA, then restored to DARPA.

283 "Historical advice": Glenn, *Combat in Hell,* 1.

Chapter Seventeen *Biological Weapons*

284 thirteen-man Soviet delegation: Alibek, 226. The other twelve members were scientists, Soviet army officers, diplomats, and spies.

285 regarded with wonderment: Alibek, 194; email correspondence with Ken Alibek, December 2013. Alibek now lives in Kazakhstan.

286 Alibekov's job: Alibek, 194.

286 he later described: Ibid., 9.

286 "It wasn't so clear": "DARPA: The Post-Soviet Years 1989–Present 2008," video available on YouTube at DARPAtv.

286 great instability: Office of the Secretary of Defense, "Proliferation and Threat Response," November 1992, 35.

287 At any given time: Hoffman, *The Dead Hand,* 330. As per Hoffman, there were 6,623 land-based and 2,760 sea-based nuclear warheads aimed at carefully selected targets inside the United States, and an additional 1,500 nuclear-armed cruise missiles and 822 nuclear-armed aircraft ready to fly.

287 helped conceive and design: Biography of Lisa Bronson, Missouri State University, Faculty DSS-73.

287 "At various stops": This account is from Alibek, 239–40.

288 reached out to Lisa Bronson: Alibek 242, also discussed with Michael Goldblatt, April 2014.

289 Vladimir Pasechnik's defection: Mangold and Goldberg, *Plague Wars,* 91–105.

289 Ultra-Pure: Hoffman, *The Dead Hand,* 327–328.

289 streptomycin: Poland and Dennis, WHO/CDS/CSR/EDC *Plague Manual,* 55.

290 "You choose plague": Hoffmann, *The Dead Hand,* 334.

290 "one of the key acts": Ibid., 332.

291 declared smallpox dead: *World Health Magazine,* May 1980 (cover).

291 Lederberg confirmed: James M. Hughes and D. Peter Drotman, "In Memoriam: Joshua Lederberg (1925–2008)," *Emerging Infectious Diseases* 14, no. 6 (June 2008): 981–983.

292 to get the Russians to admit: Braithwaite, 141–143. As the British ambassador to the Soviet Union, Braithwaite was stationed in Moscow from September 1988 to May 1992.

292 Yeltsin confessed: Braithwaite, 142–43.

293 Congress got involved: In the spring of 1992, in an interview with *Komsomolskaya Pravda,* Yeltsin acknowledged that the Soviet Union, and subsequently Russia, had been operating a biological weapons program. He blamed the arms race. In June, while visiting Washington, D.C., Yeltsin told the U.S. Congress, "We are firmly resolved not to lie any more," and promised U.S. lawmakers that Russia's illegal bioweapons programs would end.

293 "the most virulent and vicious": David Willman, "Selling the Threat of Bioterrorism," *Los Angeles Times,* July 1, 2007.

294 Alibek confirmed: Alibek, 5.

294 provided chilling details: Testimony before the Joint Economic Committee, U.S. Congress, May 20, 1998; Alibek, 40.

294 "They did not care": Alibek, 257.

295 "blindness to the pace": Cited in William J. Broad, "Joshua Lederberg, 82, a Nobel Winner, Dies," *New York Times,* February 5, 2008.

295 "very little capability in biology": Interview with Larry Lynn; "DARPA: The Post-Soviet Years 1989–Present 2008," video available on YouTube at DARPAtv.

296 "a SCIF": Quotes are from interview with Murph Goldberger, June 2013.

296 Lederberg: Nancy Stomach, "DARPA Explores Some Promising Avenues," 25.

297 unclassified findings: This section is sourced from Block, *Living Nightmares,* 39–75.

299 cancerous human tumors: Kevin Newman, "Cancer Experts Puzzled by Monkey Virus," ABC News, March 12, 1994. The subject, "The SV-40 Virus: Has Tainted Polio Vaccine Caused an Increase in Cancer?" was discussed and debated before Congress on September 10, 2003.

299 Shortly after: Block, *Living Nightmares,* 41.

299 Biological warfare defense: Quotes in this section come from DARPA Biological Warfare Defense Program, Program Overview no. 884, briefing slides (unpaginated).

300 "Star Wars of biology": Ibid.

301 Preston testified: Senate Judiciary Subcommittee on Technology, Terrorism and Government Information and the Senate Select Committee on Intelligence on Chemical and Biological Weapons, "Threats to America: Are We Prepared?" April 22, 1998.

301 "hundreds of tons": Tim Weiner, "Soviet Defector Warns of Biological Weapons," *New York Times,* February 25, 1998.

301 distributed to members of Congress: *Congressional Record,* March 12, 1998.

301 sharing information: Richard Preston, "The Bioweaponeers," *New Yorker,* March 9, 1998, 52–53.

302 private meeting at the Pentagon: David Willman, "Selling the Threat of Bioterrorism," *Los Angeles Times,* July 1, 2007.

302 Alibek became president: Executive profile, *Bloomberg Business Week,* October 14, 2013. See also Miller, Engelberg, and Broad, 302–4.

303 Popov: Quotes are from *Nova,* 1998. Transcripts online at pbs.org.

303 "enigma": Marilyn Chase, "To Fight Bioterror, Doctors Look for Ways to Spur Immune System," *Wall Street Journal,* September 24, 2002.

304 biological warfare defense: Prepared remarks of Larry Lynn, director, Defense Advanced Research Projects Agency, before the Acquisition and Technology Subcommittee, U.S. Senate Armed Services Committee, March 11, 1997.

304 "We hope": "Hadron Subsidiary Awarded $3.3 Million Biodefense Contract by DARPA," PRNewswire, May 2, 2000. In just a few years' time, Alibek's federal grant and contract money would total $28 million.

304 Ukraine: David Willman, "Selling the Threat of Bioterrorism," *Los Angeles Times,* July 1, 2007.

304 "terrorist organization": Testimony of Ken Alibek, U.S. House of Representatives, Committee on Armed Services, Subcommittee on Research and Development and Subcommittee on Procurement, October 20, 1999, 15.

Chapter Eighteen *Transforming Humans for War*

305 "weakling of the battlefield": Quotes are from interview with General Paul Gorman (retired), October 2014.

306 "On the field of battle": Colonel S. L. A. Marshall, *The Soldier's Load and the Mobility of a Nation* (Washington, DC, 1950), 7–10.

307 Gorman wrote: Gorman, SuperTroop, VIII-7.

308 radical vision: Interview with Michael Goldblatt, April 2014. This belief is common among transhumanists.

310 with the wave of a wand: Garreau, 28.

310 "rapid healing": Harry T. Whelan et al., "DARPA Soldier Self Care: Rapid Healing of Laser Eye Injuries with Light Emitting Diode Technology," September 1, 2004.

310 like hydrogen sulfide: Jason, MITRE, *Human Performance,* 22–24.

311 to control the lobes: Garreau, 28.

311 Mechanically Dominant Soldier: Tether, Statement to Congress, March 19, 2003.

311 look like Lance Armstrong: Garreau, 32.

311 "a wireless brain modem": All quotes are from Statement of Dr. Eric Eisenstadt, Defense Sciences Office, Brain Machine Interface, DARPATech '99 conference.

312 the answer was clear: Author's tour of Gina Goldblatt's high technology bedroom, April 2014.

314 the *Dark Winter* script: Quotes are from *Dark Winter,* Bioterrorism Exercise, Andrews Air Force Base, June 22–23, 2001; U.S. House of Representatives, Hearing on Combating Terrorism, "Federal Response to a Biological Weapons Attack," July 2001.

315 Nunn told Congress: Nunn, statement to Congress, July 23, 2001.

315 all BASIS could do: Interview with Dr. Alan P. Zelicoff, October 2013.

316 "Any technology": Vin LoPresti, "Guarding the Air We Breathe," *Los Alamos National Laboratory Research Quarterly* (Spring 2003), 5.

Chapter Nineteen *Terror Strikes*

319 asks Bray: Quotes are from interview with David Bray, July 2014. Per Presidential Decision Directive 39, the Bioterrorism Preparedness and Response Program was a joint effort between the CDC, the FBI, and the Association of Public Health Laboratories.

322 supercomputers would scan: David Siegrist and J. Pavlin, "Bio-ALIRT Biosurveillance Detection Algorithm Evaluation," Centers For Disease Control, *Morbidity and Mortality Weekly Report,* September 24, 2004/53, 152–158. Carlos Castillo-Chavez, "Infections Disease Informatics and Biosurveillance," *Springer,* October 2010, 6–7.

323 "It was a clear day": Cheney, 339.

323 "He grabbed me": Cheney interview with John King, CNN, September 11, 2002.

324 laying plans for war: Cheney, 341.

324 sitting in his office: Rumsfeld, 335; *Larry King Live,* December 5, 2001.

325 Davis later told: This account is from Cockburn, 1–3.

325 Secretary Rumsfeld helped: Armed Forces Press Service, September 8, 2006, photographs.

326 "Best info fast": *9/11 Commission Report,* 559; Joel Roberts, "Plans for Iraq Attack Began on 9/11," CBS News, September 4, 2002.

326 "We all knew": Rice, 83.

326 "We were embarking": Cheney, 332.

327 Rumsfeld, Known and Unknown, 356–57.

327 Tenet sent out a memo: Memorandum from George J. Tenet, The Director of Central Intelligence, "Subject: We're at War," September 16, 2001, CIA.

327 "On October first": Quotes are from interview with David Bray, July 2014.

328 "A war of nerves": R. W. Apple, "A Nation Challenged: News Analysis; City of Power, City of Fears," *New York Times,* October 17, 2001.

329 DARPA was asked: Interview with Michael Goldblatt, April 2014.

329 "a little bit of pride": Ibid.

329 "There had been": Quotes are from Cheney, 341.

330 "a virtually zero rate": Vin LoPresti, "Guarding the Air We Breathe," *Los Alamos National Laboratory Research Quarterly* (Spring 2003), 5, *Science and Technology Review,* October, 2003; Arkin, 288n.

331 "Go call Hadley": Rice, 101.

331 In New York City: Cheney, 340–42.

332 "Feet down": Rice, 101.

332 additive called bentonite: ABC News, *World News Tonight,* October 26, 2001.

332 "Iraqi intelligence agent in Prague": ABC News, *This Week,* October 28, 2001.

332 disinformation campaign: William Safire, "Mr. Atta Goes to Prague," *New York Times,* May 9, 2002.

332 indication of his significance: Anthony Tether, biography, AllGov.com.

333 five stages: Tether, Statement to Congress, March 19, 2003.

333 nearly three times: FY 2003 budget estimates, determined in February 2002.

333 "Kenneth Alibek": "George Mason University Unveils Center for Biodefense: Scientists Kenneth Alibek, Charles Bailey to Direct," press release, George Mason University, February 14, 2002.

333 "prototype biodefense products": PRNewswire, Analex Corporation, May 1, 2002.

334 $60: "National Security Notes," March 31, 2006, GlobalSecurity.org.

334 Al Qaeda spent: *9/11 Commission Report,* 169. The plotters spent between $400,000 and $500,000.

335 "The match is about to begin": John Diamond and Kathy Kiely, "Tomorrow Is Zero Hour," *USA Today,* June 19, 2002.

Chapter Twenty *Total Information Awareness*

336 nuclear physicist John Poindexter: Dr. John Poindexter, DARPA biography.

336 struck with an idea: Harris, 144.

337 Poindexter began teaching himself: Ibid., 83.

337 revitalize the Genoa program: Interview with Bob Popp, June 2014.

337 "That's funny": Quotes are from Harris, 144.

338 roughly $42 million: Ibid., 145.

338 existing Genoa program: Presentation by Brian Sharkey, Deputy Director of ISO, Total Information Awareness, DARPATech 99 conference, transcript and briefing slides.

338 let go of profit participation: Harris, 147.

339 opening slide: Ibid., 150.

339 system of systems: Popp and Yen, 409; Dr. Robert Popp, DARPA's Initiative on Countering Terrorism, TIA, Terrorism Information Awareness, Overview of TIA and IAO Programs, briefing slides.

339 Tether agreed: Interview with Bob Popp, June 2014; Harris, 150.

339 $145 million: Congressional Research Services, "Controversy About Level of Funding," memo on funding for Total Information Awareness programs from Amy Belasco, consultant on the defense budget, Foreign Affairs, Defense and Trade Division, January 21, 2003 (hereafter Belasco memo).

339 "In our view": Quotes are from interview with Bob Popp, June 2014.

340 multiple programs under the TIA umbrella: Information in this section is drawn from "Total Information Awareness Program (TIA). System Description Document (SDD)." Version 1.1, July 19, 2002.

340 EELD office: DARPA, Information Awareness Office, IAO Mission, briefing slides.

341 "techniques that allow us": Quotes are from statements of Ted Senator, DARPATech 2002 conference, Anaheim, California.

341 "capture human activities": Ibid.

341 Human Identification: Jonathan Phillips's explanation of face recognition for SPIE Defense Security and Sensing Symposium can be viewed on YouTube.

342 "the war languages": DARPA, IAO Mission briefing slides.

342 Red teaming: International Summit on Democracy, Terrorism and Security, Madrid, March 8–11, 2005.

342 "collaborations": Quotes are from statements by Tom Armour, DARPATech 2000 conference, Dallas, Texas.

344 find the snakes: Armour added, "The intelligence analyst will need to consult vast amounts of information, from both classified and open sources, to piece together enough evidence to understand their activities." Armour, DARPATech 2000 conference, Dallas, Texas.

344 "artificial automaton": Von Neumann, "The Computer and the Brain," 74.

345 lunch in Rumsfeld's office: Harris, 185.

345 at Fort Belvoir: Dr. Robert Popp, DARPA's Initiative on Countering Terrorism, TIA, Terrorism Information Awareness, Overview of TIA and IAO Programs, briefing slides.

345 a whooshing sound: Glenn Greenwald, "Inside the Mind of NSA Chief Gen. Keith Alexander," *Guardian,* September 15, 2013.

346 "initial TIA experiment": Quotes are from interview with Bob Popp; see also Harris, 187.

346 "a vast electronic dragnet": John Markoff, "Pentagon Plans a Computer System That Would Peek at Personal Data of Americans," *New York Times,* November 9, 2002.

347 Safire wrote: William Safire, "You Are a Suspect," *New York Times,* November 14, 2002.

347 285 stories: Robert L. Popp and John Yen, 409.

347 true numbers: Belasco memo; DefenseNet transfers from Project ST-28 in FY2002 to Project ST-11 in 2003.

348 No interviews: Interview with Bob Popp, June 2014.

348 "I don't know much about it": U.S. Department of Defense, news transcript, "Secretary Rumsfeld Media Availability en Route to Chile," November 18, 2002.

349 offered his resignation: John M. Poindexter to Anthony Tether, director, Defense Advanced Research Projects Agency, August 12, 2003.

349 "terminated immediately": *Congressional Record,* September 24, 2003 (House), H8500-H8550 Joint Explanatory Statement, Terrorism Information Awareness (TIA).

350 Anonymous Entity Resolution: Ericson and Haggerty, 180; Steve Mollman, "Betting on Private Data Search," *Wired,* March 5, 2003.

350 Combat Zones That See: DARPA Solicitation number SN03-13, Pre-Solicitation Notice: Combat Zones That See (CTS), March 25, 2003.

351 "to challenge the status quo": *Defense Industry Daily,* August 1, 2008.

351 came up with: Vice Admiral Arthur K. Cebrowski and John H. Garstka, "Network Centric Warfare: Its Origins and Future," *Proceedings,* 124–139.

Cebrowski says he first heard the phrase at the U.S. Naval Institute Seminar and 123rd Annual Meeting, Annapolis, April 23, 1997.

351 the whole world: Remarks by Bill Mularie, director, Information Systems Office, DARPATech '99 conference, briefing slides.

351 (C4ISR): Rumsfeld, 10.

351 internal documents: U.S. Department of Defense, *Report on Network Centric Warfare,* 2001; Vice Admiral Arthur Cebrowski (retired), speech to Network Centric Warfare 2003 conference, January 2003.

351 "great moral seductiveness": Cited in James Blaker, "Arthur K. Cebrowski: A Retrospective," *Naval War College Review,* Spring 2006, Vol. 59, no. 2, 135.

352 "The speed": Quotes are from "Transforming Warfare: An Interview with Adm. Arthur Cebrowski," *Nova,* PBS, May 5, 2004.

Chapter Twenty-One *IED War*

354 "Mission Accomplished": Remarks by the President from the USS *Abraham Lincoln,* White House Press Office, May 2003.

354 "I was a gunner": Quotes are from interview with Jeremy Ridgley, May 25, 2014; Ridgley photographs.

355 "unexploded ordnance": "Pfc. Jeremiah D. Smith, 25, OIF, 05/26/03," Defense Department press release no. 376-03, May 28, 2003.

355 Defense Department official: David Rhode, "After the War: Resistance; Deadly Attacks on G.I.'s Rise; Generals Hope Troop Buildup Will Stop the Skirmishes," *New York Times,* June 10, 2003.

356 "There's more ammunition": Abizaid, testimony before Congress, September 25, 2003.

356 greater than the number: Smith, 10.

356 soldiers killed by IEDs: Ibid.; John Diamond, "Small Weapons Prove the Real Threat in Iraq," *USA Today,* September 29, 2003.

356 "classical guerrilla-style campaign": Cited in Rick Atkinson, "Left of Boom: 'The IED Problem is getting out of control. We've got to stop the bleeding,'" *Washington Post,* September 30, 2007.

356 "A new phenomenon": Quotes are from interview with Brigadier General Andrew Smith (retired), June 2014.

357 CREW: Glenn Zorpette, "Countering IEDs," *IEEE Spectrum,* August 29, 2008.

358 study report: Clay Wilson, "Network Centric Warfare: Background and Oversight Issues for Congress," June 2, 2004.

358 "Warfare is all about": U.S. Department of Defense, *Report on Network Centric Warfare,* 2001; Vice Admiral Arthur Cebrowski (retired), speech to Network Centric Warfare 2003 conference, January 2003.

359 "Network-centric warfare": "Transformation for Survival: Interview with Arthur K. Cebrowski, Director, Office of Force Transformation," *Defense AT&L,* March–April 2004.

359 added four new slides: Office of Force Transformation, "Key Barriers to Transformation," PowerPoint, 2002; "Meeting the Challenges of the New Competitive Landscape PowerPoint, 2004. See also Donald Rumsfeld, Secretary's Forward, "Transformation Planning Guidance," U.S. Department of Defense, April 2003.

359 "That speed of advance": "Battle Plan Under Fire," *PBS NewsHour,* May 4, 2004.

360 "culture-centric" solution: Major General Robert H. Scales Jr., U.S. Army (retired), "Culture-Centric Warfare," *Proceedings,* October 2004.

360 "Knowledge of one's enemy": McFate, "Anthropology and Counterinsurgency: The Strange Story of Their Curious Relationship," *Military Review,* March–April 2005, 24–38.

360 "Combat troops": Meghan Scully," 'Social Intel' New Tool for U.S. Military," *Defense News,* April 26, 2004.

361 bringing social scientists on board: Email correspondence with Montgomery McFate; interview with Bob Popp, June 2014.

362 "punk rock wild child": Matthew B. Standard, "Montgomery McFate's Mission: Can One Anthropologist Possibly Steer the Course in Iraq?" *San Francisco Examiner,* April 29, 2007.

362 received a call: Email correspondence with Montgomery McFate.

362 majority were left-leaning: Scott Jaschik, "Social Scientists Lean to the Left, Study Says," Insidehighered.com, December 21, 2005.

362 "evangelical mission": George Packer, "Knowing the Enemy: Can social scientists redefine the 'war on terror'?" *New Yorker,* December 18, 2006.

363 An entire generation: Williamson Murray and Robert H. Scales Jr., *The Iraq War: A Military History* (Cambridge: Harvard University Press, 2003).

363 "The nature of war": Major General Robert H. Scales Jr., U.S. Army (retired), "Culture-Centric Warfare," *Proceedings,* October 2004, 32–36.

364 "When the U.S.": McFate, "The Military Utility of Understanding Adversary Culture," *Joint Force Quarterly,* issue 38, July 2005, 44-48.

364 "Soldiers and Marines": Ibid.

365 "stability operations": Dehghanpisheh and Thomas, "Scions of the Surge," *Newsweek*, March 24, 2008.

365 "I do not want": George Packer, "Knowing the Enemy: Can social scientists redefine the 'war on terror'?" *New Yorker,* December 18, 2006.

366 "Understanding and empathy": Robert Scales, "Clausewitz and World War IV," *Armed Forces Journal,* July 1, 2006.

366 McFate wrote one of the chapters: Email correspondence with Montgomery McFate.

366 "What is Counterinsurgency?": *Counterinsurgency, Field Manual* No. 3-24.

366 "the first time": http://humanterrainsystem.army.mil.

Chapter Twenty-Two *Combat Zones That See*

367 "Combat Zones That See": DARPA Solicitation number SN03-13, Pre-Solicitation Notice: Combat Zones That See (CTS), March 25, 2003.

367 "No technological challenges": Robert Leheny, "DARPA's Urban Operations Program," presentation at DARPATech 2005, August 2005, with photographs.

368 "We need a network": Tether, Statement to Congress, March 10, 2005, 11.

368 Congress had eliminated funding: U.S. Congress, H8500–H8550, Joint Explanatory Statement, Terrorism Information Awareness (TIA), *Congressional Record,* September 24, 2003.

368 "detect the clandestine production": Tether, Statement to Congress, March 10, 2005, 11.

369 "a network of nonintrusive microsensors": Leheny, "DARPA's Urban Operations Program," 38.

370 unclassified documents: Ehlschlaeger, "Understanding Megacities with the Reconnaissance, Surveillance, and Intelligence Paradigm," 50–53.

370 the HURT program: DARPA Information Exploitation Office (IXO) HURT Program Office, aerial vehicle platform documents; See also James Richardson, "Preparing Warfighters for the Urban Stage," located in *DARPA: 50 Years of Bridging the Gap,* 166–67.

371 "The [HURT] system": Pagels quoted in Clarence A. Robinson, Jr., "Air Vehicles Deliver Warrior Data," *Signal Magazine,* July 2007.

371 terrorists could sneak in: *DARPA: 50 Years of Bridging the Gap,* 169; Glenn Zorpette, "Countering IEDs," *IEEE Spectrum,* August 29, 2008.

372 DARPA's goal: This information comes from Tether, Statement to Congress, 2003; "Combat Zones That See (CTS) Solicitation Number BAA03-15, March 25, 2003. See also Stephen Graham, "Surveillance, Urbanization, and the U.S. 'Revolution in Military Affairs,' " in David Lyon, ed., *Theorizing Surveillance: The Panopticon and Beyond,* 250–54.

372 every forty-eight minutes: Rick Atkinson, "Left of Boom: 'You can't armor your way out of this problem;'" *Washington Post,* October 2, 2007.

373 the "spider": Noah Shachtman, "The Secret History of Iraq's Invisible War," *Wired,* June 14, 2011.

374 EFP: The first EFPs appeared on May 15, 2004, in Bara. DIA linked them to Hezbollah forces from 1997.

374 2,000 meters per second: Rick Atkinson, "Left of Boom: 'You can't armor your way out of this problem;'" *Washington Post,* October 2, 2007.

374 Hardwire HD: "Hardwire Receives DARPA Funding for Novel Armor Solutions," *Business Wire,* August 21, 2006.

374 rip apart soldiers' bodies: Tony Perry, "IED Wounds from Afghanistan 'Unbelievable' Trauma Docs Say," *Los Angeles Times,* April 7, 2011.

375 JIEDDO: Interview with Brigadier General Andrew Smith (retired), June 2014.

376 "We were dealing with": Quotes are from interviews with Craig Marsh, June 2014–March 2015.

376 Building 114: Interviews with Craig Marsh; Andrew E. Kramer, "Leaving Camp Victory in Iraq, the Very Name a Question Mark," *New York Times,* November 10, 2011.

377 Combined Explosive Exploitation Cell: "CEXC: Introducing a New Concept in the Art of War," *Armed Forces Journal,* June 7, 2007.

379 "Talon robots": Quotes in this section are from DARPA, Distribution Statement A, "Unmanned Robots Systems: SBIR Technology Underpins Life-Saving Military Robots," DARPA, Distribution Statement A, 2010, 1-7.

379 "Gordon the robot": Ibid., 6–8; DARPA, "Unmanned Robotic Systems: Small Business Innovation Research," *Featured Technology,* December 2010, 6.

380 Talon robots: Sargeant Lorie Jewell, "Armed Robots to March into Battle," *Army News Service,* December 6, 2004.

382 "Whether it's magic or scientific": Rod Nordland, "Iraq Swears by a Bomb Detector U.S. Sees as Useless," *New York Times,* November 3, 2009.

382 whistleblower revealed: Adam Higginbotham, "In Iraq, the Bomb-Detecting Device That Didn't Work, Except to Make Money," *Bloomberg Businessweek,* July 11, 2013.

382 more than two an hour: Rick Atkinson, "Left of Boom: 'If you don't go after the network, you're never going to stop these guys. Never,'" *Washington Post,* October 3, 2007.

382 $15 billion: Glenn Zorpette, "Countering IEDs," *IEEE Spectrum,* August 29, 2008.

383 Tether appeared: Tether, Statement to Congress, March 21, 2007.

383 "Shot. Two o'clock": Raytheon news release, BBN Technologies, Products and Services, Boomerang III.

383 CROSSHAIRS: DARPA, news release, "DARPA's CROSSHAIRS Counter Shooter System," October 5, 2010.

384 DARPA fielded fifty Radar Scopes: Quotes are from Tether, Statement to Congress, March 21, 2007; Donna Miles, "New Device Will Sense Through Concrete Walls," Armed Forces Press Service, January 3, 2006.

384 HART: DARPA Heterogeneous Airborne Reconnaissance Team (HART), Case no. 11414, briefing slides. Dr. Michael A. Pagels, August 2008.

385 TIGR (Tactical Ground Reporting): Amy Walker, "TIGR allows Soldiers to 'be there' before they arrive," *U.S. Army News,* October 13, 2009.

385 Congress was told: Leheny, Statement to Congress, May 20, 2009.

385 soldiers told: David Talbot, "A Technology Surges," *MIT Technology Review,* February 2008.

Chapter Twenty-Three *Human Terrain*

386 not one of the 1,200: Declan Walsh, "Afghan Militants Attack Kandahar Prison and Free Inmates," *Guardian,* June 13, 2008; Carlotta Gall, "Taliban Free 1,200 Inmates in Attack on Afghan Prison," *New York Times,* June 14, 2008.

387 "proto-type system": DARPA, IAO Mission, briefing slides.

387 "Based on our experience in Iraq": Thom Shankar, "To Check Militants, U.S. Has System That Never Forgets," *New York Times,* July 13, 2011.

388 On patrol: *USA v. Don Michael Ayala* (U.S. District Court for the Eastern District of Virginia, Alexandria Division), Document 33, May 6, 2009, and Document 5, November 24, 2008.

389 "An indefinable spirit": U.S. Army, "In Memory of... Paula Loyd," *Human Terrain System,* September 2011.

389 center of the alleyway: *USA v. Don Michael Ayala,* photographs.

389 A young bearded man: Gezari, 3–18.

389 He wore: *USA v. Don Michael Ayala,* photographs.

390 drew his pistol: *USA v. Don Michael Ayala,* Document 5, 4.

390 previously guarded: Ibid., Document 5, 3.

391 "the man was the devil": Ibid., Document 33, 2.

391 leniency: Matthew Barakat, "Contractor Gets Probation for Killing Prisoner," Associated Press, May 8, 2009.

391 "advise brigades": In *Human Terrain: War Becomes Academic,* Udris Films, 2010.

392 earned more: *USA v. Don Michael Ayala,* Document 33, 1.

392 "military commanders": U.S. Army press release, digital archive, http://humanterrainsystem.army.mil.

392 "dangerous and reckless": AAA [American Anthropological Association] Executive Board, Statement on the Human Terrain System Project, October 31, 2007.

393 "mercenary anthropology": Roberto J. González, "Towards mercenary anthropology? The new US Army counterinsurgency manual FM 3–24 and the military-anthropology complex," *Anthropology Today,* Volume 23, Issue 3, June 2007, 14–19.

393 Catherine Lutz: Quotes are from *Human Terrain: War Becomes Academic,* Udris Films, 2010.

393 Hugh Gusterson: Ibid.

393 Roberto González: Ibid.

394 "My very first time": Carlson quotes are from Dan G. Cox, "Human Terrain Systems and the Moral Prosecution of Warfare," 27–29.

395 "Can doctrine be applied": This account is drawn from Nigh, "An Operator's Guide to Human Terrain Teams," 20–23.

396 "clearing operation": ISAF, TAAC South, "Impacts, Contributions," 2007; U.S. Army, "Human Terrain Team Handbook," December 11, 2008.

397 replaced Paula Loyd: Korva Coleman, "Social Scientists Deployed to the Battlefield," NPR, September 1, 2009.

397 "infamous as a killing zone": Jonathan Montpetit,"Canadian Soldiers Resume Mentoring Afghan National Army After Turbulent Spring." *Military World,* October 28, 2010.

397 "Michael Bhatia was": "One Man's Odyssey from Campus to Combat," Associated Press, March 8, 2009.

398 $200,000 a year: Jason Motlagh, "Should Anthropologists Help Contain the Taliban?" *Time,* July 1, 2010.

399 "People use human networks": Tristan Reed, "Intelligence and Human Networks," *Stratfor Global Intelligence Security Weekly,* January 10, 2013.

399 "Phase Zero pre-conflict": Jim Hodges, "Cover Story: U.S. Army's Human Terrain Experts May Help Defuse Future Conflicts," *Defense News,* March 22, 2012.

400 biomedical technology program: Department of Defense, Fiscal Year 2015, Budget Estimates, Defense Advanced Research Projects Agency, 1:51.

400 "applies forecasting": Ibid., 1:130.

400 "far behind enemy lines": "DARPA Receives Joint Meritorious Unit Award," U.S. Department of Defense, press release. December 17, 2012.

401 Deep Exploration and Filtering of Text: Department of Defense, Fiscal Year 2015 Budget Estimates, Defense Advanced Research Projects Agency, 1:88.

Chapter Twenty-Four *Drone Wars*

405 "This war": Quotes are from "Remarks by the President at the National Defense University, Fort McNair," White House, Office of the Press Secretary, May 23, 2013.

406 Department of Defense reports: U.S. Department of Defense, "The Unmanned Systems Integrated Roadmap FY2013–2038," 2014, 8:13, 26.

407 "My daughter": Quotes are from interview with Bernard Crane, September 2014.

407 "Those are not insects": Quotes are from Rick Weiss, "Dragonfly or Insect Spy? Scientists at Work on Robobugs," *Washington Post,* October 9, 2007.

408 insisted that President Bush be impeached: C-SPAN, "Stop the War Rally," September 15, 2007.

408 multiple truck bombs: Damien Cave and James Glanz, "Toll in Iraq Bombings Is Raised to More Than 500," *New York Times,* August 22, 2007.

408 reportedly played a role: "A Carpet for Radicals at the White House," *Investigative Project on Terrorism,* October 12, 2012.

408 served as imam: "Al-Qaida cleric death: mixed emotions at Virginia mosque where he preached," Associated Press, September 11, 2011.

409 "Insect-size": Grasmeyer and Keennon, "Development of the Black Widow Micro Air Vehicle," *American Institute of Aeronautics and Astronautics,* 2001, 1.

410 "We have seen sparrows": Ibid., 8.

410 "micro-explosive bombs": Lambeth, "Technology Trends in Air Warfare," 141.

410 trained bees to locate: "Sandia, University of Montana Researchers Try Training Bees to Find Buried Landmines," Sandia National Laboratories, press release, April 27, 1999. In the late 1990s, the Mine Bee Program met with great success when DARPA researchers at Sandia National Laboratories worked with entomologists at the University of Montana to train honeybees to detect buried land mines.

411 Insectothopter: Author tour of the CIA museum, Langley, VA, September 2010.

412 Animal rights: Duncan Graham-Rowe, "Robo-Rat Controlled by Brain Electrodes," *New Scientist,* May 1, 2002.

413 "The tissue develops": A. Verderber, M. McKnight, and A. Bozkurt, "Early Metamorphic Insertion Technology for Insect Flight Behavior Monitoring," *Journal of Visualized Experiments,* July 12, 2014, 89.

413 animated video: online at "Armed with Science," the DoD's official science blog.

415 DARPA's hypersonic stealth drones: DARPA News, "Hypersonics—The New Stealth: DARPA investments in extreme hypersonics continue," July 6, 2012; "Darpa refocuses Hypersonics Research on Tactical Missions," *Aviation Week and Space Technology,* July 8, 2013.

415 Falcon HTV-2: Animated performance videos of Falcon HTV-2 at Lockheedmartin.com.

415 hypersonic low-earth-orbit drones: Toshio Suzuki, "DARPA Wants Hypersonic Space Drone with Daily Launches," *Stars and Stripes,* February 4, 2014.

415 Hydra: John Keller, "DARPA Considers Unmanned Submersible Mothership Designed to Deploy UAVs and UUVs," *Military Aerospace Electronics,* July 23, 2013.

416 Unmanned Ground System robots: Demonstration videos on DARPA's YouTube channel, DARPAtv.

417 LANdroids: USC Information Sciences Institute, Polymorphic Robotics Laboratory, "LANdroids," n.d.

417 what "autonomy" is: U.S. Department of Defense, "Unmanned Systems Integrated Roadmap FY2013–2038," 15.

418 "The autonomous systems": U.S. Department of Defense, "Unmanned Systems Integrated Roadmap FY2011–2036," 43.

418 "autonomous and semi-autonomous": Department of Defense Directive 3000.09, "Autonomy in Weapon Systems," sec. 4, Policy, 2, November 21, 2012.

418 fourfold process: U.S. Department of Defense, "Unmanned Systems Integrated Roadmap FY2011–2036," table 3, 46.

419 "unimagined degrees of autonomy": Ashton Carter's letter, dated (stamped) March 29, 2010, is attached to the end of Department of Defense, Defense Science Board, "Task Force Report: The Role of Autonomy in DoD Systems," Appendix C, Task Force Terms of Reference.

Chapter Twenty-Five *Brain Wars*

420 artificial brains: ArtificialBrains.com tracks scientific and technological progress toward the goal of building sentient machines. The website is maintained by James Pearn in Munich, Germany.

422 our interview: All quotes in this section are from my interview with Allen Macy Dulles, March 2014.

422 brought her brother: Interviews with Joan Dulles Talley, March 2014–May 2015.

424 The White House calls: White House Briefing Room, "BRAIN Initiative Challenges Researchers to Unlock Mysteries of Human Mind," April 2, 2013. Of note: partnering with DARPA on many of its brain programs is IARPA, the Intelligence Advanced Research Projects Agency, or the CIA's DARPA.

424 Brain programs: Information on DARPA brain-computer interface programs from Robbin A. Miranda et al., "DARPA-Funded Efforts in the Development of Novel Brain–Computer Interface Technologies," 1-17. The authors are: Robbin A. Miranda, William D. Casebeer, Amy M. Hein, Jack W. Judy, Eric P. Krotkov, Tracy L. Laabs, Justin E. Manzof, Kent G. Pankratz, Gill A. Pratt, Justin C. Sanchez, Douglas J. Weber, Tracey L. Wheeler, and Geoffrey S. F. Ling.

424 According to the Pentagon: Armed Forces Health Surveillance Center, "Summary of Mental Disorder Hospitalizations, Active and Reserve Components, U.S. Armed Forces, 2000–2012," *Medical Surveillance Monthly Report* 20, no. 7 (July 2013): 4–11.

425 SUBNETS: "SUBNETS Aims for Systems-Based Neurotechnology and Understanding for the Treatment of Neuropsychological Illnesses," Department of Defense, press release, October 25, 2013.

425 chips wirelessly transmit: George Dvorsky, "Electroconvulsive Therapy Can Erase Unwanted Memories," iO9, December 23, 2013.

425 "incorporate near real-time": "SUBNETS," DARPA News, October 25, 2013.

426 "notes on a piano": Emily Singer, "Playing Piano with a Robotic Hand," *MIT Technology Review,* July 25, 2007.

426 "The Intrinsic hand": Jonathan Kuniholm, "Open Arms," *IEEE Spectrum,* March 1, 2009.

426 Dean Kamen: Kamen interview with Scott Pelley, CBS News, *60 Minutes,* April 10, 2009.

427 yet to find a partner: Rhodi Lee, "FDA Approves DEKA Arm System," *Tech Times,* May 10, 2014.

427 "debt we owe": "From Idea to Market in Eight Years: DARPA-Funded DEKA Arm System Earns FDA Approval," DARPA News, May 9, 2014.

427 "turn a valve": Interview with Noel Sharkey, September 2014.

428 Even the cooks: Interview with LANL cooks, March 2014.

428 Kenyon and his team: Kenyon's DARPA contract is administered through the University of Michigan as part of the New Mexico Consortium (NMC). Kenyon says, "The NMC is sort of an incubator for LANL. It's a place where scientists like myself can work with a team of students and pursue risky ideas that would be hard to pull off within the confines of LANL itself."

429 simulating the primate visual system: Quotes are from interviews with Garrett Kenyon, March–November 2014.

429 world's record: "Science at the Petascale," IBM Roadrunner supercomputer, press release, October 27, 2009.

429 Tianhe-2: Lance Ulanoff, "China Has the Fastest Supercomputer in the World—Again," Mashable.com, June 23, 2014.

430 points inside: Kenyon noted that the computer room contains a number of different machines.

433 "Regeneration is really coming alive": Quotes are from interviews with David Gardiner and Sue Bryant, June 2013–October 2014.

434 children born with mutations: Ngo Vinh Long, "Vietnamese Perspectives," in *Encyclopedia of the Vietnam War,* ed. by Stanley Kutler (New York: Scribner's, 1996).

435 a human uterus: Stephanie Smith, "Creating Body Parts in a Lab; 'Things Are Happening Now,'" CNN, April 10, 2014.

435 make body parts: "Ears, Noses Grown from Stem Cells in Lab Dishes," Associated Press, April 8, 2014.

435 laboratory-grown beef burgers: Maria Cheng, "First Reaction: Lab-Made Burger Short on Flavor." Phys.org, August 5, 2013.

437 "One can imagine": S. Hawking et al., "Stephen Hawking: 'Transcendence Looks at the Implications of Artificial Intelligence—But Are We Taking AI Seriously Enough?'" *The Independent,* May 1, 2014.

437 "these [autonomous] systems": Interview with Steve Omohundro, May 2015; See also "Autonomous Technology and the Greater Human Good," *Journal of Experimental & Theoretical Artificial Intelligence,* November 21, 2014, 303–15.

438 "human-machine interaction failures": Interview with Noel Sharkey, September 2014.

Chapter Twenty-Six *The Pentagon's Brain*

438 sharing his idea: Interview with Charles Townes, April 2014.

440 SIGMA group: Interview with Doug Beason, who is a member. Beason, a physicist and the former chief scientist, U.S. Air Force Space Command,

is the author of fourteen science-fiction books, eight with collaborator Kevin J. Anderson; Email correspondence with Arlan Andrews.

440 "Those responsible": Jenna Lang, "Sci-fi writers take US security back to the future," *Guardian,* June 5, 2009.

444 brain-computer interfaces: R. A. Miranda et al., "DARPA-Funded Efforts in the Development of Novel Brain-Computer Interface Technologies," *Journal of Neuroscience Methods* (2014). The term was coined by Jacques J. Vidal, in 1971.

444 DARPA's stated goal: M. L. Cummings, "Views, Provocations: Technology Impedances to Augmented Cognition," *Ergonomics in Design* (Spring 2010): 25.

444 "Human brain activity": DARPA, Cognitive Technology Threat Warning System (CT2WS) Solicitation no. BAA07-25, April 11, 2007.

444 DARPA scientists: R. A. Miranda et al., "DARPA-Funded Efforts in the Development of Novel Brain-Computer Interface Technologies," *Journal of Neuroscience Methods* (2014).

445 "groundbreaking advances": Ibid., 3, 5.

445 DARPA program managers: Ibid., 10-13. The four DARPA program managers are William D. Casebeer, Justic C. Sanchez, Douglas J. Weber, Geoffrey S. F. Ling.

446 augmenting cognition: Quotes are from Jason, MITRE Corporation, "Human Performance," 70, 72.

447 "The Jason scientists": Quotes are from interview with Michael Goldblatt, April 2014.

448 "For commanders": Quotes are from Defense Science Board, "The Role of Autonomy in DoD Systems," 2012, 2, 19, 46, 48. "Among the key challenges moving forward," according to the DSB, "is advancing tests and evaluation capabilities to improve trust for increasing autonomy in unmanned systems."

448 "probability and consequences of failure": Department of Defense Directive no. 3000.09, November 21, 2012.

449 "the effect of narrative": Miranda et al., 9.

449 "We would all benefit": Interview with Paul Zak, October 2014.

449 "erase fear": Bret Stetka, "Can Fear Be Erased?" *Scientific American,* December 4, 2014.

450 DSB chairman Paul Kaminski: Information according to his White House biography. Kaminski had a twenty-year career as an officer in the Air Force. He served as director of Low Observable Technology and was responsible for developing and fielding the Pentagon's stealth programs. Later, as under secretary of defense for acquisition and technology, he had

responsibility for an annual budget that exceeded $100 billion. See also "Dr. Paul G. Kaminski, Former Under Secretary of Defense for Acquisition and Technology, 2011 Ronald Reagan Award Winner," Missile Defense Agency, digital archive.

450 DSB members: Email correspondence with Major Eric D. Badger, public affairs officer for the DSB Executive Director; Department of Defense press release, January 5, 2010; DSB, Appendix D—Task Force Membership, 109, Appendix E—Task Force Briefings, 110. Also participating in the DSB report advising the Pentagon on the role of autonomous weapons systems were briefers from the defense corporations Northrop Grumman, Lockheed Martin, Boeing, General Dynamics, General Atomics, SAIC, and QinetiQ.

451 "chicken-and-egg": Barber, VIII-76.

451 military-industrial complex: Dwight D. Eisenhower, "Farewell Radio and Television Address to the American People," January 17, 1961, UCSB.

452 "The battlefield is no place": Cited in Van Atta et al., *Transformation and Transition,* Volume 2, V-19.

LIST OF INTERVIEWS AND WRITTEN CORRESPONDENCE

Dr. Ken Alibek: Virologist, former deputy director Biopreparat, USSR

Dr. Jorge Barraza: Social psychologist, Claremont Graduate University

Colonel Doug Beason, Ph.D. (retired): Physicist, former chief scientist U.S. Air Force Space Command

Chris Berka: Co-founder of Advanced Brain Monitoring, Inc.

Major David Blair: Technologist, MQ-1B instructor pilot, AC-130 gunship pilot

Dr. David A. Bray: Information technologist, chief information officer, FCC; former information chief for Bioterrorism Preparedness and Response, Centers for Disease Control

Rebecca Bronson: FBI records administrator

Dr. Susan V. Bryant: Regeneration biologist, former dean of the School of Biological Sciences and vice chancellor for research, UC Irvine

Colonel Julian Chesnutt (retired): Former program officer, Defense Clandestine Service, DIA

Colonel L. Neale Cosby (retired): Former SIMNET principal investigator, DARPA

Bernard Crane: Lawyer, Washington, DC

Dr. Tanja Dominko: Biotechnoengineer, stem cell biologist, Worcester Polytechnic Institute

Allen Macy Dulles: Student of history, Korean War veteran, son of Allen Welsh Dulles

Dr. Jay W. Forrester: Computer pioneer, founder of system dynamics

Ralph "Jim" Freedman: Former nuclear weapons engineer, EG&G

Dr. David Gardiner: Regeneration biologist, professor of developmental and cell biology, UC Irvine

Colonel John Gargus (retired): Former special operations officer, U.S. Air Force

Lieutenant Colonel Peter A. Garretson: Transformational strategist, U.S. Air Force

Dr. Marvin Goldberger: Former Manhattan Project physicist, founder and chairman of the Jason scientists, science advisor to President Johnson

Dr. Michael Goldblatt: Former director, Defense Sciences Office, DARPA

Dr. Kay Godel-Gengenbach: Academic, daughter of William Godel

General Paul F. Gorman (retired): Former commander in chief, U.S. Southern Command (US SOUTHCOM), special assistant to the Joint Chiefs of Staff

Richard "Rip" Jacobs: Former engineer, VO-67 Navy squadron

Dr. Garrett T. Kenyon: Neurophysicist, Synthetic Cognition Group, Los Alamos National Laboratory

Paul Kozemchak: Special assistant to director, DARPA

Edward Lovick Jr.: Physicist, former Lockheed Skunk Works stealth technologist

Sherre Lovick: Engineer, former Lockheed Skunk Works stealth technologist

Robert A. Lowell: Radiation scientist, satellite technologist

Colonel Douglas Macgregor, Ph.D. (retired): Former squadron operations officer, Battle of 73 Easting

Master Chief Petty Officer Craig Marsh (retired): Former master explosive ordnance disposal technician, Combined Joint Counter-IED Task Force Troy, Iraq

Montgomery McFate, J. D., Ph.D.: Cultural anthropologist, former senior social scientist, Human Terrain System, U.S. Army

Cullen McInerney: Former military contractor, former U.S. Secret Service

Eugene McManus: Former technician at BMEWS J-Site, Thule, Greenland

Timothy Moynihan: Pastor, former soldier and operations officer, U.S. Army

Dr. Walter Munk: Oceanographer, former Jason scientist

Captain C. N. "Lefty" Nordhill: Former aircraft commander, VO-67 Navy squadron

Alfred O'Donnell: Former nuclear weapons engineer, EG&G

Dr. Alvaro Pascual-Leone, Ph.D.: Neurologist, Harvard Medical School, director of the Berenson-Allen Center for Non-invasive Brain Stimulation

Dr. Robert Popp: Former deputy director, Information Awareness Office, DARPA

Dr. Leonard Reiffel: Nuclear physicist

Robert E. Reynolds: Former air crewman, VO-67 Navy squadron

Michael E. Rich: Assistant U.S. attorney, Department of Justice

Jeremy Ridgley: Former soldier, Eighteenth Military Police Brigade, U.S. Army

Rob Rubio: Business director, Advanced Brain Monitoring, Inc.

Colonel Jack W. Rust: Commander, U.S. Navy, NRO
Dr. Charles Schwartz: Physicist, former Jason scientist
Dr. Noel Sharkey: Emeritus professor of artificial intelligence and robotics at the University of Sheffield, England, chairman of the International Committee for Robot Arms Control
Brigadier General Andrew Smith (Australian Army, retired): Former director, Combined Planning Group, Headquarters, U.S. CENTCOM
Colonel Edward Starbird (retired): Son of General Alfred Starbird
David J. Steffy: Former air crewman, VO-67 Navy Squadron
Lieutenant Colonel Hervey Stockman (retired): U-2 pilot, CIA and U.S. Air Force
Clifford Stoll: Astrophysicist
Robert Surrette: Former senior acquisition executive, CIA
Joan Dulles Talley: Jungian analyst, daughter of Allen Welsh Dulles
Lieutenant Colonel Troy E. Techau (retired): Former biometrics technologist, Identity Dominance Operations, U.S. CENTCOM
Elizabeth Terris: Neuroeconomics researcher, Claremont Graduate University
Kip S. Thorne: Theoretical physicist
Colonel Jack Thorpe, Ph.D. (retired): Creator and founder of SIMNET
Dr. Charles H. Townes: Inventor of the laser, Nobel Prize in Physics, 1964
Andrew Tudor: Nanofabrication and nanoscale researcher, physical intelligence, UCLA
Dr. Richard H. Van Atta: Senior research analyst, IDA
Eric Van Slander: Archivist, National Archives
Jim Wagner: Former co-pilot, VO-67 Navy Squadron
Captain Barney Walsh (retired): Former co-pilot, VO-67 Navy squadron
Tom Wells: Former engineer, VO-67 Navy squadron
Dr. James M. Wilson: Virologist, former special assistant to the director for weapons of mass destruction, U.S. Army Medical Research and Materiel Command
Dr. Paul J. Zak: Scientist, neuroeconomist, Claremont Graduate University
Dr. Joseph J. Zasloff: Social scientist, former RAND analyst for the Viet Cong Motivation and Morale Project
Dr. Alan Zelicoff: Epidemiologist, former senior scientist in the Center for National Security and Arms Control at Sandia National Laboratories

BIBLIOGRAPHY

Books

Abella, Alex. *Soldiers of Reason: The RAND Corporation and the Rise of the American Empire.* Orlando: Houghton Mifflin Harcourt, 2009.

Alibek, Ken, with Stephen Handelman. *Biohazard: The Chilling True Story of the Largest Covert Biological Weapons Program in the World— Told from Inside by the Man Who Ran It.* New York: Dell Publishing, 1999.

Arkin, William M. *American Coup: How a Terrified Government Is Destroying the Constitution.* New York: Little, Brown, 2013.

Atkinson, Rick. *Crusade: The Untold Story of the Persian Gulf War.* New York: Houghton Mifflin, 1993.

Bamford, James. *Body of Secrets: Anatomy of the Ultra-Secret National Security Agency.* New York: Anchor Books, 2002.

Barrat, James. *Our Final Invention: Artificial Intelligence and the End of the Human Era.* New York: St. Martin's Press, 2013.

Beason, Doug, Ph.D. *The E-Bomb: How America's New Directed Energy Weapons Will Change the Way Future Wars Will Be Fought.* Cambridge, MA: Da Capo Press, 2005.

Belfiore, Michael. *The Department of Mad Scientists: How DARPA Is Remaking Our World, from the Internet to Artificial Limbs.* New York: Harper, 2010.

Bradlee, Benjamin C. *Conversations with Kennedy.* New York: W. W. Norton, 1975.

Braithwaite, Rodric. *Across the Moscow River: The World Turned Upside Down.* New Haven: Yale University Press, 2002.

Broad, William J. *Teller's War: The Top-Secret Story Behind The Star Wars Deception.* New York: Simon & Schuster, 1992.

Burrows, William E. *Deep Black: The Startling Truth Behind America's Top-Secret Spy Satellites.* New York: Berkley Books, 1986.

———. *This New Ocean: The Story of the First Space Age*. New York: Random House, 1998.

Chayes, Abram, and Jerome B. Wiesner. *ABM: An Evaluation of the Decision to Deploy an Antiballistic Missile System*. New York: New American Library, 1969.

Cheney, Dick, with Liz Cheney. *In My Time: A Personal and Political Memoir*. New York: Threshold Editions, 2011.

Childs, Herbert. *An American Genius: The Life of Ernest Orlando Lawrence*. New York: E. P. Dutton, 1968.

Cockburn, Andrew. *Rumsfeld: His Rise, Fall, and Catastrophic Legacy*. New York: Scribner, 2007.

Corman, Steven R., ed. *Narrating the Exit from Afghanistan*. Tempe: Arizona State University Center for Strategic Communication, 2013.

Creveld, Martin van. *The Transformation of War: The Most Radical Reinterpretation of Armed Conflict Since Clausewitz*. New York: Free Press, 1991.

———. *Wargames: From Gladiators to Gigabytes*. New York: Cambridge University Press, 2013.

Deitchman, Seymour J. *The Best-Laid Schemes: A Tale of Research and Bureaucracy*. Cambridge: MIT Press, 1976.

———. *Limited War and American Defense Policy*. Cambridge: MIT Press, 1964.

———. *Military Power and the Advance of Technology: General Purpose Military Forces for the 1980s and Beyond*. Boulder, CO: Westview Press, 1983.

Donlon, Roger H. C., and Warren Rogers. *Outpost of Freedom*. New York: McGraw-Hill, 1965.

Dorr, Robert F. *Air Combat: An Oral History of Fighter Pilots*. New York: Penguin, 2007.

Downs, Frederick. *The Killing Zone: My Life in the Vietnam War*. New York: W. W. Norton, 2007.

Drell, Sidney D., Abraham D. Sofaer, and George D. Wilson. *The New Terror: Facing the Threat of Biological and Chemical Weapons*. Stanford: Hoover Institution Press, 1999.

Dyson, Freeman. *Weapons and Hope*. New York: Harper & Row, 1984.

Dyson, George. *Turing's Cathedral: The Origins of the Digital Universe*. New York: Pantheon Books, 2012.

Elliott, Mai. *RAND in Southeast Asia: A History of the Vietnam War Era*. Santa Monica, CA: RAND Corporation, 2010.

Ellsberg, Daniel. *Secrets: A Memoir of Vietnam and the Pentagon Papers*. New York: Penguin, 2001.

Ezell, Edward. *The Great Rifle Controversy: Search for the Ultimate Infantry Weapons from World War II Through Vietnam and Beyond*. Harrisburg, PA: Stackpole Books, 1984.

Fall, Bernard, B. *Street Without Joy: The French Debacle in Indochina.* Mechanicsburg, PA: Stackpole Books, 1994.

Fehner, Terrence R., and F. G. Gosling. *Origins of the Nevada Test Site.* Washington, D.C.: Department of Energy, 2000.

Finkbeiner, Ann. *The Jasons: The Secret History of Science's Postwar Elite.* New York: Viking Penguin, 2006.

Fleming, James Rodger. *Fixing the Sky: The Checkered History of Weather and Climate Control.* New York: Columbia University Press, 2010.

Garreau, Joel. *Radical Evolution: The Promise and Peril of Enhancing Our Minds, Our Bodies—And What It Means to Be Human.* New York: Doubleday, 2005.

Garrison, Dee. *Bracing for Armageddon: Why Civil Defense Never Worked.* New York: Oxford University Press, 2006.

Gazzaniga, Michael S. *Who's in Charge? Free Will and the Science of the Brain.* New York: HarperCollins, 2011.

Gezari, Vanessa M. *The Tender Soldier: A True Story of War and Sacrifice.* New York: Simon & Schuster, 2013.

Gilbert, Daniel. *Stumbling on Happiness.* New York: Alfred A. Knopf, 2006.

Goodchild, Peter. *Edward Teller: The Real Dr. Strangelove.* Cambridge: Harvard University Press, 2004.

Gouré, Leon. *Civil Defense in the Soviet Union.* Westport, CT: Greenwood Press, 1986.

Gravel, Mike. *The Pentagon Papers: Gravel Edition.* Volume 4. Boston: Beacon Press, 1971.

Green, Tom. *Bright Boys.* Natick, MA: A. K. Peters, 2010.

Hafner, Katie, and Matthew Lyon. *Where Wizards Stay Up Late: The Origins of the Internet.* New York: Simon & Schuster, 1996.

Halberstam, David. *The Best and the Brightest.* New York: Ballantine Books, 1993.

———. *The Making of a Quagmire: America and Vietnam During the Kennedy Era.* New York: Random House, 1965.

Hamblin, Jacob Darwin. *Arming Mother Nature: The Birth of Catastrophic Environmentalism.* New York: Oxford University Press, 2013.

Hammel, Eric. *Khe Sanh: Siege in the Clouds, An Oral History.* Pacifica, CA: Pacifica Press, 1989.

Hansen, Chuck. *U.S. Nuclear Weapons: The Secret History.* New York: Orion Books, 1987.

Hargittai, Istvan. *Judging Edward Teller: A Closer Look at One of the Most Influential Scientists of the Twentieth Century.* Amherst, NY: Prometheus Books, 2010.

Harland, David M., and Ralph D. Lorenz. *Space Systems Failures: Disasters and Rescues of Satellites, Rockets, and Space Probes.* Chichester, UK: Praxis Publishing, 2005.

Harris, Shane. *The Watchers: The Rise of America's Surveillance State.* New York: Penguin, 2010.

Hawkins, Jeff, with Sandra Blakeslee. *On Intelligence.* New York: Henry Holt and Company, 2004.

Hendrickson, Paul. *The Living and the Dead: Robert McNamara and Five Lives of a Lost War.* New York: Alfred A. Knopf, 1996.

Herken, Gregg. *Brotherhood of the Bomb: The Tangled Lives and Loyalties of Robert Oppenheimer, Ernest Lawrence, and Edward Teller.* New York: Henry Holt and Company, 2002.

———. *Cardinal Choices: Presidential Science Advising from the Atomic Bomb to SDI.* Stanford: Stanford University Press, 1992.

Hewlett, Richard G., and Jack M. Holl. *Atoms for Peace and War, 1953–1961: Eisenhower and the Atomic Energy Commission.* Berkeley: University of California Press, 1989.

Hey, Nigel. *The Star Wars Enigma: Behind the Scenes of the Cold War Race for Missile Defense.* Washington, DC: Potomac Books, 2006.

Hickey, Gerald C. *Window on a War: An Anthropologist in the Vietnam Conflict.* Lubbock: Texas Tech University Press, 2002.

Hoffman, David E. *The Dead Hand: The Untold Story of the Cold War Arms Race and Its Dangerous Legacy.* New York: Doubleday, 2009.

Hoffman, Jon T. *A History of Innovation: U.S. Army Adaptation in War and Peace.* Washington, DC: Center of Military History, 2011.

Hord, R. Michael. *The Illiac IV: The First Supercomputer.* Rockville, MD: Computer Science Press, 1982.

Jardini, David. *Thinking Through the Cold War: RAND, National Security and Domestic Policy, 1945–1975.* Amazon Digital Services, Inc., August, 2013.

Jenkins, Brian Michael. *Countering al Qaeda: An Appreciation of the Situation and Suggestions for Strategy.* Santa Monica, CA: RAND, 2002.

Johnson, George. *Strange Beauty: Murray Gell-Mann and the Revolution in Twentieth-Century Physics.* New York: Alfred A. Knopf, 1999.

Johnston, Rob, Ph.D. *Analytic Culture in the U.S. Intelligence Community: An Ethnographic Study.* Washington, DC: Center for the Study of Intelligence, Central Intelligence Agency, 2005.

Kahn, Herman. *On Thermonuclear War.* New Brunswick, NJ: Transaction Publishers, 2007.

Kaku, Michio. *The Future of the Mind: The Scientific Quest to Understand, Enhance, and Empower the Mind.* New York: Doubleday, 2014.

Kaplan, Fred. *Daydream Believers: How a Few Grand Ideas Wrecked American Power.* Hoboken, NJ: John Wiley & Sons, 2008.

———. *The Wizards of Armageddon.* New York: Simon and Schuster, 1983.

Karnow, Stanley. *Vietnam: A History; The First Complete Account of Vietnam at War.* New York: Penguin, 1984.

Keeney, L. Douglas. *The Doomsday Scenario.* St. Paul, MN: MBI Publishing Company, 2002.

Killian, James R., Jr. *Sputnik, Scientists, and Eisenhower: A Memoir of the First Special Assistant to the President for Science and Technology.* Cambridge: MIT Press, 1977.

Kistiakowsky, George Bogdan. *A Scientist in the White House.* Cambridge: Harvard University Press, 1976.

Lapp, Ralph E. *The Voyage of the Lucky Dragon.* New York: Harper & Brothers, 1957.

Leonard, Robert. *Von Neumann, Morgenstern, and the Creation of Game Theory: From Chess to Social Science, 1900–1960.* New York: Cambridge University Press, 2010.

Licklider, J. C. R. *Libraries of the Future.* Cambridge: The MIT Press, 1965.

Lyon, David, ed. *Theorizing Surveillance: The Panopticon and Beyond.* Oregon: Willan Publishing, 2006.

Lyons, Gene Martin. *The Uneasy Partnership.* New York: Russell Sage Foundation, 1969.

Macgregor, Douglas. *Warrior's Rage: The Great Tank Battle of 73 Easting.* Annapolis, MD: Naval Institute Press, 2009.

Mahnken, Thomas G. *Technology and the American Way of War.* New York: Columbia University Press, 2008

Mangold, Tom, and Jeff Goldberg. *Plague Wars: The Terrifying Reality of Biological Warfare.* New York: St. Martin's Press, 1999.

Marks, John. *The Search for the "Manchurian Candidate."* New York: W. W. Norton, 1991.

Maynard, W. Barksdale. *Princeton: America's Campus.* Pennsylvania: Penn State University Press, 2012.

Mazzetti, Mark. *The Way of the Knife: The CIA, a Secret Army, and a War at the Ends of the Earth.* New York: Penguin, 2013.

McCullough, David. *Truman.* New York: Simon & Schuster, 1992.

McMaster, H. R. *Dereliction of Duty: Lyndon Johnson, Robert McNamara, the Joint Chiefs of Staff, and the Lies That Led to Vietnam.* New York: HarperPerennial, 1997.

McRaven, William H. *Spec Ops: Case Studies in Special Operations Warfare; Theory and Practice.* New York: Presidio Press, 1996.

Miller, Judith, Stephen Engelberg, and William Broad. *Germs: Biological Weapons and America's Secret War.* New York: Simon & Schuster, 2001.

Moreno, Jonathan D. *Mind Wars: Brain Science and the Military in the 21st Century.* New York: Bellevue Literary Press, 2012.

Neese, Harvey C., and John O'Donnell, eds. *Prelude to Tragedy: Vietnam, 1960–1965.* Annapolis, MD: Naval Institute Press, 2001.

O'Keefe, Bernard J. *Nuclear Hostages.* Boston: Houghton Mifflin, 1983.

Popp, Robert L., and John Yen, eds. *Emergent Information Technologies and Enabling Policies for Counter-Terrorism.* Hoboken, New Jersey: Wiley, 2006.

Porter, John Robert. *Have Clearance Will Travel.* Bloomington, IN: iUniverse, 2008.

Poundstone, William. *Prisoner's Dilemma.* New York: Anchor Books, 1992.

Powell, Colin L., with Joseph E. Persico. *My American Journey.* New York: Random House, 1995.

Priest, Dana, and William M. Arkin. *Top Secret America: The Rise of the New American Security State.* New York: Little, Brown, 2011.

Rice, Condoleezza. *No Higher Honor: A Memoir of My Years in Washington.* New York: Crown Publishers, 2011.

Roland, Alex, with Philip Shiman. *Strategic Computing: DARPA and the Quest for Machine Intelligence, 1983–1993.* Cambridge: MIT Press, 2002.

Rumsfeld, Donald. *Known and Unknown: A Memoir.* New York: Sentinel, 2011.

Salemink, Oscar. *The Ethnography of Vietnam's Central Highlanders: A Historical Contextualization, 1850–1900.* Honolulu: University of Hawaii Press, 2003.

Schlosser, Eric. *Command and Control: Nuclear Weapons, the Damascus Accident, and the Illusion of Safety.* New York: Penguin, 2013.

Schroen, Gary C. *First In: An Insider's Account of How the CIA Spearheaded the War on Terror in Afghanistan.* New York: Presidio Press, 2005.

Schwartz, Stephen I. *Atomic Audit: The Costs and Consequences of U.S. Nuclear Weapons Since 1940.* Washington, DC: Brookings Institution Press, 1998.

Schwartzkopf, Norman. *It Doesn't Take a Hero.* New York: Bantam Books, 1992.

Shepley, James, and Clay Blair Jr. *The Hydrogen Bomb: The Men, the Menace, the Mechanism.* New York: David McKay Company, 1954.

Smith, Bruce L. R. *The RAND Corporation: Case Study of a Non-Profit Advisory Corporation.* Cambridge: Harvard University Press, 1966.

Spector, Ronald H. *Advice and Support: The Early Years, 1941–1960, United States Army in Vietnam.* Washington: Center of Military History, United States Army, 1985.

Spence, Clark C. *The Rainmakers: American "Pluviculture" to World War II.* Lincoln: University of Nebraska Press, 1980.

Stanton, Doug. *Horse Soldiers: The Extraordinary Story of a Band of U.S. Soldiers Who Rode to Victory in Afghanistan.* New York: Scribner, 2009.

Stoll, Clifford. *The Cuckoo's Egg: Tracking a Spy Through the Maze of Computer Espionage.* New York: Doubleday, 1989.

Tanham, George K., with W. Robert Warne, Earl J. Young, and William A. Nighswonger. *War Without Guns: American Civilians in Rural Vietnam.* New York: Frederick A. Praeger, 1966.

Teller, Edward. *Memoirs: A Twentieth-Century Journey in Science and Politics.* Cambridge: Perseus Publishing, 2001.

Townes, Charles H. *How the Laser Happened: Adventures of a Scientist.* New York: Oxford University Press, 1999.

Vogel, Steve. *The Pentagon: A History. The Untold Story of the Wartime Race to Build the Pentagon—And to Restore It Sixty Years Later.* New York: Random House, 2007.

von Neumann, John. *The Computer and the Brain.* New Haven: Yale University Press, 1958.

von Storch, Hans, and Klaus Hasselman. *Seventy Years of Exploration in Oceanography: A Prolonged Weekend Discussion with Walter Munk.* Berlin: Springer-Verlag, 2010.

Waldrop, M. Mitchell. *The Dream Machine: J. C. R. Licklider and the Revolution That Made Computing Personal.* New York: Viking Penguin, 2001.

Wheelis, Mark, Lajos Rózsa, and Malcolm Dando. *Deadly Cultures: Biological Weapons Since 1945.* Cambridge: Harvard University Press, 2006.

Whitman, Marina von Neumann. *The Martian's Daughter: A Memoir.* Ann Arbor: University of Michigan Press, 2013.

Whittle, Richard. *Predator: The Secret Origins of the Drone.* New York: Henry Holt and Company, 2014.

Wigner, Eugene P. *Survival and the Bomb: Methods of Civil Defense.* Bloomington: Indiana University Press, 1969.

Wills, Garry. *Bomb Power: The Modern Presidency and the National Security State.* New York: Penguin, 2010.

York, Herbert F. *The Advisors: Oppenheimer, Teller, and the Superbomb.* Stanford: Stanford University Press, 1976.

———. *Arms and the Physicist.* Woodbury, NY: American Institute of Physics Press, 1995.

———. *Making Weapons, Talking Peace: A Physicist's Odyssey from Hiroshima to Geneva.* New York: Basic Books, 1987.

Zak, Paul J. *The Moral Molecule: How Trust Works.* New York: Penguin Group, 2012.

Zasloff, Tela. *Saigon Dreaming: Recollections of Indochina Days.* New York: St. Martin's Press, 1990.

Zelicoff, Alan P., M.D., and Michael Bellomo. *Microbe: Are We Ready for the Next Plague?* New York: American Management Association, 2005.

Monographs and Reports

Advanced Research Projects Agency. *The Advanced Research Projects Agency, 1958–1974.* Richard J. Barber Associates, Washington, DC, December 1975.

———. *Combat Development & Test Center: Vietnam.* May 1962.

———."Counterinsurgency: A Symposium, April 16–20, 1962." RAND Corporation, Washington, DC, 1962.

———. *Counter-Insurgency Game Design Feasibility and Evaluation Study.* SD-301. ABT Associates, Inc., Cambridge, MA, November 1965.

———. *Guerilla Activity Defection Study.* DEC-63-1236. Defense Research Corporation, McLean, VA, December 1963.

———. *Operation Pink Rose: Final Report.* ARPA Order No. 818. U.S. Department of Agriculture–Forest Service, May 1967.

———. *Overseas Defense Research: A Brief Survey of Non-Lethal Weapons (U).* ARPA Order no. 1509. Battelle, Columbus, OH, April 30, 1971.

———. *Project Agile: OCONUS Defoliation Test Program.* ARPA Order No. 423. United States Army Biological Center, Fort Detrick, MD, July 1966.

———. *Project Agile: Remote Area Conflict Information Center (RACIC) Selected Accession List.* Battelle Memorial Institute, Columbus, OH, July 1965.

———. *Project Agile: Remote Area Research and Engineering, Semiannual Report, 1 July–30 September 1962.* AD 342163. Battelle Memorial Institute, Columbus, OH, 1962.

———. *Project Agile: Remote Area Research and Engineering, Semiannual Report, 1 July–31 December 1963.* Battelle Memorial Institute, Columbus, OH, February 1, 1964.

———. Project Agile. "The Use of a Marking Agent for Identification by Dogs." Battelle Memorial Institute, Columbus, OH, March 11, 1966.

———. *Report of the Senior Working Group on Military Operations Other Than War (OOTW).* ARPA Order No. A119. May 1994.

———. *The Utilization of ARPA-Supported Research for International Security Planning: Interim Technical Report No. 2.* AD-753476, Los Angeles, CA, October 1972.

Advanced Research Projects Division. *Identification of Certain Current Defense Problems and Possible Means of Solution.* IDA-ARPA Study No. 1. Institute for Defense Analyses, Alexandria, VA, August 1958.

AGARD-NATO. Working Group 2 of Phase I (Third Exercise) on Environmental Warfare of the von Kármán Committee. "Long-Term Scientific Studies for the Standing Group North Atlantic Treaty Organization." NATO Secret VKC-EX3-PH1/GP2. November 1962.

Ahern, Thomas L., Jr. *CIA and Rural Pacification in South Vietnam (U).* Center for the Study of Intelligence, Central Intelligence Agency, Langley, VA, August 2001.

American Legion. "The War Within: Traumatic Brain Injury and Post-Traumatic Stress Disorder: Findings and Recommendations." TBI/PTSD Ad Hoc Committee, Washington, DC, September 2013.

Betts, Russell, and Frank Denton. "An Evaluation of Chemical Crop Destruction in Vietnam." RM-5446-1-ISA/ARPA. RAND Corporation, Santa Monica, CA, October 1967.

Block, Steven M. "Living Nightmares: Biological Threats Enabled by Molecular Biology." McLean, VA, Summer 1997. [Chapter Two (pp. 39–76) of *The New Terror: Facing the Threat of Biological and Chemical Weapons.* Edited by Sidney Drell, Abraham D. Sofaer, and George D. Wilson. Hoover Institution Press, Stanford University, Stanford, CA, 1999]

Bochner, S. *John Von Neumann: 1903–1957, A Biographical Memoir.* National Academy of Sciences, Washington, DC, 1958.

Brown, James W. *Anticrop Warfare Research, Task-01.* U.S. Army Chemical Corps Research and Development Command, U.S. Army Biological Laboratories, Fort Detrick, MD, April 1962.

———. *Vegetational Spray Tests in South Vietnam.* U.S. Army Chemical Corps Biological Laboratories, Fort Detrick, MD, April 1962.

Brundage, T. W. "Military Research and Development Center, Quarterly Report," October 1, 1963–December 31, 1963. Joint Thai-U.S. Research and Development Center, Bangkok, Thailand, 1964.

Buckingham, William A., Jr. *Operation Ranch Hand: The Air Force and Herbicides in Southeast Asia, 1961–1971.* Office of Air Force History, United States Air Force, Washington, DC, 1982.

Cebrowski, Arthur K. "Transforming Defense: Trends in Security Competition." Office of Force Transformation, Defense Pentagon, June 15, 2004.

Center for Strategic and Budgetary Assessments. *Six Decades of Guided Munitions and Battle Networks: Progress and Prospects.* Washington, DC, March 2007.

Center of Military History: United States Army. *A History of Innovation: U.S. Army Adaptation in War and Peace.* CMH Pub 40-6-1, Washington, DC, 2009.

———. *Tip of the Spear: U.S. Army Small-Unit Action in Iraq 2004–2007.* CMH Pub 70-113-1. Global War on Terrorism Series, Washington, DC, 2009.

———. *United States Army in Vietnam: MACV The Joint Command in the Years of Withdrawal, 1968–1973.* CMH Pub-91-7. Washington, DC, 2006.

———. *U.S. Army Counterinsurgency and Contingency Operations Doctrine: 1941–1976.* CMH Pub 70-98-1. Washington, DC, 2006.

Chandler, Craig C., and J. R. Bentley. *Forest Fire as a Military Weapon, Final Report.* Advanced Research Projects Agency, Overseas Defense Research. June 1970.

Congressional Research Service. *Network Centric Warfare: Background and Oversight Issues for Congress.* CRS Report for Congress. June 2004.

Cosby, L. Neale. *Simnet: An Insider's Perspective.* IDA Document D-1661. Institute for Defense Analyses, Alexandria, VA, March 1995.

Davison, W. Phillips. *User's Guide to the Rand Interviews in Vietnam.* R-1024-ARPA. RAND Corporation, Santa Monica, CA, March 1972.

Defense Advanced Research Projects Agency. *Cybernetics Technology Division Program Completion Report.* Office of Naval Research, Arlington, VA, April 1981.

———. *DARPA Biological Warfare Defense Program: Program Overview.* Defense Sciences Office, Arlington, VA, n.d.

———. *DARPA: 50 Years of Bridging the Gap Powered by Ideas, 1958–2008.* Faircount, LLC., Tampa, FL, 2008.

———. *Fiscal Year 1982 Research & Development Program: Summary Statement.* AD-A101575. March 1981.

———. *A History of the Arpanet: The First Decade.* DARPA Report No. 4799. Bolt Beranek and Newman, Inc., Arlington, VA, April 1, 1981.

———. *Team Training and Evaluation Strategies: A State-of-Art Review.* AD-A 027507. Human Resources Research Organization, Alexandria, VA, June 1978.

———. "Total Information Awareness Program (TIA) System Description Document (SDD)." Version 1.1, July 19, 2002.

Defense Nuclear Agency. *Castle Series 1954: United States Atmospheric Nuclear Weapons Tests, Nuclear Test Personnel Review.* DNA 6035F, April 1982.

———. *Operation Argus 1958: United States Atmospheric Nuclear Weapons Tests, Nuclear Test Personnel Review.* DNA 6039F, April 1982.

———. *Operation Dominic I: 1962 United States Atmospheric Nuclear Weapons Tests, Nuclear Test Personnel Review.* DNA 6040F, February 1983.

Defense Science Board. *Defense Science Board Task Force on the Role and Status of DoD Red Teaming Activities.* Office of the Under Secretary of Defense for Acquisition, Technology, and Logistics, Washington, DC, September 2003.

Defense Science Board Task Group. *The Behavioral Sciences.* Office of the Director of Defense Research and Engineering, Washington, DC, May 1968.

Defense Threat Reduction Agency. *Castle Bravo: Fifty Years of Legend and Lore; A Guide to Off-Site Radiation Exposures.* Defense Threat Reduction Information Analysis Center, Kirtland AFB, NM, January 2013.

Donnell, John C., and Gerald C. Hickey. *The Vietnamese "Strategic Hamlets": A Preliminary Report.* RM-3208-ARPA. RAND Corporation, Santa Monica, CA, September 1962.

Donnell, John C., Guy J. Pauker, and Joseph J. Zasloff. *Viet Cong Motivation and Morale in 1964: A Preliminary Report.* RM-4507/3-ISA. RAND Corporation, Santa Monica, CA, March 1965.

Doolittle, James H., William B. Franke, Morris Hadley, and William D. Pawley. "Report on the Covert Activities of the Central Intelligence Agency." Special Study Group, Washington, DC, July 1954.

Eckhart, Major General George S. *Vietnam Studies: Command and Control, 1950–1969.* Department of the Army, Washington, DC, 1974.

Ehlschlaeger, Charles. "Understanding Megacities with the Reconnaissance, Surveillance, and Intelligence Paradigm." U.S. Army Engineer Research Development Center, April 2014.

Foster, John S. "Alfred Dodd Starbird, 1912–1983." *National Academy of Engineering,* Volume 3, The National Academies Press, Washington, DC, 1989.

Gates, W. L. "Rand/ARPA Climate Dynamics Research: Executive Summary and Final Report." R-2015-ARPA. RAND Corporation, Santa Monica, CA, January 1977.

Gatlin, Colonel Jesse C. *Project CHECO Southeast Asia Report, "IGLOO WHITE (Initial Phase), 31 July 1968."* HQ PACAF, Directorate, Tactical Evaluation, CHECO Division, 1968.

Glenn, Russell W. *Combat in Hell: A Consideration of Constrained Urban Warfare.* MR-780-A/DARPA. RAND Corporation, Santa Monica, CA, 1996.

Gorman, Paul F. *Supertroop Via I-Port: Distributed Simulation Technology for Combat Development and Training Development.* IDA Paper P-2374. Institute for Defense Analyses, Alexandria, VA, August 1990.

Gorman, Paul F., and H. R. McMaster. "The Future of the Armed Services: Training for the 21st Century." Statement before the Senate Armed Services Committee. Washington, DC, May 21, 1992.

Gouré, Leon. "*Quarterly Report on Viet Cong Motivation and Morale Project, October–December 1966.*" RAND Corporation, Santa Monica, CA, January 1967.

———. "Some Findings of the Viet Cong Motivation and Morale Study, January–June 1966: A Briefing to the Joint Chiefs of Staff." RAND Corporation, Santa Monica, CA, August 1, 1966.

———. *Some Preliminary Observations on NVA Behavior During Infiltration.* D-16339-PR. RAND Corporation, Santa Monica, CA, November 3, 1967.

———. "Southeast Asia Trip Report. Part 1. The Impact of Air Power in South Vietnam." RM-4400/1-PR. RAND Corporation, Santa Monica, CA, December 1964.

Gouré, Leon, Douglas Scott, and Anthony J. Russo. *Some Findings of the Viet Cong Motivation and Morale Study: June–December 1965.* RM-4911-2-ISA/ARPA. RAND Corporation, Santa Monica, CA, February 1966.

Gouré, Leon, and C. A. H. Thomson. *Some Impressions of Viet Cong Vulnerabilities: An Interim Report.* RM-4699-1-ISA/ARPA. RAND Corporation, Santa Monica, CA, September 1965.

Hansen, Chuck. *The Swords of Armageddon, U.S. Nuclear Weapons Development Since 1945, Volumes 1–8.* Chuckelea Publications, Sunnyvale, CA, August 1995.

Hanyok, Robert J. *Spartans in Darkness: American SIGINT and the Indochina War, 1945–1975.* National Security Agency/Central Security Service. Fort Meade, MD, February 1998.

Harris, Jack. *Acoustical Techniques/Designs Investigated During the Southeast Asia Conflict: 1966–1972: Final Report.* Naval Air Development Center, Warminster, PA. October 1980.

Headquarters Air Force Special Weapons Center Air Force Systems Command. "Preliminary Plan for Operation Fish Bowl (U)." AFSWC TR-61-96. Kirtland AFB, NM, November 1961.

Headquarters Department of the Army. *Tactics in Counterinsurgency.* Field Manual no. 3-24.2. Washington, DC, April 2009.

Hickey, Gerald C. *The Highland People of South Vietnam: Social and Economic Development.* RM-5281/1-ARPA. RAND Corporation, Santa Monica, CA, September 1967.

———. *The Major Ethnic Groups of the South Vietnamese Highlands.* RM-4041-ARPA. RAND Corporation, Santa Monica, CA, April 1964.

———. "The Military Advisor and His Foreign Counterpart: The Case in Vietnam." RM-4882-ARPA. RAND Corporation, Santa Monica, CA, March 1965.

Historical Division Joint Secretariat, Joint Chiefs of Staff. *The History of the Joint Chiefs of Staff: The Joint Chiefs of Staff and the War in Vietnam, 1960–1968*. Part 3. 87-F-0671, July 1970.

Historical Division Office of Information Services, Air Force Special Weapons Center. *History of Task Group 7.4 Participation in Operation Castle, 1 January 1953–26 June 1954*. Kirtland AFB, NM, November 1954.

Hundley, Richard O., and Eugene C. Gritton. *Future Technology-Driven Revolutions in Military Operations, Results of a Workshop*. National Defense Research Institute, Documented Briefing Series. RAND, Santa Monica, CA, 1994.

"Intelligence Successes and Failures in Operations Desert Shield/Storm." Report of the Oversight and Investigations Subcommittee, Committee on Armed Services, U.S. House of Representatives, August 1993.

Istituto di Fisica Teorica. *The War Physicists: Documents about the European Protest Against the Physicists Working for the American Military Through the JASON Division of the Institute for Defence Analysis*[sic] *(IDA)-1972*. Mostra d'Oltremare, Naples.

Jason Division, IDA. *Air-Supported Anti-Infiltration Barrier*. Study S-255. Alexandria, VA, August 1966.

———. *Generation and Airborne Detection of Internal Waves from an Object Moving Through a Stratified Ocean*. Volume 2. *Supporting Analyses*. Study S-334. Alexandria, VA, April 1969.

———. *Project Seesaw (U)*. Study S-307. Alexandria, VA, February 1968.

———. *Tactical Nuclear Weapons in Southeast Asia*. Study S-266. Alexandria, VA, March 1967.

Jason, The MITRE Corporation. *Biodetection Architectures*. JSR-02-330. McLean, VA, February 2003.

———. *Characterization of Underground Facilities*. JSR-97-155. McLean, VA, April 1999.

———. *Civilian Biodefense*. JSR-99-105. McLean, VA, January 2000.

———. *Human Performance*. JSR-07-625. McLean, VA, March 2008.

———. *Impacts of Severe Space Weather on the Electric Grid*. JSR-11-320. McLean, VA, November 2011.

———. *Rare Events*. JSR-09-108. McLean, VA, October 2009.

Jason, SRI International. *Tunnel Detection*. JSR-79-11. Arlington, VA, April 1980.

Joint Chiefs of Staff Special Historical Study. *The Worldwide Military Command and Control System: A Historical Perspective (1960–1977)*. September 1980.

Joint Task Force Seven. *Operation Castle: Pacific Proving Grounds, March–May 1954, Report of Commander, Task Group 7.1.* Armed Forces Special Weapons Project, September 1954.

Knarr, William. "Mazar-e Sharif Battle Site Survey Support Documents (Revised)." IDA Document D-4350. Institute for Defense Analyses, Alexandria, VA, June 2011.

Knarr, William and Robert Richbourg. "Learning from the First Victory of the 21st Century: Mazar-e Sharif (Revised)." IDA Document D-4015. Institute for Defense Analyses, Alexandria, VA, June 2010.

Lambeth, Benjamin S. "Technology Trends in Air Warfare." RP-561. RAND Project Air Force, Santa Monica, CA, 1996.

Lavalle, Major A. J. C. *The Tale of Two Bridges and The Battle for the Skies over North Vietnam.* Office of the Air Force History Office, United States Air Force, Washington, DC, 1985.

Lulejian, N. M. "Effect of Superweapons upon the Climate of the World: A Preliminary Study." C2-22190. Headquarters Air Research & Development Command, Baltimore, MD. September 1952.

MacDonald, Gordon J. "Jason—The Early Years." Presented at Jason Advisory Board, Arlington, VA, December 12, 1986.

———. "Jason and DCPG—Ten Lessons." Presented at Jason's 25th Anniversary Celebration (no location given), November 30, 1984.

Martin, Michael F. "Vietnamese Victims of Agent Orange and U.S.-Vietnam Relations." RL34761. Congressional Research Service. August 29, 2012.

McMaster, Captain H. R. "Battle of 73 Easting: Eagle Troop, Second Squadron, Second Armored Cavalry Regiment (During the war with Iraq on February 26, 1991)." Fort Benning, GA (n.d.).

McNalty, Bernard C. "Stalemate: U.S. Marines from Bunker Hill to the Hook." U.S. Marine Corps Historical Center, Washington, DC, 2001.

Melissinos, A. C. "Nicholas C. Christofilos: His Contributions to Physics." Department of Physics & Astronomy, University of Rochester, Rochester, NY, November 1993.

Military History Branch, Office of the Secretary, Joint Staff, Military Assistance Command, Vietnam. *Command History 1967.* Volume 3. AD-A955 099, June 4, 1986.

Multi-National Corps Iraq. "TF TROY Counter IED Update, USNA Alumni Association." Explosive Ordnance Disposal (EOD) Weapons Intelligence (WI) Unclassified/FOUO, briefing document, (n.d.).

Munk, Walter, Naomi Oreskes, and Richard Muller. "Gordon James Fraser MacDonald, July 30, 1929–May 14, 2002." National Academy of Science, The National Academies Press, Washington, DC, 2004.

Mutch, R. W., C. C. Chandler, J. R. Bentley, C. A. O'Dell, and S. N. Hirsch. *Operation Pink Rose*. ARPA Order no. 818. U.S. Department of Agriculture–Forest Service, May 1967.

National Academy of Sciences. National Research Council. *Civil Defense: Project Harbor Summary Report*. Publication 1237. Washington, DC, 1964.

National Aeronautics & Space Administration. "A Recommended National Program in Weather Modification: A Report to the Interdepartmental Committee for Atmospheric Sciences." ICAS Report no. 10a. Washington, DC, November 1966.

National Research Council of the National Academies: Committee on Materials and Manufacturing Processes for Advanced Sensors, Board on Manufacturing and Engineering Design, Division on Engineering and Physical Sciences. *Sensor Systems for Biological Agent Attacks: Protecting Buildings and Military Bases*. Washington, DC: National Academies Press, 2006.

National Science Foundation, Special Commission on Weather Modification. "Weather and Climate Modification." NSF 66-3, December 1965.

Nigh, Norman. "An Operator's Guide to Human Terrain Team." U.S. Naval War College, Newport, RI, 2008.

Office of the Secretary, Joint Staff, MACV, Military History Branch. *Command History, United States Military Assistance Command Vietnam: 1967*. Volume 3. AD-A955099. Department of the Army, San Francisco, CA, 1968.

Office of the Under Secretary of Defense for Acquisition, Technology, and Logistics. *Defense Science Board Task Force on Directed Energy Weapons*. Washington, DC, December 2007.

Ogle, William E. *Daily Diary, Bikini Atoll, 1954*. U.S. Atomic Energy Commission.

———. *Operation Castle: The Operation Plan No. 1-53, Task Group 7.1*. Extracted Version, December 1953.

Paolucci, Dominic A. "Summary Report of the Long Range Research and Development Planning Program." DNA-75-03055. Lulejian and Associates, Falls Church, VA, February 7, 1975.

Pauker, Guy. "Treatment of POWs, Defectors, and Suspects in South Vietnam." D-13171-ISA. RAND Corporation, Santa Monica, CA, December 8, 1964.

Peterson, Val. *Kefauver Committee Hearing: Administrator's Statement of March 3*. Federal Civil Defense Administration. Washington, DC, March 1955.

Poindexter, John. *Transcript of Remarks as Prepared for Delivery by Dr. John Poindexter, Director, Information Awareness Office of DARPA*. DARPATech 2002 Conference, Anaheim, CA, August 2002.

Polk, Charles. *Pre-Game-Theory-Based Information Technology (GAMBIT) Study.* DARPA Order no. N229. Air Force Research Laboratory, Rome, NY, October 2003.

Press, S. J. *Estimating from Misclassified Data.* RM-5360-ISA/ARPA. RAND Corporation, Santa Monica, CA, July 1967.

Reed, Sidney, Richard H. Van Atta, and Seymour Deitchman. *DARPA Technical Accomplishments.* Volume 1. *An Historical Review of Selected DARPA Projects.* IDA Paper P-2192. Institute for Defense Analyses, Alexandria, VA, February 1990.

Rego, Lieutenant Colonel Robert D. "Anti-Infiltration Barrier Technology and the Battle for Southeast Asia, 1966–1972." Air Command and Staff College, Air University, Maxwell Air Force Base, AL, April 2000.

"Report to the Commission to Assess the Threat to the United States from Electromagnetic Pulse (EMP) Attack." Critical National Infrastructures Report. April 2008.

Science Advisory Committee. Security Resources Panel. "Deterrence & Survival in the Nuclear Age." NSC 5724 (2). Washington, DC, November 1957.

Smith, Andrew. "Improvised Explosive Devices in Iraq, 2003–09: A Case of Operational Surprise and Institutional Response." The Letort Papers, Strategic Studies Institute, U.S. Army War College, Carlisle, PA, April 2011.

Solon, Jenny. *MRAP Vehicles: Tactics, Techniques, and Procedures.* No. 08-30. Center for Army Lessons Learned (CALL), Combined Arms Center (CAC), Ft. Leavenworth, KS, September 2008.

Stewart, Richard W. "The United States Army in Somalia, 1992–1994," Center of Military History, United States Army, Washington, DC, 2003.

Thorpe, Jack. "Future Views: Aircrew Training, 1980–2000," Air Force Office of Scientific Research, Bolling Air Force Base, Washington, DC, September 1978.

———. "Trends in Modeling, Simulation, & Gaming: Personal Observations About the Past Thirty Years and Speculation About the Next Ten." Interservice/Industry Training, Simulation, and Education Conference (I/ITSEC), 2010

U.S. Army Office of the Deputy Under Secretary of the Army for Operations Research. *History of Operations Research in the United States Army.* Volume 2. *1961–1973.* CMH Pub. 70-105-1. Washington, DC, 2008.

U.S. Army Ordnance Corps. Chief of Ordnance. *Soldiers Improvised Explosive Device (IED) Awareness Guide: Iraq & Afghanistan Theaters of Operation.* TC9-21-01 (093-89-01), EOD Training Department, Redstone Arsenal, AL, May 2004.

U.S. Department of Defense. *Defense Science Board Task Force on Defense Intelligence, Counterinsurgency (COIN) Intelligence, Surveillance, and Reconnaissance (ISR) Operations.* Office of the Undersecretary of Defense for Acquisition, Technology, Washington, DC, February 2011.

U.S. Department of Defense, Defense Science Board, *Task Force Report: The Role of Autonomy in DoD Systems.* Office of the Undersecretary of Defense for Acquisition, Technology, Washington, DC, July 2012.

U.S. Department of Defense, *Fiscal Year (FY) 2015 Budget Estimates, Defense Advanced Research Projects Agency, Defense Wide Justification Book,* Volumes 1–5 (unclassified).

U.S. Department of Defense. International Security Affairs and Advanced Research Projects Agency. *An Evaluation of Chemical Crop Destruction in Vietnam.* RM-5446-1-ISA/ARPA. RAND Corporation, Santa Monica, CA, October 1967.

U.S. Department of Defense. Joint Chiefs of Staff. Historical Division. *Chronology of Significant Events and Decisions Relating to the U.S. Missile and Earth Satellite Development Programs.* Supplement 3. *1 November 1959 through 31 October 1960.* December 29, 1960.

U.S. Department of Defense. Office of the Inspector General. *Defense Advanced Research Projects Agency Ethics Program Met Federal Government Standards.* January 24, 2013.

U.S. Department of Defense. Office of the Secretary of Defense. *Proliferation: Threat and Response.* November 1997.

U.S. Department of Defense, "Unmanned Systems Integrated Roadmap FY2011–2036." (n.d.)

U.S. Department of Defense, "Unmanned Systems Integrated Roadmap FY2013–2038." (n.d.)

U.S. Department of Defense and U.S. Department of Energy. "Report on the Integrated Chemical and Biological Defense Research, Development and Acquisition Plan for the Departments of Defense and Energy: Bio Point Detection." March 2001.

U.S. Department of Energy. *An Account of the Return to Nuclear Weapons Testing by the United States After the Test Moratorium, 1958–1961.* NVO-291, October 1985.

U.S. Department of Energy. Office of the Executive Secretariat. History Division. *The United States Nuclear Weapon Program: A Summary History.* DOE/ES-0005 (Draft), March 1983.

U.S. General Accounting Office. "Activities of the Research and Development Center–Thailand, Advanced Research Projects Agency." B-167324. Washington, DC, December 1971.

U.S. General Accounting Office, "Unmanned Aerial Vehicles: Department of Defense, Acquisition Efforts." Testimony, GAO/T-NSIAD-97-138. Washington, DC, 1997.

U.S. House of Representatives. Committee on Homeland Security. *One Year Later: Implementing the Bio-Surveillance Requirements of the 9/11 Act. Hearing before the Sub-Committee on Emerging Threats, Cybersecurity, and Science and Technology of the Committee on Homeland Security, House of Representatives One Hundred Tenth Congress, Second Session.* Serial no. 110-128, July 2008.

U.S. House of Representatives. House Permanent Select Committee on Intelligence. *Performance Audit of Department of Defense Intelligence, Surveillance, and Reconnaissance.* April 2012.

United States Senate Committee. *Hearings Before the Subcommittee on Civil Defense of the Committee on Armed Services, United States Senate, Eighty-fourth Congress, First Session, on Operations and Policies of the Civil Defense Program.* 1955.

University of California at Berkeley. *Social Responsibility.* Volume 2, number 1. *Information for Students on the Military Aspects of Careers in Physics.* 1989.

Van Atta, Richard H., and Alethia Cook, Ivars Gutmanis, Michael J. Lippitz, Jasper Lupo, Rob Mahoney, and Jack H. Nunn. *Transformation and Transition: DARPA's Role in Fostering an Emerging Revolution in Military Affairs.* Volume 2. *Overall Assessment.* IDA Paper P-3698. Institute for Defense Analyses, Alexandria, VA, April 2003.

Van Atta, Richard H., and Michael J. Lippitz with Jasper C. Lupo, Rob Mahoney, and Jack H. Nunn. *Transformation and Transition: DARPA's Role in Fostering an Emerging Revolution in Military Affairs.* Volume 1. *Overall Assessment.* IDA Paper P-3698. Institute for Defense Analyses, Alexandria, VA, April 2003.

Van Atta, Richard H., Sidney Reed, and Seymour Deitchman. *DARPA Technical Accomplishments.* Volume 2. *An Historical Review of Selected DARPA Projects.* IDA Paper P-2429. Institute for Defense Analyses, Alexandria, VA, April 1991.

———. *DARPA Technical Accomplishments.* Volume 3. *An Overall Perspective and Assessment of the Technical Accomplishments of the Defense Advanced Research Projects Agency: 1958–1990.* IDA Paper P-2538. Institute for Defense Analyses, Alexandria, VA, July 1991.

Wainstein, L., C. D. Cremeans, J. K. Moriarty, and J. Ponturo. *The Evolution of U.S. Strategic Command and Control and Warning, 1945–1972 (U).* Study S-467. Institute for Defense Analyses, Alexandria, VA, June 1975.

Watts, Barry D. "Precision Strike: An Evolution, Summary Report." *The National Interest,* November 2, 2013.

———. "Six Decades of Guided Munitions and Battle Networks: Progress and Prospects." Center for Strategic and Budgetary Assessments, Washington, DC, March 2007.

Weiner, Milton G. *U.S. Air Force Project Rand Research Memorandum: War Gaming Methodology*. RM-2413. RAND Corporation, Santa Monica, CA, July 1959.

White, Robert. *Anthropometric Survey of the Royal Thai Armed Forces*. U.S. Army Natick Laboratories, Natick, MA, June 1964.

Wohlstetter, Albert. "The Delicate Balance of Terror." RAND Corporation, Santa Monica, CA, November 1958.

Wolf, W. L. *Handbook of Military Infrared Technology*. Office of Naval Research, Department of the Navy, Washington, DC, 1965.

Wolk, Herman S. *USAF Plans and Policies R&D for Southeast Asia, 1965–1967*. Office of Air Force History. K 168.01-35. June 1969.

Worley, D. R., H. K. Simpson, F. L. Moses, M. Aylward, M. Bailey, and D. Fish. *Utility of Modeling and Simulation in the Department of Defense: Initial Data Collection*. IDA Document D-1825. Institute for Defense Analyses, Alexandria, VA, May 1996.

Zasloff, Joseph J. *Origins of the Insurgency in South Vietnam: The Role of the Southern Vietminh Cadres*. RM-5163/2-ISA/ARPA. RAND Corporation, Santa Monica, CA, March 1967.

———. *Political Motivation of the Viet Cong: The Vietminh Regroupees*. RM-4703/2-ISA/ARPA. RAND Corporation, Santa Monica, CA, August 1966.

———. *The Role of North Vietnam in the Southern Insurgency*. RM-4140-PR. RAND Corporation, Santa Monica, CA, July 1964.

Statements to Congress

Abizaid, General John P. Commander, U.S. Central Command, "Testimony Before Congress, Senate Armed Services Committee," September 25, 2003.

Alexander, Jane A. Acting Director, Defense Advanced Research Projects Agency, "Statement Submitted to the Subcommittee on Emerging Threats and Capabilities Committee on Armed Services," U.S. Senate, June 5, 2001.

Alibek, Kenneth. Program Manager, Battelle Memorial Institute, "Statement before the Joint Economic Committee, Terrorist and Intelligence Operations: Potential Impact on the U.S. Economy." U.S. Congress, Wednesday, May 20, 1998.

———. Chief Scientist, Hadron, Inc., "Statement before U.S. House of Representatives, Committee on Armed Services, Subcommittee on

Research and Development and Subcommittee on Procurement, Chemical and Biological Defense for U.S. Forces," U.S. Congress, October 20, 1999.

———. Chief Scientist, Hadron, Inc., Former First Deputy Chief, Biopreparat (USSR), "Testimony before the Special Oversight Panel on Terrorism of the Committee on Armed Services," U.S. House of Representatives, Tuesday, May 23, 2000.

Dugan, Regina E., Director, Defense Advanced Research Projects Agency, "Statement Submitted to the Subcommittee on Terrorism, Unconventional Threats and Capabilities, House Armed Services Committee," U.S. House of Representatives, March 23, 2010.

Fernandez, Frank. Director, Defense Advanced Research Projects Agency, "Statement before the Subcommittee on Emerging Threats and Capabilities Committee on Armed Services," U.S. Senate, March 21, 2000.

Gorman, P. F. General, USA (retired) and H. R. McMaster, Captain, Armor, USA, "The Future of the Armed Services: Training for the 21st Century," Statement before the Senate Armed Services Committee, May 21, 1992.

Leheny, Robert. Acting Director, Defense Advanced Research Projects Agency, "Statement Submitted to the Subcommittee on Terrorism, Unconventional Threats and Capabilities, House Armed Services Committee," U.S. House of Representatives, May 20, 2009.

Lynn, Larry. Director, Defense Advanced Research Projects Agency, "Statement before the Acquisition and Technology Subcommittee," U.S. Senate Armed Services Committee, March 11, 1997.

Nunn, Sam. Former Senator. "Remarks for Members of the Subcommittee on National Security, Veterans Affairs, and International Relations, Hearing on Combating Terrorism, Federal Response to a Biological Weapons Attack," U.S. House of Representatives, July 23, 2001.

Prabhakar, Arati. Director, Defense Advanced Research Projects Agency, "Statement Submitted to the Subcommittee on Intelligence, Emerging Threats and Capabilities," U.S. House of Representatives, March 26, 2014.

Preston, Richard. Author of *The Bioweaponeers* and *The Hot Zone,* "Statement Submitted before Senate Judiciary Subcommittee on Technology, Terrorism and Government Information and the Senate Select Committee on Intelligence on Chemical and Biological Weapons, Chemical and Biological Weapons Threats to America: Are We Prepared?" April 22, 1998.

Tether, Tony. Director, Defense Advanced Research Projects Agency, "Statement Submitted before the Subcommittee on Military Research and Development, Committee on Armed Services," U.S. House of Representatives, June 26, 2001.

———. "Statement Submitted to the Subcommittee on Terrorism, Unconventional Threats and Capabilities, House Armed Services Committee," U.S. House of Representatives, March 19, 2003, and March 27, 2003.

———. "Statement Submitted to the Subcommittee on Terrorism, Unconventional Threats and Capabilities, House Armed Services Committee," U.S. House of Representatives, March 10, 2005.

———. "Statement Submitted to the Subcommittee on Terrorism, Unconventional Threats and Capabilities, House Armed Services Committee," U.S. House of Representatives, March 21, 2007.

———. "Submitted to the Subcommittee on Terrorism, Unconventional Threats and Capabilities, House Armed Services Committee," U.S. House of Representatives, March 13, 2008.

Oral Histories

Abboud, A. Robert. Oral History Interview with Mark DePue. Abraham Lincoln Presidential Library, September 26, 2007.

Brueckner, Keith. Oral History Interview with Finn Aaserud. American Institute of Physics, July 2, 1986.

Deitchman, Seymour J. Oral History Project Interview by Dr. Bob Sheldon and Dr. Yuna Wong. Military Operations Research Society (MORS), September 12, 2008, and October 8, 2008.

Drell, Sidney. Oral History Interview with Finn Aaserud. American Institute of Physics, July 1, 1986.

Fitch, Val. Oral History Interview with Finn Aaserud. American Institute of Physics, December 18, 1986.

Garwin, Richard. Oral History Interview with Finn Aaserud. American Institute of Physics, June 24, 1991.

Gorman, General Paul F. (retired). "Cardinal Point: An Oral History—Training Soldiers and Becoming a Strategist in Peace and War." Combat Studies Institute, 2010–11.

Kendall, Henry. Oral History Interview with Finn Aaserud. American Institute of Physics, November 25, 1986.

Lewis, Hal. Oral History Interview with Finn Aaserud. American Institute of Physics, July 6, 1986.

Lukasik, Stephen. Oral History Interview with Finn Aaserud. American Institute of Physics, April 21, 1987.

MacDonald, Gordon. Oral History Interview with Finn Aaserud. American Institute of Physics, April 16, 1986.

Ruina, Jack P. Oral History Interview with Finn Aaserud. American Institute of Physics, August 8, 1991.

Sullivan, Ambassador William H. Oral History Interview with Major Richard B. Clement, U.S. Air Force Historical Research Agency, April 15, 1970.

Talley, Joan Dulles. Interview with Mark DePue. Abraham Lincoln Presidential Library, November 28, 2007.

Taylor, Robert. Oral History Interview with Paul McJones. Computer History Museum, October 10–11, 2008.

Wheeler, John Archibald. Oral History Interview with Finn Aaserud. American Institute of Physics, May 4, May 23, and November 28, 1988.

Woods, James L. Oral History Interview with Charles Stuart Kennedy. Association for Diplomatic Studies and Training, Foreign Affairs, Oral History Project, October 31, 2001.

Articles

ABC News. "When Anthrax Let Loose Before." October 19, 2014.

ABC News. *World News Tonight.* October 26, 2001.

ABC News. *This Week.* October 28, 2001.

Aikins, Matthieu. "Last Tango in Kabul." *Rolling Stone,* August 18, 2014.

Alpert, Bruce. "Contractor Gets Probation in Death of Afghan Prisoner." *New Orleans Times-Picayune,* May 8, 2009.

"Al-Qaida cleric death: mixed emotions at Virginia mosque where he preached." Associated Press, September 11, 2011.

"Analex's Advanced Biosystems Subsidiary Awarded $2 Million Biodefense Contract by DARPA." *PR Newswire,* May 1, 2014.

Apple, R. W., Jr. "A Nation Challenged: News Analysis; City of Power, City of Fears." *New York Times,* October 17, 2001.

Arike, Ando. "The Soft-Kill Solution: New Frontiers in Pain Compliance." *Harper's,* March 2010.

Atkinson, Rick. "Left of Boom: 'The IED problem is getting out of control. We've got to stop the bleeding.'" *Washington Post,* September 30, 2007.

———. "Left of Boom: 'There was a two-year learning curve . . . and a lot of people died in those two years.'" *Washington Post,* October 1, 2007.

———. "Left of Boom: 'You can't armor your way out of this problem.'" *Washington Post,* October 2, 2007.

———. “Left of Boom: ‘If you don’t go after the network, you’re never going to stop these guys. Never.’ ” *Washington Post,* October 3, 2007.

Barakat, Matthew, “Contractor Gets Probation for Killing Prisoner.” Associated Press, May 8, 2009.

Benke, Richard. “Right on Target.” Associated Press, January 14, 1996.

Berry, James R. “The Coldest 13 Miles on Wheels.” *Popular Mechanics,* February 1968.

Bienaimé, Pierre. “DARPA’s Incredible Jumping Robot Shows How the US Military Is Pivoting to Disaster Relief.” *Business Insider,* September 19, 2014.

Blaker, James, and Arthur K. Cebrowski. “A Retrospective.” *Naval War College Review* (Spring 2006): 134–35.

Broad, William J. “Joshua Lederberg, 82, a Nobel Winner, Dies.” *New York Times,* February 5, 2008.

Burhop, E. H. S. “Scientists and Soldiers, America’s Jason Group Looks Back on Its Vietnam Involvement.” *Bulletin of Atomic Scientists,* November 1975.

Carroll, Chris. “Report: DOD Not Tracking ‘Revolving Door’ Statistics.” *Stars and Stripes,* April 2, 2014.

Cave, Damien, and James Glanz. “Toll in Iraq Bombings Is Raised to More Than 500.” *New York Times,* August 22, 2007.

Cebrowski, Vice Admiral Arthur K., and John H. Garstka. “Network-Centric Warfare: Its Origin and Future,” *Proceedings Magazine* 124/1/1, no. 139 (January 1998): digital archive, (unpaginated).

“CEXC: Introducing a New Concept in the Art of War,” *Armed Forces Journal,* June 7, 2007.

Chase, Marilyn. “To Fight Bioterror, Doctors Look for Ways to Spur Immune System,” *Wall Street Journal,* September 24, 2002.

“Cheney Recalls Taking Charge From Bunker.” CNN.com, September 11, 2002.

Cheng, Maria. “First Reaction: Lab-Made Burger Short on Flavor.” Phys.org, August 5, 2013.

Clark, John C. “We Were Trapped by Radioactive Fallout,” *Saturday Evening Post,* July 20, 1957.

Coleman, Korva. “Social Scientists Deployed to the Battlefield.” National Public Radio, September 1, 2009.

Collins, Nick. “Britain’s First Cloned Dog ‘Made’ by Controversial Scientist.” *Telegraph,* April 9, 2014.

Cummings, M. L. “Views, Provocations: Technology Impedances to Augmented Cognition,” *Ergonomics in Design* (Spring 2010): 25-27.

DARPA. "DARPA's CROSSHAIRS Counter-Shooter System Deployed to Afghanistan." October 5, 2010.

Dehghanpisheh, Babak, and Evan Thomas. "Scions of the Surge." *Newsweek,* March 24, 2008.

Deitchman, Seymour. "An Insider's Account: Seymour Deitchman," Nautilus Institute for Security and Sustainability, February 25, 2003. Digital archive available online.

"Department of Defense to Employ UI Computer for Nuclear Weaponry." *Daily Illini,* January 6, 1970.

Diamond, John. "Small Weapons Prove the Real Threat in Iraq," *USA Today,* September 29, 2003.

Diamond, John, and Kathy Kiely. "Tomorrow Is Zero Hour," *USA Today,* June 19, 2002.

Diggins, Peter S. "Godel, Wylie Get 5 Years for Funds Conspiracy," *Washington Post,* June 19, 1965.

Douglas, Walter B. "Accused Former Aides Cite Witnesses in Asia." *Washington Post,* January 9, 1965.

Drummond, Katie. "Darpa: Do Away with Antibiotics, Then Destroy All Pathogens." *Wired Magazine,* November 11, 2011.

Dvorsky, George. "Electroconvulsive Therapy Can Erase Unwanted Memories." io9.com, December 23, 2013.

"Ears, Noses Grown from Stem Cells in Lab Dishes." Associated Press, April 8, 2014.

Elliot, Justin, and Mark Mazetti. "World of Spycraft: NSA and CIA Spied in Online Games." *New York Times,* December 9, 2013. [Also *Guardian* and *ProPublica.*]

"Embezzler Godel Sued to Repay Double." *Washington Post,* November 5, 1966.

"Executive Profile." *Bloomberg Businessweek,* October 14, 2013.

Finney, John W. "Anonymous Call Set Off Rumors of Nuclear Arms for Vietnam." *New York Times,* February 12 and 13, 1968.

———."U.S. Will Share Tiros I Pictures." *New York Times,* April 5, 1960.

"5-Year Term for Godel Is Upheld." *Washington Post,* May 21, 1966.

Gall, Carlotta. "Taliban Free 1,200 Inmates in Attack on Afghan Prison," *New York Times,* June 14, 2008.

Gardner, Amy, and Anita Kumar. "Va. Muslim Activist Denies Urging Violence." *Washington Post,* September 29, 2007.

Garner, Jay. "Army Stands by Patriot's Persian Gulf Performance," *Defense News* 7, no. 26, April 7, 1992.

Glassman, James K. "Vote of Princeton Faculty Could Lead to End of University Ties with IDA." *Harvard Crimson,* March 7, 1968.

González, Roberto J. "Towards mercenary anthropology? The new US Army counterinsurgency manual FM 3–24 and the military-anthropology complex." *Anthropology Today,* Volume 23, Issue 3, June 2007, 14–19.

Goozner, Merrill. "$100b and Counting: Missiles that Work... Sometimes." *The Fiscal Times,* March 24, 2012.

Graham-Rowe, Duncan. "Robo-Rat Controlled by Brain Electrodes." *New Scientist,* May 1, 2002.

Grasmeyer, Joel M., and Matthew T. Keennon. "Development of the Black Widow Micro Air Vehicle." *American Institute of Aeronautics and Astronautics,* 2001, 1–9.

Greenwald, Glenn. "Inside the Mind of NSA Chief Gen. Keith Alexander." *The Guardian,* September 15, 2013.

Halberstam, David. "Americans Salvage Helicopters Shot Down by Guerrillas in Vietnam." *New York Times,* January 5, 1963.

Halmos, P. R. "The Legend of John Von Neumann." *Mathematical Association of America,* Vol. 80, No. 4. April 1973, 382–394.

Hanlon, Joseph. "Project Cambridge Plans Changed After Protests," *Computer World,* October 22, 1969.

Hapgood, Fred. "Simnet," *Wired Magazine,* Vol. 5, No. 4, April 1997.

"Hardwire Receives DARPA Funding for Novel Armor Solutions," *Business Wire,* August 21, 2006.

Hawking, Stephen, et al., "Stephen Hawking: 'Transcendence Looks at the Implications of Artificial Intelligence—But Are We Taking AI Seriously Enough?'" *Independent,* May 1, 2014.

Heller, Arnie. "BASIS Counters Airborne Bioterrorism." *Science and Technology Review,* October 2003.

Helms, Nathaniel R. "The Balloon Goes Up for Army and Marines." Military.com, July 21, 2005.

Higginbotham, Adam. "In Iraq, the Bomb-Detecting Device That Didn't Work, Except to Make Money," *Bloomberg Businessweek,* July 11, 2013.

Hodges, Jim. "Cover Story: U.S. Army's Human Terrain Experts May Help Defuse Future Conflicts." *Defense News,* March 22, 2012.

Shen, Hong. "ILLIAC IV: The First Supercomputer." *University of Illinois Alumni Magazine* 1 (2012): 32–37.

Hubbell, John G. "'You Are Under Attack!' The Strange Incident of October 5." *Reader's Digest,* April 1961.

Hunter, Edward. "Brain-Washing Tactics Force Chinese into Ranks of Communist Party," *Miami News,* September 1950.

"'IDA,'"*Princeton Alumni Weekly* 60, September 25, 1959, 12.

Jewell, Sergeant Lorie. "Armed Robots to March into Battle." *Army News Service,* December 6, 2004.

Johnston, David, and Scott Shane. "U.S. Knew of Suspect's Tie to Radical Cleric." *New York Times,* November 9, 2009.

Keller, John. "DARPA Considers Unmanned Submersible Mothership Designed to Deploy UAVs and UUVs." *Military Aerospace Electronics,* July 23, 2013.

Kennedy, Patrick. "Reactions Against the Vietnam War and Military-Related Targets on Campus: The University of Illinois as a Case Study, 1965–1972." *Illinois Historical Journal* 84 (Summer 1991): 101–118.

Klein, Naomi. "China's All-Seeing Eye." *Rolling Stone,* May 14, 2008.

Kramer, Andrew E. "Leaving Camp Victory in Iraq, the Very Name a Question Mark." *New York Times,* November 10, 2011.

Kuniholm, Jonathan. "Open Arms: What Prosthetic-Arm Engineering Is Learning from Open Source, Crowdsourcing, and the Video-Game Industry." *IEEE Spectrum,* March 1, 2009.

Lang, Jenna. "Sci-fi writers take US security back to the future," *Guardian,* June 5, 2009.

Lee, Rhodi. "FDA Approves DEKA Arm System." *Tech Times,* May 10, 2014.

Licklider, J. C. R. "Man-Computer Symbiosis," *IRE Transactions on Human Factors in Electronics* HFE-1, March 1960: 4–11.

Licklider, J. C. R., and Robert W. Taylor, "The Computer as a Communication Device," *Science and Technology* (April 1968): 21–31.

LoPresti, Vin. "Guarding the Air We Breathe." *Los Alamos National Laboratory Research Quarterly* (Spring 2003): 17–22.

Madhani, Aamer. "Cleric al-Awlaki Dubbed 'bin Laden of the Internet.'" *USA Today,* August 24, 2010.

Main, Douglas. "Wooly Mammoth Clones Within Five Years? We'll Believe It When We Ride It." *Discover,* December 6, 2011.

"Marines Award Schwable the Legion of Merit." *New York Times,* July 8, 1954.

Markoff, John, "Pentagon Plans a Computer System That Would Peek at Personal Data of Americans." *New York Times,* November 9, 2002.

Mayko, Michael P. "FBI: Drone-Like Toy Planes in Bomb Plot." *Connecticut Post,* April, 7, 2014.

Maynard, W. Barksdale. "Daybreak of the Digital Age." *Princeton Alumni Weekly,* April 4, 2012.

McFate, Montgomery. "Anthropology and Counterinsurgency: The Strange Story of Their Curious Relationship." *Military Review,* March–April 2005: 24–38.

———. "The Military Utility of Understanding Adversary Culture." *Joint Force Quarterly,* no. 38 (July 2005): 44–48.

Menand, Louis. "Fat Man: Herman Kahn and the Nuclear Age," *New Yorker,* June 27, 2005.

Metz, Steven. "Non-Lethal Weapons: A Progress Report," *Joint Force Quarterly* (Spring–Summer 2001): 18–22.

Miles, Donna. "New Device Will Sense Through Concrete Walls." *Armed Forces Press Service,* January 3, 2006.

Miranda, Robbin A., et al. "DARPA-Funded Efforts in the Development of Novel Brain–Computer Interface Technologies," *Journal of Neuroscience Methods,* Elsevier, Amsterdam, Netherlands, July 24, 2014: 1–17.

Mollman, Steve. "Betting on Private Data Search." *Wired,* March 5, 2003.

Montpetit, Jonathan. "Canadian Soldiers Resume Mentoring Afghan National Army after Turbulent Spring." *Military World,* October 28, 2010. "Moon Stirs Scare of Missile Attack." Associated Press, December 7, 1960.

Newman, Kevin. "Cancer Experts Puzzled by Monkey Virus." ABC News, March 12, 1994.

Ngo, Anh D., et al. "Association Between Agent Orange and Birth Defects: Systematic Review and Meta-Analysis." *Oxford Journal of Epidemiology,* February 13, 2006.

"1991 Gulf War Chronology." *USA Today: World,* September 3, 1996.

Nordland, Rod. "Iraq Swears by a Bomb Detector U.S. Sees as Useless," *New York Times,* November 3, 2009.

NOVA. "Transforming Warfare." May 4, 2004.

Omohundro, Steve. "Autonomous Technology and the Greater Human Good," *Journal of Experimental & Theoretical Artificial Intelligence,* November 21, 2014: 303–15.

"One Man's Odyssey from Campus to Combat." Associated Press, March 8, 2009.

Packer, George. "Knowing the Enemy: Can social scientists redefine the 'war on terror'?" *New Yorker,* December 18, 2006.

Perry, Tony. "IED Wounds from Afghanistan 'Unbelievable' Trauma Docs Say." *Los Angeles Times,* April 7, 2011.

"Pfc. Jeremiah D. Smith, 25, OIF, 05/26/03," Defense Department press release no. 376-03, Military.com, posted July 26, 2003.

Pizer, Vernon. "Coming—The Electronic Battlefield." *Corpus Christi Caller-Times*, February 14, 1971.

Preston, Richard. "The Bioweaponeers." *New Yorker,* March 9, 1998.

Reed, Tristan. "Intelligence and Human Networks." *Stratfor Global Intelligence Security Weekly,* January 10, 2013.

Rhode, David. "After the War: Resistance; Deadly Attacks on G.I.'s Rise; Generals Hope Troop Buildup Will Stop the Skirmishes." *New York Times,* June 10, 2003.

Ridgway, Andy. "Cyber Moths with Backpacks Set to Fly into Disaster Zones." *Newsweek,* September 14, 2014.

Roberts, Chalmers M. "Gaither Report Said to Picture U.S. in Grave Danger." *Washington Post,* December 20, 1957.

Robinson, Clarence A., Jr., "Air Vehicles Deliver Warrior Data." *Signal Magazine,* July 2007.

Safire, William. "Mr. Atta Goes to Prague." *New York Times,* May 9, 2002.

Salisbury, Harrison E. "Soviet Shelters: A Myth or Fact?" *New York Times,* December 24, 1961.

Sang-Hun, Choe. "Disgraced Cloning Expert Convicted in South Korea." *New York Times,* October 26, 2009.

Scheer, Robert. "X-Ray Weapon: Flaws Peril Pivotal 'Star Wars' Laser, Second of Three Parts. Next: The Real Debate." *New York Times,* September 23, 1985.

"Science at the Petascale: Roadrunner Results Unveiled." Los Alamos National Laboratory Communications Office, October 26, 2009.

Scully, Meghan. " 'Social Intel' New Tool for U.S. Military." *Defense News,* April 26, 2004.

Shachtman, Noah. "The Secret History of Iraq's Invisible War." *Wired,* June 14, 2011.

Shankar, Thom. "To Check Militants, U.S. Has System That Never Forgets," *New York Times,* July 13, 2011.

Shapley, Deborah. "Jason Division: Defense Consultants Who Are Also Professors Attacked." *Science,* February 2, 1973.

Shelsby, Ted. "Iraqi soldiers surrender to AAI's drones." *Baltimore Sun*, March 2, 1991.

Shurkin, Joel. "The Secret War Over Bombing." *Philadelphia Inquirer,* February 4, 1973.

Siegrist, David, and J. Pavlin. "Bio-ALIRT Biosurveillance Detection Algorithm Evaluation," Centers For Disease Control, *Morbidity and Mortality Weekly Report*, September 24, 2004: 152–158.

Singer, Emily. "Playing Piano with a Robotic Hand," *MIT Technology Review,* July 25, 2007.

Slipke, Darla. "Vietnam War Veterans Reunite after Rescue Mission 43 Years Ago." *Daily Oklahoman,* January 8, 2011.

Smith, Stephanie. "Creating Body Parts in a Lab: 'Things Are Happening Now.'" CNN, April 10, 2014.

Solomon, Deborah. "Back From the Future Questions for William Gibson." *New York Times Magazine,* August 19, 2007.

Stannard, Matthew B. "Montgomery McFate's Mission. Can One Anthropologist Possibly Steer the Course in Iraq?" *San Francisco Chronicle,* April 29, 2007.

Sterling, Bruce. "War Is Virtual Hell." *Wired* no 1.01, March/April 1993.

"Strategic Hamlet in Vietnam." *New York Times,* May 20, 1962.

Stetka, Bret. "Can Fear Be Erased?" *Scientific American,* December 4, 2014.

Straus Military Reform Project. "DOD Office of Force Transformation." *Center for Defense Information at POGO,* September 11, 2002.

Suzuki, Toshio. "DARPA Wants Hypersonic Space Drone with Daily Launches," *Stars and Stripes,* February 4, 2014.

"10 Will Be Cited for Civil Service." *New York Times,* February 25, 1962.

Talbot, David. "A Technology Surges." *MIT Technology Review,* February 2008.

Thompson, Mark. "Why Obama Will Continue Star Wars." *Time Magazine,* November 16, 2008.

Thurber, Jon. "William P. Bundy: Advised President Johnson on Vietnam War." *Los Angeles Times,* October 8, 2000.

Tracy, Mary Frances. "Iraq Discloses Biological Weapons Capabilities." *Federation of American Scientists,* October 1995.

Trevithick, Joseph. "Firestorm: Forest Fires as a Weapon in Vietnam." *Arm Chair General Magazine,* June 13, 2012.

Ulanoff, Lance. "China Has the Fastest Supercomputer in the World—Again," Mashable.com, June 23, 2014.

"University News." *Princeton Alumni Weekly* 68, November 28, 1967, 7.

U.S. Army. "Human Terrain Team Handbook." December 11, 2008.

U.S. Army. "In Memory of... Paula Loyd." *Human Terrain System,* September 2011.

"US Looks for Bigger Warlike Computers." *New Scientist,* April 21, 1977.

Verderber, Alexander, Michael McKnight, and Alper Bozkurt. "Early Metamorphic Insertion Technology for Insect Flight Behavior Monitoring," JoVE (*Journal of Visualized Experiments*), 89 (2014): e50901-e50901.

Walker, Amy. "TIGR allows Soldiers to 'be there' before they arrive." *U.S. Army News,* October 13, 2009. Video is available online at jove.com.

Walsh, Declan. "Afghan Militants Attack Kandahar Prison and Free Inmates," *Guardian,* June 13, 2008.

Watts, Barry D. "Precision Strike: An Evolution." *National Interest,* November 2, 2013.

Weiner, Tim. "Remembering Brainwashing." *New York Times*, July 6, 2008.

———."Soviet Defector Warns of Biological Weapons," *New York Times*, February 25, 1998.

Weiss, Rick. "Dragonfly or Insect Spy? Scientists at Work on Robobugs." *Washington Post*, October 9, 2007.

Wright, Robin. "Iraqis Admit to Broad, Virulent Germ War Plan." *Los Angeles Times*, September 6, 1995.

York, H. F. "Multiple Warhead Missiles." *Scientific American*, November 5, 1973.

Zorpette, Glenn. "Countering IEDs." *IEEE Spectrum*, August 29, 2008.

INDEX

Index

Index

Index

Index